FORGOTTEN READERS

A John Hope Franklin Center Book

New Americanists   *A Series Edited by Donald E. Pease*

Forgotten Readers

Recovering the Lost History of African American Literary Societies

ELIZABETH M^cHENRY

Duke University Press Durham and London 2002

© 2002 Duke University Press

All rights reserved

Printed in the United States of America

on acid-free paper ∞

Designed by C. H. Westmoreland

Typeset in Adobe Garamond

with Weiss italic display by

Keystone Typesetting, Inc.

Library of Congress Cataloging-

in-Publication Data appear on

the last printed page of this book.

Publication of this book has

been aided by a grant from

the Abraham and Rebecca Stein

Faculty Publication Fund of

New York University, Department

of English.

For

Mom and Dad, and

Grandma and Pop

Contents

Acknowledgments

This book took shape over a number of years, and I am pleased to acknowledge the many friends, colleagues, archivists, and institutions that sustained me throughout the process of writing it. Although I began this project after I had completed my doctoral dissertation, I owe a tremendous debt to those individuals at Stanford University without whose assistance I would never have completed graduate school. First and foremost, I wish to thank Shirley Brice Heath, whose friendship, unflagging support, and scholarly integrity made a lasting impression on my work. Even before I had finished my dissertation, she encouraged me to pursue my interest in African American literary societies, and she has extended herself in innumerable ways to support me personally and professionally. I am also indebted to Rob Polhemus, George Dekker, Ramón Saldívar, and Diane Middlebrook, all of whom proved to be inspired teachers, careful readers, and constructive critics, even after my official days as a student were over.

Throughout the years, funding from several sources supported my research and writing. Much of the research for the book was conducted while I was a fellow at Harvard University's W. E. B. Du Bois Institute for Afro-American Research, where I was supported for one year by the Ford Foundation and then for another by a teaching/research fellowship from the College of the Holy Cross. Given the Du Bois Institute's enthusiastic staff and the rich intellectual atmosphere cultivated there, I was ideally situated to begin thinking about nineteenth-century African American readers and the various coalitions that supported them. In particular my thanks go to Henry Louis Gates Jr., who championed this project from its beginning; Randall Burkett, who shares my love for archival research and materials and was always willing to direct me to helpful source materials; and Richard Newman, whose astounding knowledge of black history and culture and readiness to talk with me endlessly about the project helped me to conceptualize its argument and scope.

Forgotten Readers could not have been completed without support from the National Endowment for the Humanities, which allowed me to spend a year at the National Humanities Center in Research Triangle Park, North Carolina. I wish to thank the Center's director, Robert Connor, and its deputy director, Kent Mullikin; their determination to maintain an environment that is both intellectually and socially vibrant ensured that my year there was at once productive and fun. I am grateful to the Center's staff, a remarkable collection of people who together created the conditions that would permit me to do my best writing. I am especially grateful to librarians Jean Houston, Eliza Robertson, and Alan Tuttle for their assistance in tracking down obscure references; to Karen Carroll, who patiently and meticulously edited the manuscript with skill and efficiency; and to Corbett Capps, who, in addition to his official duties, introduced us to the particular delights of a North Carolina pig pickin'. At the National Humanities Center I had the chance to work with a group of scholars who have since become some of my most valued friends. Special thanks are due Rochelle Gurstein, Jonathan Levin, Nancy and Dick Lewis, Ashraf Rushdy, and Jonah Siegal; their critical intelligence and the example of their scholarship continues to inspire me, but so too does their good humor, their spirit of friendship, and their willingness to participate in the thoroughly trivial conversations that we thrived on over long lunches at the Center.

Friends and colleagues at the University of Texas at Austin, where I was a member of the faculty for a short but enjoyable and productive time, provided invaluable support and encouragement. My special thanks go to Jim Garrison, whose respect for others continues to define my understanding of good leadership; to Koan Davis, galpal extraordinaire; and to Phil Barrish, Sabrina Barton, and Linda Ferreira-Buckley, whose friendship and generosity I remember fondly. My most profound thanks go to friends and colleagues at New York

University, my current academic home. It is sheer good fortune to have landed in a department so full of warmth and good will, in a university where teaching and research are such good bedfellows, and in a city so intellectually vibrant and culturally diverse. My students at NYU have been a pleasure to teach and to learn from, and I cannot imagine an institution more committed to supporting my research and writing. The staff and my colleagues at New York University have shown me through their example what it means to work as a team toward common goals. In particular I wish to thank Mary Carruthers, John Guillory, Cyrus Patell, Mary Poovey, and Ross Posnock for their encouragement and support. Phil Harper deserves special recognition for being a remarkable colleague and friend. I also wish to express my appreciation to the Abraham and Rebecca Stein Fund, which helped to offset publication costs for this book.

Librarians at the American Antiquarian Society, the Library of Congress, the Moorland-Spingarn Research Center (Howard University), the Boston Public Library, the Widener Library (Harvard University), the Mugar Library (Boston University), the Beineke Rare Book and Manuscript Library (Yale University), the Pennsylvania Historical Society, the Library Company of Philadelphia, the Robert W. Woodruff Library (Atlanta University), and the Avery Research Center were especially helpful. I am particularly grateful to Esme Bahn, formerly a research librarian at the Moorland-Spingarn Research Center, for enthusiastically supporting this project from its inception. I also benefited from the excellent research assistance of a number of people over the years. My thanks go especially to Anna Catone, who worked tirelessly to help me get this project off the ground, and Megan Obourn, without whose patience, dedication, and care the book would never have been completed. Thanks also to Tara Parmiter and Catherine Savini, who on short notice helped me to pull together the bibliography.

For their encouragement at crucial junctures, I wish to thank Houston Baker, Ann duCille, and Maryemma Graham, who saw the promise of this project long before it was well defined and extended themselves to support me when I most needed it. Both Carla Peterson and Shelley Fisher Fishkin listened patiently as I alternatively voiced my enthusiasm and frustrations over my work, and their words were always just the ones I needed to continue. Ken Carpenter served as my editor for the first big article I ever published, and his sound advice has guided my writing ever since. Over the years I've enjoyed many conversations with Gabrielle Foreman, Dwight McBride, and Todd Vogel, and it has been a pleasure to share ideas and materials with them. I had the good fortune to meet Jackie Goldsby at the project's beginning; she has truly become an intellectual sister who, by supplying me with endless citations, sharing instructive anecdotes from her own work, and providing stimulating discussion of the issues with which we both grapple, never ceases to remind me that scholarly work need not be a solitary endeavor.

I am grateful to Frances Smith Foster, Robert Levine, and an anonymous reader for the press for their careful readings of the manuscript and thoughtful comments on it. At Duke University Press I had the honor of working with Ken Wissoker, a remarkable editor who provided invaluable advice and support over the years. For their patience and good humor I wish to thank others at the press with whom I worked, including Leigh Anne Couch, Christine Dahlin, Laura Sell, and Cherie Westmoreland. I am particularly grateful to Lynn Walterick, who copyedited the manuscript with great skill and care.

Throughout the writing of this book it seemed as if I were the only one of my friends who was not formally a member of a book club or reading group; through the kindness of others, however, I participated in countless book club meetings, all of them contributing in no small way to my understanding of what literary societies, books clubs, and reading groups are all about. My thanks go to all those who welcomed me into their homes, sharing with me not only the critical stimulation of their literary discussions but also the warmth and fellowship that surrounded them. Special thanks are due to Lana Turner and the membership of The Literary Society in New York City; to Eugenia Guinier, Dorothy Burnham, and those who gathered with them to talk about their reading on Martha's Vineyard in the summer of 1996; and to Lois Anderson and the "Ladies Who Love Books" in Chapel Hill, North Carolina.

Finally, I wish to thank my closest friends and my family, all of whom stood by me and consistently gave me the love and the support necessary to imagine the completion of this project. Anja Hanson and Electa Sevier, my best friends since high school, spent countless hours talking with me about this book; even more appreciated is the time they dedicated to pulling me away from it for other, nonacademic, hardly intellectual pursuits. Phoebe Brown has been a wonderful friend, helping me through many difficult moments, providing inspiration when I desperately needed it, giving generously of herself and her time. Cori Field and Pat Sullivan both proved to be inexhaustibly willing to talk shop over cocktails; they provided endless encouragement, support, and much-needed sanctuary in their Martha's Vineyard homes. Esta Spalding, copilot in that unforgettable cross-country trek, has always championed my work; her enthusiasm has been indispensable. My thanks also go to Jenny Kelso Smith, whose regular Sunday morning phone calls provided the fortification I needed to face the week ahead.

Ashraf Rushdy took time away from his own work (again and again) to read and critique the manuscript with painstaking care and acuity. His investment in my project, his probing questions and critical eye, made this a better book than it otherwise would have been; equally important to it was his patience, generosity, and wit. I cherish our friendship. For countless long walks and phone calls, celebratory teas and birthday dinners, I thank Ann and Dick Behrman, who have been an unfailing source of love and encouragement in my life. I also wish to thank my brother and sister-in-law, Michael and Janice McHenry, and my aunt, Charlotte Randolph; they always kept the faith, even when mine ran low.

My sister, Christina McHenry, has always been my most ardent supporter, and it is to her that my greatest appreciation goes for providing an anchor during the seemingly endless process of research and writing. Chrissie brings tremendous energy to three of life's most demanding roles: mother, daughter, friend. And yet she always saves the time and the energy to be the best of sisters. In the most profound way we do indeed share in each other's lives, and in our steadfast commitment to the health, happiness, and well-being of one another lies the true meaning of sisterhood. Thanks also to her wonderful children, my nieces and nephew, Claire, Daniel, and Caroline, who throughout the writing of this book—which is to say, since they were born—have helped me to know when ice cream cones and a visit to the toy store were more necessary to the creative process than muddling through one last paragraph.

It is my great fortune to have Gene Assaf as a friend, colleague, and life companion. As he patiently awaited the completion of this book, he missed no opportunity to celebrate each minute sign of progress, cheering me on when I most needed it. His love, insight, humor, and steadfast commitment were instrumental to its completion and are fundamental to all that I do.

My parents, Mary W. McHenry and Donald F. McHenry, have been an unending source of love and encouragement, and the example of their tremendous success as parents and as professionals, individually and as a team, continues to inspire and motivate my own endeavors. The love, kindness, generosity, and support of my grandparents, Alphonso and Elizabeth Williamson, has served as a touchstone throughout my life, and although they did not live to see this book completed, my memory of their extraordinary lives and of our extraordinary relationship sustained me nonetheless. It is to these four remarkable people that this book is dedicated, with love and appreciation.

New York City, October 2001

FORGOTTEN READERS

Introduction

IN SEARCH OF BLACK READERS

No scene from African American literary history is more familiar than that of Frederick Douglass's learning to read. In his 1845 autobiography, Douglass describes how, when he was a young slave, his mistress taught him the alphabet and how to spell basic words. When her husband learned what she was doing, he promptly insisted she stop Douglass's lessons, telling her that "it was unlawful, as well as unsafe, to teach a slave to read." But rather than putting an end to Douglass's education, Mr. Auld's words of warning to his wife only solidified Douglass's determination to learn to read. "If you teach that nigger . . . how to read, there will be no keeping him," Auld told his wife. "It would forever unfit him to be a slave. He would at once become unmanageable, and of no value to his master. As to himself," Auld continued, "it could do him no good, but a great deal of harm. It would make him discontented and unhappy." According to Douglass, "these words sank deep into [his] heart"; they led him to understand that "the white man's power to enslave the black man" was located in his ability to maintain the black man's ignorance and his illiteracy. Without the assistance of his mistress but armed with the discovery that "what [his master] most dreaded, that I most desired," Douglass designed ingenious ways to continue his education surreptitiously.[1] Although the Aulds watched him vigilantly to prevent his learning to read, Douglass nevertheless contrived ways to "steal" literacy, first

[handwritten margin note: danger of learning to read]

from poor and hungry white boys in the neighborhood in exchange for bread and then by challenging his associates in a Baltimore shipyard to write better than he; in this way, he deceived them into demonstrating their abilities and then absorbed all that they knew.[2] Despite Douglass's confirmation that there were times when he felt that "learning to read had been a curse rather than a blessing," his life story is a testimony to his belief that literacy was "the pathway from slavery to freedom."[3] While still enslaved, Douglass began a "sabbath school" where, without the knowledge of his master, he quietly taught "my loved fellow-slaves how to read."[4] Once he was free, his career as a successful abolitionist lecturer and journalist was predicated on his literary and oratorical skills.

Let me compare Douglass's antebellum experience of learning to read with another relatively familiar scene of reading and writing from African American history: the tremendous thirst for education demonstrated by freed slaves in the years following the Civil War. Before the war, every southern state except Tennessee prohibited the education of slaves. After their emancipation, the freedpeople's desire for instruction was enormous, and they enthusiastically grasped opportunities to read and write openly and legally. "Few people who were not right in the midst of the scenes can form any exact idea of the intense desire which the people of my race showed for education," wrote Booker T. Washington of the post–Civil War atmosphere in the South. "It was a whole race trying to go to school. Few were too young, and none too old, to make the attempt to learn."[5] Although lack of funds prevented the Freedman's Bureau from itself establishing schools for ex-slaves, it coordinated the activities of the many northern benevolent and missionary societies that turned their attention to the education of ex-slaves after the Civil War. Working with organizations such as the American Missionary Association, much-needed schools were established throughout the South. Most of these schools were taught by middle-class white women, the majority of whom were from New England and received their commission from a northern freedman's aid society. W. E. B. Du Bois would later describe the arrival of the northern teachers who traveled to the South to teach the newly freed slaves as the "crusade of the New England school-ma'am," whose mission was "planting New England schoolhouses among the white and black of the South."[6]

These scenes—the first of an individual slave covertly learning and teaching others to read, the second of the great masses of former slaves being educated in schoolhouses established and run by an army of New England school teachers—constitute the most familiar representations of African American literacy in the nineteenth century. But while they are the most familiar, they are not the only examples of African American reading and writing from this period. Less well-known are stories of the efforts of free blacks in the urban North to acquire and use their literacy, or of the channels through which they gained access to and distributed books and other printed texts.[7] Although technically free, this population also faced systematic resistance to their efforts to gain and exercise their literacy. Like their enslaved brethren in the South, however, they recognized that reading was a potentially transformative activity, not only for individuals but for society as a whole. Despite their exclusion from institutions of formal education and their limited access to literary works in the first decades of the nineteenth century, despite economic conditions and social systems that were designed, in the words of Frances Smith Foster, to "repress and dehumanize, if not destroy black people," free blacks in the urban North realized the urgency of creating their own opportunities to become readers and institute systems through which to exchange and produce literature.[8] At the beginning of the nineteenth century they began establishing societies to promote literacy and to ensure that, as a group, they would not be excluded from the benefits associated with reading and literary study. Their literary societies were both large and small; they planned reading lists and provided regular opportunities for black writers to publish original literary creations, both orally and in print. Members ensured the development of their literary skills by supporting one another while also maintaining an environment where ideas could be openly discussed and honestly critiqued. In fostering the development of a literate population, literary societies furthered the evolution of a black public sphere and a politically conscious society.

To better understand the various ways black Americans have acquired and used literacy, we must further complicate our understanding of early African American literacy by considering the literary activities of free blacks and the legacy of the antebellum institutions that they built to promote reading and share texts. Of this group of black readers, we have heard almost nothing; they have been, for the most part, forgotten. Despite the enticing preliminary work of historian and librarian Dorothy Porter, whose 1936 article in *The Journal of Negro Education* presented a sizable list of what she called Negro Literary Societies, little scholarly attention has been paid to these organizations or to the readership that they cultivated and sustained.[9] While scholarship in the last decades of the twentieth century made the reading practices of enslaved African Americans increasingly visible, the reading practices of free blacks in the antebellum North and the literary activities of black Americans generally after the Civil War have remained largely invisible.

Students of African American literature, history, and culture have come to know that "invisible things are not necessarily 'not there,'" as Toni Morrison recently put it; "certain absences are so stressed, so ornate, so planned, they call attention to themselves."[10] Such, I argue, is the case with the historical invisibility of black readers, especially in the early nineteenth century. There are a series of complex and inter-related reasons for their invisibility that have as much to do with recent trends in scholarship on African American history and litera-ture as with the difficulty of conducting research on early nineteenth-century subjects, especially those concerning people of color. To intro-duce my study of the literary societies and reading practices of African Americans between 1830 and 1940 I will discuss why some early black readers and the literary productions that they created have remained invisible and then suggest some of the archaeological processes through which they can be made visible.

Much has been written about the absence of literacy skills among African Americans, from the historical past when legal codes pro-hibited slaves from reading and writing to the present when media reports inform us of the deficient reading skills of black youth. While the history and continuing ramifications of black illiteracy are un-deniable, assumptions about the illiteracy of African Americans have prevented us from seeing what is also undeniable—their literate prac-tices. The legalized withholding of literacy left a pernicious legacy that even the desire for education exhibited by ex-slaves in the years follow-ing Emancipation could not immediately erase. According to United States Census data, by 1880 70 percent of the black population was illiterate; by 1910 30 percent of the black population remained illiterate. What these and other figures document is the slow but steady rise in black literacy in the United States in the decades of the late-nineteenth and early-twentieth centuries. But today it is the persistent weakness of the literacy skills in African American communities that is most often cited and, even more problematically, assumed. Contemporary studies continue to emphasize the deficient functional-literacy skills of segments of the black population and point to their low test scores as proof of the "traditional" weakness of literacy skills in the black community.

Assumptions about African American illiteracy continue to play a part in preventing the widespread recognition of the complexity of the history of African American literacy and literary interaction; but this has not alone been responsible for rendering invisible the literate legacy of black Americans. While in recent years black verbal performance arts, from folktales and proverbs to testifying and rapping, have received wide recognition, the singular identification of African American culture as "oral in nature" has helped to push aside facts surrounding other language uses—especially those related to reading and writing. African Americans as a people and African American literary studies as a discipline have defined themselves in terms of their relationship to oral, or vernacular, culture. Denied direct forms of written expression, black Americans turned to traditional vernacular forms to communicate their sorrow and their hopefulness and deflect their anger at their subordination. In addition to sermons, folktales, and jokes, forms of music like spirituals, work songs, and the blues have historically been central to African American expression. Frederick Douglass noted the importance of spirituals to the black community in his 1845 autobiography; his observation would be revoiced in 1903 by W. E. B. Du Bois, who located spirituals, which he called the "sorrow songs," at the center of American history and culture, calling them the "singular spiritual heritage of the nation and the greatest gift of the Negro people."[11] During the Black Arts Movement of the 1960s and 1970s there was a revival of interest in other vernacular forms that influenced contemporary black oral and written expression. This interest in and revaluing of the verbal arts historically performed by African Americans led, in the 1980s and 1990s, to the compelling definition and delineation of the black vernacular as a category of African American literary study. Although this approach has been supported by a wide range of scholars, most notable is the work of Houston Baker Jr., and Henry Louis Gates Jr., which has illuminated the importance of the black vernacular to African American literature and cultural production.[12] This work has been critical and salutary. But celebrations of the black oral tradition and black vernacular have also unwittingly undermined historical evidence that points to a long and complex history of African Americans' literary interaction, not only as readers of the "canon" of European and European American authors but as creators and readers of their own literature as well.

Another reason African American readers have been forgotten is that the work of contemporary scholars has been directed toward the experiences of those who, before the Civil War, were legislated into illiteracy. Although African American expressive art forms developed in the context of a diversity of experiences, the attention of scholars of African American history and literature has largely been arrested by the experience of the southern slave and the fugitive slave narrative. The complex rhetorical aims of the slave narrative and the individual and political importance of this form have led African Americanists to situate the slave narrative as the founding paradigm of black literary production in the nineteenth century, with the slave narratives of two individuals, Frederick Douglass and Harriet Jacobs, serving as representatives of the form. While slave narratives generally, and these two texts specifically, are crucial representatives of one aspect of African American literary production in the nineteenth century, the danger of privileging them is that we risk overlooking the many other forms of literary production that coexisted alongside slave narratives. The same years that saw the greatest popularity of slave narratives, for instance, were also the years that free blacks were first organizing literary societies; these societies encouraged and supported a great variety of writing, much of which found its way into print in the early newspapers and periodicals directed toward an African American readership. The fiction and poetry, autobiographies, histories, appeals, and other forms of writing published in these and other sources, as well as the writing that was published by religious presses or was self-published, are important forms of black literary expression that have been largely overshadowed by scholarly attention to the slave narrative. In order to recover more fully the history of African American cultural production, with all of its nuances and complexity, we must be open to replacing our notion of a singular black literary tradition by attending to the many, diverse elements that form the groundwork of any tradition.

The paucity of extant records that might help us to recover the complex literary landscape of African Americans in the nineteenth century certainly complicates this work. By and large, what has been preserved as the "official" record of American literary history does not include the literature or literary activities of African Americans. With few exceptions, the words African Americans did write were not valued by libraries, museums, archives, or other institutions charged with the responsibility of preserving literary and cultural material. Although African Americans did realize the importance of and assumed responsibility for recording and preserving their own cultural artifacts, precious few of these have managed to survive. The task of locating these widely scattered fragments of African American literary and cultural history, especially in the antebellum period, is itself daunting, and the process of piecing them together presents its own particular challenges. Given these difficulties—conspicuously missing dates, identities of main characters, and other details that are the essence of "reliable" historical data—any narrative drawing on these sources and trying to tell the story of nineteenth-century African American literacy will of necessity be but a contribution to a larger enterprise.

Inquiry into the history of black readers is further complicated by the difficulty of tracking down evidence of so elusive a practice as reading. How can we know or historically document the act of reading, an activity that in our own day and age, at least, is mainly practiced in silent and individual ways that seem impossible to access? Moreover, if it is hard to know contemporary readers, how can we come to know past readers and assess their habits and the value that they assigned to the practice of reading? As Carl Kaestle notes in his introduction to *Literacy in the United States*, the very prospect of looking for readers is daunting in part because it must include the complex project of deciphering literacy, which surrounds us but proves difficult to measure and assess. Moreover, it is even more difficult to trace the meanings of literacy in earlier decades, since literacy, like all historical practices, changes with time and is defined differently in different historical epochs.[13] Even if we could agree on one precise definition of literacy, the task of delineating and portraying the American reading public of the last two centuries, let alone the African American reading public of the same period, would still present itself as a tremendous challenge. Some European American readers left elaborate paper trails to document their reading; diary accounts, subscription data from popular magazines, and the records of particular institutions, such as the Book of the Month Club, have proved effective ways of tracking the literary practices of many Americans. Sources that reflect the reading practices and literary habits of African Americans, however, especially in the early nineteenth century, are relatively few and scattered. What we have to do, I would argue, is to realize the importance of considering past reading practices by reconstructing them through what Roger Chartier has called the "sparse and multiple traces" that remain.[14] These readers existed, and their trails are important—and possible—to establish.

A number of factors make this a favorable intellectual moment in which to undertake the project of recovering forgotten African American readers and reconstructing the various processes by which their reading practices were shaped. At this writing, scholarship on print culture and the History of the Book continues to emerge rapidly. Hailed by Robert Darnton in 1989 as an important new discipline, the History of the Book has evolved into a field concerned with the "social and cultural history of communication by print."[15] Its purpose, broadly stated, is to "understand how ideas were transmitted through print and how exposure to the printed word affected the thought and behavior of mankind during the last five hundred years."[16] Emphasizing their belief that "literature is a human institution, part of a matrix of social and cultural forces from which it emerges, rather than a pure or abstract idea, independent of history," historians of the book have shifted their attention away from writers and the texts they produce to readers and the context in which literary texts are received and read.[17] The wide definition of exactly what constitutes the History of the Book has also necessitated that its practitioners abandon the boundaries that have traditionally divided the disciplines. In addition to cultural history and literary studies, their work has relied upon a variety of theoretical lenses necessary for understanding the epistemological and social conditions in a print culture. For these reasons it is a field that is particularly receptive to uncovering the many diverse communities of readers that have simultaneously existed and exposing the contexts of the actual reading practices of particular groups at particular times.

Although studies in the History of the Book have long been prominent in Europe, American scholars did not energetically enter the field until early in the 1980s; at the beginning of the twenty-first century, it has become a vital field in the United States. Centers for the study of the History of the Book, like those established by Pennsylvania State University and the University of Wisconsin, as well as the Society for the History of Authorship, Reading and Publishing (SHARP), formed in 1992, promise generous support for the development of scholarly inquiry into every imaginable aspect of book history. In conjunction with the American Antiquarian Society, Cambridge University Press is compiling a five-volume series on the History of the Book in the United States, a project that will certainly raise new questions about book history in the United States even as it answers old ones. Principal among the new directions introduced by these questions will be increased attention to the ways underrepresented cultures have interacted with books as both readers and writers. A number of recent developments attest to the extent to which scholarship of this sort is already vibrant in the United States, especially for the period after 1876. At the forefront of this research is the Center for the Study of Print Culture in Modern America, begun in Madison, Wisconsin, in 1992. A cooperative effort between the University of Wisconsin and the State Historical Society of Wisconsin, the center is dedicated to "stimulating research into the print culture collections of groups whose gender, race, occupation, ethnicity, and sexual orientation (among other factors) has historically placed them on the periphery of power but who used print sources as one of the few means of expression available to them."[18] In 1995 the center hosted its first conference, appropriately called "Print Culture in a Diverse America." A volume of selected papers from that conference, published in 1998, has been widely praised for demonstrating the scholarly shift of attention in the United States from the "cultural impact of reading and publishing the works of well-known European authors" to "exploring lesser known, but still important, aspects of America's diverse populace."[19] As Wayne Wiegand, codirector of the Center for the Study of Print Culture in Modern America, rightly points out, primary sources that document the print culture history of underrepresented groups remain "seriously understudied"; at the same time, however, Wiegand's own work attests to the fine scholarship that is already being done in the United States to document the ways minority cultures have interacted with books, as readers, writers, and publishers.[20]

If we are to gain further access to and understanding of the literate and literary practices of African Americans, we must be willing to look in new directions at the various reading cultures that existed in black communities. By slightly shifting our focus and adopting new methods of inquiry we will better understand the diverse components of the African American literary tradition and better appreciate the impact that black readers and the institutions they created to support their literacy and their literature had on the development of American and African American literary traditions. Much current research on reading examines the interpretive practices of readers and the nature of these practices across contexts—particularly the university and other institutions associated with a literary canon. New directions in the study of black readers and reading need, however, to decenter formal education as the primary institutional force behind the reading of literature. Historically, black Americans have been denied access to formal educational opportunities, and the public education that has been provided for them has been of inferior quality. They have therefore created and relied on other institutions to supplement and sustain their literary education. To uncover a more nuanced and more accurate history of their interaction with literature, we must look beyond the venues traditionally associated with reading and literary discussions and ask a series of broader questions: What institutions have centered the literary experiences of African Americans? Where has literacy been practiced and literature enjoyed, discussed, and debated? How have literary texts been acquired and exchanged?

These questions will expand our perspective beyond the classroom to a series of nonacademic venues like churches, private homes, and beauty parlors that have, since the nineteenth century, been sites for the dissemination of literacy and for literary interaction for members of the black community traditionally excluded from the nation's elite liberal arts colleges and universities. They will shift our attention away from the records of the institutions traditionally associated with the dissemination of print, like public libraries and bookstores, to the records of less familiar, less formal institutions such as reading rooms and itinerant booksellers. The exemplary story of Kathryn Johnson, a black woman who began her life as an itinerant bookseller in 1922 after returning from a post abroad with the YMCA during World War I, illustrates the importance of such a reorientation. Johnson traveled throughout the north- and southeastern United States selling books out of the back seat of a Ford coupe. By 1925 she had covered ten states and some twenty-five thousand miles in two and a half years and sold over five thousand volumes of books, one hundred volumes at a time, since that was all that she could fit in the back seat of the car. Johnson's mission was to sell books by and about African Americans to an exclusively black clientele; what she called her two-foot bookshelf— "two feet of books," she proclaimed, "that you and all the colored people ought to read"—included works by W. E. B. Du Bois, Carter Woodson, Benjamin Brawley, James Weldon Johnson, Paul Laurence Dunbar, and Silas Floyd. Her sales trips, during which she regularly received permission to address the congregation at local churches, shed light on one of the ways literacy and literature were disseminated in black communities in the first decades of the twentieth century. So too does her understanding of her occupation and her success. "I am not first of all selling books," Johnson explained. "I am first of all creating a desire for reading. . . . I knew the books that would help the Negro to understand his honorable place in the United States. The question was how to get him to buy them. . . . I knew the man or woman must handle the book, see what was in it, before he would put money down for it. So I bought my Ford and became an itinerant bookseller."[21]

What is confirmed by Kathryn Johnson's story is that evidence attesting to the activities of black readers may come from unexpected sources. It also suggests that to understand black readers, then and now, we must be willing to expand our notion of the very definition of literature and literacy, and their functions in different historical periods. Late twentieth-century definitions that associate literature with imaginative writing, usually novels and poetry, are incompatible with the "literature" that Johnson was disseminating to her readers in 1925; Johnson made explicit her understanding that her "buyers [didn't] want fiction. They look at such a book and say 'it's only a story,' and put it down. They want to spend their earnings for reality."[22] Further-

very questions that will stimulate new ways of looking at the multiple uses of literature and the various literary situations that existed in nineteenth-century African American communities.

To this point, I have noted the importance of changing our focus from formal to informal institutions, official to unofficial venues, familiar to unfamiliar definitions of literacy. One last important step we need to take is to dispense with the idea of a monolithic black community and replace it with a more accurate and historically informed understanding of a complex and differentiated black population. With few exceptions, the Africans who were brought to the United States were slaves; most would remain enslaved, as would their descendants, until Emancipation. In the years around and the decades following the Revolutionary War, however, many African Americans living in the North did gain their freedom. While the South grew more and more dependent on slave labor for its economic viability in the first decades of the nineteenth century, emancipation continued in the North. Once freed, African Americans clustered in northern cities; as the recent scholarship of Gary Nash, James Oliver Horton and Lois Horton, Emma Lapsansky, Julie Winch, and others has documented, they formed strong communities, sustained families, and built institutions through which to voice their desire for the rights and privileges of citizenship.[26]

In the past, the importance and significance of the free black population has been both overlooked and undervalued. One reason for this is that their experience was assumed to be that of a privileged few. It is true that the free black community—located primarily in the urban North and in the South's port cities like Charleston and New Orleans—never amounted to more than 10 percent of the black population in the United States before the Civil War. But the legitimacy of this group and the importance of their activities must not be discounted or dismissed because of its relatively small size. Recent scholarship has shown us the complexity of African American culture in the North and the diversity of the communities of free blacks that formed there before the Civil War. This work should dispel once and for all what Willard Gatewood, writing in 1990, called the "myth that black society is [or ever was] a homogeneous mass without significant and illuminating distinctions in background, prestige, attitudes, behavior, power, and culture."[27] It is true that the common experience of oppression and racial discrimination brought blacks of different classes together in unexpected ways; although some black Americans found various degrees of distinction within their own communities, these same individuals were equally scorned by the white population. It is nonetheless very important to realize that it has never been possible to speak of *the* black experience, and attempts to do so constitute a gross oversimplification of African American history. Equally detrimental and inaccurate are attempts to romanticize the solidarity or common experience of the black community. While examples abound of the ways that black Americans have been unified in their demand for civil rights, their different experiences and various cultural locations have made them widely and at times bitterly divided; these internal divisions and intraracial tensions demand attention. Instead of fixating on a fictional notion of black solidarity, we must try to learn all we can about what African Americans have shared as well as where they have differed; an openness to difference will move scholarship on African American history, literature, and culture to more complex and, ultimately, more important ground.

In addition to dispelling the myth of the monolithic black community, we need to reassess and complicate our ideas about what has constituted resistance for African Americans given their diverse experiences. Since the 1960s and with the rise of such disciplines as African American studies, ethnic studies, and women's studies, the impulse to document the diverse strategies of resistance employed by traditionally underrepresented groups in response to the oppression of the dominant group has been central to the research agenda of African Americanists. In looking for the overt and the hidden forms of resistance to which black Americans turned to challenge white power structures, scholars like Herbert Aptheker, Eugene Genovese, Eric Foner, and Robin D. G. Kelley have been motivated by the need to counter portrayals of black Americans as the silent and inert victims of discrimination and oppression. The result of their work is the recognition that acts of resistance among ordinary, working-class black people have taken a variety of forms, some of which have been more visible than others. Studies of black slave communities have been pivotal to reshaping our understanding of the ways in which slaves performed acts of resistance on an everyday basis; although subtle and hidden from their masters, these covert acts shaped all of antebellum southern society, politics, and daily life. In addition to expanding the very notion of what constitutes an act of resistance and raising our awareness of the ways that the "daily confrontations, evasive actions, and stifled thoughts" of working-class African Americans in the Jim Crow South "often informed organized political movements," Kelley has also identified multiple forms of resistance employed by black youth in the last decade of the twentieth century to create a space for themselves within the institutions and social relations that dominate their lives.[28] Recent scholarship on contemporary cultural productions such as rap and hip hop demonstrates the same incentive to portray the extent to which members of the black working class, although seemingly powerless and outside official structures of power, have nevertheless devised ways to participate in the political struggles that surround them, to challenge their oppression, and to express their subjectivity.

By expanding our definition of resistance to include its previously unrecognized forms, we have transformed the experience of slaves and the black working and lower classes into the paradigm for understanding African Americans and their history. The vigor with which this paradigm has been embraced across the disciplines is itself a sign of the significance and timeliness of this recuperative work and the importance of the formerly underrecognized experience of this segment of the black population. But the current tendency to present the working class as the symbolic representative of an ideal of "authentic blackness" and to view the actions of this segment of black society as the only meaningful forms of resistance is dangerous for two reasons. First, it artificially diminishes the complexity of the black community and advances the notion of a monolithic black culture that is unsupported by historical fact. Second, it ignores a significant portion of the black community whose experience was different from that of the black working class. Rather than valuing the experience of one group over that of another, we must seek to establish a perspective on the history of black Americans that takes into account the variety of their experiences and the numerous and often interrelated ways they responded to their various situations.

Although in the past it has been necessary to establish and protect the significance of the black working-class experience as a corrective to earlier assumptions about this population's disorganization and inaction, we have arrived at an important historical juncture where we can begin to bring together what we know about the diversity of black Americans' experience in the United States. The result will necessarily be a more complex historical perspective and a more balanced and more historically accurate one as well. Following the lead of recent scholarship on black Americans in the free North before the Civil War and the rehabilitative work of literary scholars Hazel Carby, Frances Smith Foster, and Carla Peterson, I submit that to achieve this goal we must reopen our critical explorations of the middle and upper classes of black society and reevaluate the ways in which we have seen and judged their various responses to the hostile climate in which they lived and the racial injustices they faced. In privileging the experience of working-class blacks as more legitimate than that of their middle- and upper-class counterparts, historians have discredited and devalued the experience of middle- and upper-class black Americans throughout the nineteenth and twentieth centuries. Against the backdrop of the "authentic" actions of their less-privileged counterparts, the perspectives of the black middle and upper classes, their activities, and their actions have been considered as indicative of one of two things: the desire to assimilate into the white middle class, or the passive acceptance of white domination and accommodation to racial segregation. This limited vision of the black middle and upper classes as assimilationist or accommodationist oversimplifies the complexity of their actions; in doing so it also grossly underestimates the complexity of the experience of black Americans in the United States.

What is called for at this critical juncture in the development of African American historical, cultural, and literary studies is a greater understanding of the common forms of oppression faced by black Americans, as well as a more complex vision of what constitutes resistance. African American literary societies provide a convenient lens through which to contemplate and develop this perspective. My study of the organized literary activities of middle- and upper-class African Americans in the nineteenth-century urban North argues that African American literary societies were formed not only as places of refuge for the self-improvement of their members but as acts of resistance to the hostile racial climate that made the United States an uncomfortable and unequal place for all black Americans, regardless of their social or economic condition. Although greater literary appreciation was one outcome of organized literary activities, it was not the only goal of African American literary societies; through their reading and writing, the members of these literary societies sought effective avenues of public access as well as ways to voice their demands for full citizenship and equal participation in the life of the nation. Their organized literary activities were a particularly effective means of educating individuals who would consider themselves capable, respected citizens.

The quest for citizenship among African Americans has often been cast as another manifestation of the desire to assimilate into white society. The establishment in 1816 of the American Colonization Society introduced in the United States the first widespread, organized attempts to "return" blacks to Africa. This development pitted those who believed blacks would never receive fair treatment in the United States and wished to emigrate against those whose identification with and commitment to remaining in the United States was firm and whose resolve to gain the rights of American citizenship unbending. Debates between emigrationists and black nationalists and those who believed that black Americans could and should be integrated into American society continued throughout the nineteenth and into the twentieth century. One of the largest mass movements among African Americans was led by Marcus Garvey, whose Africanist, nationalistic, separatist, and militant Universal Negro Improvement Association advocated that all black Americans go "home" to Africa, if not physically on the Black Star Line, the steamship company Garvey founded to transport blacks back to Africa, then psychologically by imagining themselves as in every way separate from the white population. Although ultimately unsuccessful, Garvey's movement gave voice to the disillusionment of many with the unfulfilled promises of American democracy and provided leadership to a segment of the black population disgusted with the integrationist efforts of organizations such as the NAACP and its more liberal key officials like W. E. B. Du Bois and James Weldon Johnson. It epitomizes the dichotomy tracked by historians throughout the nineteenth and twentieth centuries between those black Americans who categorically rejected the United States and wished to leave it and those who believed it could be transformed into a place that lived up to the rhetoric of its founding documents.

Historically, African American literary societies have supported the aspirations and the activism of those who wished to reform rather than leave American society; their membership believed that pursuing the freedom and equality promised to all Americans in the Declaration of Independence and the United States Constitution was not only an opportunity for African Americans but also their greatest responsibility. The earliest African American literary societies fulfilled the demands of the vision of democracy that circulated in Jacksonian America; they were schools in which free, northern blacks could learn the skills that were essential to good citizenship. As Shirley Brice Heath notes in an essay on nineteenth-century concepts of writing and education, literacy was closely linked with ideals of "citizenry."[29] Antebellum Americans believed they were part of a *new* republic; in this new republic, the exchange of information and political ideas that literacy and literature enabled was essential to sustaining a healthy democracy. As such, literacy was a key patriotic duty. Equally important as the ability to read and write was the matrix of skills that could be derived from the study of literature. Reading and responding, whether orally or in writing, to a variety of texts, analyzing ideas, and speaking critically and succinctly in conversation with others were talents deemed essential not only to the advancement of individuals but to the prosperity of the nation as well. Although officially excluded from the workings of the nation, black Americans throughout the nineteenth and into the twentieth century believed that their future in the United States depended on creating for themselves the educational and cultural opportunities that would prepare them to understand the demands of democracy. The network of literary societies they formed between 1830 and 1940 reveal their members' determination to achieve the rights of citizens in the United States; but these literary societies also challenged them to develop the skills that were essential to fulfilling the responsibilities of citizenship and achieving the promise of American democracy that ensured full participation for all.

Forgotten Readers: Recovering the Lost History of African American Literary Societies examines how literary societies have worked to promote activism, to foster resistance, and to create citizens in black communities throughout the United States. My specific focus is on the century between the height of the Anti-Slavery Movement and the Harlem Renaissance. I begin by looking at the development of literary societies in free black communities in the antebellum North in the context of early Americans' understanding of reading, writing, and print as technologies of power and political agency. Although officially excluded from the workings of the nation, free black Americans were nevertheless exposed to and understood the relationship between literacy and citizenship; they saw their literary societies and the organized literary activities that they sponsored as one way to arrest the attention of the public, assert their racial and American identities, and give voice to their belief in the promises of democracy. In the second chapter, I explore the ways the earliest literary societies interacted with the black press in the years between 1827 and the beginning of the Civil War to coordinate an African American readership and foster the sensibility of black nationalism that was essential to both the survival of the black community and their organized pursuit of civil rights.

Ironically, the years following the Civil War that saw the tremendous hunger for education and the mass pursuit of literacy by former slaves was a time when literary societies were in decline. In the aftermath of the failure of Reconstruction, literary societies were reorganized in the North; although they continued to promote the promise of democracy and encourage black Americans to develop through literary work the skills necessary to become model citizens, they were also the staging ground for black communities' increased activism. In chapter 3 I look at two prominent literary societies from the turn of the century, the Bethel Historical and Literary Association in Washington, D.C., and the Boston Literary and Historical Association. At a time when direct political agitation seemed hopeless, both organizations served their participants by providing a forum through which to design and debate alternative strategies of empowerment. Whereas chapter 3 examines two literary societies that created an environment conducive to activism, chapter 4 looks at an activist movement, the black women's club movement of the 1890s, and explores the ways it promoted literary activities and a commitment to the distribution of printed texts. Although literary work was but a component of the black women's club movement, reading and literature were essential to black women's efforts to contest racist discourses and represent themselves as moral and worthy of respect. The fifth chapter of *Forgotten Readers* looks closely at one literary society, the Saturday Nighters of Washington, D.C., and allows me to explore the ways that association with a particular literary society empowered two individuals, Jean Toomer and Georgia Douglas Johnson, to develop both personally and professionally. Finally, the epilogue of the study comments on the current interest in book clubs and reading groups among black Americans; rather than a new phenomenon, these literary societies reveal the durability of the rich African American tradition of collective literary study.

1

"Dreaded Eloquence"

THE ORIGINS AND RISE OF AFRICAN

AMERICAN LITERARY SOCIETIES

In the late 1820s and early 1830s, free blacks in the urban North formed literary societies as a place in which to read and experiment with rhetorical strategies. Embracing the Enlightenment stress on the importance of the life of the mind, they turned to reading as an invaluable method of acquiring knowledge, and to writing as a means of asserting identity, recording information, and communicating with a black public that ranged from the literate to the semiliterate to the illiterate. These individuals were vividly aware of the general perception, especially among white slaveholders in the South, that black literacy and education posed a significant threat to the future of the slave system and to maintaining black subordination generally. They were aware also of the centrality of written texts of national construction to both the legitimacy of the new nation and to their status in it. Through their own reading and writing, they sought effective avenues of public access as well as ways to voice their demands for full citizenship and equal participation in the life of the republic. Their organized literary activities were a means of educating individuals who would be prepared to perform as and would consider themselves capable, respected citizens.

How did early African Americans in northern cities come to see reading and writing as a means of forming durable communities and asserting their right to American citizenship? How did marginal literary coalitions serve to support efforts to build black communities and strengthen the resolve of their members to be recognized in the national public sphere? In what way were African American literary societies both agents for and products of an empowered black community? What, if anything, limited the effectiveness of those who believed the black condition could be ameliorated by means of increased literacy and organized literary activities?

The African American literary societies that developed from black fraternal and mutual aid societies in the late eighteenth and early nineteenth centuries are a virtually unknown chapter in African American social and literary history. The stories of free, northern blacks who used reading and writing to voice an American optimism provide a crucial counterweight to the history of southern slaves and the literary tradition of the slave narrative. The rise of African American literary societies in northern, urban black communities in the late 1820s and throughout the 1830s suggests that they became important institutions precisely because they encouraged discussion and created a forum for debate on issues of racial and American identity. Their evolution records the developing understanding and shifting uses of literary discourse by northern, free blacks for expression, interaction, and social protest in antebellum America.

The point of departure for this chapter is the case of David Walker, a black man, who in 1829 published and distributed a document that arrested the attention of white Americans. This case illustrates the extent to which free blacks living in the urban North in the first decades of the nineteenth century understood text, identity, and public access to be linked. It also serves to contextualize the belief held by many free blacks that literary texts and the ability to gain access to them could galvanize the black community and help them to give public voice to the injustice of their position and to their pursuit of civil rights.

WRITING, IDENTITY, AND PUBLIC ACCESS
The Case of David Walker's *Appeal*

On 27 March 1830, police in Charleston, South Carolina, arrested Edward Smith, a white steward on the brig *Columbo* of Boston, for distributing "some pamphlets of a very seditious & inflammatory character among the Slaves and persons of color of said City."[1] Housed in the South Carolina archives, the original transcript of Smith's sworn confession before the Guard Committee recounts how he came to possess and distribute the pamphlets. The "day before he left Boston," Smith reported, "a colored man of decent appearance & very genteely dressed called on board of the vessel and asked him if he would do a favor for him." Smith was asked "to bring a package of pamphlets to Charleston for him and to give them to any negroes he had a mind to, or that he met." Smith claimed in his confession to have been ignorant of the content of the pamphlets when he "consented & promised the man that he would do as directed"; during the voyage from Boston to Charleston he "opened one of them & read a few lines" but was called away before reading all of the pamphlet. "From what he read," Smith reported, "he found out that [the subject of the pamphlets] *was something in regard to the imposition upon negroes.*" "When he arrived in Charleston he would not on this account have delivered the Books," he claimed, "if he had not pledged his words to the Boston man to do so."[2]

In his testimony to South Carolina authorities Smith emphasized that the man from whom he received the pamphlets was a "decent looking black man whom he believed to be a Bookseller." His stress on the man's description underscores Smith's apparent determination to faithfully complete the errand in part because he was confident that a man of such genteel appearance and respectable profession would ask nothing of him that might "bring him in trouble."[3] Although Smith was indicted and found guilty of seditious libel, the jury seemed affected by his claims of ignorance and innocence and recommended clemency; his sentence was a fine of $1,000 and a prison term of one year. But, as historian Peter P. Hinks asserts, Smith's protestations are not entirely convincing.[4] In the South, anxiety over the threat of slave insurrection had been mounting since the exposure of Denmark Vesey's organized rebellion in Charleston in 1822, the plot of which had illustrated the extent to which black literacy and the printed material that supported it could provide inspiration for revolt. Southerners were well aware of the rise of abolitionist sentiment both abroad and in the North and had already taken preliminary steps to prevent the circulation of abolitionist literature in their communities. Smith's own confession that he was instructed to "give [the pamphlets] *secretly* to the Black people" suggests that he was aware of both the subversive nature and the danger of his mission; he also relayed to authorities that he was specifically told to distribute the pamphlets "privately and not let any white person know any thing about it."[5] In this Edward Smith succeeded: although arrested with at least one copy of the pamphlet in his possession, he had already managed to distribute several copies of it to black longshoremen, thus putting it into circulation in Charleston's black community.

Although it is impossible to positively identify the "decent looking black man" from whom Edward Smith received the pamphlets in Boston, what Smith carried to Charleston aboard the *Columbo* were copies of the *Appeal, in Four Articles, Together with a Preamble, to the Colored Citizens of the World, but in Particular, and Very Expressly to Those of the United States of America.* Published privately in Boston in 1829 by its author, David Walker, the *Appeal* delivered a furious indictment of American slavery and racism. That the *Appeal* called for a series of violent uprisings by blacks against their white oppressors was in part responsible for its tremendous impact. Its arrival in Savannah, Georgia, as early as December 1829 was met with concern by authorities already sensitive to the pervasiveness of insurrectionary activities. Memories of the Denmark Vesey Conspiracy, a meticulously planned slave rebellion exposed by an unnamed slave in 1822 just days before the intended uprising, were still fresh in the minds of area residents. More recent unrest had given authorities good reason to be concerned as well. In Georgetown, South Carolina, a plot of insurrection had recently been exposed. Throughout 1829 the cities of Augusta and Savannah, Georgia, had experienced repeated incidents of arson; slaves were widely suspected of having set the fires. The arrival of the *Appeal* both reinforced and augmented authorities' fears that rebellious activities led by blacks—free or slave—presented a significant threat not only to the economic stability of the system of slavery but to the personal safety of whites in the region as well. As the governor of

Georgia noted in a response to the *Appeal*, the threat of conspiracy and insurrection was increasingly understood as especially acute in urban areas: "The plots devised some years ago in Charleston, and very lately in Georgetown, South Carolina," he wrote, "the late fires in Augusta and Savannah, have shewn us the danger to be apprehended in the cities from the negroes." His closing made direct reference to Walker's *Appeal*: "The information communicated [in the *Appeal*], presents this danger in a new shape."[6]

Indeed, on a number of levels the *Appeal* did present danger "in a new shape." Although Walker's *Appeal* has traditionally been seen as a document that embodies an early model of black nationalism and critically considered for Walker's defense of violent resistance, these angles of analysis have been overemphasized.[7] In fact, as its southern white audience suspected, the *Appeal* carried with it far greater and more complicated threats as well. In it, Walker did not shy away from articulating the necessity of resisting unlawful and immoral authority by any means necessary; he exposed his own moral outrage at slavery as a crime, not only against fellow men but also against God. But the significance of the *Appeal* is not limited to this ideological message. It is crucial to consider, for instance, the extent to which Walker was influenced by America's recent revolution and the birth of the United States as a democratic republic. Walker believed that the disparity between the condition of people of African descent in the United States and the "inalienable rights" and republican principles laid out in the Declaration of Independence could be a rallying point for black Americans seeking to be recognized and treated as citizens. That he turned to strategies similar to those used by colonists such as Thomas Paine, whose own pamphlet *Common Sense*, published in 1776, had helped propel the colonies toward independence from England cannot be underestimated. Like Paine, Walker recognized the importance of claiming public voice through which to communicate with both black and white Americans, and the utility of using printed documents to do so.

In the third of the three editions of the *Appeal* printed in 1829, Walker drew explicit attention to the hypocrisy inherent in the founding documents of the United States. He recognized that this was one of the features of the *Appeal* that made it both audacious and unforgivable for its early nineteenth-century white audience. In an amendment to the fourth article of the text, Walker posed this rhetorical question: "Why do the Slave-holders or Tyrants of America and their advocates fight so hard to keep my brethren from receiving and reading my Book of Appeal? Why are the Americans so very fearfully terrified respecting my book?" Walker answers his own question later in the same amendment, referring to the very end of the *Appeal* where he quotes extensively from the Declaration of Independence: "Perhaps the Americans do their very best to keep my brethren from receiving and reading my 'Appeal' for fear they will find in it an extract which I made from their Declaration of Independence, which says, 'we hold these truths to be self-evident, that all men are created equal,' etc., etc., etc."[8]

This direct reference to the Declaration of Independence is indeed one of the most aggressive aspects of Walker's document. Although the framers focused the Declaration of Independence around the words "All Men are Created Equal," they failed to include all men in their distinction. In fact, nowhere in the Declaration of Independence or the United States Constitution do the authors refer to the people of African descent living in the new republic; the words "slave" and "slavery" are conspicuously absent from these documents. Instead, the issue of slavery—by all measures incompatible with the ideals of freedom and human equality expressed by the documents' framers—was cleverly disguised by what John Quincy Adams came to call "circumlocutions."[9] What is ironic about the *Appeal* is that while Walker condemns the hypocrisy of America and considers white Americans responsible for corrupting the principles on which the nation was founded, his most bitter passages repudiate neither his native land, the United States, nor the republican principles on which the country was formed. Although he blames white Americans entirely for their racist attitudes and hypocritical failure to recognize those of African descent as their equals, he simultaneously heralds the words and principles laid out by the Declaration of Independence, wondering why white Americans do not seem to "understand [their] own language" (75). The extended argument on the issue of colonization, which forms the fourth article of the *Appeal*, emphasizes the extent to which, however alienated he felt from the workings of the United States, Walker saw himself and sought to be considered by others as a citizen. His response to the "scheme" of "drain[ing] . . . off" (46) the black population via African colonization underscores the fact that Walker considered Americans of African descent more deserving of recognition and full citizenship than white Americans. Quoting one of Philadelphia's oldest black religious leaders, Richard Allen, Walker asserts that blacks were "the first tillers of the land" (57): "This land which we have watered with our tears and with our blood, is now our mother country, and we are well satisfied to stay" (58).

Throughout the *Appeal,* Walker contrasts the sense of allegiance black Americans feel toward their "mother country" with their perceived distance or separation from it: rather than deserving citizens they are treated by white Americans as "brutes," "talking apes" (62), and "orang outangs" (10) who "ought to be SLAVES to the American people and their children forever" (7). The terms identified rhetorically by David Walker in his 1829 *Appeal* are analogous to those defined by the Supreme Court almost three decades later in the case of *Scott v. Sanford,* more commonly known as *Dred Scott.* Were black people, the court would ask in 1857, "citizens or persons," or were they nonpersons, pieces of property no different from mules or horses? In contrast to the Court's finding that, free or slave, blacks could not be citizens of the United States within the meaning of the Constitution and were therefore entitled to "no rights which a white man was bound to respect," Walker observed in his *Appeal* that Americans of African descent were in fact the true "Americans" and more deserving of citizenship than their white countrymen. Given this status, albeit unacknowledged, Walker reminded blacks that they should be guided by the principles of civic responsibility: according to the Declaration of Independence, it was their "right" and "duty" to oppose unjust treatment and to stand as "new guards for their future security" (75). Although deprived as a group of the rights of citizenship, Walker's call for uprising is a call for blacks to nevertheless uphold the responsibilities of citizenship by protecting the republican principles on which the country was founded.[10]

In particular, Walker's *Appeal* suggests the extent to which free blacks in the late 1820s maintained faith in the nation's founding documents; they were intent on asserting their right to citizenship according to these texts. Black Americans did not wait for legislative rulings to confirm their American identities. Increasingly, they claimed what they understood as their birthright in much the same way David

Walker did: they adopted the language and habits of citizens. By illustrating their respect for the responsibilities of citizenship, free black Americans hoped to convince the white population that they were also deserving of its rights. They held up the revolutionary ideals of freedom, equality, and social justice to illustrate that their treatment was "in direct violation of the letter and spirit of [the] Constitution."[11] Walker had hope for the future: "What a happy country this will be," he advised his readers toward the end of the *Appeal*, "if the whites will listen" (70).

Rather than leave or reject racist American culture, Walker calls for African Americans to find ways to engage and question it in order to assert their status as citizens. One way of doing this was by making public the privately held sentiments of the black population with the most freedom: those living in the northern, urban cities of Philadelphia, New York, and Boston. By "making public," I refer specifically to the two public spheres accessed by David Walker through the publication of the *Appeal*. Walker's *Appeal* was able to address not only his principal audience, the public constituted by the black community, free or slave. To the extent that whites noticed Walker's text and took action to suppress it, he engaged the national public as well. While it is true that, as a black man, Walker's participation in the national public sphere would have been severely limited, it was not altogether nonexistent. As Leonard Curry emphasizes in his study of free blacks in antebellum urban America: "However much they were repressed, segregated, and restricted, urban blacks were, nevertheless, undeniably *there*. . . . They could not . . . be wholly excluded" from the workings of the white society.[12] Denied civic and political rights, Walker's means of access to this national public sphere—and its civic debate on the status of blacks in the democracy—was his literary text.[13]

That Walker was able to communicate deftly to a white audience through the *Appeal* is made vividly apparent by this population's reaction to it. After the Vesey plot had been uncovered in 1822, Charleston authorities had passed a law requiring that black sailors be quarantined at a local workhouse throughout the duration of their stay in the city. Similar restriction on the activities of black sailors were imposed by authorities after the discovery of the *Appeal* in Savannah. This policy may have complicated the means by which the *Appeal* was circulated but, as the example of Edward Smith illustrates, it did not altogether prevent its distribution. In the months after its printing, the *Appeal* was found circulating among blacks in port cities from Virginia to Louisiana. Legislators in Georgia and Louisiana became so alarmed that they banned the distribution of all antislavery literature and abruptly enacted laws to control and prevent black literacy. Similar legislation narrowly passed the Virginia house of delegates but expired in the state senate; North Carolina enacted its own versions of these restrictions in the fall of 1830. Legislation passed in the wake of the publication of the *Appeal* was focused not only on more strictly controlling the activities of enslaved blacks; it also targeted free blacks, who were increasingly seen as a dangerous element. The most extreme example of anti-free-black legislation was enacted in Louisiana, whose lawmakers passed acts expelling all free blacks who had entered the state after 1825. Mounting anxiety about the influence and potential aggressiveness of the free black population was not limited to the South; Cincinnati had attempted to rid the city of its free blacks in 1829. Horrified northern journalists joined their southern counterparts in denouncing Walker's *Appeal* as what the editor of the *Boston Centinel* called "one of the most wicked and inflammatory produc tions ever issued from the press."[14] Although impressed by the author's implacable hatred of slavery, even the antislavery spokesperson William Lloyd Garrison found the pamphlet's "spirit and tendency" to be lamentably violent and provocative.[15]

Widespread allegations that David Walker could not have been the document's author are also indicative of the extent to which Walker penetrated the consciousness of his white audience. Unquestionably, the *Appeal* was the product of an educated and active mind. Offhand references throughout the text to learned works of history, to such figures as the eighteenth-century British essayist Addison, and to American legislative debates constituted undeniable evidence of Walker's extensive reading of both religious and secular works. His precise outlining of the evils of the institution of slavery and the racist ideas used to justify it, and his tactic of systematically "expos[ing] them in their turn," attested to Walker's skill as a rhetorician (2). His prose, in keeping with the florid rhetorical preference of the day, was mature and sophisticated. His recounting of the political and civic injustices inflicted on people of African descent in the United States created a sound if uneven argument impossible for his white readers to reconcile with their perception of the status or abilities of a black man. It was precisely because of the skill with which Walker crafted his document that so many of its white readers doubted his authorship of it. "[He] who believed [the *Appeal*] to have been written by David Walker, the dealer in old clothes in Brattle Street, must have more abundant faith than falls to our share," wrote one such skeptic in a letter printed in the *Boston Daily Courier*.[16] Another letter published in the *Liberator* succinctly enumerated the reasons why a black man could not have written the *Appeal*: he could not have so perceptively acquired the necessary education.

> (1) . . . I do not believe he wrote it [began this anonymous critic]; for the matter brought forward in said pamphlet is the result of more reading than could have fallen to the lot of that man, and, at the same time, have left him so vulgar as he has been represented to me. (2) Besides, sir, he could never have read all the authors quoted in his book, and seen of what true greatness consisted, and then bestowed such unbounded praise upon one [the writer here refers to Richard Allen, the black Philadelphia leader] whose name the political, the moral, and the religious world will be found equally indifferent about handing to those who may come after us (3) To say nothing of the excellent criticisms upon the speeches of the most talented men of the age—all of which discover to us a greater degree of education than we have any reason to believe that he possessed.[17]

This reader's comments are representative of the widespread assumption held in both the North and the South that blacks did not possess the intelligence necessary to acquire an education or use it to model sophisticated and intellectually sound arguments such as those exhibited in the *Appeal*. It was not only that whites doubted blacks possessed intellectual capacity in its most basic forms; their incredulity also reflected the extent to which maintaining the balance of power between black and white Americans was dependent on maintaining the belief that blacks were fundamentally inferior to whites in part because of an inability to exhibit signs of intellectual sophistication or reason.

In this context, Walker was, in fact, quite literally "*hurtfully* indefatigable in his studies," as William Lloyd Garrison described him in his defense of Walker's authorship of the *Appeal* in the pages of the *Liberator*.[18] It was widely believed that reading and writing were dangerous skills to teach blacks, and Walker's document embodied the problem of black literacy in the most fundamental way. His explicit display of the ability of a black man to read widely, reason lucidly, and write authoritatively defied claims of black intellectual inferiority and delivered a crippling blow to the prime justification for black enslavement and oppression. It also signaled the impossibility of keeping print, especially ephemeral sources of it, out of the hands of black Americans. Certainly, the *Appeal* suggests that Walker's knowledge of the Bible was extensive. But, as Peter P. Hinks argues in his analysis of the intellectual background of the *Appeal*, Walker's most important sources of information for the *Appeal* were probably newspapers.[19] In the *Appeal*, Walker implies that he read the *African Repository and Colonial Journal* "from its commencement to the present day" (69). Founded in 1825 as the organ of the American Colonization Society (ACS), an organization whose mission was to make the United States an all-white nation by "returning" free blacks to Africa, the newspaper was printed monthly in an attempt to make public and circulate nationally the sentiments of the organization. In the *Appeal*, Walker points to this publication as a site in which blacks were particularly "abused and held up by the Americans, as the greatest nuisance to society, and throat-cutters in the world" (69). Ironically, because one of the ways the ACS made its case for African colonization was by celebrating the historical greatness of Africa, it was also one of the sources from which Walker and other blacks learned of the rich history of Africa and the achievements of its people. This information Walker used in the *Appeal* to defend the place of black Americans in the United States. Certainly Walker was also influenced by the efforts of the ACS to develop a national voice and reach a national audience through the circulation of the *African Repository and Colonial Journal*.

He was an early supporter of the first African American newspaper, *Freedom's Journal*, which similarly aspired to create a sense of nationalism among African Americans. Four weeks before its inaugural issue was released in New York, Walker hosted a meeting at his house to consider "giving aid and support to the 'Freedom's Journal.'" At the meeting, which was attended by the leaders of Boston's free black community, the group endorsed the effort of *Freedom's Journal* co-founders and coeditors John Russwurm and Samuel Cornish as one from which "great good will result to the People of Colour" and promised their "utmost exertions to increase its patronage."[20] That Walker actively participated in the life of *Freedom's Journal,* as both a contributor and distributing agent, suggests that he was also an avid reader of it. Topics discussed with great frequency during the two-year run of *Freedom's Journal,* including meditations on the history of Africa and, in particular, Egypt, the foundations of Western civilization, and the nature of slavery, are central to Walker's assertions in the *Appeal,* and Walker's principal themes and his knowledge and interpretation of history can in large part be traced back to the perspectives and interpretations that appeared in *Freedom's Journal.*[21]

Walker's ability to compel the white public to take note of his voice, his message, and his talent was indeed impressive; yet more astounding was his ability to communicate through his printed text with both free and enslaved blacks, the audience toward whom the *Appeal* was primarily directed. Ironically, the majority of this population could not read. Walker knew this, designing a document and imagining a system of distribution for it that would reach and benefit even the semiliterate and illiterate black population. In fact, Walker intended the *Appeal* to bridge the gap between the literate and the illiterate, insisting that those who could must read the text aloud to those who could not. "It is expected that all coloured men, women and children, of every nation, language, and tongue under heaven, will try to procure a copy of this Appeal and read it, or get someone to read it to them, for it is designed more particularly for them" (Pre-Preamble), he wrote in a Preamble to the third edition of the text. His direct address to the educated few who could themselves read the *Appeal* made it clear that he believed it their primary duty to deliver the text and its teachings to those less fortunate than themselves. "Men of colour, who are also of sense, for you particularly is my APPEAL designed," he wrote. "Our more ignorant brethren are not able to penetrate its value. I call upon you therefore to cast your eyes upon the wretchedness of your brethren, and to do your utmost to enlighten them" (28). By directly addressing those educated "men of sense," the growing network of black reformers and intelligentsia in the South as well as the North, Walker's text helped to strengthen liaisons between them. But the more crucial liaisons Walker set out to strengthen were between the literate and the illiterate. His literate black audience was to "enlighten" their illiterate brethren by reading the *Appeal* aloud to them and helping them to understand its content. This was, Walker indicated, not a trivial act of charity for the less fortunate but an essential act of survival for all black people. Whites judged the nation's black population as a unit, and only as a unit could they assert their rights and prove themselves to be worthy of civil rights and respectful treatment. Reading the *Appeal* aloud, Walker insisted, was part of a larger responsibility to be fulfilled by his educated black audience. "There is great work for you to do," Walker instructed these readers, "as trifling as some of you may think of it. You have to prove to the Americans and the world, that we are MEN, and not BRUTES, as we have been represented, and by millions treated. Remember," he told them, "to let the aim of your labours among your brethren, and particularly the youths, be the dissemination of education and religion" (30).

Walker was not the first black author to insist on the imperative of his text's being read by the literate to those who could not themselves read. Jupiter Hammon, the literate servant of John Lloyd, imagined a similar partnership between the literate and the illiterate when he addressed in writing the "Negroes of the State of New York" in 1787. His meditation on the importance of reading for the acquisition of religious education led him to confess the dilemma that he faced when he considered the audience his own written address might exclude.

> Those of you who can read I must beg you to read the Bible, and whenever you can get time, study the Bible, and if you can get no other time, spare some of your time from sleep, and learn what the mind and will of God is. But what shall I say to them who cannot read? This lay with great weight on my mind, when I thought of writing to my poor brethren, but I hope that those who can read will take pity on them and read what I have to say to them. If you are once engaged you may learn. Let all the time you can get be spent in trying to learn to read. Get those who can read to learn you.[22]

Although the efficacy of this system of combined written/oral literacy cannot be confirmed in the case of Jupiter Hammon's address, evidence suggests that Walker's *Appeal* was in fact productively distributed in this way. As one Boston journalist attested, the impact of the *Appeal* could not be separated from its mode of distribution. "Since the publication of that flagitious pamphlet, Walker's Appeal . . . we have noticed a marked difference in the deportment of our colored population. It is evident they have read this pamphlet, nay, we know that the larger portion of them have read it, or *heard* it read, and that they glory in its principles, as if it were a star in the east, guiding them to freedom and emancipation."[23]

What this journalist clearly acknowledges about Boston's black community and the ways knowledge was disseminated to it is important: as David Walker had hoped, the *Appeal* became a public rather than a private document, proving that a written text could be effective at communicating information, empowering and emboldening the illiterate as well as the literate. It is important to note that for Walker the imperative that the literate read the *Appeal* to the illiterate was not a straightforward endorsement of the already-scripted Western idea that those without literacy skills were also without logic. He did not assume that those without the ability to themselves read the *Appeal* were definitively without the presence of mind and sophistication of thought to eventually understand it. Rather than viewing literacy exclusively as a sign of an elevated state of reason, Walker recognized it as a powerful apparatus that might be deployed in various ways by black Americans to further their pursuit of civil rights. In fact, Walker's conviction that both "men of sense" and those without the ability to read for themselves could mutually benefit from the *Appeal* underscores his belief that literacy was neither a definitive marker of the ability to reason nor its absence a significant sign of the inability to reason. Walker recognized the importance of spreading information and knowledge by gaining what one contemporary black orator described as "access to the public mind"; the effective circulation of his *Appeal* demonstrates that Walker's certainty that this could be achieved despite the varying literacy skills of the black population was correct.[24] As a document that united the black population in their belief that they were deserving of freedom and emancipation, the impact of the *Appeal* on the black population in the United States was irrefutable, regardless of whether it was read privately by a literate individual or heard by one without the ability to read for him- or herself. Although surely there were individuals who read the text to themselves and never extended the distribution of the *Appeal* by reading it aloud to someone without literacy skills, the story of the *Appeal* points to the tentative beginnings of a cooperative system for the distribution of knowledge and pertinent information in antebellum black communities, through which printed texts were primarily consumed collectively rather than individually.

Unlike the most familiar scenes of reading from the twenty-first century, where an individual text is consumed in private by an individual reader, this early nineteenth-century reading scenario is based on the imperative that, for the welfare and the survival of the community, individuals must come together in larger group forms. The importance of building coalitions, both to create a sense of national identity and collective spirit and to extend essential knowledge to the black community, would not have been lost on David Walker. Born to a free mother and an enslaved father in Wilmington, North Carolina, in 1785, Walker left the South as a young man, arriving in Boston and setting up shop as a used-clothes salesman sometime between 1822 and 1824. In 1826 he was initiated into Boston's African Lodge of the Prince Hall Masons, which was at the time the most established and long-lived coalition of Boston's blacks. In fact, black Freemasonry in the United States had been formally established in Boston in 1775, when Prince Hall and several other free blacks were initiated into a lodge of British soldiers residing in the city during the Revolutionary War. When British troops left Boston in 1776, free blacks were left without an official lodge warrant and were therefore unable to initiate new members. After appealing to and being turned down by the white members of the Massachusetts Grand Lodge, the black Freemasons eventually received their charter from the Grand Lodge of England in 1787. African Lodge #459, as the original Boston lodge was designated, had the power to charter other lodges, and black Freemasonry soon spread to northeastern cities with large populations of free blacks. Ironically, their being denied recognition and acceptance by local, white (American) Freemasons proved to some degree fortuitous. A charter from England endowed black American Freemasons with the unrestricted authority to officially charter new lodges; at the same time, it ensured that they would have the independence they needed to establish and pursue their own agenda and operate according to their own unique political concerns.

Walker's standing in the late 1820s as a "Prince Hall Mason," as black Freemasons were designated after the death of founder Prince

Hall in 1807, is significant, as it placed him in the midst of a group of politically charged, reform-minded African American leaders whose resolve to act against slavery and racial oppression was unwavering. In the last decades of the eighteenth century, Prince Hall Masons had been instrumental in sponsoring antislavery and civil rights petitions while at the same time, through their capacity to charter new lodges, helping to forge communities of free blacks that would advance the struggle for black freedom and civil rights in other locales. As early as 1787, for instance, the African Lodge #459 tested its political strength by petitioning the legislature for some sort of program for black education. In 1788 the lodge was instrumental in abolishing the slave trade in Massachusetts. These and other political concerns were addressed by similar coalitions of black Freemasons in other cities. New lodges were chartered in both Providence, Rhode Island, and Philadelphia in 1797; by 1814, three more African lodges had been chartered in Philadelphia and one had been begun in New York City. Together these lodges laid the groundwork for a network that would create a sense of solidarity among free blacks in the Northeast. Leaders of the lodges in different cities communicated with one another through letters that reinforced their sense of common purpose despite geographic distance. Early correspondence between Prince Hall and Absalom Jones, who would eventually become the Grand Master of the first Philadelphia lodge, indicates the importance of this communication in creating a network of similarly minded free blacks united in their work toward a common goal. In response to a note of encouragement from Hall, Jones wrote appreciatively on behalf of his fraternal peers: "It afforded us much satisfaction to find that you are united with us in laboring in the same vineyard."[25]

That they were not only individually but institutionally "laboring in the same vineyard" was perhaps the feature of black Freemasonry that had the most significant effect on David Walker in the years leading up to the publication of the *Appeal.* Never had the need to organize been more acute than it was in the late 1820s. Throughout the Northeast, free blacks were more and more frequently being cordoned off as socially threatening; they were increasingly relegated to the most menial work, confined to the least attractive living conditions, and subject to more overt and aggressive racism. One effect of this climate of racial hostility was that free blacks became increasingly aware of themselves as a unified body, a distinct political entity with unique political concerns and objectives. The worsening of conditions for free blacks in the urban North in fact facilitated their organization, motivating them to look inward at the particular needs of their own communities and inspiring them to take collective action to promote change.

The Prince Hall Masons enjoyed a revival of popularity in the second half of the 1820s; in addition, during these years several other organizations were begun in Boston with similar goals. Chief among these was the Massachusetts General Colored Association (MGCA), of which David Walker was a member. Begun sometime between 1826 and 1828, the organization was designed to speak to the interest of local blacks and, by extension, to the interest of blacks throughout the United States. Although the records of the MGCA are not extant, what has survived is an address Walker delivered to the organization in December 1828. Walker's description of the MGCA reflects the growing understanding of the importance of developing associations that dominated free black communities in the late 1820s. The "primary object of this institution," he told his audience, "is, to unite the colored population." To do this, the association worked to identify the particular needs of the black community and advocated "forming societies, opening, extending, and keeping up correspondences" as one way to address the community's needs both locally and nationally. Walker used the example of the MGCA to suggest the importance of the widespread development of associations for the amelioration of the condition of black Americans. The terms of his argument merit quoting at length:

> It has been asked, in what way will the *General Colored Association* (or the Institution) unite the colored population[?] . . . to which inquiry I answer, by asking the following: Do not two hundred and eighty years [of] very intolerable sufferings teach us the actual necessity of a general among us? Do we not know indeed, the horrid dilemma into which we are, and from which, we must exert ourselves, to be extricated? Shall we keep slumbering on, with our arms completely folded up, exclaiming every now and then, against our miseries, yet never do the least thing to ameliorate our condition, or that of posterity? . . . In fine, shall we, while almost every other people under Heaven, are making such mighty efforts to better their condition, go around from house to house, enquiring what good associations and societies are

going to do for us? Ought we not to form ourselves into a general body, to protect, aid, and assist each other to the utmost of our power?

Walker closed his speech with the following rhetorical question: "Two and a half million colored people in these United States, more than five hundred thousand of whom are about two thirds of the way free. Now, I ask, if no more than these last were united (which they must be, or always live as enemies) and resolved to aid and assist each other to the utmost of their power, what mighty deeds could be done by them for the good of our cause?"[26]

As the transcript of Walker's speech makes clear, the MGCA shared with the Prince Hall Freemasons the purpose not only of working to identify the concerns and promote the welfare of the local and national black population but also to encourage the development of other coalitions that would introduce new and specific ways to address particular needs of the black community. In the late 1820s and throughout the 1830s, this impulse to organize would result in the development of broader coalitions as well as coalitions more narrowly focused in their purpose. The Negro Convention Movement, for instance, reflects a culmination of the movement toward broad coalitions that swept through free black communities in the urban North in the last years of the 1820s and the 1830s. These conventions, held annually between 1830 and 1835, were instrumental to building northern black communities, solidifying their leadership and identifying their priorities, and ensuring that a nationalist imagination would continue to develop among the growing population of free blacks. Along with local organizations, such as the Prince Hall Masons and the MGCA, whose broadly defined mission was protesting slavery and racial discrimination, the convention movement was central to identifying and focusing national attention on the critical needs of the free black population. Increasingly, these needs were presented by the various racially autonomous general organizations under four specific headings: education, temperance, economy, and universal liberty. In the late 1820s and the 1830s, these would come to be defined by community leaders as the "rallying points" around which free blacks in the United States should coalesce. "We hope to make our people," announced black leaders at the 1835 National Negro Convention, "in theory and practice, thoroughly acquainted with these subjects, as a method of future action."[27] By suggesting that "acquaintance" with these subjects could be a source of "future action," black leaders implied that attention to these tenets could form the basis for political improvement.

While all general fraternal coalitions, including the black Freemasons, the MGCA, and the Negro Convention Movement, were involved in raising racial and political awareness and advertising the imperative of working toward universal liberty, commitment to economic prudence, temperance, and education was deemed so important to the survival of the free black population as to merit the development of individual organizations and societies whose focus would be more specifically directed to these aspects of individual improvement. The rise of African American literary societies in free black communities of the urban North in the late 1820s and throughout the 1830s was a direct response to community leaders' understanding that education was essential to improving the status and condition of the nation's African Americans, free and enslaved. The tremendous impact of the circulation of such texts as Walker's *Appeal* and the first African American newspaper, *Freedom's Journal*, offered black leaders further proof of the utility of printed texts as a means of heightening the black population's awareness of their condition and introducing strategies for improvement.[28] The earliest literary societies, although specifically focused on reading, writing, and literary discussion, were similar in their dynamic to the more general societies that came before them: they depended on a sense of collective rather than individual effort. Throughout the antebellum period, these literary societies served as intellectual centers for an increasingly unified and politically conscious ethnic group. By reading and by writing about themselves, African Americans sought to become part of a historical tradition. They used these forums for collective reading, writing, and discussion to combat charges of racial inferiority, validate their call for social justice, and alert their audience to the disparity between American ideals and racial inequality. Through these institutions, African Americans took the lead in calling for a substantive democracy. As Vincent Harding reminds us, they stood, in the early nineteenth century, as "the foremost proponents of freedom and justice in the nation, demanding of the Constitution more than its slave-holding creators dared to dream, wrestling it toward an integrity that the [Founding] Fathers would not give it."[29]

"STRANGERS AND OUTCASTS IN A STRANGE LAND"

As the case of David Walker's *Appeal* makes clear, one component of the promotion of reading and the circulation of printed texts generally was the extent to which they contributed to the development of a sense of national identity among African Americans in the United States. By the late 1820s, it was readily apparent that free blacks needed to develop their own internal strength, identify and articulate their own needs, and develop their own strategies and institutions to meet these needs if they were to survive in the United States. That print could be an instrument of nation-building and a medium through which a sense of black solidarity was both communicated and achieved was masterfully demonstrated by the *Appeal*. But even earlier examples of this are equally relevant to understanding the allure of print to African Americans and the development of literary societies in the late 1820s.

In the years leading up to the American Revolution, reading, writing, and print were increasingly seen to be technologies of power. Colonists turned to written texts in the form of pamphlets and broadsides as a medium of public expression. Through these documents, revolutionary leaders were able to generate and spread the language and spirit of revolution. The ability to read and write took on special significance in the emerging nation: "literacy" became a marker for citizenship. Because writing became, in the words of historian Michael Warner, the "dominant mode of the political," the ability to read and understand these written texts became the responsibility of every (white) man committed to independence.[30] That the United States formed itself through one written document, the Declaration of Independence, and then negotiated the terms of its existence through another, the Constitution, secured the status of writing and publication as a condition of legitimacy in the new nation. "No generation," legal historian Robert A. Ferguson has suggested of the Declaration and Constitution's framers, "has looked more carefully to the written word for identity"; they relied on their "faith in the text" to "stabilize the uncertain world in which they live[d]."[31] To rhetoric the Founders assigned the most complex tasks of the new country: declaring political independence from England and creating a unified body out of the former British colonies. They believed that if rhetoric could organize individuals into a collective and move them to reshape their condition, it could also lend durability to their experience.

These early efforts at nation-building provided free blacks in the urban North with a lesson; largely if not entirely excluded from the literary practices and processes that established the republic, they were exposed to and received underlying beliefs about the purposes for which literary skills could be used. After the Revolution, manumissions and schedules to abolish slavery continued to expand communities of free African Americans but did little to ensure their civil liberties or political rights. While guaranteeing the eventual extinction of slavery, judicial and legislative maneuvers also guaranteed that free blacks would face disenfranchisement and untold social and economic obstacles.[32] In an effort to band together to promote their own interests and to support each other financially, free blacks began to organize themselves into mutual aid societies in the last decades of the eighteenth century. Although mutual aid societies would also become important institutions among free black women in the early nineteenth century, the earliest and largest mutual aid societies were composed exclusively of men. The first for which records exist was formed in Newport, Rhode Island, in 1770. A similar organization was begun in 1787 in Philadelphia, the city with the largest population of free blacks, and in Boston a society was formed in 1796. These "Free African Societies," as they were called, as well as the hundreds of smaller mutual aid societies that developed in the first half of the nineteenth century, all worked on much the same principle.[33] Members paid a sum to join and a monthly fee, which was held "for the mutual benefit of each other." The society was then able to "hand forth to the needy" a certain amount each week or at a time of crisis, "provided this necessity [was] not brought on them by their own imprudence."[34]

The significance of these societies was not primarily in their role as relief organizations, although records indicate that mutual aid societies acquired tremendous amounts of money, which were distributed in various ways to address both individual and community needs. Their very existence—the first independent institutions formed and run by blacks themselves—was crucial to creating the nationalist imagination that allowed free blacks to recognize themselves as a community. The extant constitutions of the Philadelphia and Boston Free African Societies underscore the extent to which, from their use of Preambles to their Articles of Association and Constitutions, black leaders turned to the rhetorical structures used by white Americans to establish their own autonomous government. Implicit in their efforts to "declare" these organizations was a desire for independent recognition. Consider the Articles of Association of the Free African Society of Philadelphia (1787): "We, the free Africans and their descendants, of the City of Philadelphia . . . do unanimously agree, for the benefit of each other" (Douglass, *Annals*, 15), or the Preamble to the Constitution of Boston's African Society, written in 1796: "We, the African Members, form ourselves into a Society, under the above name, for the mutual benefit of each other, which may from time to time offer; behaving ourselves at the same time as true and faithful citizens of the Commonwealth in which we live; and that we take no one into the Society, who shall commit any injustice or outrage against the laws of their country."[35] By shaping texts that echo the "official" documents of United States government—in the case of the Boston Society, the "official" text is the United States Constitution, which was ratified in 1787—the "African Members" produce a document that is "almost the same, but not quite."[36] My understanding of this distinction is informed by the work of Homi Bhabha, who in *The Location of Culture* suggests the complicated ways in which "mimicry" is "at once resemblance and menace." Like the colonists of the revolutionary period, these free Africans employed written constitutions to give themselves recognition and, at least in their own communities, authority. In this case, however, their process of representation "is itself a process of disavowal." While modeled on those of the United States, the documents that define the free African societies and express their political desire stand in opposition to American nationalism. Recognizing the paraphernalia of authority inherent in the United States Constitution, they appropriate and challenge it by conferring similar privileges on a segment of society that, according to the drafters of the "official" Constitution, has no claim to that authority.

Once organized, the first mutual aid societies in Newport, Philadelphia, and Boston functioned as units of solidarity. The societies identified and promoted black leaders. They sponsored petitions and letters to the public addressing concerns of the African American community. The issues most important to members are documented in the societies' minutes: how they felt about themselves and how best to contend with their position in society; how financial assistance might be given to struggling members; how to develop the religious life of the community; how to address the question of emigration to Africa; and, increasingly, how to improve educational opportunities for themselves and their children.

The records of Newport's Free African Union Society and of Philadelphia's Free African Society confirm that the members of both societies were eager to compare their experiences as "strangers and outcasts in a strange land" (Douglass, *Annals*, 26). A visit by Mr. Henry Stewart, an active member of the Philadelphia organization, to the Newport and Boston societies in 1789 suggests the importance of such exchanges to forming a network of support for free blacks in the northeastern cities. All accounts indicate that Mr. Stewart was received hospitably when he arrived in Newport, where he made contact with the Newport Free African Society. Before leaving Newport he secured the following recommendation to serve as an introduction to Boston's Free African Society: "Mr. Henry Stewart, one of the members of the Freeholders, African Society, established in the city of Philadelphia for the benefit of the sick of said society, and other commendable purposes, has been with us a traveler, and has behaved himself as a truly worthy member, and as such we recommend him to all our friends, more particularly to the African Company now in the town of Boston."[37] This letter of introduction combined with Mr. Stewart's report to the "Boston Company" on the nature of the Newport society prompted communication between Boston and Newport: "These lines come to acquaint you that we have your recommended brother, Mr. Henry Stewart, and [are] happy to hear that you have such a society built on so laudable a foundation." The letter continues by informing its recipients of the activities of the Boston society: "We here are not idle, but are doing what we can to promote the interests and good of our dear brethren that stand in so much need at such a time as this" (Newport, 25–26).

Stewart's visit also prompted the Free African Union Society to write directly to the Philadelphia society, telling their membership that during Stewart's visit they had "had the pleasure of being informed of [the Philadelphia society's] formation" (Douglass, *Annals*, 25). Although the greetings exchanged by the societies in Newport and Philadelphia were typically warm, their correspondence suggests the diversity of opinions held by early African Americans. In a letter to the Philadelphia Free African Society, the members of the Newport Free African Union Society expressed their stand in favor of African colonization, citing Africa as a place where blacks might be "more happy than they can be here" (Douglass, *Annals*, 26). In response to their inquiry about the Philadelphia society's position on the issue of colonization, the members replied without enthusiasm: "With regard to the emigration to Africa you mention, we have at present little to communicate on that head" (Douglass, *Annals*, 28). More interested in remaining in the United States and proving "every pious man is a good citizen of the whole world" than being returned to Africa, the Philadelphia society presented its argument for working toward a day when "captivity shall cease, and buying and selling mankind have an end" (28, 29).

The commitment expressed by Philadelphia's Free African Society to establish themselves as upstanding members of the community and to work together for the public good is in fact central to their rules of organization and conduct. Originally organized by two black leaders, Richard Allen and Absalom Jones, who "beheld with sorrow . . . [the] irreligious and uncivilized state" of free blacks in Philadelphia, the society instituted a code of conduct that would disseminate positive images of African Americans as upstanding citizens (Douglass, *Annals*, 15). "No drunkard or disorderly person" could be admitted as a member, and if any member "should prove disorderly after having been received, the said disorderly person [was to be] disjoined from . . . [the society], without having any of his subscription money returned" (16). Strict rules monitored the payment of dues and attendance at society meetings. Members were instructed to "lay aside all superfluity of naughtiness, especially gaming and feasting" (31) and were visited regularly by "overseers" to ensure that "no breach of good order was observed" (41). Given its historical association with the institution of slavery, the title "overseer" seems an odd if appropriate designation. As historian Julie Winch argues, the rules of the Free African Society "gradually moved from regulating the lives of its members to defining the standards of behavior which were acceptable for the community as a whole."[38] Members of the society placed increasing faith in the belief that "imprudent conduct stops the mouths of our real friends, who would ardently plead our cause," and "enables our enemies to declare we are not fit for freedom" (Douglass, *Annals*, 32).

Efforts to prove themselves "respectable" in the eyes of the white community did not, however, prevent the free African societies from asserting their separate identity by directing themselves to the needs of the black community. Records of the Newport Free African Union Society and Philadelphia and Boston's free African societies indicate that ensuring proper burial for the deceased was a motivating force behind the organization of mutual aid societies. One of the first collective efforts of Philadelphia's Free African Society was to petition the city of Philadelphia to allow that "the burial-ground called the Potter's field, [be] in part appropriated for the burial of black persons" (Douglass, *Annals*, 34). The term "potter's field" was used to designate a burial place for "strangers" or those not accepted in other places. Contrary to the implications of these spaces, the members' "[desire] to have the said burial ground under the care of [the Free African Society]" and their willingness "to pay the same rent that hath been offered by any other person, and a year's advance as soon as said ground is enclosed" suggest the importance of proper burial and lasting memorials to the maintenance of their fragile community (34).[39]

The treatment of the deceased had special significance to early African Americans because of their African religious heritage, which emphasized the interdependence of the living and the dead. But, given the difficult and uncertain conditions of their lives, free blacks' concern for proper burial was a means of seeking some degree of dignity, security, and remembrance—if only in the form of a respectable place to be buried. The relegation of blacks to potter's fields and strangers' burial grounds was in keeping with efforts of slaveholders to strip slaves of all legitimate family ties and community relationships when enslaved; in the antebellum North, it suggested the indifference with which people of African descent were viewed. Through the efforts of mutual aid societies, free blacks were able to develop and protect areas in which to remember their relatives. Determined that their lives would be marked by respect, they sustained a belief that respect for the dead would help define the humanity of the living.[40]

Paradoxically, the development of independent African American

institutions and the movement toward self-determination they represented were met by the rapid deterioration of conditions for free
blacks in northern cities at the beginning of the nineteenth century.
Instead of recognition for their impressive accomplishments, black
Americans faced revitalized charges of innate black inferiority and the
escalation of exclusionist policies. Although technically "free," blacks
were increasingly subject to open hostility and discrimination, and the
passing of the Fugitive Slave Law in 1793 led to increased incidents
of kidnapping. While the first decades of the nineteenth century saw
the expansion of suffrage to all white men, free blacks gradually lost
the right to vote that had, during the late eighteenth century, been
granted to them in most of the northern states. In the urban North,
competition with foreign immigrants for jobs often left black Americans without work. Emerging Jacksonian capitalism contributed to
unprecedented economic upheaval and accompanying social chaos.
Rapid economic development and the resulting fluctuation of status
among the white population created new anxieties, which were re-
lieved through increased racial violence and expressions of white su-
premacy. By seeing themselves as better than blacks, the lowest classes
of white Americans ensured their superiority over at least one segment
of society. In this hardening racist atmosphere, almost every social and
educational institution and mechanism of support in the northern
cities was closed to free blacks. Religious and secular organizations
alike were unwilling to accept African American membership or participation, or to extend their beneficent support to free blacks in need
of assistance.[41]

Mutual aid societies were essential to fostering economic security,
but there was also a need for public voice, particularly a public voice
seen as "learned." As early as the first decade of the nineteenth century,
some mutual aid societies began to call for the revision and expansion
of their functions to include more deliberate writing and public presentation of their condition. In an address to the New York African
Society for Mutual Relief in 1809, William Hamilton commended an
essay cowritten by two "colored" men of the community not only for
its important subject, the abolition of the slave trade, but also for
being an example of the kind of writing in demand. He urged others
to write equally carefully constructed and powerful essays: "If we

continue to produce specimens like these," he said, "we shall soon put our enemies to the blush; abashed and confounded they shall quit the field, and no longer urge their superiority of souls."[42] Underlying Hamilton's comments is an understanding of both the ubiquity of and the difficulty of disproving the discourse of black intellectual inferiority. His concern that "we have not produced any to excel in arts and sciences" was based in his belief that literary and intellectual contributions would alter the standing of African Americans in American society. Among other things, it would enable them to make economic gains and move into trades from which they were largely excluded: "what station above the common employment of craftsmen and labourers," he wondered aloud, "would we fill, did we possess both learning and abilities?" (Hamilton, 36). Although Hamilton's address indicates the broad focus of the New York African Society for Mutual Relief on economic, social, religious, and political issues, it is immersed in concerns for literary style and production. He advocates an agenda for promoting black opportunities and equality that is grounded in African American literary practice.

Throughout the first three decades of the nineteenth century, free blacks expressed increasing consciousness that they were living in "the golden age of Literature" and subscribed to the theory that interaction with "the Literature of the day . . . brings in regular succession the condensed learning of past ages; and all the erudition of the present."[43] In the midst of a dominant society for whom knowledge of the arts, sciences, and literature was highly valued, blacks increasingly believed that they needed to read widely and produce documents that were sophisticated in their presentation, as well as their content. "The age in which we live is fastidious in its taste," acknowledged William Whipper in an address to an early literary society in Philadelphia in 1828. "The orator [and writer] must display the pomp of words, the magnificence of the tropes and figures, or he will be considered unfit for the duties of his profession." But, he continued, "such high-wrought artificial [presentations] are like beautiful paint upon windows, they rather obscure than admit the light of the sun. Truth should always be exhibited in such a dress as may be best suited to the state of the audience, accompanied with every principle of science and reason" (Whipper, *Address*, 107).

"DREADED ELOQUENCE"

As they increased in number and grew, African American mutual aid and artisan societies continued to function as working-class support systems: by 1849, Philadelphia had 106 mutual aid societies, to which more than half of the African American population belonged.[44] Coalitions established around reading and writing developed alongside these institutions and flourished in the vibrant black communities of the urban North. Literary societies were both formal and informal, large and small; they organized discussion groups and supported libraries and reading rooms. Some instructed beginning readers, while others supported those more advanced. Literary societies planned reading lists and schedules; they provided regular opportunities for authors to "publish" original literary creations and for audiences to encourage, discuss, and criticize their ideas and presentation. The societies helped train future orators and leaders by sponsoring debates on issues of importance to the black community. In supporting the development of a literate public they furthered the evolution of a black public sphere and politically conscious society.

The mechanics of societies organized around reading and literature were much the same as those of mutual aid societies, so much so that the Constitution of the Colored Reading Society of Philadelphia, organized in 1828 for "Men of Colour, who are citizens of the City and Liberties of Philadelphia,"[45] reads simply: "All persons initiated into this Society shall become members in the same mode as is customary in all benevolent institutions, with the same strictness and regard to the moral qualifications as is necessary in all institutions to secure their welfare" (Whipper, *Address*, 107). Members were to pay an initiation fee and monthly dues.[46] The bylaws of the society made it clear that their focus would be literary and not more generally beneficent. The fourth item in the constitution stipulated that "all monies received by this Society" be "expended in useful books, such as the Society may from time to time appropriate." The fifth item stated that "all books initiated into this Society shall be placed in the care of the Librarian belonging to said institution, and it shall be his duty to deliver to said members alternatively, such books as they shall demand" (107–08). The members of the society agreed to "meet once a week to return and receive books, to read, and express whatever sentiments they may have conceived if they think proper, and transact the necessary business relative to this institution" (108). "It shall be our whole duty," they resolved, "to instruct and assist each other in the improvement of our minds, as we wish to see the flame of improvement spreading amongst our brethren, and friends" (108).

The guiding principle of Philadelphia's Colored Reading Society was that "the station of a scholar highly versed in classic lore . . . is indeed higher than any other occupied by man" (Whipper, *Address*, 109). Members adopted a "course of study" that would allow them to cultivate both intellectual competence and artistic sensibility. They subscribed to the belief that the "acquisition of knowledge is not the only design of a liberal education"; in addition to amassing knowledge, a goal of their reading was to "discipline the mind itself, to strengthen and enlarge its powers, to form habits of close and accurate thinking, and to acquire a facility of classifying and arranging, analyzing and comparing our ideas on different subjects" (110). The "cultivation of taste" required attention to "the study of belle lettres, to criticism, to composition, pronunciation, style, and to everything included in the name of eloquence" (113). They believed that classical texts would facilitate the fulfillment of their ambition. From these texts, "a fund of ideas is acquired on a variety of subjects; the taste is greatly improved by conversing with the best models; the imagination is enriched by the fine scenery with which the classics abound; and an acquaintance is formed with human nature, together with the history, customs and manners of antiquity" (111). In addition to the classics and works by "our best English writers," the society filled its library with "books treating . . . the subject of Ancient Modern and Ecclesiastical History, [and] the Laws of Pennsylvania" and subscribed to at least two important journals of the time, the *Genius of Universal Emancipation* and the first African American newspaper, *Freedom's Journal*.[47] The founders of the Colored Reading Society believed that exposure to all of these texts and the conversations they inspired would allow the society's membership to "contribut[e] something to the advancement of science [and literature] generally amongst our brethren," while also providing opportunities to "become acquainted with the transacting of public affairs" (Whipper, *Address*, 118, 110).

Like that of most early literary societies, the fate of the Colored Reading Society is uncertain. When Joseph Willson outlined the most prominent of the active literary societies of Philadelphia in his 1841 *Sketches of the Higher Classes of Colored Society*, the Colored Reading Society was not mentioned.[48] One of its founding members, William Whipper, was part of a group that began the Philadelphia Library Company of Colored Persons in 1833, which suggests that the Library Company of Colored Persons may have absorbed the membership of the Colored Reading Society. Modeled after the Library Company of Philadelphia, begun by Benjamin Franklin in 1731 for "literary and scientific discussion, the reading of original essays, poems, and so forth," the membership of the Library Company of Colored Persons was composed of free black males.[49] From its first announcement, the Library Company of Colored Persons boasted it was neither "sectarian" nor "a mere fractional effort, the design of any single society among us." Rather, the Library Company was formed in recognition of the "necessity of promoting among our rising youth, a proper cultivation for literary pursuits and improvement of the faculties and powers of their minds," and designed "to embrace the entire population of the City of Philadelphia."[50] The members' request for "such books or other donations as will facilitate the object of this institution" accompanied the public announcement of their organization. Books were to be made accessible at minimal cost. Members could read on their own or participate in a reading schedule. In addition, in order to promote research, discussion, and debate, the Library Company sponsored a weekly lecture series, which ran from October through May. The Library Company of Colored Persons was still a strong institution in 1837, when James Forten Jr., at a meeting of the American Moral Reform Society, cited it as an example of the state of learning among the colored population of Philadelphia. "Our Library Association is gaining strength every day," he reported. "We have a well supplied stock of books collected from the most useful and varied productions of the age."[51] By 1838 the Library Company had more than 600 volumes in their collection and at least 150 members.[52]

Begun in 1833, New York's Phoenix Society, which included a broader segment of the African American community than the Colored Reading Society, was founded on the theory that the "condition" of African Americans could "only be meliorated by their being improved in morals, literature, and mechanic arts."[53] The directors called on "every person of color to unite himself, or herself, to [the Phoenix Society], and faithfully endeavor to promote its objects" (Phoenix, 141). To facilitate this, the Society had a unique policy on fees: its constitution stipulated that membership would be open to "all persons who contribute to its funds quarterly, any sum of money they may think proper." Despite this provision, the directors set ambitious goals. The first of these was to "immediately" raise "at least Ten Thousand Dollars" for the "establishment and sustaining of a Manual Labour School" (142). The ultimate goal of the Phoenix Society was to transform New York City's entire black population into a "useful portion of the community" (141). Their first step was to divide the black communities into "wards" and to form committees to "make a register of every colored person" that documented whether "they read, write and cipher" (144). By making contacts throughout the community they would "induce" not only children but also adults to attend school. They planned to "establish circulating libraries in each ward for the use of people of colour on very moderate pay,—to establish mental feasts, and also lyceums for speaking and for lectures on sciences" (144).

It took only eight months for the Phoenix Society to begin fulfilling its goals. In a letter dated 7 December 1833 and printed in the *Colonizationist and Journal of Freedom*, Samuel Cornish outlined the goals and activities of the "library and Reading Room lately opened by the executive committee of the Phoenix Society." "The objects of the institution are generally improvement and the training of our youth to habits of reading and reflection," he explained. In addition to a "course of lectures . . . on morals, economy, and the arts and sciences generally," the Society conducted three "class[es] of readers," each consisting of "25 or 30 or more." Each class was to have "selected its course of reading and appointed the readers, whose duty it shall be to read for one hour. All classes shall note prominent parts, and then retire into the adjacent room to converse on the subjects, together with occurrences of the day, calculated to cultivate the mind and improve the heart."[54]

References such as this one to the appointment of readers, as well as descriptions of societies whose focus was memorization and public reading rather than strictly individual literary study, indicate the importance placed on the practices of reading aloud and recitation by some early African American literary societies. By the early nineteenth century, reading aloud had long been a prominent feature of European and European American reading circles. In the case of the earliest African American literary societies, the emphasis on the performative aspect of literary learning and on the sharing of texts indicates that membership in a literary society and basic literacy—the ability to read—did not necessarily go together. Some societies, such as Boston's Minors' Exhibition Society, were founded expressly "for the laudable purpose of improving [young black people's] minds by committing to memory and reciting select articles of prose and poetry."[55] Reading texts aloud fostered an environment in which a truly democratic "sharing" of texts could take place, and it ensured that cohesive groups could be formed from individuals with widely divergent literacy skills. Because the process of silent reading of the text was not privileged over its oral performance, subsequent discussions could involve those who listened to the text's performance as well as those with the ability to read it for themselves. In this sense, "cultivating the mind" had less to do with basic literacy skills than it did with fostering exposure to literary texts and the discussions which they prompted.

Cornish's letter to the *Colonizationist and Journal of Freedom* includes an appeal for "donations from the favored people of New York, in books, maps, papers, money, etc., for the benefit of our feeble institution." The acknowledgment of a number of donations in a February 1834 issue of *The Emancipator* indicates that this appeal was well-received.[56] The Phoenix Society's library was reported to be a "good collection of valuable books" that included "much that is rare and choice in English Literature [and] a considerable amount of History and Science."[57] Despite this success, the Phoenix Society was unable to maintain its momentum. Although their rooms continued to serve for a time as a community space, the literary society folded.[58] In an 1839 letter to the editor of the *Colored American*, an anonymous member of another literary society, the Phoenixonian Society, reported that the " 'Phoenix Society' has gone out of existence." His interest was in the Phoenix Society's library, which was apparently still intact. Reminding his readers that the bulk of the Phoenix Society's texts had been originally donated to the society "for the improvement of the colored population of this city," he lamented that "these books now are not serving any high interest, or adding to the mental stature of that class for which they were designed." "I am connected with a Literary Society which has enrolled among its members a considerable portion of the young and active talent of our city . . . a society that has done considerable . . . [good] in the cause of Literature, and the members of which are putting forth exertions to improve their minds, and prepare themselves for usefulness among our people," he wrote. "This society has no Library, and as I hear the Library of the 'Phoenix Society' is to be given to some Literary Association, I have thought our destitute state a demand for this Library, and an inducement for us to put in our claims. The amount of good the possession of this Library would affect among us, I will not pretend to calculate. Our destitute state, and inability to obtain books we sorely feel. Doubtless the influence of a good Library—such a Library as the 'Phoenix Society' are about to dispose of, would be salutary in the highest extent."[59]

The Phoenixonian Literary Society was structured differently than the Phoenix Society; they sponsored a lecture series each year to which the public was invited. Lectures were given by members as well as guests from other cities. Topics included "Astronomy," "Duty of Young Men," "Patriots of the American Revolution," and "Music—Its Practical Influence on Society."[60] Interest in the lectures seems to have varied from year to year. The society's fifth anniversary celebration, for instance, which took place in 1838, was something of a disappointment to one attendee, who arrived to find "but few of [the society's] members, and several ladies." "Surprised at the emptiness of the hall," he was told that "a new Society has appointed a meeting in the neighborhood of the Hall, at the same hour, and that this arrangement had detained many of the members, and disappointed many persons who were deeply interested in both meetings." Of the meeting, the spectator commented: "Though we were well entertained, the audience did not enjoy so great an intellectual feast as they anticipated that the society would furnish." The disappointing anniversary meeting occurred at a particularly unfortunate time, lending reinforcement to the "impression . . . among the public, that this Society has gone by the board."[61] In fact, the Phoenixonian Society joined with the Philomathean Literary Society to sponsor a public exhibition on behalf of the captives of the *Amistad* in September 1839 at which $104.83 was raised.[62] It held regular business meetings and supported an especially diverse lecture series through 1841, when it celebrated its eighth anniversary.[63]

For African Americans in the early nineteenth century, these societies offered a protected, collective environment in which to develop a literary background as well as the oral and written skills needed to express and represent themselves with confidence. Nowhere is this made clearer than in the description of the Female Literary Association, an association for which William Lloyd Garrison expressed particularly high praise in the pages of the *Liberator*. In an address to its members on the occasion of the first anniversary of their coalition, words written "by a member" and later published by the *Liberator* in 1832 draw a parallel between the role of the literary society for its members and the "vault" Demosthenes built to provide him with the needed privacy to overcome the defects of his speech. "On his first attempt to speak in public, he was hissed." Still, Demosthenes developed the will to overcome his ridicule in a vault he built where "he might practice without disturbance." By referring to this particular story in her anniversary address, the writer of these words insists that the "brilliant success" that resulted from Demosthenes' "seclusion" is also available through the protective "vault" created by the women's literary society itself. She equates the words Demosthenes masters during his time spent in the vault with powerful weapons: as the "first orator of the age," his "eloquence was more dreaded . . . than all the fleets and armies of Athens."[64]

In the hostile racial climate of the United States, such "dreaded eloquence" was a necessity. Literary societies provided free blacks in the urban North with opportunities to practice and perform literacy and allowed them to experiment with voice and self-representation in ways that approximated the ideals of civic participation. One result of this experience was the immutable connection established by black Americans between the forms of literacy cultivated in African American literary societies and political activity. Just as literary societies were modeled as political communities, complete with constitutions, amendments, and elections, the open discussion and sharing of opinion that took place in the sheltered environment of the literary society were suggestive of the ways that political voices might be exchanged in an ideal democracy. So important was this atmosphere that, largely excluded from any meaningful political activity, the founders of the Phoenix Society saw the need to divide New York's black community into "wards," not for electoral strategy but to determine and enact a plan to systematically augment the levels of literacy in the city. That expressions of public and political voice by African Americans were unwelcome in the larger American society gave the literary activities of free blacks an aspect of resistance. Rather than using their literacy and literary skills to function openly as citizens, free blacks in the urban North were forced to use them as a means of self-defense and to fight for the right to enter the sphere of politics. Increasingly, this use of literacy was represented metaphorically in the language of the military and of weaponry.[65] These metaphors suggest the extent to which African American literary societies, however protective as institutions, worked to prepare their members to interact in a larger American society where they needed to defend themselves against the condemnation and ridicule they regularly confronted.

"TO CULTIVATE THE TALENTS ENTRUSTED TO OUR KEEPING"

African American women found literary societies to be especially important and popular resources. In 1831 the number of female mutual aid societies in the city of Philadelphia outnumbered male mutual aid societies 27 to 16.[66] Black women, working in even lower-paying situations than black men, were in greater need of the financial safety net that mutual aid societies provided. This numerical balance may also have been true of literary societies. Although deprived of the advantages of formal schooling, black women had a desire to educate themselves. Evidence suggests that women's literary societies from 1830 to 1850 may have outnumbered men's, even though they did not exceed them in size or prominence.[67] Whereas men's literary societies typically consisted of a large membership and sponsored public lectures and debates, women's societies were more likely to assemble in small groups in a member's home. In contrast to the formal documents that represent many of the men's literary societies, one-line announcements in journals of the day are often all that remain to record early African American women's literary societies. One such small entry in the 24 August 1827 issue of *Freedom's Journal* reads, "A Society of Young Ladies has been formed at Lynn, Mass., to meet once a week, to read in turn to the society, works adapted to virtuous and literary improvement."[68]

Largely because it attracted the attention of William Lloyd Garrison, one black women's literary society from the early nineteenth century stands as an exception to this pattern. Dedicated to the success of their own association and determined to see their effort duplicated by other black women throughout the North, the Female Literary Association of Philadelphia sent a copy of their constitution to Garrison for publication in the *Liberator* soon after their organization in the fall of 1831. Although "accidently mislaid" for a time, the constitution was printed in the paper on 3 December 1831.[69] Garrison's own report of his visit to "a society of colored ladies, called the female literary association," appeared in the Ladies' Department of the *Liberator* in June 1832. "The members assemble every Tuesday evening," he told his readers, "for the purpose of mutual improvement in moral and literary pursuits. Nearly all of them write, almost weekly, original pieces, which are put anonymously into a box, and afterward criticized by a committee." "If the traducers of the colored race could be acquainted with the moral worth, just refinement, and large intelligence of this association," Garrison concluded, "their mouths would hereafter be dumb." His impression of the literary society resulted from the "intellectual promise" he perceived from the group's conversation, but he equally admired the very fact of their coalition. "Having been permitted to bring with him several of [their] pieces [of writing]," Garrison "commence[d] their publication [in the *Liberator*], not only for their merit, but also to induce the colored ladies of other places to go and do likewise."[70]

No less than their male counterparts, the members of the Female Literary Association of Philadelphia felt it a "duty incumbent upon us, as women—as daughters of a despised race—to use our utmost endeavors to enlighten the understanding, and cultivate the talents entrusted to our keeping."[71] They saw collective reading, recitation, and writing as a way to "break down the strong barrier of prejudice, and raise ourselves to an equality with those of our fellow beings who differ from us in complexion, but who are, with ourselves, children of one Eternal Parent." Although this clause from the Female Literary Association's constitution suggests that its members were intent on proving themselves the intellectual equals of white citizens, their literary association was equally informed by their desire to manifest the affiliation they increasingly felt with those who remained enslaved.

The Pennsylvania legislature's 1831 consideration of measures to further restrict the rights of free blacks and to strengthen fugitive slave laws had underscored the tentative nature of black freedom, even in the "free" North. The uncertain freedom of free blacks was further exposed by the fact that, despite the relative safety of the urban North, they were increasingly subject to kidnapping and "return" to the South by overeager slave hunters. In this deteriorating racial climate, the fact that free, northern black women were more and more often in direct contact with fugitive slaves worked to dispel the sense of distance they perceived between themselves and those who remained enslaved. All of these factors came together to stimulate a renewed commitment to antislavery efforts in free black women that was embodied in their literary activities.[72]

Sarah Mapps Douglass, the daughter of black abolitionists Robert and Grace Bustill Douglass and a member of the Female Literary Association, communicated this sentiment in an address to the Association in 1832. Beginning with a quote from an unidentified English writer who advised, "We must feel deeply before we can act rightly," Douglass shared the story of her own awakening to activism with the membership of the Female Literary Association. "One short year ago, how different were my feelings on the subject of slavery!" she told her audience,

> It is true, the wail of the captive sometimes came to my ear in the midst of my happiness, and caused my heart to bleed for his wrongs; but, alas! the impression was as evanescent as the early cloud and morning dew. I had formed a little world of my own, and cared not to move beyond its precincts. But how was the scene changed when I beheld the oppressor lurking on the border of my peaceful home! I saw his iron hand stretched forth to seize me as his prey, and the cause of the slave became my own. I started up, and with one mighty effort threw from me the lethargy which had covered me as a mantle for years; and determined, by the help of the Almighty, to use every exertion in my power to elevate the character of my wronged and neglected race.

Douglass believed that one way to help elevate her "wronged and neglected race" was through literary activity. The exercises of the Female Literary Association were a means of refining and asserting the intellectual abilities of black women while also creating documents, such as the address that Douglass composed and read before the Association, which was later printed in the pages of the *Liberator*, that would give public expression to their "feeling of deep sympathy for [their] brethren and sisters." Their "mental feasts" were not only opportunities for the free black women to "feed [their] never-dying minds"; they also hoped to publicize through their literary work their own intellectual abilities and the injustice of slavery and racism. Douglass's description of the meeting's events as she hoped they would unfold underlines the group's sense of dual focus: "I would respectfully recommend that our mental feast should commence by reading a portion of the Holy Scriptures. A pause should proceed the reading for supplication. It is my wish that the reading and conversation should be altogether directed to the subject of slavery. The refreshment that may be offered to you for the body, will be of the most simple kind, that you may feel for those who have nothing to refresh the body and mind."[73]

The authority with which Douglass proposed the meeting's agenda at the end of her address suggests that the Female Literary Association did not assemble haphazardly. A sense of their mission and their goals directed their literary activities. In 1832 Douglass served as the Female Literary Association's secretary; but it is likely that she was responsible for setting the Association's agenda on that day because she had prepared and delivered the principal address rather than because of her leadership role within the Association. That the meeting proceeded more or less as Douglass suggested is confirmed by this account, written by a white woman invited to attend the meeting and printed in the *Liberator* alongside Douglass's address:

> Soon after they were all quietly seated, a short address, prepared for the occasion, was read by the authoress [Sarah Mapps Douglass], a copy of which is herewith sent. The fifty-fourth beautiful and encouraging chapter of Isaiah was then read. After sitting a short time under a solemn and impressive silence that ensured the reading of the chapter, one of the company vocally petitioned our Heavenly Father for a continuation of his favor, &c. The remainder of the evening was occupied principally by their severally reading and relating affecting slave tales, calculated to bring forcibly into view the deplorable situation of our fellow creatures at the south—both the oppressor and the

oppressed. This interesting interview was closed with singing an appropriate hymn.[74]

As described by Sarah Douglass and confirmed by the white visitor to the Female Literary Association, the activities of this group defy simple definition. Members functioned alternatively as producers, distributors, and consumers of texts whose variety ranged from the religious to the poetic to the political. One self-conscious objective of their reading was to refine their sensibilities by producing emotional expressions of sympathy for those less fortunate. Another was to give active form and voice to the social and historical contexts in which they lived and to their own burgeoning political perspectives. They believed that by cultivating their talents they were primarily serving God, whose intellectual gifts were a source of power and whose will dictated that this power be both developed and disciplined. All of these purposes came together under the rubric of self-improvement and moral and intellectual growth.

Approximately twenty women formed the initial membership of the Female Literary Association. Like the men's societies, it was governed by the offices of president, vice president, secretary, and treasurer. An Agent was chosen and a Purchasing Committee formed annually to "procure suitable books" and journals for the society; the librarian's responsibility was to ensure the books were properly returned to the library at the end of each meeting. The society operated on an annual subscription basis, and the cost for one year's membership was $1.50. Because one of the central activities of this society's membership was writing, the society appointed a Committee of Examination whose task it was "to inspect and read to the Association such papers as might be [anonymously] placed in the box."[75]

This practice of submitting their writing anonymously, to be criticized by members of the Association, warrants further analysis, especially as the members' desire for anonymity seems to contradict the sense of safety and intimacy that was implied by the small group, single-sex setting. The circulation of writing without attaching the given name of the author to it was in keeping with antebellum literary practice, when anonymous and pseudonymous authorship was common. But in the case of a literary society like the Female Literary Association, this culture of anonymity and masking was uniquely able to contribute to the development of a wide variety of practices particularly well-suited to helping antebellum free black women to position and reposition themselves in multiple and productive ways. Like the strategy of attributing their literary work to the will of God, which provided a veneer of passivity to their literary efforts that protected them from accusations of impropriety and arrogance, the mask of anonymity allowed black women to confidently experiment with roles that might otherwise have remained socially and culturally outside the realm of accepted norms. The exclusion of women from most of the antebellum political and intellectual associations organized by black men reflects the male-oriented and male-dominated nature of the political and intellectual world they imagined. In keeping with the boundaries of this world, free black women seem to have understood that their engagement with serious political issues should be limited. Middle-class black women, like their white counterparts, were taught to cultivate dispositions that were amiable and meek, and they were made to understand that "the voice of a woman should not be heard in public debates."[76]

Faced with what Sarah Mapps Douglass described as the "iron hand" of slavery and oppression, however, free black women were increasingly reluctant to remain in a "little world of [their] own." In this context, paradigms of nineteenth-century American life that associate the activities of men with the public sphere and women with the domestic provide an inadequate framework for understanding the importance of literary societies for African American women. In many respects, the common conditions under which black men and black women lived made their agendas and means of pursuing them more similar than different: it was these similarities that prompted Frances E. W. Harper in 1869 to argue that "when it [is] a question of race we let the lesser question of sex go."[77] Black women as well as black men were called on to articulate their responses to racist ideology. Historical associations of the black female body with unbridled sexuality made black women particularly susceptible to the public perception of being shiftless. This particular interpretation of black womanhood, debasing both psychologically and materially, radically refigured black women as Other.[78] It heightened black women's racial identity and made them keenly aware of the great work to be done in the struggle for equality.

The practices of free black women in literary societies such as the Female Literary Association embodied the contradictory demands that they faced to be simultaneously meek and vocal, submissive and assertive. Literary associations allowed their members to occupy what Carla Peterson has called a "state of liminality," which Peterson, quoting Victor Turner, argues situated them "betwixt and between the positions assigned and arrayed by law, custom, [and] convention."[79] Members of the Female Literary Association's adoption of pseudonyms and the Association's use of the box demonstrates the way anonymity mediated the two poles of submissiveness and assertiveness between which the members oscillated. In the setting of the literary society, women might politely disagree with one another; but under the veil of anonymity provided by the practices of taking on pseudonyms for publication and submitting their writing anonymously to the box, these disagreements could develop into extended, political conversations that expressed sharp dissension from the perspectives of their male counterparts or, more to the point, from those of one another. Similarly, literary societies provided a setting where women could express themselves in lyrical poetry; but through various strategies of masking and anonymity, it was also a place where black women found ways to voice radical political convictions in fiery rhetoric.

An example of this can be seen in the writing of Sarah Forten, one of the daughters of Philadelphia sailmaker and community leader James Forten Sr., and a member of the Female Literary Association. Socially imposed constraints of both race and gender would have forbidden Sarah Forten to engage in public and political conversation. By taking on a pen name, however, Forten shielded herself from accusations of impropriety that would come with directly addressing her audience in both a public and a political way. Using the alias "Ada," and, less frequently, "Magawisca," Forten became a regular contributor of occasional poetry to the *Liberator* and other antebellum publications.[80] The name "Ada," derived from the first female name in the Old Testament, was a popular pseudonym for female writers in the antebellum period.[81] The name "Magawisca" may have been less familiar to her antebellum audience. It was drawn from the name of a character in Catherine Maria Sedgwick's *Hope Leslie; or Early Times in Massachusetts*, published in 1827. Sedgwick's novel revolves around two strong female characters. Hope Leslie is the daughter of Puritan Governor John Winthrop; but it is the other female character, Magawisca, the daughter of a Pequot chieftain, that Forten evokes by appropriating her name. "Although marked by the peculiarities of her race," writes Sedgwick of Magawisca, she "was beautiful even to an European eye." Despite the oppression she suffers because of her race, Magawisca is a strong young woman of noble birth, described in terms that both epitomize feminine ideals and challenge the idea that women are weak and must be passive. She is "slender, flexible, and graceful; and . . . tempered with modesty." Yet she is also able to withstand unwarranted insults and racist slurs with dignity. Forten's choice of the name Magawisca implies her desire to attach to her own prose and identity the passionate nature of Sedgwick's character, whose articulateness, courage in the face of oppression, and fierce, unwavering loyalty to the ideals of universal liberty she would have found admirable.[82]

Many critics have noted that extensive analysis of the writing of the Female Literary Association is particularly challenging because of the impossibility of positively matching pseudonyms with group members. Nevertheless, as Marie Lindhorst has illustrated in her own work on the Female Literary Association, it is possible to identify some writers with a degree of certainty and to trace the dynamics of the group through their anonymous submissions to the box.[83] Instrumental to this process is Garrison's promise to publish in the pages of the *Liberator* the writing of members of the Female Literary Association after his visit to the group in June 1832. Garrison's offer to publish this writing in the "Ladies' Department" of the *Liberator* is telling: it underscores the assumptions under which he operated regarding the circumscribed place of women's voices and their intellectual work in the abolitionist movement. But despite the limits he undiscriminatingly imposed on women's writing, Garrison's newspaper is a source of great insight into the creative work, the discussion, and the debates that took place in the context of the Female Literary Association. Included in Garrison's initial report in the *Liberator* on the Female Literary Association is a piece by "Zillah," a name frequently used by Sarah Douglass, titled "To a Friend." Zillah's piece is an excerpt of a conversation that took place at one of the Association's meetings that focused on the bill pending before the Pennsylvania legislature that proposed limiting the movement of free blacks into and out of the state and forcing free black residents of the state to register themselves and carry identification at all times. "You ask me," meditated Zillah, rhetorically, "if I do not despair on account of the Bill now before our Legislature? I am cast down but not in despair." She exemplified both the courage and the hope inherent in her response by referring to the story of a brave Quaker martyr: if "a double portion of her humility and fortitude may be ours," mused Zillah, the United States would be transformed into a place where true freedom and equal rights were available to all.[84]

Zillah's prose demonstrates the way in which members of the Female Literary Association referred to literary texts and characters that they discovered in their reading to illustrate and reinforce their own ideas and assertions. While meditations such as Zillah's suggest the extent to which these women were concerned with issues of slavery and their own status as free blacks, other extant writing attributed to members illustrates that the Association also promoted the exchange of ideas. Polite discussion may have reigned at the meetings themselves; but the system of submitting pieces of writing to the box encouraged open (if anonymous) dialogue and provided black women with a protected way to engage with one another, to assert their opinions, and to debate the efficacy of various strategies of resistance. In July and August 1832, the *Liberator* printed a series of articles that had been taken from the box and processed through the Female Literary Association's system of anonymous review. The catalyst for their writing was an article written by "A Colored Female of Philadelphia" on the subject of emigration; it is unclear whether she was a member of the Female Literary Association, or whether its members had seen her article as avid readers of the *Liberator*. While the author unquestioningly rejected the idea of the black population's emigrating to Africa or even to Canada, she proposed Mexico as a possible place for American blacks to reestablish themselves. "The government of these United States is not the only one in this hemisphere that offers equal rights to men," she wrote,

but there are others, under whose protection we may safely reside, where it is no disgrace to wear a sable complexion, and where our rights will not be continually trampled on, on that account. . . . [I] believe that the time has arrived, when we too ought to manifest that

spirit of independence which shines so conspicuously in the character of Europeans, by leaving the land of oppression, and emigrating
where we may be received and treated as brothers; where our worth
will be felt and acknowledged; and where we may acquire education,
wealth, and respectability, together with a knowledge of the arts and
sciences. . . . Where is that country to which we may remove, and
thus become free and equal? I believe that country to be Mexico. . . . I
would not wish to be thought pleading the cause of colonization, for
no one detests it more than I do. I would not be taken to Africa, were
the Society [American Colonization Society] to make me 'queen of
the country' . . . I am informed that the population of Mexico is eight
millions of colored, and one million of whites; and by the rapid
growth of amalgamation amongst them, there is every probability
that it will ere long become one entire colored nation.[85]

While the idea of "one entire colored nation" held great appeal for
this writer, submissions to the Female Literary Association's box illustrate the extent to which members of the Female Literary Association
debated the issue of colonization. In a piece printed in the *Liberator* on
21 July 1832, Zillah rejected emigration to "Hayti" or Mexico as unsafe.
She did not support any emigration plan for black Americans, however, not primarily because of the risk involved but because the United
States "is our home," even as it "unkindly strives to throw me from her
bosom." In a letter printed in the 18 August 1832 issue of the *Liberator*,
another member of the Female Literary Association, whose adopted
pen name was "Woodby," began her address by making it clear that
she was writing in response to "[Zillah's] reply to 'A Colored Female of
Philadelphia,' read at our last meeting." Zillah had, Woodby believed,
misunderstood the author's position on emigration to Mexico. Like
many others, Woodby abhorred the idea of colonization and would
resist being "obliged to leave this place." But, she emphasized, blacks
had to anticipate that the time might come when "the people of these
United States should make such compulsory laws" that African Americans might be forced to emigrate. It was wise, Woodby implied,
especially given the increasingly hostile racial atmosphere that pre-
vailed, to consider viable options before such a time of crisis arose.

Zillah's reply to Woodby, also printed in the 18 August 1832 issue of
the *Liberator*, was direct and to the point. "My friend has entirely
mistaken the design of the communication placed in the box last

week," wrote Zillah. Under no circumstances, she believed, should blacks discuss or be willing to consider the question of emigration. Woodby had urged Zillah to reconsider "A Colored Female of Philadelphia" 's comments on Mexico as a possible locale for black emigration. Zillah's refusal to discuss emigration as a viable option for American blacks was unqualified. "Believe me, my friend, were I to read it [the article by 'A Colored Female of Philadelphia'] a thousand times, it could not alter feelings and opinions which have entwined themselves round every fibre of my heart, from my childhood; even at that early period, when I heard encomiums lavished upon this favored country, my heart exulted, and I said, 'This is my own, my native land.'" "Cease, then," she advised Woodby and the diverse set of readers she would have reached through the pages of the *Liberator*, "to think of any other city of refuge."

Given the few sources of information available on the activities of the Female Literary Association or, for that matter, of the activities of any African American women's literary societies from the antebellum period, this brief exchange provides a rare and invaluable window onto the experience of black women who dedicated themselves to organized literary study. Apparent from their dialogue is their confidence and sense of purpose; evident in their prose is an eloquence and a taste for rhetoric that could only have been the result of exposure to a variety of texts. For these members of the Female Literary Association, the rubric of literary study provided a forum through which black women could challenge the limitations of gender and begin the process of changing the role of women in American society. The coalitions served as the institutional bases from which black women distinguished themselves by assuming responsibility for the authoring of their own presentation. Convinced that "the degraded station that we occupy in society is in great measure attributable to our want of education," the members of black women's literary societies were able to act on their belief that "cultivating [their] intellect" was essential to their efforts to "contradict the constant assertions of our enemies that so low is our situation we can never rise to an equality with those of a fairer complexion."[86] Immediately, literary exercises provided multiple avenues to attaining political voice, even if a significant venue for the publication of their voices remained qualified by its delegation to the "Ladies' Department" of the black and abolitionist press. But the development of black women's literary societies had future implications as well. One of the most significant ways literary societies were instrumental in establishing the place of African American women was by exposing them to education generally. Before formal educational opportunities became available for black women, literary societies served as "school[s] for the encouragement and promotion of polite literature."[87] They were invaluable means of educating black women beyond what was considered their "proper sphere," preparing them instead to participate in the "gentleman's course" of study at schools like Oberlin in the 1860s.[88]

Despite these fairly radical associations, black women's literary study remained an acceptable means of civic participation, as it embraced the image of feminine virtue associated with the literary. When the study of polite literature remained a domestic activity, black men seem to have supported black women's efforts to establish literary societies. A woman's reading was considered an important if relatively passive form of intellectual exercise and an essential component of her image of refinement and her role as caregiver to future generations. Through black women's "vigorous action," black children would believe themselves to be "not inferior in intellect, but . . . as capable of improvement as any people under heaven."[89] This influence would be felt not only in the domestic sphere. Women were also responsible for extending the proper values and moral order that shaped their homes and families to the larger community. Their endeavors would inspire black men to persevere in their own undertakings. In the words of William Lloyd Garrison to a member of the Female Literary Association, "there is not a glance of your eye, not a tone of your voice . . . but has a direct connexion with the results of masculine actions and pursuits."[90] Through their efforts, black women would enable Americans of African descent to become "highly distinguished and intelligent people."[91]

While the tension between claiming feminine virtue and asserting what might be best described as masculine voice proved productive for many free black women, it was never without ambiguities and contradictions. These are illustrated in the experience of black antebellum author and orator Maria Stewart. When Stewart addressed a meeting of Boston's Afric-American Female Intelligence Society in the spring of 1832, she received an unenthusiastic welcome from its members. The Afric-American Female Intelligence Society was begun in September 1831. According to their constitution, motivated by "a natural feeling for the welfare of our friends," the society's membership "thought fit to associate for the diffusion of knowledge, the suppression of vice and immorality, and for cherishing such virtues as will render us happy and useful to society." This clause suggests that the Afric-American Female Intelligence Society formed their coalition with similar objectives to those of Philadelphia's Female Literary Association. The two organizations shared similar principles of organization as well: the Afric-American Female Intelligence Society collected twenty-five cents at the first meeting of the year and then twelve and a half cents at every monthly meeting thereafter and used the money "for the purchasing of books, the hiring of a room, and other contingencies."[92] But rather than fully support the developing public, political voice of another black woman, at least some members of the group seem to have disapproved of Stewart's outspokenness.

Stewart had been warned by one of the Society's members to anticipate a cool reception: "A lady of high distinction among us," she relayed to her audience, "observed to me that I might never expect your homage" (Afric-American, 54). With this information in mind, she scripted much of her address defensively "The frowns of the world shall never discourage me," she began, "nor its smiles flatter me" (50). In her address Stewart emphasized again and again that it was not vanity that made her seek an audience for her meditations; rather, her public advocacy was a sign of her devotion to God and to her community. Her writing and public speaking constituted what she imagined as a sort of temporary crisis intervention. "The only motive that has prompted me to raise my voice in your behalf," she told her audience, "is because I have discovered that religion is held in low repute among some of us; and purely to promote the cause of Christ, and the good of souls, in the hope that others more experienced, more able and more talented than myself, might go forward and do likewise" (52). Stewart's justification for her activities lay in the will of God. "I believe that God has fired my soul with a holy zeal for his cause," she explained. "It was God alone who inspired my heart to publish the meditations thereof; and it was done with pure motives of love to your souls, in the hope that Christians might examine themselves, and sinners become pricked in their hearts" (52). For Stewart, these were the purest of motives, and her audience's negative response to her work came as a surprise. "Little did I think," she lamented before the Afric-American Female Intelligence Association, "that any of the professed followers of Christ would have frowned upon me, and discouraged and hindered its progress [she refers here to the pamphlet *Religion and The Pure Principles of Morality*, published in Boston in 1831]." Although she had come to "expect to be hated of all men, and persecuted even unto death," she was especially disappointed to find that the women with whom she believed she had the most in common also considered her an adversary. "I am not your enemy," she told them, "but a friend to both you and your children" (52). She closed her address by underscoring her disappointment at being received with such hostility in an environment where she hoped to find comraderie. "There is not one of you, my dear friends, who has given me a cup of cold water in the name of the Lord, or soothed the sorrows of my wounded heart. . . . Cruel indeed, are those that indulge such an opinion respecting me as that" (54–55).

To speculate more insightfully as to the complex reasons behind the Afric-American Female Intelligence Society's reaction to Maria Stewart, one must delve more fully into her short career as a writer and an orator in Boston between 1831 and 1833. Born free in Hartford, Connecticut, Maria Stewart was a member of the same black middle class in Boston that included the political activist David Walker. Stewart's admiration for Walker and the extent to which she respected him as both a political and intellectual mentor is apparent in her designation of him as "the most noble, fearless, and undaunted David Walker."[93] His death in 1830, which followed one year after that of her husband, led Stewart to reassess the place of religion in her life. As her religious commitment deepened, so too did her resolution to speak out against injustices as they appeared around her. To Stewart, these commitments were fundamentally linked. "In 1831 [I] made a public profession of my faith in Christ," she wrote in her earliest publication, titled *Religion and The Pure Principles of Morality*.[94] Stewart understood social activism to be an expression of her faith and considered herself a "strong advocate for the cause of God and for the cause of freedom" (Afric-American, 52).

As an advocate for both of these causes, Stewart felt obliged to voice her criticisms of both the white and the black community directly. Stewart appreciated that the root of black oppression and suffering lay in the larger white society. But her main focus of attention rested on what blacks needed to do to help themselves. She made these observations without disguising her political convictions with lyrical rhetoric or hiding under the mantle of anonymity. Disapproval of the personal and leisure habits of some in the black community prompted her to assert that dancing, while not "criminal in itself . . . [had] been carried on among us to such an extent that it has become absolutely disgusting." Of the black community's economic habits, Stewart admonished, "our money, instead of being thrown away as heretofore, [should] be appropriated for schools and seminaries of learning for our children and youth. We ought to follow the example of whites in this respect. Nothing would raise our respectability, add to our peace and happiness, and reflect so much honor upon us, as to be ourselves the promoters of temperance, and the supporters, as far as we are able, of useful and scientific knowledge."[95] Although she acknowledged the centuries of "deprivations, fraud, and opposition" the black population had been subject to, she nevertheless used blunt language to assert, "Our condition as a people has been low for hundreds of years, and it will continue to be so, unless by true piety and virtue, we strive to regain that which we have lost."[96] These criticisms of the black community itself are significant, not only because they point to dissident points of view despite the community's burgeoning sense of nationalism, but also because inherent in them was a direct and definitive challenge to the black community's male leadership as well. Stewart did not hesitate to specifically take this group to task when justifying her own presence in the lecture hall. "Had those men among us who had an opportunity, turned their attention as assiduously to mental and moral improvement as they had to gambling and dancing," she told an audience gathered at the African Masonic Hall in February 1833, "I might have remained quietly at home and they stood contending in my place."[97]

That Stewart did not remain quietly at home, or adopt more "feminine" and thus more acceptable means of acquiring public voice, points to precisely what made her public presence intolerable. "O ye sons of Africa," Stewart would challenge those in her audience, "when will your voices be heard in our legislative halls, in defiance of your enemies, contending for equal rights and liberty?"[98] For black men, whose place in the lecture halls Stewart albeit briefly but no less effectively usurped, her aggressive rhetorical questions were a direct assault on their authority, their manhood, and their sense of a woman's place. As the reaction of the Afric-American Female Intelligence Association attests, however, Stewart's presence was no less of an affront to some of Boston's most intellectually ambitious black women. Even those middle-class black women who "thought fit to associate for the diffusion of knowledge, the suppression of vice and immorality, and for cherishing such virtues as will render us happy and useful to society," considered Stewart to be something of an adversary.[99] From her first appearance on the public stage, one of Stewart's primary objectives was to appeal to black women to recognize and rise up to their particular responsibilities by developing their intellectual abilities. "Ye daughters of Africa, awake! . . . Arise! . . . distinguish yourselves," she wrote in *Religion and The Pure Principles of Morality*. "Show forth to the world that you are endowed with noble and exalted faculties."[100] She believed that only by developing their intellects could black women transcend the paralyzing conditions assigned to them by race and gender. Stewart's own "bitter experience" as a domestic servant qualified her to testify that "continual hard labor deadens the energies of the soul, and benumbs the faculties of the mind." She noted that the "most worthy and most interesting of us [women were] doomed to spend our lives in gentlemen's kitchens."[101] "How long," she asked, "shall the fair daughters of Africa be compelled to bury their minds and their talents beneath a load of iron pots and kettles?"[102] Rather than succumb to the limitations imposed by race and gender, Stewart advised African American women to band together; together, she believed, black women could improve themselves and, in turn, achieve great things for their community. One of the things that Stewart envisioned was an institution for formal education that would not be subject to restrictions based on race or gender. Were they to unite, Stewart asserted, it would be a short time before black women "might be able to lay the corner stone for the building of a High School, that the higher branches of knowledge might be enjoyed by us."[103]

The Afric-American Female Intelligence Society clearly embraced the spirit of union and mutual aid that Stewart advocated. Given the lukewarm reception that Stewart received from the Society, however, it is safe to assume that the group's goals were less ambitious than those they attributed to Stewart. Although they wished to improve themselves intellectually, they were not prepared to abandon the facade of feminine propriety that dictated that even their activism be veiled in passivity, their voices tempered by virtue. However pleased she was with their efforts to organize, Stewart was obviously disappointed in what she perceived as the modest "progress" of the Afric-American Female Intelligence Society. "It is useless for us any longer to sit with our hands folded," she reprimanded the membership of this ostensibly active, progressive organization (Afric-American, 53). Stewart believed that, given their historical condition, women were not only entitled to express themselves in public; it was their duty. In addressing the Afric-American Female Intelligence Society, she was clearly disappointed not to get more support for her own efforts at public expression from a literary society whose professed goals were theoretically in keeping with her own. In turn, the chastising and condescending tone Stewart adopted in her address appears to have alienated the membership of the Society instead of persuading them to share her methods.

The conclusion that she was entirely comfortable in her outspokenness fails to take into consideration the extent to which Stewart in many ways herself embodied the tentative nature of the members of the Afric-American Female Intelligence Society. Like those members of the Afric-American Female Intelligence Society who considered her appropriation of public voice to be unwarranted, Stewart at times conservatively embraced the very norms of domestic womanhood that her vocation as a public speaker tested. While she urged black women to develop their intellectual abilities, she also advised them to become "chaste keepers at home, not busy bodies, meddlers in other men's matters."[104] Rhetorically, she supported conventional notions about the importance of women's influence in the domestic arena, counseling her female audience to remember that "upon [their] exertions almost entirely depends whether the rising generation shall be anything more than we have been or not." "O woman, woman!" she wrote, in support of the notion that a woman's work was in fact political because of her influence over her family, "your example is powerful, your influence great; it extends over your husband and your children, and throughout the circle of your acquaintance" (Afric-American, 55). Supporting conventional associations of women and femininity, she urged black women to appreciate that their "forms [are] as delicate, and [their] constitutions as slender" as those of white women. She encouraged them to "strive to excel in good housewifery, knowing that prudence and economy are the road to wealth."[105]

Surely these instructions could have been a part of a facade erected in order not to completely alienate the very women Stewart hoped to influence, whose investment in the ideals of domesticity seemed unwavering. It is more likely, however, that like other black women of her class in antebellum Boston, Stewart was genuinely torn between the dictates of convention and what she saw as the demand that she and all black Americans do what they could to nurture black leaders and create a sense of black nationalism within the United States that could pose a formidable challenge to American racism. Stewart repeatedly embraced the terms of domesticity, hoping, perhaps, as Lora Romero argues, that it could "[provide] a model for writing women into the leadership of nationalist movements," but her words and actions are also in keeping with the contradictory understanding that circumstances were such that the relatively passive place assigned to women by middle-class domestic ideology must be supplemented with more overt and deliberate political activism.[106] Stewart turned to the Bible to explain to black women that their social and historical circumstances made it forgivable—made it, in fact, imperative—for them to go against its teachings by finding and using their voices in public forums and in political ways. Citing Paul's admonitions to women to remain silent on religious matters and to defer to their husbands' judgment generally, she argued, "Did St. Paul but know of our wrongs and deprivations, I presume he would make no objection to our pleading in public for our rights."[107] Stewart even imagined that the need for women's public advocacy was a temporary situation; in almost all of her addresses she invokes the hope and anticipation that "God will surely raise up those among us who will plead the cause of virtue, and the pure principles of morality, more eloquently than I am able to do."[108]

Given the restrictions of the gender expectations under which women lived, association with literary activity promised to alter the very character of a woman's nature: through her writing and other forms of public address, a woman could "possess the spirit of men, bold and enterprising, fearless and undaunted."[109] Even so, Maria

Stewart understood that oral and written expression remained imbedded in gender distinction. For a woman to write and express her political thoughts publicly was to inhabit gender in a particular, contradictory way. On the one hand, literary activities ushered her into an implicitly male community that was constituted in writing; on the other hand, her "membership" in this community was based on the emphasis—not the elimination—of gender. In a letter to Maria Stewart written almost a half century after the close of her literary and oratorical career in Boston, William Lloyd Garrison captured the chasm between Stewart's gendered person and her literary presence. He relayed his first impression of her in terms of her femininity: he remembered her "in the flush and promise of ripening womanhood, with a graceful form and a pleasing countenance." But it is through her literary work that Stewart became "known" to Garrison. "Soon after I started the publication of The Liberator," wrote Garrison to Stewart in April 1879,

> you made yourself known to me by coming into my office and putting into my hands, for criticism and friendly advice, the manuscript embodying your devotional thoughts and aspirations, and also various essays pertaining to the condition of the class with which you were complexionally identified—a class "peeled, meeted out, and trodden under foot." You will recollect, if not the surprise, at least the satisfaction I expressed on examining what you had written—far more remarkable in those early days than it would be now, where there are so many educated persons of color who are able to write with ability. I not only gave you words of encouragement, but in my printing office put your manuscript into type, an edition of which was struck off in tract form, subject to your order. I was impressed by your intelligence and excellence of character.[110]

Garrison attributes his initial respect for Stewart and for her work not to her gender but to the fact that it was atypical in the early 1830s to discover someone of her race with the literary abilities that she possessed. Yet it is important to note that the tract of her writing that he printed at and distributed from the *Liberator*'s offices, *Religion and The Pure Principles Of Morality,* was marketed as the work of a "respectable colored lady." Furthermore, her name could not stand alone on the pamphlet's cover; after Stewart's name was a clause that identified her as "Widow of The Late James W. Stewar[t], of Boston."[111] His subsequent relegation of virtually all women's writing submitted to the *Liberator* to the paper's "Ladies' Department" underscores the way in which he sorted out the contradiction inherent in the idea of a literary woman. Even in print, where it would have been possible to publish texts unmediated by designations of gender, women's writing was distinguished by labels; their writing appeared in the "Ladies' Department" or was signed "a colored lady" or "a female of color." The differences between men and women and their designation to different spheres, Garrison's editorial decisions seem to be saying, must remain intact.

Maria Stewart believed that these conventional associations need not be entirely restrictive. Throughout her unusual career as a public speaker, Stewart grew more and more sure of her conviction that the most effective race leader would be one who "joined the charms and accomplishments of a woman to all the knowledge of a man."[112] She explicitly criticized black men for their reluctance to participate in the public, civic debates of the time. She accused them of refusing to "let [their] voices be heard, [or raise] their hands . . . in [*sic*] behalf of their color."[113] Such statements were intolerable. Regardless of the soundness of her skills or her dedication to the welfare of the community, it was considered inappropriate for a woman to speak out so boldly.[114] Stewart left Boston in 1833, but not without asserting the potential "power of [a woman's] eloquence" and defending a woman's right to active engagement with the world.[115] She moved to New York, where she joined one of the city's female literary societies. Although she never again addressed the public as she had in Boston, Stewart found opportunities to "publish" her "compositions and declamations" regularly as a member of the literary society. She was described by one person who knew her in this context as "full of literary aspirations and the ambitions of authorship."[116]

It is impossible to definitively gauge the degree to which Stewart's involvement in a female literary society influenced her later writing. Soon after her departure from Boston, a volume of her collected work, *Productions of Mrs. Maria W. Stewart*, appeared and was advertised for sale with other antislavery publications. In 1878 Stewart became eligible to receive a pension as the widow of a veteran of the War of 1812; she dedicated the first payments she received from this pension to the publication of a new volume of her collected works. As Marilyn Richardson notes, the autobiographical and historical document that introduces Stewart's essays in this volume is a "curiously hybrid document." In it Stewart draws from and experiments with a variety of narrative techniques. "Telling her story at times in the first person, at times in the third, this former practitioner of the graphic and indeed theatrical jeremiad drew inspiration from both fiction and the theater, shaping an original text with considerable creative authority," Richardson observes. Stewart "exploit[ed] techniques popularized in the sentimental novels and drama of the day . . . introduced cliff-hanging moments of uncertainty, cruel misunderstandings which compromise the heroine's reputation, a scene of bleak despair set on Christmas Eve, and, of course, prayers answered in the fullness of the time." A comparison with Stewart's earlier writing suggests that, between 1833, when she left Boston, and 1879, when *Meditations From The Pen of Mrs. Maria W. Stewart* was published, Stewart had developed into a much more practiced and skillful writer. In the introductory essays that frame *Meditations*, Stewart experimented with and even anticipated sophisticated literary techniques that were just evolving among black American writers. It is impossible to tell to what extent Stewart was exposed to these literary techniques through her independent reading and to what extent her developing literary consciousness is attributable to the activities in which she participated as a member of a New York female literary society. Although Stewart is largely if not entirely overlooked as a literary foremother by late nineteenth-century African American women intellectuals and activists, many of the themes and techniques that distinguish Stewart's late writing "emerged as characteristic of the new black women's writing." As Richardson notes, these characteristics "figure in the work of Frances Harper, Emma Kelley, Alice Dunbar-Nelson, and Pauline Hopkins, the best known among the early generation of black women novelists and writers of shorter fiction."[117]

That Stewart was able to find in New York a sympathetic "small literary circle" composed of young women who, like herself, were "full of the greed for literature and letters" points to the importance of such enclaves to the intellectual training of antebellum black women. As the attitude of members of the Afric-American Female Intelligence Society toward Maria Stewart's candidness attests, black women's confidence in their mission to redesign themselves in order to participate in efforts to redesign the society in which they lived was often diluted by the domestic ideology to which they clung, which also seemed to offer black women a model for refiguring themselves and writing themselves into positions of power and of leadership. The practices and the activities of the earliest black women's literary societies exhibit both the fear and the fearlessness of the women who populated them; like Maria Stewart herself, they wished to be disruptive of the social and political status quo while at the same time remaining within the bounds it prescribed for women.

Although these dual aims may have decreased the speed with which black women overtly claimed public podiums and became part of the political landscape, it may also have increased the effectiveness of those who believed that literary study would ultimately offer women a means to these ends. The praise that women's literary coalitions received from curious onlookers, for instance, suggests that they were prudent to experiment with public voice through their tentative literary activities without entirely forfeiting the claims of domesticity, which seemed also to promise access to the political arena. So prevalent and so impressive were the meetings of black women's literary societies in 1834 that they were used by one writer to epitomize the benefits for the whole population, black or white, of what were increasingly called "mental feasts." Defining a mental feast as "a convocation of rational beings, who come together . . . to enjoy the sublime and exalted pleasures of intellectual cultivation and improvement," the writer of the *Liberator*'s occasional column "Moral" suggested that the mental feasts organized by black women were the sorts of activities that ought to be pursued by more members of the community. While reserving high praise for "our colored female friends, in divers places, [who] have adopted the practice of holding mental feasts," the author did not disguise the segment of the population to whom his observations were primarily directed. "While many of their fairer and more privileged sisters are spending their precious time at the theatre or the ball-room, they, more rational and wise, are cultivating those qualities of the soul which are indispensable," he wrote. To black women's "more privileged sisters," he said, "Let the fair daughters of the Columbia take example from those, whom too many have regarded as unworthy of their notice." One week after his meditation on mental feasts, the same author focused his column again on the educational activities of black women. In a letter addressed "To the Societies of Colored Females for Mutual Improvement," he called the members of these societies "more rational and wise" for the "ardent pursuit" of intellectual stimulation than those women who spend their time cultivating their "personal charms." He praised them for their efforts to "direct [their] thoughts and [their] exertions to the improvement of the mind."[118]

The phenomenon of the organized, educational activities of black women attracted considerable attention from those skeptical of a black woman's ability to engage in respectable practices and "civilized" activity. Numerous commentaries in contemporary publications suggest that the meetings of African American women's literary societies often included a steady stream of observers who later documented their impression of the proceedings. Calling himself a frequent visitor to the Female Literary Association and the Minerva Literary Association in Philadelphia, one such observer reported that he was "highly delighted" with the meetings he attended: "My anticipations were more than realized, to see and hear my oppressed sisters (who the colonizationists have the audacity to assert can never be elevated in this country) read and recite pieces, some of which were original, and which would have done credit to the fairest female in America—the republican land of liberty!" He concluded his observations by urging black women to "establish societies," and "give them strict attention." Encouragement like this contributed to the association of literary activities and membership in literary societies with a gendered notion of civic participation, in which reading and writing in organized groups was central to the "enlighten[ment] of [the female] mind" as well as the proper "adornment of the female character."[119]

"THE CHARACTER AND CONDITION OF THE COUNTRY"

Throughout the 1830s, black leaders continued to promote their conviction that literary coalitions would shape their membership into educated individuals who would be considered exemplary, respected citizens. At the first meeting of the American Moral Reform Society in 1837, James Forten Jr. declared this to be the goal of African American literary societies: "As soon as we engage in any enterprise having for its foundation the mighty principles of mental illumination, we are at once noticed and respected. Thus we see that, whatever tends to disseminate the principles of education, tends to raise us above the tide of popular prejudice; and whatever tends to raise us above the chilling influence of prejudice, must of reason tend to elevate our condition. . . . Such, I conceive, our Literary Institutions to have the power of doing."[120] In preparation for the meeting, Forten had distributed a circular in June 1837 that he hoped would give him an accurate count of the active black literary societies from Nashville, Tennessee, to New Bedford, Massachusetts. Although only a small number of the existing societies replied, Forten indicated their significance beyond the reported numbers by focusing much of his address on the work of the colored population's "many Literary institutions." Calling the development of African American literary societies in the free North "an intellectual and moral reformation," Forten explained the importance of literary activities to the future of the race: "I know of but few better ways to effect this [reformation] than by reading, by examining, by close comparisons and thorough investigations, by exercising the great faculty of thinking; for, if a man can be brought to think, he soon discovers that his highest enjoyment consists in the improvement of the mind; it is this that will give him rich ideas, and teach him, also, that his limbs were never made to wear the chains of servitude; and he will see too that equal rights were intended for all."[121]

As they built institutions from which to become increasingly vocal and active in the public sphere, free blacks increasingly expressed their belief that their reading and writing would lead to the formation of American roots. They could build no physical monuments or even transport African culture to their new shores as ways of taking possession of the United States. They looked instead to upholding the spirit of the nation's founding documents and to creating their own intellectual monuments and monuments of language. Participation in literary societies came to be seen as a means of doing so and consequently of changing the status and condition of African Americans in the United States. One proponent of African American involvement in literary coalitions went so far as to refer to the societies as "durable monuments" in a letter to the *Colored American.* He urged the more educated members of the black community to "act as volunteer professors" and serve as the leaders of such societies, substantiating the vitality of their role in this way: "Mr. [Thomas] Jefferson, we know, complained that he had never heard of a colored man who expressed a thought above narration. On this and other facts of the kind he hazarded the conclusion that colored men are inferior to white. Others contend that colored men never improve their talents and privileges, and especially, that if they have any knowledge of superior education, they cannot teach others. Will not the educated and the privileged ones among us think of these charges, and leave their intellectual monuments?"[122]

Literary societies quickly became crucial to African Americans' assertions of their right to a place in the democracy. "We consider these institutions as of more importance than any others in the present age of societies and Associations," announced one assessment of African American literary societies in 1839. The editorial continued by underlining the importance of literary institutions to the development of confident individuals:

[Literary societies] have a tendency, when properly conducted to unite talent and abilities which would otherwise be [lost?]; and the commendable spirit of competition which generally exists, engenders and fosters a taste for literary pursuits. A person [may] possess the necessary qualifications to become a public speaker, or the talent, which, if encouraged, and properly applied would eventually make him a good writer, but for the [existence?] of an association with kindred spirits he is deprived of the opportunity of exercising his natural abilities, he requires a field for practice where he can measure his talents and acquirements with others, so that he may judge his own [tendency?] by the merit of those with whom he [is] in competition, and when he is aware wherein he lacks, he can by study and perseverance easily attain an eminence equal with those who were formerly his superiors.[123]

Although it is impossible to recreate the discussion that took place in the earliest African American literary societies, the "intellectual monuments" erected by their membership can be seen in the documents created by African Americans that were published as newspaper articles, pamphlets, petitions, and addresses. Literary interaction allowed

African Americans to develop sophisticated uses of language that announce their knowledge about dominant discourse and social and political "rules" while simultaneously subverting, overcoming, and sidestepping them. Language was used to disguise from unknowing audiences "unacceptable" ideas and yet to convey to kindred spirits a commonality of intentions. Strategies of representation included the ability of black authors to "signify" or, as Henry Louis Gates Jr., has suggested, to embody a "black double-voicedness" that seems to reiterate texts from Western literary tradition but does so with a "signal difference" that is located in the authors' use of black cultural forms.[124]

Without question, literary societies and their activities functioned as vehicles of empowerment for their African American members. In a nation increasingly divided over issues of race and gender, they provided forums where issues of importance to the black community might be discussed. These discussions had definite goals: "As [members] of a despised race [it becomes a duty] to cultivate the talents entrusted to our keeping, that by doing so, we may break down the strong barrier of prejudice."[125] One way literary societies contributed to this effort was by conferring to their membership the confidence to interact in the world of print that surrounded them. It was not simply "immensely important that the public should see what blacks can do," as abolitionist Theodore Weld argued in 1834; more to the point, it was immensely important that the public see black people engaged in the particular activities and discourse valorized by the white majority. Literary societies positioned them well to be "their own letters of introduction on the score of energy, decision, perseverance, and high attempt."[126]

Although the societies alone could not break the barrier of prejudice, they were able, to some extent, to penetrate the national consciousness and to attract the attention of whites interested in black progress. In an 1833 edition of the *Genius of Universal Emancipation*, an anonymous resident of Philadelphia who had attended a meeting of an African American literary society had this to say: "Discussions were conducted with a degree of spirit and propriety and displayed a cogency and acuteness of reasoning, and an elevation and elegance of language for which he was little prepared." Speaking more generally, the editorial continued: "[The societies] are numerous, united and bitterly conscious of their degradation and their power. To this let the pride, the independence and ambition which [learning] ever imparts be added, and the consequences[,] though beyond the reach of conjecture, would doubtless be such as to involve the character, and condition of the whole country."[127] Surely African Americans *did* mean to change the character and condition of the country through their literary societies. Their reading and writing were motivated by a desire to expand ideas of liberty and justice and to communicate an identity that was black, American, and, above all, human. Literary societies provided the literal and psychological space where their membership might develop the ability and confidence to speak for themselves rather than be spoken for. In this, despite the obvious allegiance to the assumptions and dominant ideologies established by early nineteenth-century white culture, African American literary societies had the potential to serve the free black population as points of access to social and political arenas from which they were otherwise excluded.

It should be emphasized, however, that even as they worked optimistically through literary coalitions to cultivate public, political voices and the literary habits respected by the white community, free blacks struggled with the realization that their organized literary activities did little to temper white racial prejudice or alter the negative image of black Americans in the white imagination.[128] An ongoing theme in the history of African American literary societies is the tension between the faith placed by their members in literary study as a pathway to respect, political voice, and citizenship and their consciousness that, regardless of the sophistication of their literary endeavors and accomplishments, the white community remained largely unable to see black Americans as anything but mentally inferior, servile, and fundamentally unworthy of equal access to American society. As they worked diligently through their literary societies to fashion themselves into "respectable," model citizens, the tremendous racial animosity they faced, which manifested itself daily in physical and psychological ways, served as a constant reminder of the limited effectiveness of this strategy. Inclusion in American society would demand more than attention to literary skills. Fundamental change was needed, not just within the black community, but within the entire racial, political, and class structure of American society.

2

Spreading the Word

THE CULTURAL WORK OF THE BLACK PRESS

To fully understand the development of a readership and literary culture among free blacks in the antebellum United States, we must look not only at the contexts and situations in which reading and other literary activities took place but also at the avenues of production and distribution that gave free black Americans in the urban North access to printed texts. As the well-known example of Frederick Douglass illustrates, it was necessary for slaves to acquire reading and writing skills surreptitiously: Douglass records in his 1845 autobiography how, as a slave, he contrived ways to "steal" literacy from his white associates in a Baltimore shipyard.[1] Less well-known are stories of the efforts of free blacks in the urban North to acquire and use their literacy, or of the channels through which they gained access to and distributed printed texts at a time when bound books were, for the most part, prohibitively expensive and hard to come by. How did free black Americans come to value reading and how did they come to understand the uses to which printed texts could be put? How was reading presented as a compelling attraction for free blacks as they made choices about what to do with relative financial stability and increasing leisure time? And what were they reading, both within and outside of their literary societies?

It is no coincidence that the rise of the African American press paralleled the development of literary societies and literary culture in northern antebellum black communities: a primary goal of these texts was to foster the development of what one early contributor to the black press called "a literary character."[2] As Henry Louis Gates Jr., and others have persuasively argued, since the Enlightenment, "the index of any race's 'humanity' was its possession of reason, which was to be known through its representation in writing." Particularly admired was writing "in its more exalted or 'literary' forms," but all association with literature, as readers and writers, was seen by free black Americans living in the urban North as a means to becoming exemplary citizens who could fully participate in the civic life of their community. Evidence of literary skill and demonstrations of literary character would refute the claims of racists and proponents of slavery that the African was innately inferior and therefore, "by nature," fit for nothing but slavery.[3] The pursuit of literary culture in black communities that culminated, in the final years of the 1820s, in the formation of African American literary societies and the institution of an African American press must be seen as part of a constant and ongoing campaign launched by black Americans to prove the sublimity of the black mind by demonstrating literary abilities and a propensity for developing "literary character." Literary character offered black Americans a way to refute widespread claims of their miserable, degraded position; examples of it, made visible at meetings of African American literary societies or through the pages of an African American newspaper, would counter assumptions of African inferiority with displays of black genius.

Beginning in 1827 with the inaugural issue of *Freedom's Journal*, newspapers published by and for the African American community were able to advance and advertise the existence of literary character in the black community. They provided black readers with common reading material that was relatively easily obtained and could be shared among multiple readers who possessed a range of literacy levels. Equally important was the key role played by newspapers in shaping a black readership by disseminating a sense of the importance of reading and literary activity to the future of the black community. The antebellum black press both responded to and stimulated interest in literary interaction among antebellum free blacks, providing a context through which its readers could see how literary texts and the activities fostered by literary societies could be a source of empowerment for

African Americans. It offered them a means to express themselves and instructed them in the ways that literature, both oral and written, could publicly mediate the radical disjuncture between "African" and "American." In doing so, it assisted free blacks in asserting agency in the construction and representation of themselves as new subjectivities and allowed them to position race within the context of an American identity.

In this chapter I explore the ways in which and the extent to which the antebellum African American press promoted the development of literary character and extended the formation of literary community among free blacks in the urban North. I argue that central to the mission of two of the earliest African American newspapers, *Freedom's Journal* and *The Colored American*, was the development of a black readership; they worked to illustrate the existence of a vibrant tradition of black literary arts while also encouraging black Americans to consider themselves integral to the future viability of that tradition. These publications launched a campaign to promote reading and literary activity as a component of citizenship and the responsibility of all free blacks living in the North. These newspapers advocated through their content and style as well as through the very fact of their existence that reading and a commitment to literature were an essential means of assuming an intellectual identity and introducing oneself to the public conversations of civic life. They were a means of assuming a quality of respectability that, for African Americans who were presumed in the white imagination to be in every way inferior and incapable of rational thought, must be seen as both polite and political gesture. Rather than an alternative to political action, the pursuit of literary character became, in the decades that preceded the Civil War, a strategy that leaders in the free black community believed would open the doors of American society to black people. The antebellum black press was a chief agent in the emphatic delivery of this message. The extent to which it penetrated the black community is manifest in the extensive literary record that survived within its pages and in the sheer number of literary institutions that developed throughout the urban North in the decades that preceded the Civil War. I close this chapter by illustrating how vibrant the "literary character" of a significant portion of the free black community was and how determined they were to claim what they considered their literary rights as the

Civil War began, even as the threat of imminent emancipation intensified debates about the character and the nature of "the Negro" and
augmented hostility toward all African Americans, free and slave. In
this turbulent time literary publications by and for the black community thrived, and the publishing division of the A.M.E. Church, the
Book Concern, was able to claim that it was "really in a prosperous
condition."[4]

The texts I consider here, first *Freedom's Journal*, the *Colored American*, and *Frederick Douglass' Paper*, and later the *Repository of Religion
and Literature, and of Science and Art*, the *Weekly Anglo-African* and the
Anglo-African Magazine, and the *Christian Recorder*, were crucial to
the formation of an ideal of community that affirmed reading and
other literary activities as acts of public good on which the intellectual life and civic character of its members could be grounded. The
sense of community created by these texts approximated the sort
of "nationalism" Benedict Anderson defined as "an imagined political community—and imagined as both inherently limited and sover-
eign."[5] In the case of the black readership of the newspapers I address
here, the "imagined community" was racially bounded and its sov-
ereignty was perceived as free from the control of whites. In urban areas
throughout the North, black men and women personally unknown to
one another sought to realize a common destiny despite white attempts to derail this project. Their community was also imagined,
since tensions and conflicts within the black community, between
emigrationists and those who believed that their future lay in achieving
full citizenship rights in the United States, for instance, coexisted
alongside assumptions of a "deep horizontal comradeship."[6] Anderson
points specifically to the role of print in the formation of nationalism.
He cites the newspaper as an institution that connects its "assemblage
of fellow-readers" by articulating a sameness of purpose and by defining specific cultural, social, and intellectual activities as common
means of executing designs; in this way, newspapers help to create and
sustain "imagined community."[7]

"WE WISH TO PLEAD OUR OWN CAUSE"

Generalizations about black illiteracy in the first half of the nineteenth century, coupled with the scholarly attention given to the slave narrative as the primary form of literary expression by black Americans between 1830 and 1865, have contributed to misrepresentations of the black press in the early nineteenth century. Traditionally, antebellum black newspapers have been examined as abolitionist publications whose primary focus was to expose the evils of slavery in order to free the slaves and put an end to the institution of slavery in the United States.[8] In keeping with that perspective, scholars have assumed that the newspapers' primary audience was located in the white population. But, as historian Frederick Cooper notes of the first African American newspaper, *Freedom's Journal,* "in the two-year lifetime of [the paper], slavery was mentioned with some frequency, but rarely was it the subject of the featured article or the editorial."[9] Although the newspapers demonstrate that the free black population was sympathetic to the plight of the southern slaves and that they recognized the institution of slavery as "cruel in its practice and unlimited in duration," they also suggest that free blacks believed the prejudice to which they were victim was, to quote an anonymous contributor to the *Colored American,* "more wicked and fatal than even slavery itself."[10] In the inaugural issue of *Freedom's Journal,* the editors lamented that "no publication, as yet, [had] been devoted to their improvement."[11] To focus exclusively on the antebellum black press as an antislavery concern is to misrepresent the newspapers' actual content and artificially limit the complex role they played in antebellum American society.

Given the extent to which literacy was broadly defined and widely practiced by free blacks well before the Civil War, a reconsideration of *Freedom's Journal* and other antebellum African American newspapers as a source of literature by and reading material for African Americans is especially pertinent. Systematic analysis of the content of the newspaper supports the editors' statement that their journalistic effort was specifically "designed for the reading of their coloured brethren."[12] *Freedom's Journal*'s coeditors Samuel Cornish and John Russwurm estimated that "FIVE HUNDRED THOUSAND free persons of color [were among the total population of the United States], one half of whom might peruse, and the whole be benefitted by the publication of the Journal."[13] A network of agents located throughout the urban North and informal systems of distribution that enabled the publication to reach black readers as far away as Canada, the Caribbean, and England ensured that *Freedom's Journal* would transcend its local New York City area to become a national newspaper. Even if verifiable circulation figures were available they would also be unreliable as indicators of the number of *Freedom's Journal*'s readers, as placement in reading rooms and the sharing of copies among whole congregations and associations as well as between friends and neighbors distinguishes the newspaper's actual readership from its list of subscribers. Systems of combined oral and written literacy, where those who could read to those who could not, further confounds assumptions that the African American "readership" of the early black press was insignificant.

The newspaper was at the heart of a new political strategy for the free black community: because of its ability to communicate a common message to a wide audience and thus facilitate organization, the editors believed it to be a "most economical and convenient method" of ensuring the "moral, religious, civic and literary improvement of the injured race" that was "daily slandered."[14] Indeed, whites' resentment of free blacks intensified throughout the antebellum period, paralleling the rising visibility of African Americans in urban spaces. In the 1820s and 1830s this was captured by the white popular press with increasing frequency in print and caricature.[15] Scholars have blamed increasing racial antipathy in the rapidly growing urban centers of Philadelphia, New York, and Boston after the War of 1812 on growing competition for jobs, housing, and political voice among the lower classes. Changing theories about race and racial difference, and a proliferation of arguments refuting the idea of human equality, encouraged middle- and upper-class white Americans to reconsider previous sympathies and voice concerns about the dangers of intermixing white "superior" blood with black "inferior" blood, both sexually and in terms of shared public space. Deteriorating race relations were exacerbated by the growing numbers of free blacks and their increasing social and, to some extent, economic stability. The rising aspirations of free black Americans—especially in terms of their rejection of subservient roles and claims of full citizenship rights—threatened to upset the established social order.[16] In this hostile climate, the white community was more and more willing to adopt the perspective advanced by the American Colonization Society, which argued in 1825 in the pages of its journal, the *African Repository*, that free blacks were "notoriously ignorant, degraded, and miserable, mentally diseased, brokenspirited, acted upon by no motive to honourable exertions, [and] scarcely reached in their debasement by the heavenly light."[17] "Bond or free," proclaimed one writer for the *African Repository* in a June 1828 issue, black Americans were "the subjects of a degradation inevitable and incurable. The African in this country belongs by birth to the lowest station in society; and from that station he can never rise, be his talent, his enterprise, his virtues what they may."[18]

In response to such pronouncements, and with forms of political power like the ballot largely unavailable to them, free blacks developed alternative strategies to assert themselves and act on their determination to achieve equality in the United States.[19] The daily behavior and activities of black Americans, they believed, would sway public opinion and dispel negative attitudes toward free blacks. The newspaper was designed as a medium of socialization that would disseminate to the black community the standards of behavior that would make this strategy effective. Blacks must be encouraged to adopt and exercise visibly those habits that would help them to become and to be seen as useful in society: these included personal morality, temperance, industriousness, and, most importantly, an intellectual identity that was the result of the active pursuit of a literary education. Were white Americans to see blacks engaged in these activities, the editors idealistically believed, they would recognize them as worthy of democratic treatment regardless of their skin color. "When our too long neglected race shall have become proportionally intelligent and informed with the white community, prejudice will and must sink into insignificance and give place to liberty and impartiality," declared one writer in an early column promoting the need for perseverance in education.[20] The editors placed great faith in an ideal of American democracy that could embrace the black community, and they used their paper to outline for their readers what they must do to propel themselves to the point where they would be judged by their merit and morality and not by their skin color. Placing their belief in the ideal that the "world has grown too enlightened, to estimate any man's character by his personal appearance," they imagined a national community that transcended race and that could be achieved through, among other things, the presentation of a broad intellectual persona within the black community.[21]

To some extent, Samuel Cornish and John Russwurm identified discrimination against the free black population as a problem of misleading representation. The majority press's erroneous and incomplete reports on free blacks led to inaccuracies about black people becoming lodged in the white imagination. "From the press and the pulpit we have suffered much by being incorrectly represented," they announced. "Men, who we equally love and admire have not hesitated to represent us disadvantageously, without becoming personally acquainted with the true state of things, nor discerning between the virtue and vice among us." The editors acknowledged that there were many examples of corruption among African Americans, but they signaled that these were largely attributable to the lack of educational and economic opportunities in black communities. They asserted that without their own representation the black community was portrayed unfairly and inaccurately: while "our vices and our degradation are ever arrayed against us," they lamented, "our virtues are passed by unnoticed." Literary activities would mark black Americans as public and refined figures, giving them the positive reputation that they lacked. It would also help them to find and use their own voices. "We wish to plead our own cause," wrote Cornish and Russwurm in their inaugural editorial. "Too long have others spoken for us. Too long has the publick been deceived by misrepresentations, in things which concern us dearly." Coupled with strict adherence to "acceptable" forms of behavior, this simple act of self-representation, the editors believed, would "arrest the progress of prejudice, and . . . shield [the free black community] against the consequent evils."[22]

To this end, much of the content of *Freedom's Journal* was loyal to the editors' commitment to represent more fully the plight and achievements of black people and to document the white community's sympathetic response to unprejudiced representation of them. The newspaper balanced accounts of black delinquency alongside stories of black accomplishments, highlighting the fact that both existed in the community. Reports of social outcasts such as murderers, counterfeiters, and those who fell victim to the evils of alcohol were included not only to document the very real failures of the black community but also to provide a context through which to consider examples of the disciplined, orderly lives that enabled others to make contributions to the advancement of the race. A biographical article on Paul Cuffe, a successful black shipowner, was reprinted serially from the pages of England's *Liverpool Mercury* in the first five issues of *Freedom's Journal*'s two-year run. By detailing Cuffe's life, the text emphasized how he came to be a recognized man by overcoming the difficulties and discrimination associated with his race.[23] To emphasize that such balanced representation of blacks elicited positive responses from the white community, *Freedom's Journal* also reprinted from other newspapers letters and occasional pieces written by sympathetic whites that dramatized their awakening to the cruelty inflicted on black people in the United States, free and slave, and to the depth and danger of American racism. A letter signed "Omega" and printed in the first issue of *Freedom's Journal* is representative. Writing of an unspecified injustice recently witnessed, she explained her horror at what she had seen: "It took hold of my feelings in a very particular manner, and excited within my bosom a greater detestation of slave dealings as well as of those who engage in this nefarious practice, than I ever realized before."[24]

While stories establishing fair representation of the black community and the white community's appropriate response to it served one of *Freedom's Journal*'s purposes, the miscellaneous articles that filled the pages of each issue served another. They were lessons in literacy for both the young and the adult student. In subject matter at least, much of the miscellaneous material was unrelated to the immediate lives of its readers. The content of the paper's "Varieties" column exemplified this. In one early issue it included instructions for the proper burial of corpses alongside a table outlining the consumption of wheat and other grains in the United Kingdom. Other "newsworthy" items printed in the same column were titled "A Polish Joke," "Rare Instances of Self-Devotion," and "Curious Love Letter." The "Domestic News" column generally carried accounts of tragic but spectacular accidents in which victims suffered greatly before dramatically "expiring." "Foreign News" published in *Freedom's Journal* consisted of equally diverse items. The paper's first edition carried articles on the egg trade in Ireland as well as on Chinese fashions. Later accounts of parliamentary activities and the installation of royalty in England were only slightly more pertinent to the immediate lives of free blacks in the United States.[25]

However random, these stories provided the free black community with narratives and reports that were educational tools. They supplied their readers with a steady stream of interesting and diverse reading material consumable by a readership of various ages and literacy levels. The vignettes included in the newspaper were interesting and compelling, if often sensational. Brief enough to be consumed in short periods of time, they were also convenient to read. Stories included in *Freedom's Journal* were written for sharing, in a format that lent itself to their being read aloud. In addition to their informational value, these features made the *Journal* an important resource for newly and semi-literate readers.[26] Furthermore, unlike bound books, *Freedom's Journal* was readily available; it could be read in the home and was also a primary text in the libraries of local reading rooms and literary societies. At least one of New York's African Free Schools received the newspaper, where it was used as a makeshift textbook. When Charles C. Andrews, a teacher at the African Free School on Mulberry Street, wrote to the editors to thank them for "furnishing gratuitously, the regular weekly numbers of the 'Freedom's Journal,' for the benefit of the Library in the School," he assured them that the newspaper was being put to use: "much good," he reported, "may be calculated to result from such a journal being perused by such readers, as will have access to its pages."[27]

As a means of facilitating the continual practice of literacy and encouraging the development of literary sophistication, *Freedom's Journal* was a timely addition to the free black community. As its editors pointed out, one paradoxical effect of the acquisition of the most basic literacy skills by many free blacks in the urban North was to mask the need for more profound literacy and the continued pursuit of education. "The day has been," they wrote, "when if any one of us could read it was considered a 'passing strange;' and we believe that this has been unfavorable to our improvement. This wonderment and praise from our fairer brethren, instead of exciting, has been the cause of many halting in their career of acquiring knowledge." The journal advanced the notion that the astonishment expressed by the white community over black Americans with even the most basic literacy skills served only to maintain an educational and intellectual disparity between blacks and whites. For the "youthful mind, unsupported by the sage counsels of age and wisdom," the flattery that ostensibly praised blacks who possessed only basic skills was crippling; it was even more "dangerous to the middle-aged and intelligent." Rather than be content to "read and write a little," or "cypher and transact the common affairs of life, almost as well as other men," *Freedom's Journal* submitted that blacks needed to be more demanding of themselves and of their educational institutions.[28]

The newspaper itself responded to this imperative in two ways: it became a forum for the announcement of schools and other educational opportunities as well as the site of educational programs in themselves. Its pages were filled with advertisements for "Coloured schools" and other small, local institutions where children might be taught the rudiments of "reading, writing, arithmetic, English grammar, geography with the use of maps and globes, and history."[29] Along with advertisements for other commodities desperately needed by the black community—primarily cheap clothes and boardinghouses where they would be welcome—announcements of the opening of schools were among the most prominent features of *Freedom's Journal*. Most of these listed the name of a single individual, usually a man, who served as the school's primary instructor. Jeremiah Gloucester's notice of his Philadelphia school is typical of efforts that ran weekly to attract students to such institutions: "The subscriber wishes to return thanks to his friends, for the liberal encouragement of patronizing his school; and would be permitted to say, he still continues to teach in the same place, and hopes by increasing exertions, to merit a share of public encouragement." At Gloucester's school, "the branches attended to" were "Reading, Writing, Cyphering, Geography, English Grammar, and Natural Philosophy"; female students were taught "Needle Work."[30]

Increased opportunities for and improvements in the education of black children such as those offered by informal academies like Jeremiah Gloucester's and the network of Free African Schools in New York and Boston allowed leaders in free black communities to focus more of their energy on the educational needs of older African Americans. *Freedom's Journal* communicated to its readers that adults had to rely on diverse and independent means of educating themselves.

Reading was depicted as a panacea for the sort of adult instruction needed in the free black community, and *Freedom's Journal* presented itself as a proper and practical source of that reading. In the first issue of the newspaper, Cornish and Russwurm promised that a central function of their publication would be to assist their readers in selecting "such authors as will not only enlarge their stock of useful knowledge, but such as will also serve to stimulate them to higher attainments in science." This service would help readers avoid "time . . . lost, and wrong principles instilled, by the perusal of works of trivial importance."[31] Evident in this promise is the extent to which *Freedom's Journal* sought to influence its readers, not only in terms of what they read but in how they used their time generally. Articles included in *Freedom's Journal* were exemplary of the ways a written text might serve as a manual to self-improvement and the standards of good character and "respectable" behavior. Titles such as "Formation of Character," "Duty of Wives," "Duties of Children," "Accurate Judgement," and "Economy" suggest the way readers were provided with guidelines to "proper" behavior and the attitudes that would strengthen the moral condition of the individual, the race, and the nation.[32]

As educational reading, lessons that emphasized the parameters of respectable behavior and inspired discipline, especially in the disposal of excess time and money, were particularly popular. Early in its two-year run *Freedom's Journal* published the story of "Dick the Gentleman," whose fine clothing and dapper lifestyle suggested the superficial trappings of success but who was ultimately devoid of the qualities most needed in the black community. His story warned readers of the dangers of excess and alerted them as to how not to behave:

DICK THE GENTLEMAN—Dicky Dash was born in the midst of a fine, flat, fertile county of the west, where there were plenty of potatoes, cabbage, and corn—but no gentlemen. Dicky had small hands, thin face, an idle disposition, and a bushy head. Dicky said he was a gentleman. The squire looked from top to toe of Dicky, and said he was a gentleman. The lawyer cross-examined him and said "Dicky's a gentleman," This being ascertained beyond a doubt, Dicky immediately kicked the potatoes from him—tossed away the cabbages— and gave the plough over to satan. Dicky put a new shirt into his pocket, jumped on board the steamship, and hallowed out to the captain to start away his nine inches of steam for the city.

After setting himself up as a merchant, Dicky neglected to cultivate the qualities most important to the success of the black Americans, both individually and as a group. He supported his extravagant lifestyle with credit, "got a horse and a saddle and went to the races," and became a regular at the theater, the opera, and at concerts, where girls smiled at him and women "praised him." According to the story, he eventually became so debt-ridden that he had to leave the city and return to the country "as he came from it, with a shirt in his pocket and a flea in his ear."[33]

This satire reinforces the extent to which readers of *Freedom's Journal* were encouraged to see the disposition of free time and relative wealth as a novel dilemma: what should be done with them? Neither idleness nor superficial displays of culture and class had a place in the lives of even the most well-to-do African Americans in the antebellum urban North. Fine clothing, attendance at the races or the theatre—these activities would only provide opportunities for blacks to reinforce negative stereotypes of themselves as aimless and undisciplined, confirming white assumptions that black people were nuisances to society. In contrast, reading and other forms of literary study were depicted as ideal activities, providing the means not only of "edification, but merely to employ an idle hour."[34] The frequency with which the term "useful knowledge" is associated with literary study in *Freedom's Journal* suggests the extent to which a commitment to reading and other forms of literary activity had moral and, for blacks striving to be seen as Americans, political implications. *Freedom's Journal* worked to develop in the minds of its readers a binary opposition between what was "useful" and morally "good" and the many forms of "evil" that threatened to destroy black people, individually and as a group, by perpetuating racial stereotypes. Reading was presented as a vehicle of instruction, a positive elective for an African American population who had to negotiate on a daily basis a dense landscape of tempting hazards that included intemperance and lack of economy, the central targets of the moral reform movement that was sweeping the nation as a whole. As a habit, reading was a responsible way to engage the mind and give shape to what would otherwise be time lost. An alternative to the various forms of moral decay that threatened to bring down the individual and, ultimately, the race and nation, reading would convert "the many moments now spent in idleness" into hours "employed storing [free African Americans'] minds with all kinds of useful knowledge, and preparing themselves for future usefulness."[35]

The campaign launched by *Freedom's Journal* to promote literary study as an alternative to idleness and moral decay manifested itself institutionally in the development of African American literary societies, which were advertised in the pages of *Freedom's Journal* as definitive elixirs for societal "evils." Letters to the editor, original contributions, and other notices on the topic of literary associations in the first volume of *Freedom's Journal* record the escalation of literary activity in the free black community in 1827 and underscore the extent to which organized literary coalitions reinforced the political purposes that the newspaper advanced. "That man must be blind indeed," observed one correspondent in a letter to the editors of *Freedom's Journal*, "who does not discover that the people of color, in these parts are rapidly improving in knowledge and virtue, notwithstanding all the great disadvantages to which they are subjected by prejudice." "Much of this improvement," the writer contended, "has arisen from the societies formed among themselves, and on these more than ever, must their future advancement depend." Believing that the intellectual achievements that resulted from participation in literary coalitions would promote the equal treatment of African Americans, the writer posed the rhetorical question: "Wha[t] man can attend an orderly . . . literary, or charitable institution of coloured persons, and not feel the injustice of ranking t[h]em as inferior beings, while there are multitudes of white men, who never associate for any virtuous, or honourable purpose whatever?" Equally important to the writer's sense of the value of these institutions, however, was his contention that literary societies were "highly beneficial," not only "to their members," but to "society at large."[36]

From its earliest issues, *Freedom's Journal* devoted pages of print to supplying its readers with a sense of the rich history of black literary arts. It regularly published literary criticism, which appeared mainly in the form of biographical summaries of eighteenth-century black poets followed by brief extracts from their works. In the paper's first year of existence, Ignatius Sancho, Olaudah Equiano, Ottobah Cuagono, and "Cesar" were all reviewed. Hailed by the editors of *Freedom's Journal* alternatively as "our poetess" and as the "African genius," Phillis Wheatley was frequently evaluated and presented as a model of literary achievement. Her story and her literary work were important not only as examples of black achievement but also because they had had such a tremendous impact on those who believed the African to be inferior. Acknowledging that from the "want of education had also arisen the idea of '*African inferiority*' among many, who will not take the trouble to inquire into the cause," one correspondent for the *Freedom's Journal* submitted to the editors an account of Wheatley in November 1827, in which she was identified as a hero of the race:

> Boston is the place where that sweet poetess of nature, *Phillis Wheatley*, first tuned her lyre under the inspiration of the Muses, putting to shame the illiberal expressions of the advocates of slavery in all parts of the globe. So incredible were the public concerning the genuineness of poems, that they are ushered into the world with the signature of the Governor, the Lieutenant-Governor, and other distinguished men of Massachusetts affixed to them. O Liberality, thou art not certainly a being of this lower sphere! for why should the natural powers of man be rated by the fairness of his complexion?[37]

In an effort to create another, contemporary literary hero, the editors of *Freedom's Journal* launched a campaign in 1828 to free the slave-poet George Moses Horton. Described in a front-page story printed in an August 1828 issue of the paper as "an extraordinary young slave . . . who has astonished all who have witnessed his poetic talent," Horton soon became a primary focus of *Freedom's Journal*'s articles and correspondence. "It is with much pleasure that we inform our readers that measures are about to be taken to effect the emancipation of this interesting young man," the editors of *Freedom's Journal* wrote later that month. The importance of literary figures and their value to members of the free black community in the urban North is evident in the speed with which the campaign to free Horton became a principal concern. Horton quickly came to represent the belief of free blacks in the urban North that association with literature would lead to freedom. Their hopes for the elevating power of association with literature are reflected in the urgency they felt about the emancipation of this representative of black literary arts. "*Something must be done—George M. Horton must be liberated from a state of bondage,*" the editors wrote in a September 1828 issue of *Freedom's Journal.* "Were each person of colour in [the city of New York] to give but one penny, there would be no danger about obtaining his liberty."³⁸ Although a significant amount of money was raised to secure Horton's freedom, his master would not permit his sale. Horton's publication in 1829 of the twenty-two-page volume of his poetry, "The Hope of Liberty," reveals the extent to which antebellum blacks believed that in their literacy lay the key to liberation. Horton's hope that, with the proceeds of his volume of poetry, he might be permitted to purchase his freedom was in keeping with the perspective advanced by free blacks in the urban North, who connected their literary activities with the eventual literal freedom of all blacks in the United States and the immediate elevation of free blacks in the eyes of whites, many of whom doubted their very humanity.

Literary activity, engaged in through the pages of *Freedom's Journal* and in the context of the literary society, was presented as a prime means by which African Americans could contribute to their own self-improvement and, in turn, the making of "good society." It was considered a necessity for the community's young men, who were otherwise in danger of being lured into unproductive patterns of behavior. Disappointment that too many black men of promise were neglecting substantive activities in favor of more superficial forms of entertainment was the sentiment behind one writer's letter to the editor, printed in a July 1827 issue of *Freedom's Journal.* "Many of our young men, whose situation in life afforded them the means to improve their minds, and whose prospects were so fair that they needed nothing except their assiduous attention to direct their course through life, after having obtained their rudiments of a liberal education, have degenerated into such insignificance, that their very existence has been a matter of no great concern," wrote "Muta." "This, I am sorry to say, has too long existed among us, and it is partly from the want of literary institutions."³⁹ Because, in this writer's assessment, they further not only intellectual development but also conversation and exchange, literary societies were the essential arena to ensure the lasting value of one's educational efforts. Much of the benefit of literary associations was the connection they established between sociability and the acquisition of knowledge. Literary societies, the author argued, "create a spirit of emulations, and, of course, a disposition for reading, which would tend to mature the judgement and expand the mind, causing it to germinate in all its native beauty, to contemplate on objects which ignorance had before veiled in obscurity. . . . They will remove the very illiberal views which may have been taken of people of color."[40]

Certainly one effect of adopting positive habits such as reading and the associated activities of discussion and debate was to illustrate a readiness to learn. Through these activities, the negative stereotypes associated with blacks would be replaced with images of industry, economy, and intellectual competence. But another outcome of literary activity was the development of literary character, an attribute that, when acquired and properly maintained, would serve not only to divert African Americans from the many "evils" that threatened to corrupt society but also endow them with the personality needed to participate in the civic debates that would sustain a healthy democracy. Literary activities and the character cultivated through them provided a means of equipping oneself with lasting benefits that would ensure the success of the individual and, in turn, the community. Developing literary character, the components of which included morality, self-discipline, intellectual curiosity, civic responsibility, and eloquence, was cast as both a private virtue and a civic duty: it benefitted the individual, but it was essential for the common good as well. For Americans of African descent, the implications of the correlation between personal responsibility and civic duty were potentially far-reaching. In developing literary talents, they contributed not only to their own improvement but to the improvement of their race. In the words of Samuel Cornish, the acquisition of these skills would lead to the "good principles [that] will soon break down the barriers between [the black] and the white population."[41]

In this context, it is interesting to note that the editors of *Freedom's Journal* did not question the need for distinctions in their society: "We have never contended," they wrote, "that there should be no distinctions in society: but we have, and are still determined to maintain, that distinctions should not exist merely on account of a man's complexion."[42] Rather than skin color or economic criteria, the quality of one's literary character should define one's standing in society. It also dictated one's usefulness in the struggle to obtain civil rights. Eloquence, for instance, one component of literary character, was considered a powerful attribute that would be instrumental in dismantling both institutionalized racism in the North and the institution of slavery in

the South. Inspired to write to the paper on the "importance of forming a Debating Society, among our brethren of [New York City]," one
writer, who signed his name "A Young Man," asserted that "no one at
the present day, will presume to dispute the extensive influence which
Eloquence exerts upon mankind." In the context of this writer's comments, "Eloquence" gained from reading, writing, and debating in the
company of others became a vital weapon. "What caused the Abolition of the Slave Trade," he argued, "but the glowing language and
vivid colouring given to its abominations? I do not expect a Debating
Society will make us all Sheridans, but it will enlarge our powers of
reasoning by teaching us to express our thoughts as brief as possible,
and to the best advantage. It will also enable us to detect at a glance
whatever sophistry is contained in the arguments of an opponent."[43]

Such rehearsals of eloquence were essential to preparing black
Americans to fully participate in the democratic culture advocated
and exemplified by *Freedom's Journal.* As a forum for literary exchange,
Freedom's Journal encouraged its readers to consider themselves and assume the responsibilities of citizens; giving voice to their opinions and
perspectives through the pages of the newspaper was one way of doing
this. Responses to the editors' appeals to "the pens of many of our respected friends" to contribute "practical pieces, having for their bases,
the improvement of our brethren" filled the publication with "Original Communications." These took the form of letters to the editors,
testimonials, contributions to the "marriage and death" column, and
poetry and occasional pieces.[44] Distinguished by the heading "For the
Freedom's Journal," original contributions to the newspaper included
a "short and imperfect account" of the eighteenth-century black poet
Phillis Wheatley and a biographical sketch of Toussaint L'Ouverture.
Poetry by the "masters" of European literature was published alongside the verses of "Amelia" and "Emma." Black readers' appetite for
this material, and the extent of their desire to themselves become a
part of the literary exchange, is recorded in the pages of the newspaper
itself. A brief column called "To our Correspondents" encouraged
readers to become contributors and informed them of the status of
their submissions. In one 1827 issue of the paper the editors used this
column to report that " 'ACROSTIC' is under consideration" and to
inform the author of "CLARKSON, No. 3" that it "has been received
and will appear next week." They encouraged "ROSA, of our sister

city," to "write frequently," but related that "Poetical lines by 'AME-
LIA,' of N. York, we cannot insert, being too personal."[45]

Through the contributions of these and other writers, *Freedom's
Journal* quickly became a forum for discussion and debate in the black
community. Cornish and Russwurm were true to their promise that
their "columns would ever be open to a temperate discussion of interesting subjects." In providing this "public channel" through which to
communicate, they created for the black community a social and
cultural space in which to articulate their opposition to white oppression while also providing an invaluable lesson in literary interaction
and the power of print. The object of a literary education, they relayed
through the pages of their newspaper, was not merely to learn how to
read; black Americans needed to understand the public uses to which
literature could be put. In the pages of *Freedom's Journal*, reading was
not presented as a passive or solitary activity; rather, it was an invitation to participate, a means of orienting the individual toward
social and communal models of exchange, be they written or oral,
that would enhance civic life and facilitate involvement in the public
sphere. Readers were encouraged to respond to what they read as the
basis for further exchange. In this sense, the ability to read was not an
end in itself; it was a part of a larger process of training individuals to
claim the authority of language and effectively use it to participate in
reasoned and civil public debate.

"THERE IS A PEOPLE HERE . . ."

From 1827 until it folded in 1829, *Freedom's Journal* urged free African
Americans to educate themselves by becoming readers and involving
themselves in both the life of the newspaper and in literary societies
and other associations through which they might exercise their intellects and make their voices heard. Blacks were encouraged to become
active participants in the goals of a national society by taking part in
literary activities and public discussions in hopes that by doing this,
they would be considered a part of that society. Despite the sense of
discouragement and disillusionment that dominated the final issues of
Freedom's Journal, evidence that an appetite for "literary character" had
taken hold in the black community filled the pages of the newspaper

from its inception. Even before the first issue of *Freedom's Journal* was released, free blacks in the urban North indicated their desire for a newspaper and their readiness to foster its success in their individual communities. The inaugural issue of the paper was released on March 16th, 1827, but almost four weeks earlier a group of black Bostonians had gathered in the home of David Walker to discuss the prospectus of the new venture and consider "giving aid and support to the Freedom's Journal." Those present agreed that "the enterprise is one of a laudable nature, reflecting great credit upon the projectors, and well worthy of our countenance and support." Their decision was not merely to give *Freedom's Journal* their "aid and support" as subscribers to and readers of it; in their determination "to use [their] utmost exertions to increase its patronage," they expressed their deep commitment to the life of the paper, from which they believed that "great good will result to the People of Colour."[46] This democratic assessment of the newspaper and the commitment of members of black communities throughout the urban North to work cooperatively toward its success indicate the extent to which *Freedom's Journal* was truly a communal effort and not merely the creation of its New York City editors. David Walker, whose own literary work and belief in the importance of spreading literacy throughout the black community was in keeping with the mission of *Freedom's Journal*, himself became a distributing agent for the newspaper. When the Boston supporters of *Freedom's Journal* met a year later, in April 1828, "for the purpose of enquiring whether the Freedom's Journal had been conducted in a manner satisfactory to the subscribers and the Coloured community at large," Walker argued that indeed it had. In his comments in support of the newspaper he pointed specifically to the "disadvantages the people of Colour labour under, by the neglect of literature." He identified *Freedom's Journal* as a medium that was taking important steps to remedy that situation. The "very derision, violence, and oppression, with which we as a part of the community are treated by a benevolent and Christian people," he remarked, "ought to stimulate us to the greatest exertion for the acquirement of . . . literature."[47] *Freedom's Journal* was instrumental in facilitating that goal.

This appetite "for the acquirement of literature" filled the pages of the *Colored American* from its beginning in 1837. While the form and content of *Freedom's Journal* had promoted basic literacy, the *Colored*

American assumed it and instead encouraged its readers to use their literary skills to acquire cultural literacy. Whereas *Freedom's Journal* had primarily encouraged black communities to form literary societies and avail themselves of their benefits, the *Colored American* acted as a coworker of these societies, operating in conjunction with them to further their shared mission. Like *Freedom's Journal*, the *Colored American* was deeply sensitive to promoting reading as an activity that expanded opportunities and encouraged moral conduct. "He that would be an intelligent person must be a reading person," announced one of the many articles published in the newspaper that underlined the role of reading in the productive use of leisure hours. "By reading you may visit all countries, converse with the wise, good, and great, who have lived in any age or country, imbibe their very feelings and sentiments and view every thing elegant in architecture, sculpture, and painting. By reading you may ascend to those remote regions where other spheres encircle other sums, where other stars illuminate a new expanse of skies, and enkindle the most sublime emotions that can animate the human soul." The extraordinary power of literature to expose readers to this expansive world is starkly contrasted to the dreary existence of nonreaders in the single sentence that composes the item's next paragraph. "Without being a reading person, your information must be limited, and of a local nature."[48] In addition to articles giving general counsel on reading, the *Colored American* reprinted articles from European American newspapers like the *New York Observer* that instructed the middle class how to choose the "right" books and chronicled the decline of "solid" reading and the rise of genres of literature, such as the novel, which were considered "fanciful and imaginative."[49]

One of the things communicated in this juxtaposition is the perceived difference between a program of "solid" reading and the informal, relaxed reading implied by the very nature of fiction and other "fanciful and imaginative" texts. Articles printed in the *Colored American* on the subject of reading reinforced the belief that to derive full benefit from one's reading required discipline, diligence, and direction; imaginative texts suggested a certain casual freedom, a release from the very moral and civic responsibility and sense of engagement with others that was at the heart of literary study. This distinction serves to underscore the extent to which reading was deemed a suitable activity only in terms of its association with notions of the appropriate use of leisure time. Like *Freedom's Journal,* the *Colored American* communicated to its readers that reading was not, in fact, to be thought of as a "pastime" in the casual sense of the word. The consumption of entertaining, imaginative literature was considered a passive, frivolous activity, one that threatened to falsely release readers from both civic responsibility and social interaction. "Proper" reading was associated with study or work rather than with amusement, and it required vigorous attention and active mental application for full benefit and appreciation.

This understanding of literary activity dictated that the *Colored American* would also share with *Freedom's Journal* a particular interest in promoting organized literary study as a positive alternative to the host of negative and "immoral" distractions that faced the free black community daily. Particular concern was expressed again and again for what one anonymous contributor to the *Colored American* described as "the rising generation," by which was meant those "young men whose evenings are unemployed, and who now spend their leisure hours in the theatre or porter house, (which leads to the brothel and gaming tables)." In an article titled "Literary Societies" this writer called these institutions "of more importance than any others in the present age of Societies and Associations." With more of them in the black community, susceptible young men "might be induced to make the reading room their place of resort, and thus instead of injuring their health, wasting their money, and acquring immoral habits, they might be storing their minds with useful knowledge, and erecting a reputation which would be far superior to the ephemeral renown which pleasure confers on their votaries, and they might also establish for themselves a character which time itself could not destroy."[50]

Announcements of new opportunities for literary study and interaction appeared regularly in the *Colored American* and expressed similar concern for the many obstacles to the development of literary character in the black community. Like the one placed by David Ruggles in the 16 June 1838 issue, most made reference both to the distractions of urban life and to the difficulties of finding access to literary texts or appropriate environments for their appreciation. Observing that "intelligence can only be acquired by observation, reading and reflection," Ruggles condemned the exclusion of African Americans "from

Reading Rooms, popular lectures, and all places of literary attractions and general improvement" by those he termed "our fairer and more favored citizens." Ruggles expressed the commonly held fear that "without some centre of literary attraction for all young men whose mental appetites thirst for food, many are in danger of being led into idle and licentious habits by the allurements of vice which surround them on every side." He tried to remedy this situation by opening a "READING ROOM, where those who wish to avail themselves of the opportunity, can have access to the principal daily and leading anti-slavery papers, and other popular periodicals of the day." He concluded with an invitation and an exhortation: "We hope that the friends of literary improvement, among all classes of our citizens, in this part of the city, will encourage our enterprise."[51] Inherent in this and similar announcements that appeared in the *Colored American* is the insistence that literary texts and the institutions that would provide access to them were vital to the "present and future prosperity of young men in this community."[52] Without them, black Americans could not cultivate public voices capable of withstanding the demands of any situation or subject.

Despite these similarities, however, the *Colored American* assumed a different kind of readership than had *Freedom's Journal*, with a different set of expertise and expectations. It was itself a testimony to the improved literacy skills and changing needs of black readers. As a "channel of communication for the interchange of thought," the newspaper provided a forum for energetic discussions that revolved around a variety of subjects.[53] Sophisticated debates—including the debate over the racial name by which blacks in the United States would be known—were waged in its pages, largely replacing the sensational domestic tragedies and international trivia that had padded the columns of *Freedom's Journal*. Indeed, one reason for this debate and another significant way that the *Colored American* differed from *Freedom's Journal* had to do with the question of emigration, which the earlier *Freedom's Journal* had contemplated but which the *Colored American* thoroughly repudiated. When it dealt with the political issues of colonization and racial names, the *Colored American* did so with a combination of sharp political assertiveness and distinguished literary prose. "Many would gladly rob us of the endeared name, AMERICANS, a distinction more emphatically belonging to us, than five-sixths of this nation, and one which we will never yield," wrote Samuel Cornish, in his role as the *Colored American*'s editor. The newspaper's first numbers were issued under the name the *Weekly Advocate*; by renaming the paper the *Colored American,* Cornish effectively stymied "enemies, who would rob [blacks] of [their] nationality and reproach [them] as exoticks" by moving beyond their terms of discussion.[54]

Although themes from *Freedom's Journal,* such as self-improvement and economy, formed a familiar foundation for the new publication, the *Colored American* presented itself from its beginning as a paper with a different attitude toward and different assumptions about the black community. According to the editorial address published in the first issue of the *Weekly Advocate* and titled "Our Undertaking," the new paper would be "devoted to the moral improvement and amelioration of [the] race"; no shift in objective took place when the name of the paper was changed to the *Colored American.*[55] Contributors to the *Colored American* expressed themselves largely without cushioning or disguising the authority they claimed through the very act of writing for publication. The words of one writer, who identified himself only as a "Free Man of Colour," exemplify the boldness and literary confidence largely absent in the contributions to *Freedom's Journal.*[56] Calling the term "free man of color" an "empty name" and "a mockery," his editorial asserted that "no man of color, be his talents, be his respectability, be his worth, or be his wealth what they may, enjoys, in any sense, the rights of a freeman."[57] This statement, with its directness and lack of artifice and the firmness and intensity that give it resonance, was exactly the sort of expression called for by Samuel Cornish in his first editorial for the *Colored American,* titled "Why we should have a paper." Because of the great distances that separated free people of color from one another, Cornish declared they must use the press, "that mighty vehicle for the transmission and transfusion of thought," to "speak out in THUNDER TONES, until the nation repents and renders to every man that which is his just and equal." The *Colored American* was to convey the grievances of black people expressly in order "to rouse them up" and "call their energies into action."[58]

Armed with the nickname "The American" and the place it asserted for free blacks in the United States, the newspaper proceeded to publish pointed political statements that disseminated the message that equal rights and citizenship were due "all men." The *Colored American* promised to be the organ through which free blacks would obtain these rights and sustain themselves.[59] It would be the "Advocate and Friend" of the free black population by making public specific incidents of injustice and inequality, as well as the efforts of black leaders and organizations to effect change in black communities.[60] This promise stimulated reports that reflected the subscribers' hopes for the new publication: "all we ask is light on [a] subject," wrote one reader, "full, free, and unbiased discussion,—for the sake of arriving at truth and correct principles."[61] Without exception, the *Colored American* was "to be looked on as their own, and devoted to their interests." It was to serve as a vehicle through which free blacks could "communicate with each other and their friends," and "make known their views to the public."[62]

In exchange for the rights of citizenship, the *Colored American* suggested that claiming an American identity brought with it its own set of responsibilities; with the acquisition of basic literacy assumed to be one of these, the *Colored American* pushed its readers toward greater attention to intellectual exercise. "Our people must be supplied with mental resources," insisted the writer of an introductory editorial printed in the newspaper's inaugural issue.[63] The *Colored American* offered itself to the free black population as a means of access to these needed resources. "The paper is adapted in form, in matter, and in price to nearly the whole of our friends," this writer claimed; it would be instrumental in "persuad[ing] unthinking men (and women) to leave the haunts of vice and wretchedness" and join "the enviable ranks of virtuous, intelligent, and useful men."[64] One form of needed knowledge among the *Colored American*'s target population was perceived to be a certain level of cultural literacy, not only about their own expanding and prosperous democracy but also about the distant regions increasingly within the national consciousness. The first three issues of the paper included a series of articles written for the *New York Weekly Advocate* on various historical and organizational aspects of the United States. After recounting the general history of the country from its "discovery," these articles outlined the origins of and relevant statistics on each state. Included in the knowledge communicated in this series as "useful for present and future reference" was the structure of local and Federal government, anticipated population figures for the various states in 1837 based on the population in 1830, and a listing of the "Vessels of War, in the United States Navy, 1836."[65] Subsequent issues of the *Colored American* featured an extensive article titled "Principal Features of the Various Nations of the Earth," compiled specifically for the newspaper, as well as a biographical sketch of Benjamin Franklin.[66] By offering its readers a kind of advanced course of study on national history, state statistics, and eminent American lives, the *Colored American* was implicitly demonstrating the kind of cultural literacy its editors believed necessary for creating an informed African American citizenry.

The acquisition of cultural literacy was also something that would be fostered in the literary societies that the publication supported. Like *Freedom's Journal*, only to an even greater degree, the *Colored American* announced the meetings of African American literary societies, generally supporting their efforts and forming an alliance with them that advanced the mutual work of both institutions. By advertising and covering the activities and the events, such as public lectures and debates, that were sponsored by African American literary societies and were increasingly open to the public, the *Colored American* contributed to the societies' visibility and facilitated the spread of their influence. An early edition of the newspaper carried a review of "Our Literary Societies" that boasted of the status of literary societies in New York City's black community. "It is certainly gratifying to know that there is in existence, in this city, a number of associations, male and female, devoted to the mental and literary improvement of our people," the writer observed. "They will do us good." He suggested that the impact of literary societies was to be felt not from their numbers but from their activities. "These societies," he claimed, "will be productive of the happiest, and most beneficial results" and will "prove a readiness in us to avail ourselves of every means of improvement which lies within our reach." Literary societies would be responsible for the development of a new generation of black leaders, preparing them to be "useful and honorable members of society."[67]

In the pages of the *Colored American*, such general commentary on the benefits of organized literary study was combined with articles that systematically enumerated African American literary societies in the northeast and reprinted their founding documents. An article titled

"Highly Important" and printed in the second issue of the *Weekly Advocate* issued a call to the black community for "a concise account" of the various literary societies. It was announced that a listing of these would "occupy a prominent place" in the paper's "forthcoming numbers."[68] Appearing periodically throughout the publication history of the paper, this list of literary societies across the nation suggests just how extensive the network of reading associations was and how diverse they were in their activities. Even more than cataloguing the names of various literary societies, the *Colored American* also published pertinent information on their organization and sometimes reprinted their founding documents. For instance, in the 24 June 1837 issue of the paper, the editors printed the constitution of the Philadelphia Society for the Moral and Mental Improvement of the People of Color; on 2 September 1837, the constitution and bylaws of Pittsburgh's Young Men's Literary and Moral Reform Society were featured. "Feeling the necessity and demand of literary talent among us," the society was established by and for "young [men] of known moral habits and respectability" between the ages of eighteen and thirty-five. In a brief note written on behalf of the society, a member elaborated on its nature: "We have as it were only begun to exist," wrote the correspondent, as if to explain their membership of "only sixteen." He reported that "Our society has regular meetings which are spent for the improvement of our minds." He closed his communication by praising the *Colored American* and expressing the society's appreciation "that we have a press of our own, and a paper edited by a colored man." His description of the importance of the newspaper is noteworthy: through its pages, "the world might know there is a people here and [that] they have life."[69]

Indeed, the *Colored American* used its pages to publish not only the constitutions but also the statements of purpose, bylaws, and schedules of upcoming topics to be discussed or debated in the meetings of local literary societies. On a practical level, this public information on the operation of reading groups served as a guideline for the formation of new literary societies. It also promoted the expansion of this alternative system of improvement by reiterating the imperative relationship that was believed to exist between the "moral and intellectual improvement" of people of color and their "civil and political elevation."[70] That the newspaper was a crucial institution through which the literary skills developed in the context of the literary society might be employed to reach a larger public was not lost on the organizers of African American literary societies, which often incorporated a commitment to support African American and abolitionist newspapers into their founding documents. Included in the constitution of the Phoenixonian Literary Society, for instance, was a resolution to "ascertain those persons who are able to subscribe for a newspaper that advocates the cause of immediate abolition of slavery and the elevation of the colored population to equal rights with whites."[71] Other literary organizations, such as New York's Ladies Literary Society, regularly held fairs and festivals "for the benefit of the Colored American." Engaged in the same project, the newspaper and the literary societies also shared the same economic troubles and were comfortable enough in their relationship to ask for mutual aid. As it struggled to succeed in November 1837, the *Colored American*'s general agent, Charles Ray, felt at liberty to issue a general call to the members of literary societies to "send us of the funds they may have on hand, not wanted for present use, to aid us at this crisis, in sustaining our paper."[72]

As a coworker in the drive to "give our people a literary character," the *Colored American* documented the proceedings of African American literary societies in such a way as to approximate the experience of being present.[73] Associating its readers with the tangible social space of the lecture hall and the intellectual community implied by the activities practiced there was one reason for doing this. By revealing how literary characteristics were valued in the context of a specific literary society meeting, the reports also offered incentive to those who were not present to consider, critique, and correct their own literary performance. In addition, they reinforced the rigor and demands of literary study, a perspective easily lost when reading in solitude. These multiple purposes are perhaps best illustrated through the report of a meeting of the Phoenixonian Society that was included in the 18 February 1837 issue of the newspaper. In all, eight presentations had been made at the meeting of this "rising and deservedly popular institution"; due to time constraints, one presenter "read only extracts from his address." Although the correspondent, whose article was signed with only the initial "W," described the evening as "an affair which the members of the 'Phoenixonian Society' have every reason to be proud of," he also felt it his duty "to make some passing remarks on the general character" of the "original compositions which were delivered on the evening in question."[74]

What "W" chooses to focus on and report in the pages of the *Colored American* suggests the ways in which readers of the newspaper were trained and encouraged in literary pursuits even as they were informed of actual events at which they may or may not have been present. His comments also illustrate the extent to which speaking in public in nineteenth-century African American literary societies elicited a spectrum of critical discernment potentially as sophisticated as that which, within the modern rhetoric of literary study, would be applied to written texts. "W"'s "reading" of the orally presented texts includes not only summaries of the arguments made and examples given; a complex inventory of stylistic gestures, physical presence, and vocal quality suggests the virtual lack of distinction between the oral and written features of texts. While an essay titled "The Influence of the Press" was praised for its evidence of "profound thought and extensive enquiry," for instance, "W" noted with equal emphasis that the document was "not read with that spirit and energy which usually characterizes the author." Mr. G. Downing, whose address was called "The Possibility of Great Changes," was advised to "exert himself more"; "this young man has power," remarked his reviewer, "but he is not conscious of it." Only Mr. Thomas Sidney received unqualified praise from "W" for his address on "The Influence of Intellectual Ability." "It is not our province to flatter . . . ," remarked "W," "but we must say candidly, this gentleman has abundant reason to congratulate himself on being endowed with so large a share of that which was the subject of his discourse. . . . He show[ed] an imagination, and depth of research, truly astonishing for his years."[75]

"W"'s criteria for a successful lecture imply the limited authority of written text on its own. They point toward a social model of knowledge oriented toward the importance of communication. Carefully chosen words, whether written or oral, were meaningless unless compellingly conveyed to the audience. Well-spoken, effectively communicated words, on the other hand, asserted the authority, prestige, and power of the speaker and indicated his readiness to contribute to civic debate; they also inspired his audience to respond and stimulated the conversations that were essential to the workings of community. By reporting on literary performances as if the reader were a participant, the *Colored American* embraced this social model of knowledge and attempted to duplicate it through its own content and structure. As a teacher of and model for an ideal of democratic culture, literary societies offered the free black community an extraordinary environment in which to read, exchange ideas, and study uses of language in relation to their ability to inform their membership and inspire them to find and use their own voices. By attempting to replicate the structure of a literary society and reproducing the experience of being present at a meeting in its pages, by reprinting the constitutions of literary societies and applauding their activities at every turn, the *Colored American* embraced the values assumed by the term "society": only in the company of others and through conversations with others could the ideal of democratic culture be realized and a comprehensive literary character develop.

Like the libraries and reading rooms of literary societies, the *Colored American* aspired to supply its readers with access to lasting texts that would be central to their acquisition of "useful knowledge" while also providing a basis for engagement with others in productive conversation. Singlehandedly, it fulfilled the role of a reading room by distributing texts on a diverse range of subjects to an audience that could then come together to discuss and debate what they had read. In this, the *Colored American* considered itself a valuable resource that should be preserved for future rereading and later reference. Beginning with the first issue of the paper, the editors regularly published this reminder to "File Your Papers": "As the advocate will not only be devoted to the passing events of the day, but also in a great measure to useful and entertaining general matter, which may be perused at any future time with as much interest as at the present, we would suggest to our readers the importance of preserving a file of the journal. By doing this, they will, at the end of a year, have a neat little volume, and also have at hand the means of amusing and improving their minds during leisure hours."[76] This advice is telling, especially when contrasted with the anxiety expressed over the modest size of the publication by the paper's editor in its first issue: "Our paper, though somewhat small in size, will be found valuable in contents."[77] Taken together, a year's worth of individual issues of the newspaper would form a "neat little volume"—practically a book. In the same way that the *Colored American* presented reading as an imperative activity, it presented books as items to be treasured: they were promoted as the agents and, increasingly, the emblems of an appropriately cultivated intellect. Later issues carried advertisements for "whole libraries" containing the "most valuable Standard Religious and Scientific Works," which were available for purchase for "only twelve dollars."[78] A library was advertised as something "every family ought to have," and the *Colored American* printed at least one list of guidelines to help its readers establish their own.[79] Those with the financial security to do so were to consider themselves "blessed."[80] For the unblessed majority, however, access to and the ownership of books was not impossible. The *Colored American* presented itself as an affordable substitute. For the sum of $1.50 per year, it provided free blacks with both an encyclopedia of "useful information" and a source of appropriate entertainment. Although its issues would remain unbound, possession of a full year's run of the *Colored American* was something of which to be proud. Like a library of bound books, the collection would testify to the social, civic, and moral standing of its owner.

"WE MUST DO JUST WHAT WHITE MEN DO"

I have shown so far that the connection between literary societies and *Freedom's Journal* and the *Colored American* is explicit, and the newspapers' deliberate involvement in the project of spreading literacy and literary culture throughout the communities of free blacks in the urban North is directly visible. Both newspapers included in their pages instructions on what and how to read; they also made readers aware of the development and rising popularity of literary societies in northern, urban free black communities. Literary societies were promoted in these newspapers as alternatives to society's evils, including idleness, financial irresponsibility, intemperance, and moral decay. The mere frequency with which meetings of literary societies were announced and their activities positively reviewed gives some indication of the partnership that developed between these early African American newspapers and African American literary organizations. Both *Freedom's Journal* and, to a greater extent, the *Colored American* carried detailed accounts of discussions surrounding literature that took place at meetings of literary societies, approximating for their readers the experience of being present at these meetings. In essence, these articles scripted for their readers—whether themselves members of literary societies or not—how literature might be discussed, debated, and put to use.

In contrast, all three of Frederick Douglass's newspapers, the *North Star, Frederick Douglass' Paper,* and *Douglass' Monthly* (the last of which I will not discuss here), took for granted that the black community understood the contexts in which literature would be enjoyed and the uses to which literature could be put. Unlike the earlier papers, the *North Star* and *Frederick Douglass' Paper* did not include didactic articles instructing readers on the importance of reading and the benefits of literary conversation, nor did it explicitly encourage black readers to consider literature within the context of organized literary activities. Instead, these newspapers served as libraries for what they assumed to be skilled and sophisticated readers, including in their pages all of the material, literary and political, that was the subject of literary discussions, both within the context of literary societies and in the larger community. In this, their connection to the organized literary activities of free blacks in the urban North that proliferated in the decades before the Civil War was no less definitive. That their relationship with black readers generally and with antebellum African American literary societies specifically is implicit rather than explicit points to a significant evolution in black literary culture and underscores the observation that the antebellum black press accommodated literature and served black readers in a variety of different ways.

It should be noted that Douglass's newspapers were complicated entities that served many purposes; but I am interested in uncovering some of the literary objectives in the *North Star* and *Frederick Douglass' Paper.* Because Douglass was able to assume that his readers understood the importance of reading—were themselves readers, whether literate or not—he was able to focus on more complex literary goals than were the editors of *Freedom's Journal* and the *Colored American.* First, Douglass hoped to make the pages of the *North Star* and *Frederick Douglass' Paper* a forum for black writers, whose work he actively solicited and reviewed and who eventually came to see his newspapers as a primary site for the publication of their work. Second, Douglass sought to capture the nuances of an emerging American literature that included the poetry and prose of European American authors like Ralph Waldo Emerson, Nathaniel Hawthorne, and John Greenleaf Whittier as well as the slave narratives and other writing composed by black authors. From Douglass's perspective, one important aspect of this emerging American literature was its dual positioning as both political and imaginative. In the work of white writers this duality was taken for granted; but one of Douglass's literary goals in his newspapers was to claim artistic license for black literary arts and the work of black authors, whose writing, with the rising popularity of the slave narrative in the 1830s and 1840s, had come to be valued only for its veracity and political force. Finally but perhaps most significantly, Douglass sought to advance the unprecedented idea of the creative parity between black and white writers. Although discussions that took place in the pages of Douglass's papers underscored the extent to which material equality between blacks and whites did not exist, Douglass's placement of the work of the most celebrated white European and European American writers next to that of black writers insisted on the equality of their literary, cultural, and artistic pursuits.

Douglass's motivation in establishing the *North Star* in 1847 was in keeping with these aims. His objective was to create a "colored newspaper" that would "attack SLAVERY in all its forms and aspects, advocate UNIVERSAL EMANCIPATION; exalt the standard of PUBLIC MORALITY; promote the moral and intellectual improvement of the colored people; and hasten the day of FREEDOM to the THREE MILLION of our ENSLAVED FELLOW COUNTRYMEN."[81] Colored newspapers, he realized, were sometimes "objected to, on the ground that they serve to keep up an odious and wicked distinction between white and colored persons," but this distinction, while odious, was also very real. "Facts are facts," he wrote in an editorial that appeared early in the life of the *North Star*, "white is not black, and black is not white. There is neither good sense, nor common honesty, in trying to forget this distinction." "The distinction which degrades us," he continued,

> is not that which exists between a *white* MAN and a black MAN. They are equal men: the one is white, the other is black; but both are men, and equal men. The white man is only superior to the black man, when he outstrips him in the race of improvement; and the black man is only inferior, when he proves himself incapable of doing just

what is done by his white brother. In order to remove this odious distinction, we must do just what white men do. It must no longer be white lawyer and black woodsawyer [*sic*],—white editor, and black street cleaner: it must be no longer white, intelligent, and black, ignorant; but we must take our stand side by side with our white fellow countrymen, in all the trades, arts, profession[s] and callings of the day.[82]

That Douglass was relatively successful in helping black Americans "take their stand" in the arts was readily apparent by September 1854, when *Frederick Douglass' Paper* printed a review of Frances Ellen Watkins [Harper]'s *Poems on Miscellaneous Subjects.* Calling Watkins's collection "a credible production and . . . one tending, both on account of the excellence of its sentiments, and the source from which they emanate, to interest and improve the hearts of those who may peruse it," the reviewer hailed *Poems on Miscellaneous Subjects* as "one of the increasing number of evidences of the gradual and certain advancements of our long enthralled and deeply injured people." "We observe, in the papers, that Miss Watkins has recently taken the field as a lecturer, and that the impression made by her addresses is highly beneficial to the cause of Freedom, and the elevation of our people," the reviewer noted. His closing remarks seem equally directed to her literary accomplishments and her political presence: "It must have required no slight stretch of conviction, and no small amount of moral courage, to bring one, identified as Miss W. is with a despised race, publicly before the oppressors, to plead the cause of her people." "Let her be encouraged and cheered on in her good works," this reviewer wrote, shifting the focus of his comments directly to black readers who needed to be conscientious in their support of black authors and public figures. "Colored people, especially, should be forward in sustaining Miss Watkins, and affording her the means of prosecuting her literary and oral labors in behalf of the slave."[83]

There are many noteworthy aspects of this review, and we will return to it later for the emphasis that the reviewer places on the coexistence in Watkins's writing of literary excellence and political power. For the time being, however, I want to focus on the way that Watkins's collection came to the attention of Douglass and his staff: it was sent to *Frederick Douglass' Paper* "by the author." That Watkins herself sent a copy of her volume of poetry to Douglass underscores the extent to which she considered *Frederick Douglass' Paper* an appropriate venue not only for the publication of her literary work but also for its critical analysis and its promotion. By 1854 the literary arts of African American authors filled the pages of *Frederick Douglass' Paper*, often accompanied by sophisticated literary criticism that analyzed both its content and its impact. As this review indicates, black readers still needed a bit of prodding to remind them of the importance of supporting authors of their own race. But Watkins's voluntary submission of *Poems on Miscellaneous Subjects* to Douglass in 1854 stands in striking contrast to Douglass's earlier struggle to solicit the work of black writers for the *North Star* and gives some indication of Douglass's challenge and his success in his bid to make his newspapers a literary forum for the work of black authors. Initially, the *North Star* struggled to be seen by authors and their promoters as a place where literary news would appear, and Douglass was more apt to stumble on the work of a promising African American author than to receive his or her work directly. Douglass's readers were first informed of the existence of Henry Bibb's *Narrative of the Life of Henry Bibb*, for instance, by Gerrit Smith, a white abolitionist and longtime supporter of the *North Star* and *Frederick Douglass' Paper*. In an early August issue of the *North Star*, Douglass printed a letter from Smith to Bibb written in July 1849. Smith's letter commends Bibb on his "deeply interesting Narrative" and expresses his wish that "every reader in the nation and in the world might read it." In his role as the *North Star*'s editor Douglass appended a note to the bottom of Smith's letter. "Why have we not seen this Narrative?" he asked rhetorically. "We should be glad to see it. Will the author favor us with a copy[?]"[84]

Whether Bibb did indeed forward a copy of his *Narrative* to Douglass, or whether Douglass gained access to the *Narrative* from another source, is unclear. A review of it, however, appeared in the *North Star* two weeks later. "Although we dislike the principle just acted on," Douglass wrote in reference to his belief that Bibb had overlooked him as the black editor of a black newspaper, "we are disposed to do justice to his book." Calling it "one of the most interesting and thrilling narratives of slavery ever laid before the American people," Douglass "deem[ed] the work a most valuable acquisition to the anti-slavery cause." Douglass's positive assessment of Bibb's narrative and his understanding of its potential impact seems straightforward; to under-stand its subtlety, however, we must return momentarily to Gerrit Smith's letter to Bibb reprinted by Douglass in the *North Star*. The primary function of Smith's letter was to anticipate challenges to Bibb's credibility and assure potential readers of the character of the author and the authenticity of his story. "What a horrible thing slavery is in the light of your Narrative!" Smith wrote. "And your Narrative is true," he concluded, "for I know you to be a man of integrity." In his own review of Bibb's *Narrative*, Douglass also praised Bibb for the "exposure which the author makes of the horrors of slavery." He noted, however, that while Bibb's "narrations of the cruelty of slave-holders" was "natural," it was probably "not in every essential particu-lar true."[85]

At first glance, it is easy to consider this comment as intended to be critical, prompted perhaps by Douglass's frustration and even anger or bitterness that Bibb did not immediately present his *Narrative* to Douglass for consideration by the *North Star*. In the antebellum polit-ical climate, Douglass's comments, which question the veracity of Bibb's *Narrative*, might well have threatened to undermine and de-value the *Narrative* by raising suspicions that it was untrue. As Gerrit Smith's letter affirming the quality of Bibb's character and the authen-ticity of his *Narrative* suggests, the issue of truth-telling that Douglass raises here was particularly relevant. "True" or verifiable slave narra-tives such as that written by Douglass himself were becoming more and more important to the abolitionist movement and to antislavery discourse; in fact, the political force that was believed to result from relaying the "truth" about slavery was the sole criterion by which the quality of black writing and black writers was assessed. As illustrated by the earlier case of James Williams, a black ex-slave who in 1838 dictated the story of his life in bondage and escape from slavery to the abolitionist poet John Greenleaf Whittier, the truth of which was later challenged by the southern press, slave narratives that were deter-mined to be "false," no matter how compelling or effective they were in conveying the abolitionist message, were ultimately considered det-rimental to the antislavery cause. Williams's narrative had been widely circulated both in book form and as a serial in the *Anti-Slavery Exam-iner*. But in the wake of the brouhaha surrounding its determination as "wholly false," the publisher was ordered to discontinue sale of the work. In 1838 there was no place, it seemed, for works of literature that were, in the words of one commentator, "purely of the Negro imagination."[86]

Douglass's own experience as an antislavery lecturer and the author of a slave narrative would have made him familiar with the potentially fatal consequences of implying that Bibb's *Narrative* was "not in every essential particular true." But he was also aware of the extent to which the exclusive demand for "truthfulness" in the slave narrative threatened to effectively silence black writers whose perceived value lay in the political effectiveness of their stories while their creative, artistic abilities and literary style went unrecognized. Located in Douglass's apparent criticism of Bibb's work is an affirmation of the creative abilities of black writers and a desire to reclaim imagination as a feature of their literature. At the core of Douglass's dual assertion in his review of Bibb's *Narrative*—that Bibb's *Narrative* was probably not entirely true coupled with his assessment of it as "one of the most interesting and thrilling narratives of slavery ever laid before the American people" and "a most valuable acquisition to the anti-slavery cause"—is a powerful argument: literature by black Americans, Douglass contends, can be both political and imaginative. By positioning the imagination as a valuable and viable feature of black literary arts, Douglass refutes those who would judge it exclusively in the context of racial politics and for its political effectiveness. As the transcribers of slave narratives that provided firsthand accounts of slavery, black Americans had received wide recognition; yet the heavily mediated genre of the slave narrative threatened to become, for many black writers, a form of verbal bondage. These verbal bonds Douglass knew well. Readily embraced by William Lloyd Garrison, a principal sponsor of his 1845 *Narrative*, and others in the New England antislavery group as an effective spokesperson, Douglass never felt that he was recognized by them as an independent thinker, a creative writer, or a dynamic leader in his own right. This was one of the factors leading him to split with that group. His desire to break the verbal bonds that he came to feel had dominated his 1845 *Narrative* and infected his participation in Garrison's antislavery movement and to exercise authorial control over both the narrative he told and the way in which that narrative was told manifests itself in Douglass's pursuit of bolder and more independent literary efforts, of which his venture into journalism is but one example. In this light, Douglass's review of Henry Bibb's *Narrative*, with its potentially inflammatory suggestion that Bibb's work could be both artistically imaginative and politically powerful, is a bold and contentious statement. The dual criteria for the assessment of African American literature he outlines in it, still resonant in African American critical discourse today, would come to guide much of the literary criticism and assessments of literary value in the *North Star* and *Frederick Douglass' Paper*. Recall, for instance, the 1854 evaluation of Frances Ellen Watkins's *Poems on Miscellaneous Subjects*, which was praised simultaneously for the "excellence of its sentiments" and because Watkins's work would "interest and improve the hearts of those who may peruse it."

Douglass's critical voice would take on still greater and more deliberate force as he worked through the pages of the *North Star* and, later, *Frederick Douglass' Paper* to assert the place of black literature. In the fall of 1849, Douglass included in the *North Star* an extensive review of the *Narrative of Henry Box Brown*. Like those of other slave narrators, Brown's story offered an eyewitness account of the horrors of slavery, and Douglass's straightforward recommendation to his readers to "Get the book" reflects his assessment of the narrative's success as both a powerful indictment of slavery and the compelling story of one man's heroic pursuit of freedom.[87] Douglass's review of Henry Box Brown's *Narrative* was the occasion for a brief but resonant critical meditation on the emergence of American slave narratives as a literary genre. "America has the melancholy honor of being the sole producer of books such as this," Douglass wrote in his review. "She is so busy talking about the doctrine of human rights, that she has not time to put it in practice. Boasting forever of her republican institutions, where shall we find a nation that has less reason to boast? Shouting continually about freedom, and human equality; but in practice denying the existence of either."[88] Douglass points here to the ironic dichotomy between the romantic but ultimately insincere rhetoric of American revolutionary ideals and its genuine expression in the narratives of fugitive slaves. He believed that the hunger for freedom and human justice that had given shape to the American republic was exemplified in stories of the pursuit of freedom in the narratives of former slaves. This hunger for freedom and its passionate expression had given rise to what Douglass identified in his review of Henry Box

Brown's *Narrative* as a uniquely American literary form. In advancing this perspective, Douglass echoed that of Boston Unitarian minister and abolitionist Ephraim Peabody, whose review-essay "Narratives of Fugitive Slaves" Douglass had excerpted in an earlier issue of the *North Star*. In his review of three prominent slave narratives, *Narrative of the Life of Frederick Douglass, an American Slave* (1845), *Narrative of William W. Brown, a Fugitive Slave* (1847), and *The Life of Josiah Henson, Formerly a Slave, Now an Inhabitant of Canada* (1849), Peabody called slave narratives a "new department" in the "literature of civilization" whose appearance it was America's "mournful honor" to claim. Peabody went so far as to argue that this literature was superior to much of the fiction being produced: the "ordinary characters" of literature, he wrote, seem "dull and tame" when compared with those slave narrators "who have sufficient force of mind and heart to enable them to struggle up from hopeless bondage."[89] This perspective would also be advanced by transcendentalist and activist Theodore Parker, who argued in 1849 that "all of the original romance of Americans is in [slave narratives], not in the white man's novel."[90]

These comments indicate the extent to which, in the 1830s, 1840s, and into the 1850s, the narratives of fugitive slaves increasingly gained literary as well as political significance. Abolitionists hoped that slave narratives, by exposing the courage and perseverance of slaves in contrast to the cruelty of slavery, could potentially serve as powerful weapons in the fight against slavery because of their power to change prevailing skeptical attitudes lodged in the public imagination toward blacks in the United States. But Douglass, Peabody, Parker, and others asserted that in the narratives of fugitive slaves lay the basis of a distinct and distinctly American literature, one inseparable from the nation in which it was created and one which epitomized its national experience and its character. Slave narratives were in keeping with Ralph Waldo Emerson's 1837 assertion that a "cultural revolution, a democratization of literature, was underway." Emerson insisted that, "instead of the sublime and beautiful," American literature must instead explore "the near, the common." The best of the slave narratives, notes literary historian William Andrews, fulfilled this objective by "restor[ing] political and literary discourse on the subject of slavery to first considerations—the tangible experience and direct perceptions of the individual." It was the slave narrative's "absence of conventional art," Andrews continues, "its rejection of elegance and classic form, its apparent spontaneous rhythms of consciousness, and its dependence on plain speech and empirical facts" that contributed to its being recognized by a handful of black and white intellectuals of the day as a model for American literature's potential to combine spiritual self-examination, romantic self-consciousness, and democratic individualism in a format that was rhetorically eloquent yet resounded with language that was unpretentious, vibrant, true.[91]

That the *North Star* and *Frederick Douglass' Paper* were focused in part on capturing this emerging American literature in all its complexity and variety is apparent in the literary selections and critical discussions about literature that took place in the newspapers. Slave narratives and other writing by black Americans were a vital component of this emerging American literature; Douglass included literature by a variety of American writers of European descent that he considered notable as well. A partial catalogue of these authors reveals the names of some of the most significant literary figures of the nineteenth century. References to and the writing of Henry Wadsworth Longfellow, James Fenimore Cooper, Henry Beecher Ward, and Lydia Maria Child appeared frequently in the pages of the newspapers. Ralph Waldo Emerson was regularly discussed, his lectures announced and reviewed, and his work excerpted. Nathaniel Hawthorne's short story "The Pine Tree Shilling" was included in the 14 December 1849 issue of the *North Star*; a selection from Herman Melville's *Typee*, titled "Tatooing," appeared in the 2 June 1848 issue.[92] John Greenleaf Whittier was heralded as a major poet worthy of extended study by readers of the newspaper. His verses were frequently included in the "Poetry" column and often matched with biographical data and critical discussions of the author's work. The terms for his praise and that of other European American writers typically recalled the new standards for American literature that were embodied in the narratives of fugitive slaves. Whittier, one writer asserted, "has made more than verses. He has not only written, but done something. . . . He has perhaps, fulfilled the truest vocation of the poet in this transition age by being in some sort the voice of one crying in the wilderness."[93]

By situating the work of these emergent European American writers next to that of black writers, by implying that these authors, black and white, were responsible for negotiating the terms of an emerging and distinct American literature, Douglass effectively advanced the un-precedented idea of their creative parity. While much of the content of the *North Star* and *Frederick Douglass' Paper* attested to the dramatic differences in the material condition of the nation's black and white populations, the juxtaposition of the creative literary work of black and white American writers in the pages of the newspapers was a testimony to their shared cultural pursuits. Like W. E. B. Du Bois's strategy of pairing Negro spirituals with European verse as the epigraphs of each of his chapters of *The Souls of Black Folk* (1903), Douglass is able to emphasize both the creative symmetry and the complementarity of these forms of expression, all of which he considered as indigenous, American literature.

To say the least, Douglass's assertion of the creative parity of black and white writers was subversive to the cultural hierarchy of the time; many Americans questioned the very humanity of black people, and even among sympathetic abolitionists their ability to create literary art was viewed skeptically. By printing the work of the most celebrated European authors alongside that of black and white American writers Douglass posed a further challenge to early nineteenth-century assumptions about literary value, which held that works of European literature were far superior to those of American literature. The writing of Sir Walter Scott, Samuel Coleridge, and Felicia Hemans appeared regularly in the *North Star* and *Frederick Douglass' Paper*. Douglass's efforts to highlight the work of one of the most popular English writers, Charles Dickens, is particularly notable. The editorial decision to serialize Dickens's latest novel, *Bleak House*, in the spring of 1852 is another sign of Douglass's determination to expose black readers to a variety of literature, including that which was more immediately associated with white readers. *Harper's Monthly*, a publication with increasing prestige as a literary journal, had secured an agreement with Dickens for the right to publish *Bleak House*; without securing such an agreement, Douglass seems to have taken the liberty of simultaneously publishing the novel, the installments in *Frederick Douglass' Paper* running slightly behind those in *Harper's Monthly*.

There is no shortage of questions to be asked and observations to be made about both Douglass's decision to print *Bleak House* and his readers' response to it. For the purposes of this discussion, it must suffice to leap straight to one of the most significant observations.

Douglass promoted the publication of *Bleak House* as a significant event, supplying his readers with the supplemental texts, including biographical sketches of Dickens and notices informing readers of the record-breaking sales of his work abroad, that were traditionally employed by newspaper editors to stimulate and maintain their readers' interest in serialized fiction. Nevertheless, during the eighteen-month serialization of *Bleak House* in *Frederick Douglass' Paper*, the main literary attraction of the newspaper was not Dickens's novel but, rather, critical discussion of Harriet Beecher Stowe's *Uncle Tom's Cabin*. The serialization of *Bleak House*, which ran weekly with one exception from 15 April 1852 until 16 December 1853, coincided directly with extensive debates on the literary and political merit of *Uncle Tom's Cabin*. Black readers of *Frederick Douglass' Paper* were more focused on Stowe's novel, which was reviewed in the "Literary Notices" column of the newspaper on the same day that the commencement of *Bleak House* was announced. The one exception to the weekly inclusion of *Bleak House* in *Frederick Douglass' Paper* points to the literary and political priorities of Douglass's readers: on 1 October 1852 an editorial decision to reprint the text of Charles Sumner's speech addressing his motion to repeal the Fugitive Slave Act left no room for the weekly installment of the novel. Slavery and the future of black Americans in the United States were issues directly addressed by Stowe's novel. Initially serialized in the *National Era*, *Uncle Tom's Cabin* was, in the spring of 1852, released as a single volume. Frederick Douglass's review of that volume, issued before he had in fact seen it and based almost entirely on Stowe's reputation and on his knowledge that the book took up the question of slavery, posited his belief in its ability to work political wonders. "The touching portraiture [Stowe] has given of 'poor Uncle Tom' will, of itself, enlist the kind sympathies, of numbers, in behalf of the oppressed African race, and will raise up a host of enemies against the fearful system of slavery," concluded an early review of the novel.[94]

That Stowe's subject matter and the potential political impact of her novel were of more interest and personal concern to Douglass's readers than was Dickens's *Bleak House* is unsurprising, and editorial notices indicate that Douglass was certainly aware that some readers were critical of his decision even to include *Bleak House* in *Frederick Douglass' Paper*. More to the point, the timing of the publication of the two novels seemed to have put them in direct competition with one another, an impression that the newspaper's editors seemed aware of and worked to dispel. As early as the end of April 1852, a note to readers in the newspaper's "Literary Notices" column highlighted this tension: "We make no apology to our readers for devoting our fourth page to 'Bleak House,'" it began. "To those among them who have read 'UNCLE TOM'S CABIN,' (and who has not read it ere this?) we commend this attractive story of the most popular of English writers."[95] In this implied contest, *Uncle Tom's Cabin* was the definitive victor; while *Bleak House* inspired little critical commentary, letters to the newspaper concerning the literary and political merits of Stowe's novel abounded.

It bears emphasizing that Douglass might have suspended the serialization of *Bleak House* at any time, either in order to make more room for the publication of critical perspectives on *Uncle Tom's Cabin* or because he sensed his readers' waning interest in the novel. That he did not serves to underscore Douglass's literary priorities and commitments. As I have already argued, Douglass was intent on laying the work of European, American, and African American writers side by side in *Frederick Douglass' Paper*. His purpose in doing so was to prove by association that this writing was equal and to insist, at the same time, that literary talent was transracial. In the juxtaposition of all of this literature—fiction about legal injustice in *Bleak House*, fiction about racial injustice in *Uncle Tom's Cabin*, and nonfiction about slave experience in the slave narratives—the newspaper's readers were able to see them as connected by theme (injustice) and in political intent (to reform the justice system, abolish slavery).

Douglass's editorial choice to serialize *Bleak House* alongside critical debates about *Uncle Tom's Cabin* demonstrates his commitment to producing both literature and literary criticism, both primary texts and the discussions that surrounded them, in the pages of *Frederick Douglass' Paper*. As I have argued, the ways in which Douglass's journalism supported efforts to foster the development of literary skills in the black community are not explicitly communicated in the pages of the newspapers. But a desire to enhance these talents and a keen sense of their importance was inherent in Douglass's literary decisions. His determination to provide his readers with both a variety of literature and an array of critical voices serves to illustrate the extent to which

Douglass advocated an agenda for promoting black liberation and equality that was grounded in African American literary practice. The tangible focus of the critical debates waged in the pages of *Frederick Douglass' Paper*, the most visible and well-documented of which was that between Douglass and his former coeditor, Martin Delany, was Stowe's *Uncle Tom's Cabin*; but while the novel provided a concrete center for these conversations, it served as a point of departure for literary and political discussions that would shape and galvanize both black readers and the black community generally in myriad ways. Behind the various critical commentaries on the novel lurked a variety of questions crucial to the future of black Americans and the development of their literary and political voices. Did Stowe's novel, as Douglass initially believed, have the power to improve the condition of blacks in the United States? How was this impression of the novel compatible with its final chapter, in which Stowe promoted colonization? What were the limits of religious piety, and when was resistance not only justified but demanded? Could a white writer such as Stowe faithfully represent the black experience in slavery?[96]

Douglass's own response to these questions seems at once straightforward. Editorial pieces contributed to the newspaper in the years after the publication of *Uncle Tom's Cabin* attest to Douglass's belief in "Mrs. Stowe's power to do us good," and there is no doubt that he used the pages of *Frederick Douglass' Paper* to orchestrate a positive reading of *Uncle Tom's Cabin*, defending the novel valiantly against even its troubling advocacy of colonization. But at the height of his defense of the novel, Douglass included in the pages of *Frederick Douglass' Paper* a novella that he wrote which delivered a searching critique of Stowe's work. "The Heroic Slave," serialized in the paper early in 1853, tells the story of the slave Madison Washington who, in 1841, led a successful revolt against the slave ship *Creole*. Douglass's novella confirms in fictional form the belief he expressed in the context of his comments on *Uncle Tom's Cabin*: working in concert with black Americans, sympathetic whites could help to bring about the liberation and elevation of African Americans. At the same time, "The Heroic Slave" pointedly counters or revises some of the images put forth by Stowe's novel. Most notably, Washington is presented to the reader as a rebellious rather than a docile slave. He does share some of Uncle Tom's attributes: "A child might play in his arms, or dance on his shoulders," Douglass writes in a description of him. Yet unlike Stowe's Uncle Tom, Washington is also described as a man with the capacity to think for himself and act decisively: "He had the head to conceive, and the hand to execute. In a word, he was one to be sought as a friend, but to be dreaded as an enemy."[97]

Douglass's novella is an early example of African American fiction based on the conventions of the slave narrative. Douglass's familiarity and frustration with the slave narrative needs no further documentation, and his experimentation with fiction writing in "The Heroic Slave" is a tangible demonstration of his desire to assume control over both narrative strategy and creative voice. Taken in concert, Douglass's fictional response to *Uncle Tom's Cabin* and his critical assessments of the novel, laid side by side in the pages of *Frederick Douglass's Paper*, make visible a less straightforward, more complex response to it than allowed by either source alone. On the one hand, he embraced it because he believed it had the potential to mobilize Americans in support of the interests of both free and enslaved blacks. On the other hand, he used "The Heroic Slave" to posit a critical revision of some aspects of it. That Douglass relied on two different kinds of literary texts, imaginative and critical, to communicate the nuances of his thinking on Stowe's novel points to the important work Douglass relied on literary texts to do in 1853 and suggests the extent to which, in the 1850s and on the eve of the Civil War, he trusted literary texts to provide free blacks with a means of discussing questions to which definitive answers were scarce. One need only look as far as the rift between Douglass and Delany that found expression in the pages of *Frederick Douglass' Paper* as a debate over the value of *Uncle Tom's Cabin* to see the complicated and often divisive nature of these discussions. The immorality of slavery and racist practices in the North, the validity of the Fugitive Slave Law, the complexity of issues of colonization and emigration, the intricacies inherent in the pursuit of freedom and citizenship, the desirability of religious otherworldliness, the advocacy of various strategies for effective leadership and representation and their political consequences—sorting through these issues presented great challenges to black Americans as they struggled to maintain their focus on effecting communal change while remaining true to differences in perspectives on race and nation, political vision and public stance. Douglass's journalism reinforced for its black readers the extent to which literary texts could provide the basis for fruitful discussions; it is in these productive literary conversations that Douglass and other free blacks continued to struggle for their rights as well as to suggest how that struggle might best be waged.

"AN INTIMATE COMPANION OF ALL CLASSES"

Literary historians have noted with surprise that the first African American newspapers focused decisively on literature and the first African American literary magazines produced in and for the black community were launched in the politically turbulent 1850s, when legislation like the passage of the Fugitive Slave Act and court decisions like the *Dred Scott* case made fugitive slaves and free blacks more vulnerable than ever. Although the law and the Supreme Court decision exacerbated the situation of blacks enslaved in the South, they proved particularly problematic for the free black population who were now threatened with kidnapping and had their hopes for citizenship dashed by Judge Taney's firm assertion that all blacks constituted a "subordinate and inferior class of beings" who essentially had "no rights or privileges but such as those who held the power and the government might choose to grant them."[98] But against this desolate background, newspapers focused more decisively on literature like *Frederick Douglass' Paper* and the first black literary magazines were published; in this political situation, these publications counseled new strategies for literacy and literary work.

In the midst of deteriorating conditions, attention to literary pursuits generally and specifically to the development of journalism more literary in nature was one way to "uphold and encourage the now depressed hopes of thinking black men, in the United States." In the words of Thomas Hamilton, publisher of the *Anglo-African Magazine*, this population had, "for twenty years and more . . . been active in conventions, in public meetings, in societies, in the pulpit, and through the press, cheering on and laboring on to promote emancipation, affranchisement [*sic*] and education." The "apparent result of their work and their sacrifices," however, was "only Fugitive Slave laws and Compromise bills, and the denial of citizenship on the part of the Federal and State Governments."[99] Despite their sense of discouragement, these individuals remained committed to achieving social and racial justice in the United States; once literary character spread throughout the black community, they believed, prejudice and discrimination would disappear and the promise of democracy would be fulfilled. "If ever there was a time when our people should read," wrote one contributor to the *Christian Recorder* in 1854, "it is now, in order to improve their understanding, and cultivate their minds. We should read and study every book and paper, any thing and every thing that tends to religion, morality, science, and literature." Exposure to such literary learning, this writer advocated, would allow black Americans to "cultivate and improve ourselves, that we may be able to stand in juxtaposition with our friends, who think themselves the favoured of God."[100]

I close this chapter by looking summarily at two newspapers, the *Christian Recorder*, established in 1852, and the *Weekly Anglo-African*, begun in 1859, and two literary magazines, the *Repository of Religion and Literature, and of Science and Art* and the *Anglo-African Magazine*, begun in 1858 and 1859, respectively. All of these publications supported the concerns expressed by *Freedom's Journal*, the *Colored American*, and the *North Star* and *Frederick Douglass' Paper*: they regarded the need for self-representation as central to the future of black Americans in the United States and saw their columns as places where black voices would find a receptive audience. "We know that there are many well-educated, strong and powerful minds among us, that have need only to be discovered . . . in order to become the wonder and admiration of the world," wrote the editor of the *Christian Recorder* in an early issue of the newspaper. "Come friends, one and all, who are interested for [*sic*] the spread of useful knowledge . . . let us hear what you have to say upon these great questions."[101] Five years later, Thomas Hamilton used his introductory remarks in the *Anglo-African Magazine* to reiterate the imperative of creating a platform from which to counter what he recognized as a concerted "endeavor to write down the negro [*sic*] as something less than a man." " 'The twelve millions of blacks in the United States and its environs,' " he wrote, "must speak for themselves; no outside tongue, however gifted with eloquence, can tell their story; no outside eye, however penetrating, can see their wants; no outside organization, however benevolently intended, nor however cunningly contrived, can develope [*sic*] the energies and aspirations that make up

their mission."[102] Hamilton promised that "all articles in the Magazine, not otherwise designated, will be the products of the pens of
colored men and women."[103] He told his readers of his intent, "if the
requisite editorial matter can be furnished, to make this magazine 'one
of the institutions of the country'."[104]

Hamilton's desire to create a publication composed exclusively of
literature by black authors reflects an approach to fostering the development of "literary character" in the black community that differed
significantly from that of Frederick Douglass. Their goals, however,
were not dissimilar. In addition to providing a place in which literary
production by African Americans would find a readership, the *Anglo-
African Magazine* also furnished a forum in which black writers used
sophisticated works of literature to engage in debates about the nature
and function of black art and its role in racial uplift. Writers of such
different political persuasions and artistic sensibilities as Frances E. W.
Harper and Martin R. Delany published significant pieces in the first
volume of the *Anglo-African Magazine*. Published serially throughout
1859, Delany's *Blake: or the Huts of America* is the story of Henry
Holland, a free black who attempts to organize a revolt among the
slaves not only in the United States but throughout the western hemisphere. Harper's short story "The Two Offers," which also appeared
serially, presents a radically different literary representation of black
life. She contrasts the lives of two cousins to argue against complacency
and to assert that marriage is but one option for women of intelligence
and social conscience. While one cousin lives an unhappy life after
marrying someone she does not love, the other does not marry; she
becomes a writer and dedicates her life to "mak[ing] the world better
by her example [and] gladder by her presence." Like Harper herself,
her fictional character "had a higher and better object in all her writings than the mere acquisition of gold, or acquirement of fame . . . she
had a high and holy mission on the battlefield of existence."[105] Harper
and Delany represent two extremes in their aesthetic beliefs and social
politics; like other authors who published in the *Anglo-African Magazine*, the *Weekly Anglo-African*, the *Repository*, and the *Christian Recorder*, both found an audience for their diverse agendas.[106]

In their quest to become monuments to the intellectual abilities and
the cultural achievements of black Americans, these publications
shared with the earlier newspapers a commitment to working cooper-

atively with other institutions of literary activity. The *Christian Recorder*, for instance, was a product of the African Methodist Episcopal (A.M.E.) Church's Book Concern, a committee formed in 1817 to ensure the distribution of moral and religious texts to the black community. The newspaper was central to fulfilling the Book Concern's mission of extending literacy throughout the black community and seeing that black Americans were well represented in print. Founders of the *Christian Recorder* considered the publication a principal means of presenting the black community in its best light and "pledged to make it a paper—in print, in size, in type and in general appearance—that shall give respectability and credit to us."[107] The literary content of each issue of the newspaper supported this commitment, as well as the Book Concern's dedication to the distribution of texts and of literary knowledge generally. In addition to the original contributions written by both well-known and amateur black writers, the *Christian Recorder* published bibliographic essays and discussions about literary theory and reviewed and recommended recently published books by both African American and European American authors. Early in 1864, a column called "Books For Our Times" recommended Louisa May Alcott's "Hospital Sketches" and a collection of speeches and lectures by Wendell Phillips as well as William Wells Brown's recently published *The Black Man* and a biography of Toussaint L'Ouverture.[108] Some books received special acknowledgment. Under the heading "Book Notices," a slave narrative by Rev. J. W. Loguen of Syracuse, New York, was called "a wonderful book" that "narrates the life of Bro. Loguen with startling power."[109] This and all other books mentioned in the *Christian Recorder* were available for purchase through what was advertised as "Our Very Own Bookstore." A full catalogue of "Books for Sale at the Book Depository of the A.M.E. Church," located on Pine Street in Philadelphia, was regularly included in the *Christian Recorder*. In addition to "Sabbath School Books" and "Public School Books," the Book Depository also had available a vast array of titles aimed at a general audience.[110]

The *Repository of Religion and Literature, and of Science and Art* was formed in conjunction with not one but many literary institutions. It was first published by select "Literary Societies of the African Methodist Episcopal Church." By January 1862 the *Repository*'s sponsorship shifted to "all the Literary Societies that will contribute the annual sum of $24 for its support." Many of the features that were included in the *Repository* were lectures that had been given before or were prepared in the context of men's and women's literary societies, and the editors appealed regularly to members of the literary societies that sponsored the magazine to employ "their rich thought and polished pen" toward the production of "contributions of great value."[111] The *Repository* included "Literature" and "Poetry" sections as well as a "Young Ladies' Lecture Room." Stories for children were found in a section called the "Children's Room" and short reviews of books, pamphlets, and magazines appeared in the "Monthly Book-Table" section, or under the heading "Literary Notices."

So oriented toward literature was the *Weekly Anglo-African* that it inspired the formation of both informal literary coalitions and a formal reading room. Writing to the editors of the *Weekly Anglo-African* in October 1859, one of its readers, the Reverend Amos Gerry, made the following observation: "Long winter evenings are before us— many hours are to be disposed of," he wrote. "How shall they be occupied?" "Now is the time to form Social Improvement Circles," Gerry suggested, "where the few, if no more are willing to join, may meet at least *one* evening in each week, and read such selections as may be agreed upon, or recite from the great poets such portions as will expand the mind, strengthen the understanding, and improve the taste." He recalled one such "little company of five or six individuals," who gathered "to hear one of their number read through David Walker's Appeal to the Colored People of America." Gerry commended this activity, not only because of the importance of Walker's text specifically ("Would that that book could be read by every person within these United States," he wrote of it. "Its pages thunder, its paragraphs blaze"), but also because such reading circles were one way to expose African Americans to black authors and, in so doing, preserve black literary arts. It was an opportune time to think about the formation of such circles, Gerry believed, for several reasons. Surely free blacks such as those who had access to the *Weekly Anglo-African* were in need of improving their literary skills, and the approach of shorter days and colder weather made a renewed commitment to indoor activities like reading and extended literary discussion appropriate. It was the existence of the *Weekly Anglo-African*, however, and the unprecedented access to literary texts that it facilitated, that made it a particularly auspicious time for free blacks to form literary circles. The "opportunities for gaining useful knowledge now presented, especially by the 'Anglo-African'" were tremendous, Gerry argued. He considered the newspaper an invaluable source of reading material as well as a forum through which the thinking and writing of black people could be appreciated and preserved. This was, in fact, one of Gerry's principal concerns. "An effort should be made to preserve the writings of colored persons, and we know of no better way than to form such 'improvement circles,' and to gather up all the books and writing so far as may be which refer to us as a people. If this is faithfully done," he concluded, "there will be many a library formed of no small value—of inestimable value—and of increasing interest."[112]

Indeed, the contents of the *Weekly Anglo-African* did form a library of no small value, each issue containing abundant material to support the activities of a reading circle. In addition to letters, essays, and extended book reviews, a regular feature of the newspaper was a "Poems, Anecdotes and Sketches" column. The content of this column was entirely explained in its title. In one issue, Frances Ellen Watkins's poem "Be Active" was followed by an anonymously authored poem called "He's None The Worse For That" and two works of short fiction, "The Negro of Brazil" by "An Old Tar" and "The Lost Diamond" by Mrs. F. D. Gage.[113] Short, moralistic vignettes appeared alongside excerpts from recently published novels. The close relationship between the *Weekly Anglo-African* and the *Anglo-African Magazine* ensured that a steady stream of texts would appear in both journals. James McCune Smith's "Chess," originally published in the September 1859 issue of the *Anglo-African Magazine*, was also included on the front page of the issue of the *Weekly Anglo-African* published on 10 September 1859, and Frances E. Watkins's contribution to the August 1859 issue of the *Anglo-African Magazine*, "The Dying Fugitive," also appeared in the *Weekly Anglo-African* on 20 August 1859. Even the extended book reviews that were included in the *Weekly Anglo-African* offered readers significant literary texts that enhanced their critical perspective as they suggested further reading. Reviews and advertisements for Douglass's *My Bondage and My Freedom*, a biography of the Reverend Jermain W. Loguen, and William C. Nell's *The Colored Patriots of the American Revolution* shared space with recommendations for Lydia Maria Child's "The Right Way, The Safe Way."[114] The number as well as the diversity of texts supplied on a weekly basis by the *Weekly Anglo-African* was appreciated by readers, who recognized the advantages that would accompany such literary exposure. In the words of one of the newspaper's patrons, through active interaction with the literary texts included in the *Weekly Anglo-African*, "readers are taught to think for themselves, and are stimulated to express their thoughts in appropriate language. By this means," this reader recognized, "they will make rapid advances in literature."[115] Evidently, the newspaper's audience's eagerness to consume its literary offerings sometimes came at the expense of their reading of another text commonly associated with African American readers: the Bible. A small item included in a February 1860 issue of the newspaper and titled "Popularity of the 'Anglo-African'" reported that one New York City preacher had complained to his congregation that "he knew Christians who could be found sitting up late at night reading the 'African Paper,' while their Bibles were totally neglected."[116]

Capitalizing on the interest in literature and literary texts in part created by the *Weekly Anglo-African*, its editors moved to open their own reading room in November 1859. Located in 178 Prince Street in New York City, the Anglo-African Reading Room opened with much fanfare. To publicize the existence of the reading room and ensure its immediate popularity, the committee responsible for organizing the Anglo-African Reading Room instigated "a course of popular lectures" to be held periodically at the reading room. Although they chose to promote the lectures, rather than the reading room itself, in their initial announcement, the text of it makes clear that "the object of the course [of lectures]" was to "aid in the establishment of a reading-room." By providing ready access to literary material and promoting attention to literary character in the black community, the reading room, this group recognized, would constitute an essential and lasting addition to the black community. Organizers hoped that the reading room would be inviting to "the masses," a space "where the barriers of complexion, sect, or party shall have no existence whatever—a place where young and old may resort to inform themselves upon the current events of the age, and enjoy the various and piquant pleasures produced by the learned review or the well stored magazine." Intergenerational as well as interracial, the Anglo-African Reading Room was envisioned as a "place . . . not for the *colored man*, and not for the *white man*, but for the PEOPLE."[117]

To this end, the "list of lecturers" was to "comprehend the representatives of color and those who are not." Speakers were to encompass a wide range of subject matters and perspectives, representing "the pulpit, the bar, the bench, the editorial chair—the Presbyterian, the Congregationalist, the Methodist, the Baptist, the Universalist—learning, eloquence, and enthusiasm."[118] Meetings were often sponsored by independent literary societies, including those whose membership was female. Reports of lectures and meetings held in the Anglo-African Reading Room suggest that these events, serious or playful, were dominated by a spirit of interaction rather than opposition. Speakers assembled could be contentious, their addresses challenging, but they were thought-provoking as well. Exposure to this sort of environment and the intellectually challenging climate it encouraged seems to have been precisely the type of exercise the reading room hoped to provide. Surely gatherings advertised as "A little literature and lemonade—a few declamations and doughnuts!" were playful and entertaining; but they were serious and academic, too. As had traditionally been the case with African American literary coalitions, the success of the reading room was in its combination of intellectual exercise and society. "To sit alone and gorge one's self with venison and wine, is not our taste," wrote one correspondent for the *Weekly Anglo-African* in praise of the reading room's activities. "An association of kindred spirits can sometimes find profitable conversation over a cup of coffee, refreshing our minds as well as bodies, and sharpening the ideas by social interchange of sentiment."[119] This understanding was shared by readers of the *Weekly Anglo-African* who did not live near the Anglo-African Reading Room. Writing from Hartford, Connecticut, "Sigma" used these words to express her belief in the advantages of the social aspect of literary study afforded by reading rooms, for both men and women: "We feel glad to know that a reading room has been started in your city, and although we cannot enjoy its benefits yet we console ourselves with the idea that it will be productive of good, especially if the ladies patronize it and enter into discussions upon the merits of the different periodicals on the files. Nothing calls into action and better strengthens one's judgement as this habit of conversing on what we read."[120]

Despite the emphasis of all of these publications on nurturing black readers and writers and preserving a record of their accomplishments, most have until recently been overlooked by literary historians as sources of early African American literature. An exception to this is the *Anglo-African Magazine*, widely considered the first literary magazine produced by and for the black community. Contemporary definitions of journalism have prevented us from dissociating our understanding of the newspaper's coverage of "news" from the actual literary contexts of early nineteenth-century African American newspapers. Furthermore, contemporary distinctions between church and state, between "high" and "popular" literary productions, have limited our ability to see either the *Repository* or the *Christian Recorder* as anything other than religious publications. But, as Frances Smith Foster has recently reminded us, "the Afro-Protestant press rarely if ever confined itself to what we might understand as 'religious' subjects. To the publishers and contributors, as to their intended readers, the sacred and the secular were not discrete elements of their lives and their experiences."[121] Foster's own recovery of three novels by Frances E. W. Harper that were published serially in the *Christian Recorder* between 1868 and 1888 reinforces her argument that the Afro-Protestant press must be reconsidered as a major source of literature by and for African Americans. By ignoring or dismissing such sources, scholars of African American literary history will necessarily perpetuate what Foster calls "ahistorical and overdisciplined ways of thinking" about the literary habits of and literary production by African Americans in the mid-nineteenth century.[122] The diverse literary content of publications like the *Repository of Religion and Literature, and of Science and Art* and the *Christian Recorder* serves as an important reminder that many non-religious documents were included in church-based sources, and that the black church encouraged African American readers to acquaint themselves with literature that was not limited to the Bible.

Scholarly neglect of these critical sources has had tremendous repercussions, not only in terms of our knowledge of early African American literature but also in terms of our understanding of the habits of African Americans as readers as they faced the definitional crises that marked the 1850s. During this time, for instance, the *Repository*, the *Anglo-African Magazine*, and the *Christian Recorder* all shared what in the *Colored American* had been a fledgling concern with the creation of an enduring record of African American accomplishments and cultural production. The editors considered the durability of their publications a prime aspect of their appeal; in promoting them, they distanced the publications from the ephemeral qualities of a newspaper by representing them as booklike. This was true even of the *Christian Recorder*, which was published more frequently and printed on sheets larger than the new literary magazines. The founders of the *Christian Recorder* emphasized in the prospectus that it would be "in a form so as to be folded as a book or pamphlet, that families and individuals may have books made of it and preserved for future references."[123] A statement regularly included in issues of the *Repository* cited the magazine's durability as a principal appeal when it enumerated the reasons it should be patronized. "Because being in book form," this announcement stated, "it is better adapted to preserve the current literature of our Church, and of sister denominations for the use of posterity—for where you will find one copy of our newspapers fifty years hence, you will doubtless find fifty copies of the Repository." Although the *Repository* would remain unbound, it was as good as having a book: "People seldom preserve newspapers, but almost always preserve their books. Indeed, books preserve themselves." The creation of durable sources of literature was considered critical to the support of black authors and the development of an African American literary tradition. The *Repository* claimed that "because of [its] conservative power it is better adapted to develope [*sic*] the talents of our young people, and to furnish data for future comparison."[124] This and similar assertions offer further insight into the literary aesthetics of early African American readers, who were reminded in multiple ways that literature was, above all, functional. It could not serve to educate or inspire the people if it did not survive to reach multiple generations of black readers.

What finally distinguishes the literary journalism of the period just before the Civil War is that, in addition to attempting to recreate the shared space of literary societies, as *Freedom's Journal* and the *Colored American* had, it also encouraged independent reading and fostered the development of individual reading habits. A distinctive feature of the new literary magazines was their portability; individual issues of the *Repository*, for instance, were but twenty-two pages, bound by a single thread, and small enough to fit conveniently in a pocket. The

Repository highlighted its portability as a primary appeal to subscribers in a statement repeated monthly on the back cover of the publication. "If you bind newspapers into book form it then becomes too large to be portable, too unhandy for use," explained the editors, "but the Repository *will always be portable, always easily used.*"[125] This portable source of literature was designed to convey the experience and the benefits of organized literary activity to individual readers and to each solitary reading experience. The implication here is that, because of its portability, the magazine insisted on being read; it was, according to the *Repository*'s editors, "an intimate companion of all classes," capable of providing the individual reader with opportunities to engage in a communal model of literary activity even when away from the company of peers at the literary society meeting or in the lecture hall.[126] Literary magazines would provide constant company for black readers, ensuring that they were kept in regular contact with appropriate literature. As if they were at a meeting of a literary society, readers of the new literary magazines would be tutored in the civic responsibilities and democratic process that formed the basis of all literary engagement as they read. In this way, the editors of the *Repository* suggested, the solitary reading experience would be another means of exposing black Americans to the literary environments that would contribute to their becoming "fit for society, [and] better neighbors in any community."[127]

The design of these publications to expand the literary habits of black readers to include more attention to individual, solitary reading is representative of notable changes taking place in the black community on the eve of the Civil War. Despite significant restrictions on their freedom, free blacks responded to the legislative assaults of the 1850s through different and more decisively political organizational channels than they had in earlier decades. In response to the political setbacks of the 1850s, some black Americans revisited the idea of emigration, not only to Africa but also to Canada and Haiti. Others became involved in greater numbers in antislavery societies and the activities that directly supported the abolitionist effort. African Americans in New York and Ohio renewed their dedication to organizing annual conventions, and throughout the North blacks held meetings to consider how to respond to the infuriating disregard for their rights and their freedom. In this increasingly polarized, increasingly hostile pre–Civil War environment, black Americans had less energy to dedicate to organized literary efforts, and the number of organizations specifically focused around reading and literature declined. Literary study, however, remained no less important, and the literary publications of the 1850s and early 1860s addressed this continued need for attention to literature by cultivating the development of more solitary and individual reading habits. Although they appreciated the institutions that continued to support organized literary activities, the idea of literacy communicated by these publications was not tied to the specific context of the literary society or reading room. It is not that the communal context associated with literary societies became any less important in the decade preceding the Civil War. In fact, never had there been greater need for free blacks to assert in strong, public voices their commitment to liberty and equality. The terms of literary practice shaped and communicated by the literary journalism of the 1850s and early 1860s insisted that individual readers must remain oriented toward uses of literacy and language that allowed them to forcefully enter into public debates about the future of black Americans in the United States and to raise the voice of conscience in a society seemingly deaf to its own ideals.

3

Literary Coalitions
in the Age of Washington

In this chapter I shift my attention from the literary societies formed by black Americans in the urban North in the first half of the nineteenth century and the culture of reading promoted by the early nineteenth-century black press to two post-Reconstruction literary societies, the Bethel Historical and Literary Association and the Boston Literary and Historical Association. The Bethel Literary, as it was commonly called, was founded in Washington, D.C., in 1881 and remained active until at least 1915. The Boston Literary and Historical Association was begun in 1901 and remained active into the 1920s.[1] The membership of these postbellum organizations shared with their antebellum predecessors the ideals that had motivated African Americans early in the nineteenth century to involve themselves in literary associations. They believed that association with literature was one way of definitively asserting a positive, learned identity far removed from the intellectual poverty associated with slavery. They also trusted that literary study would expose them to the set of useful knowledge through which black Americans would enlighten themselves, thus becoming, as a race, better prepared for the demands of citizenship and the particular challenges of the twentieth century. By demonstrating their capacity for improvement and elevation, they hoped that the white racist image of black Americans would be transformed, and their political rights and respectability among the world's most "civilized" peoples would be established.

While this shared commitment to the construction of literary identity and shared belief that literary production and exchange provided a means to contest racial caricatures and to respond to racial violence and inequity links the earliest African American literary societies of the nineteenth century to those instituted at the turn of the century, the postbellum societies I explore here are remarkable for their subtle differences, too. Most immediately striking is their size and the format of their activities. Both the Bethel Literary and the Boston Literary and Historical Association were large, formal institutions; their meetings took place in public places and were regularly attended by hundreds of people. Although punctuated by music and literary readings, meetings were focused around a formal presentation delivered by an invited speaker, and the audience participated in the program by taking part in the discussion that followed the lecture. The emphasis on this format serves to highlight the ways that the activities of these postbellum societies were directed at fostering a different sort of "literacy" than that which had been the primary interest of earlier societies. Antebellum literary societies had operated in such a way as to meet the needs of an emerging democratic culture. Their emphasis on creating a community of black readers and nurturing public speakers with sophisticated rhetorical and oratorical skills was crucial to the future of the nation's free black population who, before the Civil War, sought effective avenues of public access and ways to voice their demands for full citizenship and equal participation in the life of the republic. In contrast, while they continued to nurture and value the development of literary and rhetorical skills, postbellum societies like the Bethel Literary and Boston Literary and Historical Association sought to cultivate a new form of cultural and political literacy among their participants.

Although antebellum literary societies had provided early black Americans with a forum in which to discuss the benefits of emigration and express concern for the racial name by which they would be known, the membership of postbellum literary societies focused on questions of intraracial politics in a new and more concerted fashion. The questions that had dominated antebellum literary societies had mainly been ones of intraracial morals—how African Americans might best avoid the temptations of alcohol as well as brothels and gaming tables and use their leisure time in productive ways—and interracial politics—how to best counter the racism and hostility of the white community. Even as they continued to appreciate the "respectability" with which literary activities were associated, the membership of the Bethel Literary and the Boston Literary and Historical Association focused on intraracial politics to an unprecedented degree. This can be seen most clearly in their active participation in the explosive political debates about the future of the Negro in the United States at the end of the century and the best social strategies for racial advancement. The most prominent and most persistent of these debates surrounded the question of Negro education, a question that was inseparable from the more general issues of racial identity that assumed increasing urgency at the end of the nineteenth century. In their respective communities, the Bethel Literary and the Boston Literary and Historical Association provided the primary forum in which middle-class black Americans discussed and debated these issues. It is notable that the two most prominent political figures from this time who would come to embody two opposing perspectives on both Negro education and racial identity, Booker T. Washington and W. E. B. Du Bois, addressed the membership of the literary societies I discuss here.

The debate between these two leaders over whether Negro youth were better served by industrial or higher education, and the contradictory definitions of race consciousness and racial politics their work has come to epitomize, provide a framework from which to consider the differences between the Bethel Historical and Literary Association and the Boston Literary and Historical Association. While both societies used the same weekly format to promote the importance of an informed democratic citizenry and foster a renewed faith in literary accomplishments as a means of addressing social problems, the subtle differences between these literary associations offer important insight into the different historical situations at the end of the nineteenth century and the beginning of the twentieth century, two distinct periods often considered as one. Although it has been widely documented that, by the beginning of the twentieth century, middle-class blacks in the urban North had grown critical of Washington's accommodationist policies and his advocacy of industrial education for Negro youth, the Bethel Historical and Literary Association's records document a period before this perspective had fully evolved. In the last decade of the nineteenth century, the membership of the Bethel Literary struggled to understand their leadership role in the context of the tensions, contradictions, and disillusionment of what has since been called the "nadir" of black life in the United States. This struggle reached its pinnacle during the Bethel Literary's 1895–96 season. The death of Frederick Douglass and the ascent of Booker T. Washington to a position of national prominence with the delivery of the Atlanta Exposition Address in the fall of 1895 brought questions of black leadership to the fore. What is most clearly expressed through the considerable debate spawned by their attention to these questions, including the question of industrial or higher education, is the degree to which middle-class black Washingtonians associated with the Bethel Literary struggled to determine the path most likely to fulfill their political, civil, and social aspirations. Social and political conditions in the North and the South by the last decade of the nineteenth century were such that members of the Bethel Literary knew that the approaching twentieth century demanded more effective expressions of black identity; but discussions surrounding the nature of that identity were fraught with the uncertainties and anxieties of the age.

In contrast, the intraracial friction that characterizes the debates that took place at the Bethel Literary in the last decade of the nineteenth century is virtually absent from the Boston Literary and Historical Association. Organized in 1901, the Boston association was intended by its founders to be a direct attack on the leadership and racial policies of Booker T. Washington and his by-then considerable "Tuskegee Machine." Convinced that the underlying objective behind industrial education was the maintenance of a hierarchical society in which blacks would remain subservient, and vehemently opposed to spreading this "social gospel" throughout the black population, the membership of the Boston Literary and Historical Association were united in their opinion of Washington. Rather than debate this position, they designed a program that *assumed* the ideals of higher education and the importance of racial consciousness and pride. In the topics that they discussed and the issues that they raised, the members of the Boston Literary and Historical Association confidently embodied the New Negro voice that would be epitomized by

W. E. B. Du Bois's *The Souls of Black Folk* in 1903. Although the nature of their discussions may appear less overtly political than those of the Bethel Literary, they ascribed to a form of cultural politics that, given the context of the deeply racist society in which they lived, they believed promised to do more to organize and empower the black community than direct political agitation.

In order to make sense of the political debates waged in post-Reconstruction literary societies, it is important to understand the social and historical conditions of the last third of the nineteenth century. I begin this chapter by outlining the historical events that provide the backdrop for the formation of the Bethel Historical and Literary Association and the Boston Literary and Historical Association, as well as the turn-of-the-century black women's clubs that are the subject of the next chapter. Emancipation spread hope throughout the black community that the future of black Americans in the United States would be bright. This optimism, however, was short-lived. What followed was a period of intense social, economic, and political upheaval that affected both the rural South and the rapidly industrializing North and reached its pinnacle in the last decade of the nineteenth century. African Americans at the turn of the century found themselves enmeshed in a complex system of oppression and further from enfranchisement in the workings of the American political system than ever before. In this context, literary societies re-emerged in the last decades of the nineteenth century as institutions crucial to the shaping of black intellectual and political thought.

"WHAT SHALL WE DO WITH THE NEGROES AFTER THEY ARE FREE?"

The Civil War had begun with the singular purpose of preserving the Federal union from the secession of eleven states into the Confederacy. It soon became clear, however, that the "peculiar institution" of chattel slavery on which the South's whole economic, political, and social life was based was the real issue underlying its claim for independence. Thus, by 1862, setting free the slaves became one of the North's war aims. As the war effort intensified, and as the emancipation of slaves became a tangible possibility, debates about the character and nature of "the Negro" heated up throughout the nation and hostility toward all African Americans—free and slave—intensified. When General Robert E. Lee surrendered in the spring of 1865, the Union had officially won the war, and the Thirteenth Amendment, ratified later that year, irrevocably abolished slavery throughout the nation. But complex questions of peace, reconciliation, and reunion had yet to be faced. Above all, the nation, North and South, had to address Abraham Lincoln's plaintive question: "But what shall we do with the Negroes after they are free?"[2]

The passing of the Fourteenth and Fifteenth Amendments to the United States Constitution, which made African Americans citizens and enfranchised black men, signaled the advent and the promise of Reconstruction. Created in 1865, the Freedmen's Bureau was empowered to protect the legal rights of former slaves; in addition to leasing land to black families and overseeing labor contracts between emancipated slaves and their former masters, it established hospitals and social agencies throughout the South. Significant legislation to protect freedpeople and the establishment of public schools to educate black children inspired further optimism that the promises of full citizenship would be realized. But white southern backlash to these efforts was powerful and effective. Peonage and sharecropping quickly came to replace slave labor, and locally enforced "vagrancy" charges sent many blacks back to their former owners to work off their "sentences." Unusual taxes and other forms of economic repression kept blacks from many jobs, and grandfather clauses and other locally imposed regulations kept black voters away from the polls. The Supreme Court's nullification of the restrictive features of the Civil Rights Act of 1875 opened a path for the institution of Jim Crow laws, which segregated public facilities and socially isolated blacks and whites in virtually all aspects of public and private life. A campaign of extreme and extensive violence directed at black people by secret organizations such as the Ku Klux Klan intimidated freedpeople and their few white allies into silence and inactivity. This brutal violence, combined as it was with increased interest in "scientific" explanations for black inferiority in the last decades of the nineteenth century, confirmed that many whites continued to question the very humanity of black people.

In 1877 the last Federal troops were withdrawn from the South, effectively ending the period known as Reconstruction by restoring state and regional power to white racists in the South. The consequences were predictable and disastrous and extended not only throughout the South but to the North as well. In the South, a system of Jim Crow laws and decrees intended to isolate, subordinate, and degrade African Americans was enforced through barbaric lynchings that, by the 1890s, had reached epidemic proportions. The segregation of African Americans in northern cities, coupled with the rampant economic discrimination and political impotence they faced, provides evidence of the extent to which race relations were rapidly and steadily deteriorating there as well. Their antebellum positions of service and subordination reinforced in postbellum forms, black men and women found little cause for renewed or sustained optimism by the last decade of the nineteenth century. The Supreme Court's 1896 decision in *Plessy v. Ferguson*, which ruled that segregation did not violate the Fourteenth Amendment's guarantee of equal protection before the law as long as facilities for the races were "separate but equal," confirmed that African Americans could not depend on the Federal government for protection and would have to devise their own strategies of collective empowerment and social and political advancement. In light of the intensity of political repression and brutal racial violence in the 1890s, Rayford Logan's description of this period as the "nadir" of black experience in the United States is appropriate. With a stunning swiftness, the advances of Reconstruction were arrested and black Americans' dreams for what it had promised—full citizenship and a more inclusive democracy—were dissipated.

The end of Reconstruction and the escalation of racial violence and hostility throughout the last decades of the nineteenth century left African Americans in the leadership classes searching for political and social solutions to the intractable problems of legalized violence, institutionalized racism, and widespread discrimination. When compared with African Americans in the South, this group of educated, middle-class, black northerners had always enjoyed a relative measure of freedom and, during the Reconstruction years, many of them had been directly involved in the apparent political and social advances of Reconstruction. In the face of imperiled citizenship and a mounting tide of racist sentiment, however, they found themselves as powerless as their southern counterparts. Betrayed by the Federal government in which they had placed their trust, their social aspirations thwarted by the indignities of widespread segregation and discrimination, middle-class black Americans were confronted with the question of how they might take control of their social and political milieu. As they struggled to answer this question, black communities turned increasingly inward, and black institutions such as literary societies provided a place in which to critique white America's racial domination and devise their own strategies through which it might be contested. Like the black churches that often housed them, literary societies were a social space in which public concerns could be discussed and questions of Negro leadership and identity debated.

The decades that immediately followed the Civil War were hospitable to little in the way of literary community for African Americans. As the Civil War drew to a close, widespread efforts to educate ex-slaves were coordinated by black and white missionaries from the North as well as the Union army and the Freedmen's Bureau; in addition, former slaves who could read and write held informal classes and established small schools throughout the South. Perhaps in part because of the demand for concentrated efforts to spread literacy throughout the ex-slave population in the South, and because the population that had once dedicated their leisure time to literary pursuits was preoccupied with Reconstruction efforts, participation in the organized literary communities that had flourished in the urban North before the Civil War declined, as did the publication of literary texts in book form.[3] As Henry Louis Gates Jr. has noted, although "the historical period known as Reconstruction seems to have been characterized by a dramatic upsurge of energy in the American body politic, the corpus of *black* literature and art . . . enjoyed no such apparent vitalization." It seemed as if "the great and terrible subject of black literature—slavery—found no immediate counterpart when blacks were freed." In contrast, with the collapse of Reconstruction in 1877 and the social chaos that resulted from it, black Americans "regained a public voice, louder and more strident than it had been even during slavery."[4]

As the effects of the dismantling of Reconstruction were felt, literary societies reemerged as crucial institutions in black communities from Boston to Washington, D.C. In the wake of African Americans' failure to gain true and lasting political power during Reconstruction, in the face of mounting obstacles and diversifying forms of resistance to their desire to be seen and treated as American citizens, the renewed effort of black Americans to use literary forums to become "thinkers and contributors" to American culture and its central institutions was an astute, if controversial, political strategy. While they continued to hope that demonstrations of their capacity for improvement and "elevation" would transform white racist images of black Americans and bring to them the political rights and recognition they deserved, middle-class black Americans defined their political mission in terms of racial uplift.[5] Rather than direct political or economic protest, middle-class black Americans saw their literary work as a means of instilling pride in their own community; stressing the importance of racial solidarity and self-help, they struggled to turn the pejorative designation of race into a source of dignity and self-affirmation. Central to the success of this strategy was the formation of a self-conscious black intelligentsia, and literary work in organizations such as the Bethel Historical and Literary Association presented itself as a prime means of shaping and defining this group.

BETHEL HISTORICAL AND LITERARY ASSOCIATION

In July 1879 a writer for Washington, D.C.'s black newspaper the *People's Advocate* lamented that "Washington has nothing to boast of in the way of literary organizations."[6] By the end of 1881, however, the newspaper noted that interest in literary societies had risen dramatically. "We feel encouraged to see that our people are beginning to appreciate the usefulness to [*sic*] literary societies," announced one article that appeared on 10 December 1881. Titled "A Good Sign," it commended Washington, D.C.'s black community for recognizing literature as an institution around which it might come together to investigate and address the inequalities that defined its existence. Literary coalitions would foster "that solidarity which would enable us to stand intact against the shocks which a change of political conditions would now produce." Anticipating the strategy of developing a public voice to combat the inhuman treatment and social and political turmoil that would face all African Americans by the last decade of the century, the article continued: "The importance of investigating the forces which have culminated in the present civilization must be apparent to all thinking colored men. An accurate knowledge of them will enable us not only to understand the philosophy of enlightened society, but also to become thinkers and contributors to the rapidly growing institutions of America—moulders and remodelers of the forms of thought adapted to human institutions."[7]

The same issue of the *People's Advocate* carried a letter written by Lewis H. Douglass, who praised the Bethel Historical and Literary Association for what he called a "good beginning." Commending its focus on what he believed was "the most important factor in the upbuilding of the race—self-respect," Douglass asserted that the literary organization had "opened . . . the way to much needed thoughts on subjects that have been shamefully neglected by the colored people of this country." It was not only the poverty and disappointments of the black community that needed to be given voice, Douglass wrote, but the positive aspects of black history and culture as well. "Our people are apparently the only class in this land, composed of so many different races and classes of the human family, who fail to discover among themselves heroes and heroines and to honor and respect the memory of those of their kind who have performed deeds worthy of emulation, or who have been martyrs as grand and noble as any treated of in the annals of any other race or people in the world," he lamented. "We must cease to believe that all learning, all noble deeds, all devotion to principles and all glorious martyrs are confined to the race or class that has done so much toward degrading the Negro in this country." Encouraging its members to "persevere" in their work, Douglass applauded the Bethel Historical and Literary Association for its "good work in bringing out the names of great men and women of our race that remind us that we may make 'our sublime.' "[8]

In addition to publishing reports of its meetings, the *People's Advocate* continued to print letters and editorials that documented the rise of the Bethel Literary, which, by 1883, was widely recognized as an institution that had intervened in important ways in the lives of black Washingtonians. "A striking illustration of the utility of literary associations is seen in the operations and influence of Bethel Literary," wrote author "Le Duke" in December 1883. Comparing the Bethel Literary favorably against the "narrow" literary associations that had previously been formed in Washington, D.C., Le Duke's comments underscore the social and intellectual good that was perceived as resulting from the literary society's activities. The Bethel Literary, he wrote, "is the most popular and at the same time the most influential and worthy institution which has ever been instituted among us. The character of the topics discussed is generally of the highest order and those who are invited to furnish subjects for discussion [are] intelligent and sometimes learned. This society is largely attended, and if we are to judge anything from the interest manifested among the young men and women, it is wielding a most powerful influence for good." Le Duke's passionate article ends with a reminder to his readers: "We must not forget our duty to our people." Suggesting that regular attendance at meetings was one way to fulfill this duty, he urged the Bethel Literary to continue to "open the doors and let all find the glorious light of instruction." "I have no doubt," he concluded, "that it will be said to the credit of the Bethel Literary, that the community has been highly benefited and that the race as a whole has been lifted higher in the scale of civilization and respect."[9]

As these comments attest, the rise of the Bethel Historical and Literary Association represented a new and highly significant development in the cultural and political life of African Americans in Washington, D.C., and in the cultural politics of the nation as a whole. Rather than present a history of this organization from its inception through its decline, what I aim to do here is give some sense of the ways in which the Bethel Literary became a unique forum for black political debate in the last decades of the nineteenth century. As a public or "popular" forum that permitted a growing middle and upper class to mingle and converse and encouraged them to engage one another in healthy and productive debate on the political matters that affected them most directly, the Bethel Literary was itself a prototype of the post-Reconstruction black public sphere, and, at the same time, a model for the development of African American literary societies nationwide. After outlining the rise and development of the Bethel Literary, as well as some key features of its development, I will look at how, during the height of its popularity, the Bethel Literary struggled to address the most immediate and pressing issues that faced the black community in the last decade of the nineteenth century: the questions of Negro education and black leadership.

Founded on 9 November 1881 by Bishop Daniel A. Payne, the

Bethel Literary was named after the hall in which the Association met, Bethel Hall in the Metropolitan A.M.E. Church, located on M Street between 15th and 16th Streets. The Bethel Literary's Board of Officers included a president, two vice presidents, a secretary, librarian, treasurer, and a five-member Executive Committee; five of the original officers, including both vice presidents, were women and, with one exception, all of the original officers were, at the time of their appointment, associated with the Metropolitan A.M.E. Church. The majority of its seventy-five original members were also members of the congregation of the Bethel A.M.E. Church who "responded to the call given out in church the previous Sunday, without regard for their qualification or interest."[10] What was unique about the Bethel Literary, however, was that it was essentially a public and popular institution.[11] While the society maintained a core membership whose weekly contributions supported the lectures and other activities of the organization, black Washingtonians throughout the city were welcome to attend the regularly scheduled presentations. The society printed ready-to-mail postcards that announced future speakers and urged those in the black community to "Come and Bring Your Friends"; as a result, "new faces were always eager to be introduced."[12] From its inception, this feature set the Bethel Literary apart. Although there were other literary societies in existence in 1881, "admission to [these] was based more on certain social tests rather than always on sound literary qualifications or ambitions."[13]

Meetings of the Bethel Literary, which convened at eight o'clock in the evening, often began and ended with the reading of poetry or a dramatic selection and musical entertainment. The highlight, however, was a lecture or the reading of at least one and sometimes several prepared papers by a member or invited guest and the stimulating discussion that followed. The Bethel Literary was originally scheduled to meet once a month, but "interest was such that they almost immediately became weekly sessions."[14] This "interest" did not at first translate into active participation; while "there was quite a large audience" at the first three meetings of the Literary, and the audience reportedly listened to the papers read "with rapt attention," the presentations "led to no discussion."[15] It was only after the audience grew and diversified that the Literary began to take on the energy and integrity that would make it "the intellectual center of Washington."[16] According to Bethel

Literary historian John W. Cromwell, by the fourth meeting of the Literary, the "audience had steadily grown larger, and their character had visibly changed from the brothers and sisters of the 'amen' corner, of which they were [originally] nearly exclusively composed, to those brought out by their interest in the topics discussed."[17] By the final meeting of the first season, held on 20 June 1882, commitment to the Literary, as well as active participation in its activities, was strong. This meeting was as well attended as those in the winter had been, "thus showing that the interest was kept up even after warm weather had fully set in."[18]

The Bethel Literary's original association with the Metropolitan A.M.E. Church provided it with a place to conduct its meetings and assured it of an initial membership. The literary society's determination to remain independent from the church resulted, however, in one of the first threats to its survival. During the first year of its organization, the Bethel Literary moved its meetings to the Berean Baptist Church for "several weeks" rather than give up its autonomy. According to Cromwell, "Dr. J. W. Stevenson, the pastor of the Metropolitan Church, not being able to control the Literary, as he had dominated all other church interests, drove the Literary out of doors, thinking that in this way he would destroy the Association and prevent the development of that free speech and action which was diametrically opposed to his ideas of government and methods of church promotion."[19] The membership's resolve to remain independent from the church and to continue their intellectual work served to underscore the timeliness of the Bethel Literary's development. The Bethel Literary's success proved "that an appeal to the intellect would receive as ready a response [from the black community] as would one to the pleasurable emotions" and was evidence that "there was ample material ready and willing to supply all the people's intellectual needs."[20] This last point was confirmed by the selectivity of the Association's Executive Committee, who in overseeing the program sought to maintain the quality and intellectual rigor of the papers delivered before the Association. According to Cromwell, even as it struggled to establish itself, "many a paper which might have lowered our standard . . . was declined with thanks."[21]

Combined with newspaper reports of individual meetings, Cromwell's early *History of the Bethel Historical and Literary Association* provides the most complete record available of the Association's activities from 1881 through 1896. Although documents at Howard University's Moorland-Spingarn Research Center, where the Association's records are housed, indicate that the Bethel Literary remained active until at least 1913, minutes for the years 1881–95 and 1899–1913 are incomplete.[22] These gaps are due, it seems, to inconsistencies in record keeping in the early and later years of the organization. The difficulties encountered by Cromwell in 1896 as he attempted to write a history of the Bethel Literary on the occasion of its fifteenth anniversary celebration are only exacerbated today. "It is impossible for me to write a comprehensive history of this organization," Cromwell wrote, "for there is no accessible official record covering the entire existence of this Literary. Different secretaries having had vastly different conceptions of what constituted an adequate record—some recording the barest outlines; others going into details, their journals even were they at hand, would render but meagre assistance."[23] Cromwell's history of the Association ends by emphasizing the "healthy condition" of the Literary in 1896 and its "firm hold on the community."[24] Another history of the Association, compiled for the Founder's Day celebration in 1901, is brief and not nearly as detailed as the one written in 1896, but it also suggests the continued good health of the Bethel Literary in the first years of the twentieth century.

From the scant records that do exist, what is well documented about the Bethel Literary is the extent of its popularity. Black Washingtonians knew that there they would find a forum in which to present their views and discuss the most pressing issues of race and society, as well as science and letters. In addition to hearing lectures, they would also have the chance to participate in stimulating debates and enjoy musical and literary entertainment. Regularly, attendance at the Bethel Literary exceeded the capacity of the hall in which the organization met. This description from a 1883 newspaper account gives some sense of the sheer numbers that attended the Bethel Literary's weekly meetings: "Not only was every seat of the pews filled, but the space on either side of the pulpit and within the altar was occupied, and the aisle from the front to the rear of the hall was crowded with people, who contentedly stood from the beginning to the close."[25] Those who packed themselves into Bethel Hall on the night of the meeting were not the only ones who benefited from the Association's activities. As Cromwell notes in his history of the Association, the conversations that took place at the Bethel Literary "in one form and another were echoed throughout the country." Travelers attended meetings of the Bethel Literary when they were in Washington, D.C., taking news of the Association's interests and debates back to their local communities on their return. In addition, "every Washington correspondent of the Colored press . . . gave conspicuous notice to this institution, and the editors of their home papers often continued the discussions," sometimes dissenting from the opinions of the members of the Bethel Literary.[26]

Although the Bethel Historical and Literary Association lacked the intimacy of smaller, more informal literary societies such as those that met in the homes of some black Washingtonians in the last decades of the nineteenth century, in its size lay some advantages. As Willard B. Gatewood has noted in his study of upper-class black social life at the turn of the century, one benefit was that the Bethel Literary remained a relatively inclusive organization: it was always able to embrace what Gatewood describes as "representatives of both the upper and middle classes." Gatewood rightly notes that "almost invariably . . . members of the upper class held the most important offices and made the major decisions," and Cromwell confirms that, particularly during its first year of existence, the "presence night after night of the very highest social elements among us" was not without impact on who participated in discussions that took place at the Literary. During this time, he comments, "no one without some prestige would dare to venture on the sea of discussion without some definite message, on the penalty of manifest popular disapproval."[27]

These observations confirm that class did play a role in the organization of the Bethel Literary, and that some were intimidated by the discussion and reluctant to speak at the meetings. However, they disguise the extent to which the cultivation and widespread dissemination of sharp critical thinking skills and oratorical eloquence were the desired outcome of the Literary's activities for all its members. The common purposes that they sought to achieve forged a certain unity among members of the Bethel Literary, and those who attended their meetings tried to transcend the boundaries of class and color for which Washington's black community is notorious. Repeatedly, it was the inclusiveness rather than the exclusivity of the Association that was celebrated by those who regularly attended its meetings. In a column that appeared in the *People's Advocate* on 15 December 1883, one Washington, D.C., resident active in the Bethel Literary communicated his appreciation for it with these words of praise: "Bethel Literary, while it consists of clerks, school teachers, professional men and others occupying the higher grades of labor, offers inducements and entry to all persons who desire to avail themselves of the benefits it is able to offer. It is democratic in its character and reaches out its arms to encompass all the people. As a consequence Bethel Literary is the most popular and at the same time the most influential and worthy institution which has ever been instituted among us. The character of the topics discussed is generally of the highest order and those who are invited to furnish subjects for discussion [are] intelligent and sometimes learned."[28] Rather than accentuating class differences, this writer emphasizes the extent to which the Bethel Literary worked to create a forum through which black Americans might "build up a community." According to this and other accounts of the Bethel Literary, the very "secret of its usefulness [was] its liberality. It opens the door and invites all who desire to hear and be heard to enter."[29]

In large part the sense of "community" that emanated from the Bethel Literary was the result of explicit conversations about African American history and culture and the unprecedented atmosphere of racial consciousness they fostered. That the Literary sought to instill racial awareness in its membership is evident in the topics they chose to address. The first meeting that inspired energetic discussion and debate was one at which two papers were presented: "Eminent Men of the Negro Race," by Reverend A. W. Upshaw and "Racial Connection of the Zulus" by Reverend R. M. Cheeks. Both papers stimulated an audience that had in previous weeks listened attentively but passively to the lectures to become active participants in the proceedings, albeit in different ways. Reverend Cheeks's paper, which included his own "reminiscences of the Zulu War," was "entertaining, thrilling, instructive and eloquent," and the audience was impressed with the "prowess, skill and intrepidity of the Zulus."[30] Reverend Upshaw's paper on eminent Negro men inspired those present not only to "[supplement] the information contained in the paper" with their own opinions of those men who qualified as "eminent" and why; it also prompted them to consider the eminent women of the race, a conversation that was continued as the subject of the next meeting.[31] In early February 1882 renowned black leader Frederick Douglass presented a paper on "Self-Made Men." Shortly thereafter, Mr. L. H. Douglass read a paper titled "Race Pride" and on the same evening the Association also heard Reverend J. L. Davis's presentation on "The Moral and Statistical Status of the Colored Church."[32] That issues of race and black identity were explicitly or tangentially the focus of most of the papers presented before the Literary in its first year of organization is apparent from this partial list of paper titles: "The Negro in the 10th Census," "Cooperation," "The Future of the Negro," "African Experiences," "Mohammedanism vs. Christianity," "The Negro in Journalism," "The Negro in Business," "Heroes of the Anti-Slavery Struggles," "Skepticism among Negroes."[33]

For many, the result of rising racial consciousness was an overwhelming sense of race pride; others expressed concern, however, that by accentuating race and advancing black Americans as a separate cultural group, they risked delaying or preventing altogether their integration into American society. In 1883 an address on the subject of "Individual Development," in which the speaker, Dr. O. M. Atwood, argued that "in laying stress upon race pride [the black community] is apt to lose sight of individual development," prompted a vigorous debate among those who attended. Some members questioned whether "the tendency of the exclusive policy of individual development led to indifference to the needs and conditions of the masses"; others agreed that a policy of individual development might best serve northern blacks but expressed their suspicion that the same policy applied to the "millions who live in the South" would be ineffective. The extent to which the audience of the Bethel Literary held separate and often incompatible views is best seen in the perspectives of two men who attended the meeting, Mr. Wears and Mr. Price. Early in the discussion Mr. Wears contended that "the Negro ought to forget the fact of his race because there was nothing in it of which he had cause to be proud, either as related to its past or present." In contrast, Mr. Price's position was that "in our upward struggle it was not necessary, nor should we lose sight of the fact that we are Negroes any more than the Irishman, the German or the Frenchman."[34]

The Bethel Literary welcomed this public exchange of such disparate political ideas and cultivated an atmosphere in which participation in the discussion that followed the evening's presentation was crucial to the meeting's success. As Cromwell emphasizes in his *History*, the first meetings of the Bethel Literary, during which the audience listened politely but did not share their thoughts after the speakers' presentations, were not considered productive. As the limited avenues of public and political voice they had achieved during Reconstruction were gradually but definitively blocked, the Bethel Literary sought to become for black Washingtonians an alternative space where they might publicly sort through the most pressing issues that they faced and debate the relative merits of different approaches to addressing them. The issues that the Bethel Literary took up at their weekly meetings were often both deeply personal and political, pertaining both to individuals and their families and to the future of black Americans as a group in the United States. A spirited discussion on the question of separate schools for Negro children, for instance, took place during the 1881–82 season; so controversial was the question of Negro education and so divided was the audience on the issue that "two evenings did not exhaust the list of those eager for the fray."[35]

Neither the membership nor the governing board of the Bethel Literary wished to avoid the respectful disagreements that resulted from the debates among members of the audience or between members of the audience and the invited speaker. On the contrary, these were considered essential to deriving the best and most complete education and training possible from the meetings. Conviction of thought and the confidence with which to speak publicly and forcefully were the important and desired results of the Bethel Literary's activities, and it sought to provide a challenging atmosphere in which every black man and woman could practice and develop these skills. A respectful appreciation for the speaker was expected of everyone present at a meeting, but speakers were not coddled or protected from the dissenting views of the audience. At one meeting, for instance, Benjamin T. Tanner, editor of the *Christian Recorder*, presented to the Association a paper titled "The Year 2000 and What of It?" The paper was certainly assertive; Bishop Tanner, a reverend at the time, "left little uncertainty as to his beliefs and boldly advocated his views." Perhaps because of the strength of his convictions or the deficiencies of the essay, the "criticisms on his paper were merciless." "The prelate stood all very well until a somewhat unknown and unpretentious youth humbly arose. After apologizing for his venturesomeness, he subjected the Doctor's argument to the tests of cold logic, and so exposed the weakness of his positions that at the conclusion of the youth's remarks, there was nothing left of the good editor's lecture but the paper on which it was written." Bishop Tanner stormed out of the room, but not before criticizing the officers of the Literary for "inviting a stranger to read a paper to the Association and then permitting it to be picked to pieces," and promising "I will never read for you again." The "unknown, the unpretentious, youth, then a collegiate student who fairly paralyzed Dr. Tanner's paper disappeared" from the Literary's meetings, "but after a lapse of several years he became a regular visitor." He was none other than future Howard University professor Kelly Miller, who would attend meetings of and address the Bethel Literary regularly throughout his career.[36]

The topic most intensely debated during the lifetime of the Bethel Historical and Literary Association was the kind of education best suited to elevating the race. Not surprisingly, attention to this subject and the related questions it raised about black identity and leadership at the turn of the century intensified in the fall of 1895. Frederick Douglass, the foremost African American spokesperson of the century and a tireless advocate for civil rights, had died earlier in the year. Booker T. Washington's address at the Cotton States and International Exposition at Atlanta on 18 September 1895 drew national attention and brought him into the spotlight as the next leader of and spokesperson for black Americans. His speech, which became known as the "Atlanta Compromise," maintained that the black community could accommodate white domination and segregation. "In all things that are purely social," he assured the white members of his audience, "we can be as separate as the fingers, yet one as the hand in all things essential to mutual progress."[37] Rather than civil rights, Washington stressed economic initiative and self-help and championed industrial training as more appropriate for black Americans than literary or higher education. This position drew immediate support from influential whites, who were quick to endorse Washington as a sensible leader for black America.

Two weeks later, on 2 October 1895, the Literary abandoned the usual structure of its meetings and dedicated the evening to an open discussion of Washington's Atlanta Exposition address. Records do not reveal the tenor of the conversation that took place. But the Literary's dedication, in January 1896, to weekly discussions of the question of Negro education in the context of the future of black Americans in the United States suggests the extent to which their views about Washington and his leadership remained unresolved. On 14 January 1896 the Reverend Sebastian Doyle, pastor of the A.M.E. Church, read a paper titled "The Old Problem in the New Century," in which he "advocated strongly 'higher education for the Negro' and insisted that the first requisite in solving the great problem of this age is 'mind development,' 'brain cultivation[,]' a training of the mind sufficient to comprehend the great problems of science, the vastness of everything, and the intricacies of law and business." Reverend John M. Henderson's presentation on the "New Negro" on 21 January 1896 raised similar questions about education in the context of the future of the race and its social recognition. On 28 January 1896 the Literary returned to the subject of the Atlanta Exposition speech, sponsoring a symposium and asking five members to share their impressions of Washington's address and its implications. Finally, on 4 February 1896 Mr. Lewis Douglass presented a paper titled "Have We A Cause?," in which he argued that "Education of the Masses [must be] Education . . . in its fullest sense, the combined training of the hand and culture, of the brain. Not manual training only, but science, art[,] literature and the higher mathematics, and all accompanying accomplishments is what we need[,] is what we should strive for, is what we should encourage."[38]

On 17 March 1896 Booker T. Washington himself addressed the Literary, delivering a paper titled "Industrial Education of Colored Youth." In it he expressed his belief that "Perfection in Industrial Education enabling the Colored man to compete with the skilled laborer on all lines will solve the race problem."[39] He "likened the problem of the Colored man in America to two unfortunate frogs in a can of milk, struggling to get out." Although Washington's parable of the two frogs does not appear in *Black Diamonds: Gems from the Speeches, Addresses and Talks to Students*, the collection of his writings selected and arranged by Victoria Earle Matthews and published in 1898, it would be right at home there. "One frog weary with the

struggle *died*," he told his audience, apparently as a means of counseling them on the untold advantages of patience and self-help, but

> The *braver* frog, undaunted still,
> Kept *kicking on* with a right good will,
> Until with joy too great to utter
> He found he'd churned a lump of butter;
> And climbing on that chunk of grease
> He *floated round with greatest ease.*[40]

According to the secretary's notes, Washington's wisdom drew laughter from his audience, even if they were not entirely sympathetic to the
program he advocated. Respectfully, members of the Literary supported and approved of Washington's address, and as a tangible expression of their "vote of approval," they collected $37.93 at the meeting to
contribute to Washington's efforts at Tuskegee.[41] This reaction dramatizes the aura Washington held, even for this educated elite, and the
extent to which few blacks were openly critical of his approach or his
leadership in the final years of the nineteenth century. Whether out
of respect for Washington's stature or out of intimidation, members of
the Literary waited until the next meeting to give their true impression of his views. One week later, on 24 March 1896, the "subject of
the evening'[s] discussion was Industrial Education[,] the basis being
[Washington's] paper of the previous week." Begun by Professor Kelly
Miller, "who spoke about twenty minutes on the side of *higher education*," the evening's conversation reveals the extent to which Washington's theories sparked more controversy among the members of his
audience than they had revealed in his presence the week before.
Miller's own comments "discountenanc[ed] the popular Industrial
Education schemes"; he cited as his "chief reason" for not believing in
them "that not one of the ten graduates of these Industrial schools
follows his trade 'for a livelihood'."[42]

Although Miller's was the most overtly critical voice on record, the
tenor of discussions on the subject earlier in the year suggest he was
not alone in his condemnation of industrial education. But others
disagreed. At least one person at the 24 March 1896 meeting of the Literary was directly critical of Miller and his observations. Professor J. T.
Jenifer "cited many instances . . . where young colored men were

employed in Cotton Seed Mills, dash factories, etc."[43] Still others made general remarks that, while not especially supportive of Washington's program of conciliation, compromise, and accommodation, adopted its language by using words such as "co-operation," "self-help," "self-respect," and "efficiency."

The variety of reactions to Washington and his program illustrate the complex intraracial debate that was sustained during the Bethel Literary's 1895–96 season. On the one hand, Washington's Atlanta Exposition speech with its adherence to a politics of compromise was displeasing to this group in that it offered the white community a way of thinking about all black people and their "place" in the United States that undermined middle- and upper-class African Americans' aspirations for fair treatment and full citizenship rights. Furthermore, Washington's theory that "if education does not make the Negro humble, simple, and of service to the community, then it [should] no longer be encouraged" was fundamentally incompatible not only with the educational background they themselves had achieved but also with the guiding principles of the Bethel Literary, whose primary ambition in gathering weekly was to create "a forum in which maturity of thought, breadth of comprehension, sound scholarship, lofty patriotism and exalted philanthropy could find a cordial welcome."[44] On the other hand, Washington's policies were largely untested, and there were definite advantages to the black community's presentation of a unified front. Expressions of discord between members and the indecision of many members of the Bethel Literary as they struggled to determine whether they should support Washington and his policies serve as important reminders that difficult questions plagued this group as they wrestled to understand the best strategies for racial advancement and their responsibilities as educated, financially stable black Americans.

What is clear from the extended discussion and debate on Negro education and Washington's leadership is that all understood the urgency of breaking away from the white constructions of blackness that had dominated the nineteenth century and establishing ways to see and present themselves in a new and different light. Questions about what form Negro education should take were inseparable from the larger questions of racial identity that faced the black community in the last years of the nineteenth century. How would the Negro of the

Channing H. Tobias leads a group of African American
men in a literary discussion. *Jesse Alexander Photograph
Collection, Prints and Photographs Division, Schomberg
Center for Research in Black Culture, The New York
Public Library, Astor, Lenox and Tilden Foundations.*

twentieth century be seen and defined? More importantly, how would the New Negroes of the twentieth century see and define themselves? Should they strive for civil rights or, in exchange for some measure of material and economic success, give up or at least patiently postpone a bid for equality? Should they advocate vocational training for the masses despite their own obvious allegiance to obtaining higher education for themselves and for their children?[45]

Based most fundamentally on the rejection of those properties commonly associated with the "old Negro"—such as enslavement, poverty, and illiteracy—the idea of the New Negro being considered, debated, and, ultimately, defined in the last years of the nineteenth century presented a conundrum for members of the Bethel Literary. By 1896 the term "New Negro" was a part of the vocabulary of members of the Bethel Literary but its meaning was unclear. In 1895 an editorial published in the *Cleveland Gazette* used the term in reference to "a class of colored people" with "education, refinement, and money."[46] When members of the Bethel Literary tentatively and inconsistently used it to refer to themselves, the element of New Negro identity most consistently emphasized was a race consciousness that must have seemed at times downright dangerous in the increasingly hostile racial environment of the turn of the century. Another was a rejection of the status quo and a fiery claim to equality, protection by law, and citizenship that was difficult to reconcile with Washington's advocacy of patience, compromise, and accommodation. To some, the mere idea of a New Negro identity was so ambiguous and unsettling that the concrete strategies of Booker T. Washington, to the extent that they heralded the potential for economic survival through the acquisition of what were perceived by some as basic and "practical" survival skills, were profoundly appealing. "The 'new negro' is something I don't understand," one man inserted into the Literary's discussion of the "New Negro" on 21 January 1895. "The Negro of today is a problem," he continued. "You take a thousand vigorous, able-bodied colored men, give them twelve months' supplies and place them on the prairies of the west in favorable surroundings, and in six months they will all be dead or gone. But look at Mr. Booker T. Washington's work for our race. Take his young men educated at Tuskegee. They can support themselves. You could place a thousand of them with six months' supplies on the western prairies, and in eighteen months you would find them [there]."[47]

Despite the reservations articulated in this statement, the fact that the possibility of a New Negro identity could be fleetingly imagined and discussed at all, especially given the increasingly hostile racial climate of the last years of the nineteenth century, points to an extraordinary and unprecedented moment in the history of African American political development and intellectual thought. Racial identity, black leadership, Negro education—these issues remained largely unresolved for the members of the Bethel Literary during their 1895–96 season. But what was most important was that the Bethel Literary provided a space in which these issues and the questions that they raised could freely circulate and be openly and hotly debated, even if not definitively answered. In 1896 Cromwell asserted that the Bethel Literary was responsible "for the growth and development of a public spirit among the people that has made possible the success of enterprises the mere contemplation of which would have been regarded as a sure evidence of a possession of an unsound mind half a generation ago."[48] While the Bethel Literary would go on to involve itself in more publicly demonstrative forms of protest against such matters as lynching and Jim Crow practices, no enterprise was more important to the future of the black community than the development of the institution itself as a thriving black public sphere and forum for intraracial debate.

BOSTON LITERARY AND HISTORICAL ASSOCIATION

By the time the Boston Literary and Historical Association was founded in 1901, Booker T. Washington was at the height of his political power. This development signals the most significant difference between the Boston Literary and Historical Association and the Bethel Literary, which was most popular during its 1895–96 season, the very year that marked the introduction of Booker T. Washington as a political force and the beginning of his ascendancy. It also provides a key to understanding some of the differences in the ways the two societies operated. Although the membership of the Bethel Literary was comprised of a class who, for the most part, owed their own status and social and economic mobility to higher education, this did not prevent them from debating the relative merits of Washington's politics, including the potential benefits of industrial education, or from inviting Washington himself to address the society in 1896. Even those with initial misgivings could appreciate the importance of maintaining optimism about Washington's leadership and recognized the advantages of supporting Washington if only to present a unified front. They had been willing to wait and see where Washington and his policies might lead.

By 1901, however, there was little doubt that Washington's "compromise" was not producing desirable results. Conditions in both the South and the North had only worsened for black Americans in the last years of the nineteenth century. From educational and employment opportunities to political involvement and protection under the law, African Americans were further from equality and enfranchisement in the workings of the American political system than ever before. Against this background, the Boston Literary and Historical Association was founded by a group of relatively successful members of Boston's black professional class with a keen sense of political purpose: their intention was to launch a self-conscious attack on the prestige and racial policies of Booker T. Washington and his "Tuskegee Machine." Unlike the Bethel Literary, neither the leaders nor the membership of the Boston Literary were willing to discuss or debate the relative merits of Washington's leadership or his policies. Rather, Washington was assumed to be an antagonist, and the Boston Literary was itself considered a means of contesting his politics and his educational policies. That this was understood implicitly was evident in every aspect of the Boston Literary, from its leadership to its membership, from its choice of speakers to the range of subjects it addressed. Whereas the Bethel Literary had encountered Washington's policies at a time when debating their merits was a meaningful political exercise, the Boston Literary never explicitly discussed Washington's policies and ideas. Everything that they stood for and did, however, was diametrically opposed to his politics.[49]

Most prominent and outspoken in the group that organized the Boston Literary was William Monroe Trotter who, with partner George Forbes, founded the militant *Boston Guardian* in the same year.[50] Trotter considered his involvement in both of these institutions a form of public service. He credited his determination to organize them at the turn of the century to two things. The first was the worsening of conditions for the Negro in the South, a reality made painfully obvious by daily reports of racial violence, and the worsening of the effects of the institution of a legalized Jim Crow system in all areas of southern life. The second was the equally obvious fact that the racial attitudes traditionally associated with the South were infiltrating the North. In Boston, as in other urban areas, the black community was experiencing the slow deterioration of the rights and respect that they had long taken for granted.[51] Trotter believed that the racial policies of Booker T. Washington were directly responsible for exacerbating the social conditions for African Americans in both the South and the North. From the relative calm of twenty-five years later, Trotter succinctly summed up what motivated him in 1901 to orient his life's work toward countering what he saw as the destructive influence at work in the turn-of-the-century United States and finding strategies that might bring about racial and civic equality. "The conviction grew upon me," he wrote in retrospect, "that pursuit of business, money, civic or literary position was like building a house on the sands, if race prejudice and persecution and public discrimination for mere color was to spread up from the South and result in a fixed caste of color."[52]

Although Washington and Trotter differed radically on many questions, none was more central to the future of black Americans in the United States than that of Negro education. Himself an 1895 graduate of Harvard University, Trotter believed that Negroes must be encouraged to seek and succeed in the highest forms of liberal arts education; from this sort of education came the capacity for strong intellectual and political leadership. Although he believed that schools for industrial education like Hampton and Tuskegee had their value, he opposed the widespread effort to institute manual training exclusively throughout the black population because he believed "the idea lying back of it is the relegating of a race to serfdom." Trotter saw the underlying objective behind industrial education as maintaining a hierarchical society in which whites would remain dominant and their views of black people as innately inferior and therefore, subordinate, would remain intact. This, Trotter argued, "must be admitted to be the reason why industrial education is more popular with the general white population than advanced or classical education." Like many black Americans in the growing middle class, Trotter felt that Washington's discouragement of higher education for all black Americans would undermine the fundamental interest in civil rights that he believed should be shared by all black people in the United States. He would come to be one of Boston's most outspoken black leaders, expressing his opinion from the pages of the *Boston Guardian.* "The colored people see and understand you," he warned Booker T. Washington. "They know you have marked their very freedom for destruction."[53]

Trotter understood that with the North's legacy of relative freedom came a great responsibility: the northern Negro must stand at the forefront of demands for justice for all black Americans. "The north is the battleground," Trotter declared in 1903, contradicting Washington's belief that the battle for Negro rights was best fought in the agrarian South, "and the northern Negroes are the soldiers."[54] He and his associates believed that the Boston Literary and Historical Association would provide a basis for cultural and literary accomplishments that would do more to alter the dim views of the future of the Negro in the United States than direct attempts to make economic or political gains. Their biweekly literary activities became a forum for a different sort of political activity, one intended to discredit the ideas of Booker T. Washington and undermine his political agenda. After preliminary discussion about the nature and function of the new organization, a formal constitution and bylaws were adopted on 18 March 1901. According to the constitution, the stated purpose of the Association was "to promote the intellectual life of the community." The Association was founded by Boston's black elite, Trotter would write to a prospective speaker, noted black author Charles Chesnutt, within the first month of its organization, in order to "improve and quicken the intellectual life of the Colored people of Boston and to have a body to represent their best interests."[55] Still another account of the Association's founding and objective contributes to a more nuanced understanding of its purpose: according to one history, the Boston Literary and Historical Association was begun in order to "arouse men and women to the grave danger of mental starvation as a result of their absorption in the strife of commercialism so characteristic of the age."[56]

Like the Bethel Literary, the Boston Literary and Historical Association was a popular institution that appealed to middle- and upper-class blacks but had a constitution that mandated inclusiveness. According to the constitution, "Any person over eighteen years of age proposed for membership by any member may be admitted to this association by a majority vote of the members present and by signing the constitution." Twenty-seven people were involved in the initial planning of the organization; thirty-three new members were introduced and approved at the first official meeting, bringing the membership roster to sixty. When nine more people were approved for membership at the next meeting, the Association felt the need to revise the procedures for accepting members to efficiently accommodate the sheer numbers of those interested.[57] By 1908 the Association revised their admissions procedures again, this time in order to limit their membership. In a clause added to the constitution, it was decided that "no person shall be admitted to this association when its membership numbers reach three hundred."[58]

Despite these regulations for membership, the Association's regularly scheduled meetings and exercises were public, and it was not necessary to be a member to attend. All were welcome, and the Association was particularly proud of that fact. "From the outset the meetings have been opened to the public without charge," boasts a printed history of the Association.[59] This openness served to expand the population that benefited from the cultural activities of the Association beyond the most highly educated of Boston's black community. By organizing a series of cultural events and miscellaneous activities, the Association acted on behalf of the public and for the good of the community. Although periodically throughout the year those in the audience who were not members were invited and encouraged to join, the Association never closed itself off as a private organization. As it had for the Bethel Literary, this policy served multiple purposes, not the least of which was to provide a place of intellectual exchange in Boston for an increasingly mobile black population. Attendance rosters included in the Association's records contain the names of out-of-town guests who chose to attend meetings of the Literary and Historical Association while visiting Boston from New York, Philadelphia, and Washington, D.C.

The Boston Literary's structure and organization were similar to those of the Bethel Literary. From their official membership the Association filled the offices of president, vice president, secretary, assistant secretary, and treasurer. An executive committee consisting of seven members was also appointed, and the chaplain was also considered an officer. The job of the seven members of the executive committee appointed by the president was to "provide all the public exercises of the association."[60] Typically, the committee would be "busy all summer" procuring speakers and making arrangements for the following year's program.[61] According to the constitution, the Association was to meet biweekly from the first Monday in October through the last Monday in May. During the winter months of December, January, and February they met weekly, and following the standard academic calendar no meetings were scheduled for the summer months when members were more likely to be out of town. Meetings were to begin promptly at eight o'clock and last until "not later than half-past ten o'clock." The general course of each meeting and a mandate to strictly follow parliamentary procedures as laid out in *Cashing's Manual* were also stipulated in the constitution. After a "Call to Order," the membership was led in prayer and the roll taken. Minutes from the previous meeting were read and approved, and all "Unfinished Business" was addressed. Next, nominations were taken for new members, and a vote was taken to formally admit those previously nominated. With this necessary business out of the way, the membership could get on with the real "work" of the association: the speaker's presentation and the subsequent discussion.[62]

To each meeting, one or more principal speakers were invited. "At the conclusion of the principal speaker or speakers," the floor was opened for discussion, and "any member" was invited to "speak on the subject of the evening." No member—"except the principal speaker or speakers"—was to "occupy the floor for more than five minutes," and no member was "entitled to the floor more than once until every other person desirous of speaking shall have spoken." Nonmembers were also invited to share their thoughts on the presentation after "being recognized by the chair."[63] An amendment to the constitution passed in April 1902 revised this policy, giving nonmembers the right to speak "when presented by a member of the association or when asked by the president of the association."[64] The last ten minutes of each meeting were reserved for the principal speaker or speakers, who might use this time to respond to points introduced during the evening's discussion.

These and other guidelines were not intended to restrict the voices of the Association's membership; rather, they were in place and closely followed to serve as a reminder to all that the proceedings must remain dignified, collegial, and, above all, intellectually productive. At the first meeting and periodically thereafter, the president took the time to remind members of the importance of maintaining this spirit of the Association. "If members find it necessary to differ," he insisted, "let it be done in a manly and dignified manner, as ladies and gentlemen."[65] Members were reminded that they were themselves responsible for the success or failure of their enterprise and each member must therefore "exert himself or herself to securing [as large an] attendance as possible." In addition, they were encouraged to contribute to the quality of the proceedings by making "such criticisms as they may desire in the meetings."[66]

Having outlined something of the origins and structure of the Boston Literary and Historical Association, I want to turn now to look in detail at how the political stance of this association manifested itself in its work. Specifically, I want to look at the way the Boston Literary addressed three areas that were of particular concern to the Association in its first years of organization. Discussions of literature undertaken by the Boston Literary were conducted with an eye toward establishing the parameters of a proper literary curriculum for a higher, liberal arts education. Historical topics allowed them to discuss larger issues of representation and forced them to weigh the need for unity in the black community against the differences of opinion which were bound to exist among the membership. Finally, the Boston Literary's interest in international topics and the different ethnic communities that surrounded them in the United States suggested ways of thinking about their own community and oppression and introduced the possibility of creating a unified front with other "darker races" throughout the world. My attention to these areas exposes the extent to which the Boston Literary was, from its inception, engaged in implicit rather than explicit political dialogue with Booker T. Washington. It also offers insight into how the cultural activities of the Boston Literary prepared its members for the more overtly political battles yet to come.

Literary offerings from the 1895–96 season of the Bethel Historical and Literary Association, such as "What Walt Whitman Means to the

Negro," "Phyllis [*sic*] Wheatley, Her Life and Times," and "Recollections of the Poet Whittier," suggest the extent to which its literary discussions tended to be celebratory or inspirational rather than critical. By contrast, the Boston Literary rarely limited its focus to the celebration of a particular author or genre. Rather, the membership's interest was in debating literary standards, determining the value of particular authors and genres, and establishing the texts they deemed essential to a classical, liberal arts education. Reverend Frank F. Hall's January 1902 address, "The Companionship of Books," and the Boston Literary's reaction to it provide an example of the issues of literary standards and values debated by the Literary, as well as the members' interest in why and how reading took place. No one argued with Hall's general comments about the importance of reading and the ease with which a literary education could be achieved. "Association with books, is a company into which one can enter without other ticket than the ability to read," Hall counseled the audience. "One great advantage is that book friends come at any and all times." Hall's address included advice on how, as well as what, they should read to consider themselves well-educated in literary matters. "Don't try to enter into the companionship of too many books," he warned, "but know something about the really great literature of Homer, Virgil, Dante, Shakespeare[,] and don't slight the really great works for the latest publication." Hall's standards of literary value were both endorsed and challenged in the discussion that followed his address. One man echoed the speaker's flowery respect for the literary "masters" by contributing the observation that "whatever one's station in life the one company from which one cannot be excluded is the company of master minds of all ages." But other members of the Association questioned the very definitions of "proper" reading that the speaker's address had sanctioned. Mrs. B. R. Wilson and Miss Eva Lewis "defended the new novels and thought that in the mass of literature launched in the last two years there are examples of books of considerable worth." Mr. Sargent argued that the "indiscriminate love of books [was] as pernicious as the lack of love for books" and warned those present of what he considered to be the great danger of "taking as incontrovertable [*sic*] facts the statements of the Anglo-Saxon" found in "great" books. Books, he insisted, must not prevent people from thinking for themselves. In response to this opinion, Mr. Trotter responded with an alternative perspective: "while it is well to have original thoughts it is better to have thoughts worth while [*sic*]." Trotter's opinion came from his own experience with literature. While he "never felt the need of reading books for amusement," he read them "for the refinement they gave him."[67]

Although the membership of the Boston Literary could agree that one of the black community's "needs of the hour" was "more reading and thinking," they took great pleasure in intricate debates about the kinds of reading that were most appropriate and why.[68] In the spring of 1902 the Boston Literary engaged in two critical literary discussions. The first concerned Sir Thomas More's *Utopia*. The other was about the genre of biography, which was considered both as a literary and a historical genre.[69] Later that spring a list of the "best" authors was offered to the Association by George W. Forbes, a graduate of Amherst College, an employee of the Boston Public Library system, and a cofounder and coeditor of the *Boston Guardian*. One component of Forbes's paper, titled "A Short Excursion into the Provinces of Letters," was a breakdown of all literature into the five genres he considered basic to literary study: epic, tragedy, lyric, didactic, and ode. His presentation also included a listing of who were, from his perspective, the standard-bearers of each category: Milton, Spenser, and Homer were the best writers of epic; Aeschylus's writing epitomized tragedy; Longfellow, Lowell, and Emerson were selected as representatives of lyric writers; Dryden, Pope, and Browning were classic "didactic" authors; and the works of Pindar and Sappho were exemplary of writers of the ode. Forbes's own liberal arts education and his multiple literary associations suggest that his opinion might have carried great weight for the membership of the Boston Literary. His audience, however, had several objections to his classifications. Reverend Parrish criticized Forbes's presentation because he "thought that too much praise was given to philosophy and not enough to the novel," a genre Forbes had failed even to mention. "We need something recreative," posited Reverend Parrish to justify his assertions about the novel. Suggesting that novels were more of a "diversion . . . than a recreation," another member, Mrs. Hazel, seemed to agree. Mr. Lee argued that Forbes had overlooked another genre as well: theology. Further discussion centered on the question of whether the Bible should be considered literature or left outside of the realm of criticism as an "inspired Book."[70]

This and other discussions that revolved around the "classics" of European literature reveal the literary proficiency of the membership of the Boston Literary and their dedication to determining the "proper" curriculum for literary education. Their unwavering belief in the value of classical, liberal arts education illustrates their great distance from Booker T. Washington, whose ridicule of African Americans' need for higher education is extensively documented. For those involved in the Boston Literary, however, discussions about literature and literary canons were essential to undertake, not only for their own sake but also as a prelude to the establishment and maturation of an African American literary tradition. Those who participated in discussions about literature at the Boston Literary appreciated classical European attitudes toward literature and literary genres; but that did not diminish their sense of racial consciousness or quell their interest in developing and giving value to their own, individual forms of expression. The cultural productions of African Americans, they believed, and specifically the literature and intellectual thought that resulted from the writing of African American authors, would bring recognition to black Americans similar to that afforded to Europeans for their literary contributions. This interest was captured by one member, whose comment opened the discussion after Forbes's presentation, when he expressed his "hope the great American epic of the joys and sorrows of our blood and kindred, of those who have gone before us[,] would one day be written."[71] The idea that literature might be the vehicle through which the past, present, and future of the American Negro could be presented epitomized the group's intellectual commitment and their cultural focus.

Whereas the Bethel Historical and Literary Association had introduced historical topics as a means of instilling race pride and racial consciousness in its membership, historical discussions at meetings of the Boston Literary and Historical Association were the catalyst for the debate of intricate issues of historical representation, misrepresentation, and self-representation. Participants in the Boston Literary were acutely aware of the importance of creating their own portrayals of African Americans' role in the history of the United States to refute racist accounts of it produced by whites. "The history of the American negro [*sic*] is written by persons afflicted with colorphobia," one member asserted with disgust in response to a presentation by Charles Gould Steward on Negro soldiers. Steward's talk, delivered in April 1901, is representative of the interest among African Americans at the turn of the century in black militaristic achievement. This emphasis was at least in part a reaction to an article written by Theodore Roosevelt and published in *Scribner's Magazine* in 1899 in which he claimed that inherent racial weakness would prevent the Negro from effectively commanding his own troops. As one member remarked at the end of the meeting, presentations such as Steward's were crucial to ensuring that black Americans, at least, understood that "the Negro of this country can never be separated from its grandeur."[72] Only then could they hope to make this noble history known to white Americans.

The issue of how the black community would present itself and its perspective on the historical past was also the subject of a 1901 meeting at which the Boston Literary's president, Archibald Grimké, presented a paper on Abraham Lincoln. It was "time for the colored people to form their own opinion of Abraham Lincoln," Grimké argued in his paper. Although it had been "the vogue to sing the praises of Lincoln," Grimké suggested that in fact "at no time either before or after the war was [Lincoln] such a friend of the slave" as was William Lloyd Garrison. Rather than the best interest of the slaves, Lincoln's primary concern had been the preservation of the Union. "Could it have been accomplished without the abolition of slavery," Grimké asserted, "the south would have retained its bondsmen." Although Grimké saw Lincoln as "a great American and a great states man [*sic*]," he advanced the argument that Lincoln was "no friend to humanity as evidenced by the negro [*sic*]." He was a "political abolitionist which is vastly different from a moral abolitionist," Grimké concluded.[73]

Given Lincoln's reputation in the black community, it is no surprise that Grimké's paper was, according to the secretary's report, "provocative of much animated discussion." One point of disagreement among the members concerned Grimké's perspective on the nature of Lincoln's leadership. While Mr. John J. Smith "thought the paper was a perfectly fair representation of conditions at that time," Mr. Forbes was "surprised and amazed at the sentiments expressed by the speaker." He believed that while "Garrison's influence in the anti-slavery movement was but slight," Lincoln was "at heart an abolitionist." Maria Baldwin contributed to the discussion by suggesting that "Mr. Lincoln moved above the feeling of the public [and] that Garrison in Lincoln's place would have meant utter failure."[74]

It was not until Reverend Stevens's comment that the real source of many of the members' discomfort with Grimké's comments became evident. Rather than contributing his own perspective on Lincoln's leadership, Stevens's remarks are directed toward the appropriateness of Grimké's paper and his critical perspective given contemporary political realities. In his opinion the paper was untimely because it was "too pessimistic in its tone." Instead, Stevens implied, the times called for black people to temper their dissenting voices and critical stances in favor of maintaining a positive attitude and giving the impression of a unified front. Supporting Stevens's perspective, Mr. Morgan underlined this imperative, urging those present to "be careful in discussing matters that have already been settled. This is too critical a time to attack Lincoln who is held in the highest esteem by all liberty lovers."[75]

The questions underlying the Boston Literary's discussion of Grimké's presentation on Lincoln are particularly revealing, especially in light of the Literary's history as an organization that emerged from a division within the black community over the best strategies to be used toward its advancement. Leaders of the Boston Literary had vocally and visibly opposed the politics and policies of Booker T. Washington; yet in the context of their own discussions, they faced lingering questions about whether black people in the United States could afford to be seen as divided. As the comments of Morgan and Stevens attest, some believed that they could not; from their perspective, the black community must present itself as unified. Others, like Grimké, questioned the very possibility, as well as the desirability, of suppressing differences of opinion and perspective in order to present a unified front. Grimké insisted that the issue of how the black community could and should represent itself was crucial to consider, and this was precisely the discussion he had intended his paper to introduce. What was the black community's reading of its own past, especially as it pertained to national heroes and race leaders? Was it realistic—much less desirable—for the black community to be united in their reading of the past and to accept would-be heroes without questioning the nuances of their actions? Was it indeed possible to deny division among African Americans and uniformly "settle" matters of historical representation or leadership? Given the anxieties inherent in these questions for an African American population struggling to determine the best course toward its future advancement, Grimké had known that his paper "would raise a storm of protest"; rather than being discouraged by it, however, Grimké "enjoyed the criticisms very much" because he believed that such heated discussions concerning questions of representation were of utmost importance to the future of blacks in the United States.[76]

Questions of historical representation remained so important to the Boston Literary that its membership decided to strengthen the "Historical" aspect of the Association to ensure that historical research would be conducted and publications written to augment their understanding of their own past. Anxieties about the suitability of what was written and interest in exerting control over dissenting voices in matters of representation, however, remained a visible aspect of their endeavor. In October 1903 the constitution was amended with the following statement: "The President shall appoint, by and with the consent of the Association, a Committee of five persons who shall be known as 'The Historical Committee.'" According to this amendment, the duties of the Historical Committee were "to select and approve historical topics and data, to choose competent persons who shall write history expressly for the Association, and to direct and control all matters pertaining to the writing, printing, purchasing, publishing, and preserving of such history, provided that no history shall be written, printed, purchased, published, or preserved at the expense and in the name of this association except by a vote of the Association at any regular meeting."[77] The Boston Literary's mandate that only histories supervised and approved by the Association would go out under its name stands in stark contrast to its status as a public or popular institution and its initial belief in the importance of maintaining an atmosphere in which differences of opinion could constructively be expressed.

Questions about representation, the importance and possibility of unity, and the appropriateness of expressions of dissent within the Boston Literary continued throughout the life of the institution. In 1915, however, two significant events proved decisive in uniting the group's membership in one voice. The first was the death of Booker T. Washington. Washington had continued to promote and defend his philosophy of African American education and social and economic progress; with his death, the Boston Literary lost its primary adversary. The second event was the widespread distribution of the "photo-play" *The Birth of a Nation*, which had its Boston premiere on 10 April 1915. Even before its arrival, participants in the Boston Literary and Historical Association recognized the film for what it was: the most destructive representation of African Americans and their history ever created. In an era marked by gradual advances in Negro literacy and economic independence, the film vilified black people, portraying them as little more than vicious animals who posed a tangible threat to white civilization. Its release on the fiftieth anniversary of the Civil War encouraged its white viewers to romanticize the lives they might have led under the institution of slavery and to celebrate racial discrimination, residential segregation, closed ballot boxes, and Jim Crow accommodations. Its portrayal of the United States during Reconstruction as a place of terror and violence caused audiences to cheer at the creation of the Ku Klux Klan and to applaud its inhumane tactics of restoring the black population to its "proper place" of subordination. The most influential aspect of *The Birth of a Nation* was perhaps its unprecedented scope; it was, according to President Woodrow Wilson's concise and colorful sound bite, which enticed thousands of Americans to see the film, "like writing history with lightning."[78]

Collective efforts to organize and launch a protest against *The Birth of a Nation* consumed participants in the Boston Literary throughout the spring of 1915. Delegates from the Boston Literary were among those members of the black community who demanded a public meeting with the mayor of Boston, James Curley. At this meeting, which was attended by the film's director D. W. Griffith, they argued for the film's censorship, citing the excessive and misleading representations of black sexuality and the film's blatant promotion of racial hatred and discrimination. Modest cuts were made to the film before its Boston premiere, and although Curley emphasized that these were made as a concession to the black community and not as an act of conscience, it was still a small victory. Beginning with the meeting held on 15 April 1915, the usual format of the Boston Literary was abandoned as the membership dedicated their attention to preparing themselves for what Reverend C. C. Alleyne described as the "strenuous duties which must inevitably fall to our lot." Alleyne had traveled from Providence, Rhode Island, to address the Boston Literary, but he willingly "reserved his address for some future date" and participated in the group's exchange of strategies to decide the most effective means of demonstrating their disapproval of the film. On this occasion, in the face of a racist representation that demanded unity, a consensus was reached. The membership of the Boston Literary decided that the best way to proceed would be to "attack the play on the grounds of immorality and the fact that it would create race prejudice." They drafted a "motion of condemnation for 'Birth of a Nation,' " a copy of which was delivered to the mayor. They also planned a demonstration, which took place two days later in front of the Tremont Theater, where the film was being shown. Over two hundred police officers were reportedly brought out to disperse the crowd.[79]

From its first season, debates about unity within the black community that took place at meetings of the Boston Literary existed alongside debates that encompassed the possibility of African Americans' unity with those of other races and ethnic identities. The topics they chose to pursue reveal the membership of the Boston Literary's burgeoning sense of being part of a larger community of oppressed and misunderstood people. Their efforts to educate themselves about the history and customs of China and the Chinese, for instance, illustrates their tentative explorations of the possibilities for coalition that existed among the world's "darker races." At the Boston Literary's first substantive meeting, which took place on 1 April 1901, George W. Forbes presented a paper titled "Is the Attitude of the Christian Nations toward the Chinese Justifiable?" Forbes's paper began by placing China's political situation in a cultural and historical context. China was a "very old civilization," Forbes explained to his audience. Understanding its strict class structure as well as its educational system of advancement through exams was crucial for comprehending current relations between China and the Christian nations of the world. The introduction of Christian missionaries to the country was at first a great success, Forbes recounted, but eventually the missionaries became another "class" and thus separated themselves off from the very people they were trying to convert. "One way or another the various Chris-

tian nation[s] have forced China to make numerous valued conces-
sions to them so that affairs has [*sic*] gone on until the Boxer movement of last summer when Chinese people rose in the night against
the Christian nations."[80]

Although, at the outset of the meeting, China may have seemed
utterly foreign to those present, Forbes was able to make it familiar in
part by proposing parallels between Chinese history and the history of
the United States. According to the secretary's notes, although he
made it clear that "the Chinese government is a monarchy, Mr. Forbes
traced resemblances between China with its nineteen provinces and
the United States with its territories." What followed Forbes's address
was described as an "animated discussion which was participated in by
a number of persons"; it revolved around the question of whether the
"Christian missionaries were . . . being judged fairly as to their responsibility for the present trouble in China."[81] The discussion was equally
animated on 15 April 1901 when the topic of the evening was "Cuba
and the Cubans." Once again the audience was challenged to consider
another culture and, in doing so, to contemplate American customs
and character and expand their notion of difference. Some discovered
profound connections between the Cubans' experience and their own
identities and positioning in the United States. One member determined that "Miss Huidobro's remarks [in her paper on Cuba and the
Cubans] should be an inspiration to the so-called inferior races of the
earth." Although another "took issue with [this] position on the matter," all were offered by the lecture the context in which to begin to
think of black Americans as one of a number of "darker races" in the
world maneuvering for power in an unwelcoming political system.[82]
Through the numerous addresses on other nations presented before
the Boston Literary, members came to see the possibility of forming
alliances with others around the globe struggling for full acceptance
and equality in the face of debilitating assumptions about their capacity for self-rule.

In addition to international populations, the Boston Literary was
also curious about those ethnic groups in the United States whose
cultures persistently differed from that of the white majority. Rabbi
Charles Fleischer was invited to address the Boston Literary to "explain facts and explode fictions concerning the Jews"; all hoped that
this would lead to a greater understanding of and sense of affinity with

them. In his address "Fact and Fiction Concerning the Jew," Fleischer spoke bluntly about the stereotypes associated with the Jewish people, challenging their reputation as "unscrupulously shrewd" by presenting information on the historical circumstances they faced. "In so far as this [reputation] is true," he told an attentive audience, "this is due to the fact that this people who lived in one country, Palestine, and were engaged wholly in agriculture, were uprooted and made to wander over the earth, subject to persecution. They found money alone was power, their wealth had to be portable, they felt that every man's hand was against them. Hence, they became traders, money-makers, ready to take advantage." Certainly some became "unscrupulous," Fleischer conceded, but he emphasized that not all Jews should be seen in this light. "Jews are not to be judged by their worst, or even by the average of them, but by the best of them for any body of people is as strong as the strongest and as good as the best." His next comments drew applause from his audience: "Such [is] true of every race, for human beings are what they are in their best moments. The highest type shows the possibility of a race and what the race really is and every race should be measured by its highest possibilities."[83]

Questions posed to the Rabbi after his presentation suggest that the Boston Literary provided a safe and comfortable atmosphere in which to learn about other cultures and their habits. Concern for what was perceived as an interest in maintaining separate and segregated institutions prompted one member to ask the Rabbi "why the Jews have a hospital." The Rabbi's response served to further demystify the Jewish people by educating the Association's membership on the religious practices of some Jews. The Rabbi explained that "the Jewish religion demanded that the Jews should not eat food prepared by a non-Jew." Although the "liberal Jews" were "bitterly opposed" to the Jewish hospital, the "older Jews and those recently arrived are so strict that they would die of starvation if taken to an American hospital." "Besides," he added, "many cannot understand our language and so cannot indicate their wants to American attendants."[84]

The Boston Literary's fascination with Chinese civilization, Cuban customs, and Jewish culture reflects one aspect of their struggle to transform the pejorative concept of race into an affirming vision of cultural distinctiveness. Explorations of a diverse range of experiences of alienation allowed those who attended the meetings of the Boston

Literary to develop a perspective on the positioning of African Americans in the United States in the context of that of other oppressed people throughout the world and across time. What was developed through these conversations was a sense of historical perspective and an appreciation of cultural origins that would be manifest in W. E. B. Du Bois's celebration of black culture and the contributions of African Americans to the nation, *The Souls of Black Folk.*

It was this sense of cultural identity that Du Bois encouraged when he addressed the Boston Literary in January 1903. In order that "all who wish[ed] to hear this distinguished Negro thinker" could have the opportunity, the meeting was moved to a large auditorium and its date changed from a Monday to a Wednesday evening. Despite inclement weather, the auditorium was "filled . . . with Bostonians."[85] As the *Boston Guardian* observed in its report of the event, "the very presence of this educated Negro must have won over everyone present to positive advocacy of the higher education of the race." Although on this occasion "Prof. Du Bois said nothing of the subject," he "gave evidence of a knowledge and a grasp on the world's history past and present" that his audience found admirable. Du Bois used his address before the Boston Literary, titled "Outlook for the Darker Races," to further develop a political vision that would not be fully articulated until his later writings. The "greatest question at the beginning of this new century," Du Bois declared, "is the question of the Color line." Drawing a parallel between black Americans and the "darker races" throughout the world, Du Bois argued that because they were beginning to unite in their oppression, "there was grave danger to the white races in dealing cruelly and unjustly with the darker races." Touching on the "struggle of the Chinese, the natives of East India, the Fillipinos [*sic*], the Negroes of America" and reviewing "each in their oppression by the invading or dominating white races," Du Bois emphasized that all of these peoples were "really engaged in one great common struggle for a self-preservation and a fair chance to live." Du Bois insisted that "a unification of interests on the part of the Negro here with the darker people [of the world]" was crucial to their survival. "The future of the darker races [is] critical," Du Bois argued, "and the American Negro [stands at the lead] in the world contest in behalf of the darker races [*sic*]." In this, a "great responsibility rested upon" black Americans. They must act as leaders in the effort to "do away with the Color line, to strive to the end that the dominant whites may be willing to give the dark skinned individual the place in social, civil, religious and in political life that his individual merits entitle him to without regard to the condition of his race or class."[86] Du Bois's address offered members of the Boston Literary the theoretical language and framework through which their own historical research could be interpreted. United in ambition not only with one another but with oppressed peoples throughout the world, members of the Boston Literary took from this and other addresses and from their own conversations a cultural sensibility and sense of collective destiny that reinforced their confidence in black identity.

"OUR ONE HAVEN OF REFUGE IS OURSELVES"

The activities of the Bethel Historical and Literary Association and the Boston Literary and Historical Association are representative of an important chapter in the long history of African American literary societies. Both institutions captured the imagination of highly literate middle- and upper-class black Americans who struggled to find new strategies to promote racial advancement and develop self-confidence at a time when overt political involvement offered little hope. In this hostile environment, black Americans turned to institutions such as the Bethel Literary and the Boston Literary as places where racial consciousness and confidence could develop. Both were crucial to sustaining African Americans' hopes for civil rights and full recognition as citizens of the United States. As leaders of thought and missionaries of culture, the membership of these literary societies took the lead in the effort to "conserve [the] physical powers, intellectual endowments, [and] spiritual ideals" of the Negro people. "Let us not deceive ourselves at our situation in this country," Du Bois counseled his audience in a presentation. "Weighted with a heritage of moral inequity from our past history, hard pressed in the economic world by foreign immigrants and native prejudice, hated here, despised there and pitied everywhere; our one haven of refuge is ourselves."[87] As explicitly political avenues to freedom and security were closed, Du Bois urged black Americans to focus their energies on the formation of a black consciousness and an identity less susceptible to racist untruths.

"There is no power under God's high heaven that can stop the advance of eight thousand thousand honest, earnest, inspired and united people," he continued. But "such a people must be united . . . in serious organizations, to determine by careful conference and thoughtful interchange of opinion the broad lines of policy and action for the American Negro."[88] Du Bois made these comments to the literary organization to which he belonged, the American Negro Academy, in 1897. Ironically, this call for unity was made before the all-male Academy that had purposely and emphatically excluded women from membership.

The dates of the greatest activity of both Bethel Historical and Literary Association and the Boston Literary and Historical Association coincided with the black women's club movement, which began in the last decade of the nineteenth century and remained vibrant into the first decade of the twentieth century. Black women also participated in both the Bethel Literary and the Boston Literary; they were in fact welcomed into both institutions not only as members but as central players in the governing bodies of the institutions. Five women were on the Bethel Literary's original board of officers, and two of them occupied the position of vice president. Women were also represented in similar numbers on the original board of officers of the Boston Literary. Included on the membership roster of the Boston Literary was author and editor Pauline E. Hopkins, and the membership of that association welcomed presentations by such female lecturers as Frances E. W. Harper.[89] Women were active participants in the weekly activities of both organizations, and their presentations covered not only the range of topics traditionally associated with women but a host of other subjects as well. Certainly the number of women associated with the institutions encouraged their attention to issues of particular concern to Negro women. The comments of black women in a discussion of "Eminent Negro Men" early in the life of the Bethel Literary, for instance, inspired the organization to reserve the next week's meeting for a full discussion of "Eminent Women of the Negro Race." A paper written by Miss Mattie Bowen covered a wide range of accomplished black women, including poet Phillis Wheatley, educators Sarah Mapps Douglass and Fanny Jackson Coppin, author and lecturer Frances Ellen Watkins Harper, and sculptor Edmonia Lewis.

Present at this meeting was Mary Ann Shadd Cary, whose contribution to the discussion suggests the extent to which women felt comfortable voicing their opinions before those in attendance. Reminding those present of the "scores of colored women who in every walk of life had ennobled the race," she asserted that "the very low estimate in which the colored woman is held is attributable to colored men."[90] Despite this contentious statement, Cary was invited to present her own work before the Bethel Literary the next week; the paper she read, "Heroes of the Anti-Slavery Struggle," was the first of many public presentations she made before the Association. As a regular participant in the Bethel Historical and Literary Association, Cary found what her biographer Jane Rhodes describes as an "ideal outlet" for her intellectual energies.[91] The esteem in which she was held by her colleagues at the Bethel Literary, and their respect for her oratorical skills, are captured in one member's description of her as "a speaker whose clear, high treble voice and epigrammatic sentences were a signal for death-like stillness and oracular sayings that nearly always met popular approval."[92]

In 1892 Mary Church Terrell was elected as president of the Bethel Literary. Hers was a controversial appointment; according to one source, "many knowing ones regarded it as a mistake," although it turned out that she did "preside with ease and grace, plan with foresight, and execute with vigor."[93] It is telling that Terrell served in this capacity for only one year, and that she mentions her presidency of the Bethel Literary only in passing in her autobiography, *A Colored Woman in a White World*.[94] There is no doubt that the Bethel Literary offered Terrell and other educated black women like her a significant outlet for their intellectual energy. But the range of the Literary's work could not contain her passion for women's issues or her pragmatic, gendered racial concerns. Rather than finding a public forum, these interests seemed likely to become submerged by the larger racial struggle that required black men and black women to work effectively together. Terrell saw black women as a distinct social and political force in need of the opportunities and environment that would allow them to become effective race leaders and to have their political role taken seriously. The same year that Terrell served as president of the Bethel Literary she played a central role in the formation of the Colored Women's League, one of the many women's groups formed in the last decade of the nineteenth century as part of the fledgling black women's club movement that would serve as a precursor to the organization of the National Association of Colored Women. By the time Terrell became the first president of this organization in 1896, the black women's club movement was in full swing.

4

Reading, Writing, and Reform
in the Woman's Era

I begin this chapter with a scene from African American literary history. It comes from Frances E. W. Harper's fourth and most well-known novel, *Iola Leroy, or, Shadow Uplifted,* a fictionalized history of slavery and Reconstruction published in 1892. Near the end of the novel, the chapter "Friends in Council" depicts the meeting of a community of blacks distinguished by their northern, private-school educations and professional lives as educators, ministers, and doctors. Harper's description of Iola's evening suggests the liveliness of the meeting, held in "Mr. Stillman's pleasant, spacious parlors," which Harper describes as "overflowing with a select company of earnest men and women." The evening's "program" includes the reading of papers written by the group's membership, on topics ranging from "Negro Emigration" and "Patriotism" to Iola's paper on the "Education of Negro Mothers." Lively discussion of the issues raised follows each reading, and the recitation of poetry and other genres is interspersed with the essays. One regular member of the group who "regrets" she cannot attend the meeting contributes a poem to the session, which is read by a member in attendance. Members leaving Mr. Stillman's house at the end of the evening remark how "interested and deeply pleased" they are with the proceedings. Iola Leroy is more clarified in her goals and her ambitions than she was when she arrived; she feels deeply inspired to "do something of lasting service for the race," a desire that she relays to her companion, Dr. Latimore. " 'Doctor,' " Iola says, " 'I wish I could do something more for our people than I am doing.' " The Doctor's response seems to confirm Iola in her direction: "Why not . . . write a good, strong book which will be helpful to them?"[1]

This depiction of a meeting of a literary society only begins to suggest the place occupied by literature and literary activities for some African Americans at century's end. Association with African American literary culture was considered fundamental to the agenda of racial uplift and social reform and one potential avenue to the assertion of political agency. Harper's *Iola Leroy* underscores this message in two ways: while it dramatizes the process of transformation to race consciousness and pious activism experienced by the members of the fictional literary society, the novel offers itself as a means of making that process available to its readers. As a fictional heroine, Iola Leroy presented late nineteenth-century readers with an example of virtue, compassion, and high moral character; at the same time she is intelligent, ambitious, and committed to public service. By the end of the novel, Iola Leroy has not yet satisfied her desire to write a "good, strong book" but her creator, Frances Harper, has; by stimulating the racial and sexual consciousness of her intended readers, Harper's novel fulfilled the ambition of its author to "awaken in the hearts of our countrymen a stronger sense of justice . . . and thus add to the solution of our unsolved American problem."[2]

In the last decades of the nineteenth century, literature resurfaced as one of the practical tools black Americans envisioned using not only to reflect but also in fact to redefine themselves and their roles in the larger community. Men and women like Iola Leroy whose literary activities left them "inspired to do something of lasting service for the race" believed that interaction with print—producing it, reading it, and allowing it to direct their social and political conversation—was a potential vehicle for constructing identity and regulating social change that carried with it the power to elevate and enlighten the race. Literary activities constituted an attempt to complicate and reformulate both individual and group identity and, equally important, to exert control over self-representation. In the words of one literary woman of the time, "thoughtful, well-defined and intelligently placed [literary] efforts" would supply "influential and accurate information, on all subjects relating to the Negro and his environments, to inform the American mind."[3]

The growing numbers of educated black men and women considered reading and other literary work as essential to the project of refashioning the personal identity and reconstructing the public image of African Americans in the last decade of the nineteenth century. Although black men also put literature to good use in single-sex organizations as a means of defining themselves and asserting a new place in the larger American society, my focus in this chapter on the literary activities of middle-class black women at the turn of the century allows me to look at the ways reading and literary activity gave direction to the women's associations that proliferated during this time. Although most black women's clubs at the turn of the century were not exclusively literary in nature, club membership offered black women a variety of literary and textual means through which to experience and exercise individual and collaborative agency, and a primary impact of the black women's club movement was the increased production, circulation, and readership of printed texts. As Doctor Latimore's advice to Iola Leroy suggests, authorship was one of the single most important roles a black woman could assume. And while authorship was not for everyone—as Iola Leroy points out, "besides money and leisure, [the writing of a book] needs patience, perseverance, courage, and the hand of an artist to weave it into the literature of the country"—the ideologies of literacy disseminated by the black women's club movement emphasized that practical knowledge and authority could be derived simply from reading "a good, strong book."[4] Even as literary work implied a gendered, corresponding role for black women in the advancement of the race, it also allowed them to transcend the models of literacy endorsed by contemporary institutions and the dominant cultural expectations that prohibited all women from sharing the same educational opportunities, voting rights, and professional roles as white and, for that matter, black men. While the particular status of black women in the United States further limited their presumed need for even the most basic literacy, definitions of the meaning and uses of literacy and print developed in and communicated through black women's clubs effectively allowed black women to inhabit new discourses and introduced them to different ways of thinking about themselves and their positions in the larger social world. The great variety of literary interaction that took place in the context of African American women's clubs effectively functioned as activities that would "[open] the door for the entry of a nobler and better way of thinking of ourselves."[5]

This chapter explores the intricate connection forged between the shared literary work of African American clubwomen at the turn of the century, after whom Iola Leroy is modeled, and the identities they put forth. To understand their literary activities, I look first at clubwoman Victoria Earle Matthews's address "The Value of Race Literature," delivered before leaders of the women's club movement at a crucial juncture of its organization. I then look to place Matthews's call for clubwomen to become "literary activists," which I argue served as the manifesto of the black women's movement itself, in a broader context by illustrating the ways that other black women in the last decade of the nineteenth century used public forums to articulate their understanding of the political implications of literary work. Next, I turn to the literary clubwork itself, focusing first on two products of black women's literary practices, the club paper and a newspaper produced by one club in particular, Boston's Woman's Era. Begun in 1894, the *Woman's Era*, which became the official organ of the National Association of Colored Women in 1896, is representative of the ways that black women created through their literary work a collaborative space in which to represent themselves and expand their identities. Finally, I look at clubwomen's reading, the variety of which demonstrates both their desire to appropriate the prestige of those texts associated with dominant notions of high culture and their interest in challenging the traditional boundaries of culture to expand what was considered literature to include, among other things, the writing of women and of African Americans. Concluding the chapter with an assessment of the public institutions, especially local libraries, that resulted from clubwomen's commitment to literature, I also offer a sense of the "costs" of clubwork for these literary women, whose commitment to public service often interfered with their literary ambitions.

THE VALUE OF RACE LITERATURE

On 30 July 1895 Victoria Earle Matthews delivered an address titled "The Value of Race Literature" to an audience of her peers assembled in Boston. Matthews's argument was that the literature written by African American men and women—whether it specifically confronted issues of race or not—was crucial for a people in need of publicly communicating their past accomplishments, present injustices, and future ambitions. Literature, she noted, was widely used to disseminate vivid mischaracterizations of black people. Why should it not also become a principle medium through which African Americans countered these racist mischaracterizations with more accurate and more praiseworthy representations of themselves? What was needed from the black community were "thoughtful, well-defined and intelligent [literary] efforts . . . to serve as counter-irritants" against the destructive images produced and sustained by racist white Americans (177). Matthews believed that "race literature" would serve the black community in at least three ways. First, she believed that by associating themselves with the creation, distribution, and consumption of literature, African Americans would reap the benefits of its stature. Second, Matthews considered literature uniquely able to communicate "influential and accurate information, on all subjects relating to the Negro and his environs" (177). Through literature, Matthews believed, African Americans could themselves make public specific information about the diversity of black life in the United States, and in doing so "undermine and utterly drive out . . . the subordinate, the servant as the type representing a race whose numbers are now far into the millions" (173). Finally, Matthews asserted that these nuanced and accurate literary portraits of black Americans would be "a revelation to our people, [which] will enlarge our scope," fostering racial consciousness and the development of race pride among African Americans (173).

The occasion for Matthews's address on the value of race literature was the First Congress of Colored Women, which met for three days in July 1895. Black women had for some time been discussing their desire to hold a national assembly; they were prompted to do so by the publication of an incendiary letter written by J. W. Jacks, president of the Missouri Press Association. Jacks's letter attacked antilynching crusader Ida B. Wells-Barnett, denigrating her in particular and black women generally as having "no sense of virtue and being altogether without character."[6] Coupled with other efforts to malign black womanhood and insults such as the refusal of white women's clubs to accept African Americans as members, this attack made vividly clear how desperately African American women needed to form coalitions and devise strategies to defend and "reflect credit" on themselves. The conference was, therefore, part of an organized effort on behalf of black women to identify the particular political challenges they faced and determine the best strategies to meet those challenges. Their meeting galvanized the black women's club movement; in addition to strengthening the commitment and visibility of black women's local organizations, it led to the founding of a federation of black women's clubs that would eventually evolve into the National Association of Colored Women (NACW).

Although Matthews modestly described the address she delivered at the First Congress of Colored Women as "a cursory glance at . . . the past, present, and future of our race literature" (185), the context in which she delivered "The Value of Literature" compels us to consider her address in much more significant terms: it was nothing less than a manifesto of the women's club movement itself. The impetus for their assembly and coalition in the summer of 1895 was the problem of how black women might counter ignorant and racist representations such as that advanced by Jacks, who described black women as "wholly devoid of morality." In her address Matthews asserted that an effective means of meeting the political challenges faced by black women lay in literature. In addition to allowing black Americans to represent themselves in more accurate and nuanced ways, Matthews believed that race literature, by which she meant "a general collection of what has been written by [African American] men and women" (170), would also inspire pride in black people by allowing them to see themselves in a positive light. By articulating "the value of race literature" in the context of the First Congress of Colored Women, Matthews was intent on acknowledging the centrality of various kinds of literary work to black women's political struggle. She wished to pose a challenge to black clubwomen to become politically active by dedicating themselves to literary activities which, in addition to writing, included the consumption, preservation, and circulation of printed texts.

In "The Value of Race Literature" Matthews used several means to illustrate for her audience the power of literature and literary representation. She began by reviewing negative representations of black people in literature by white authors in order to reveal "the kind of types of Negro characters eminent writers have taken exceeding care to place before the world as representing us" (176). The prejudice inherent in the work of the nation's most popular writers, Matthews argued, and the offensiveness of their prose, was wide-ranging. Singling out the author of a story that appeared in *Harper's Magazine* as "representative of the spirit of the writers of today," Matthews exposed as fraudulent the "pathetic picture . . . drawn of [the] character generally known as the typical 'Darkey'" (174). Describing Samuel Clemens as the "Negro-hating Mark Twain," she condemned his portrayal of "an educated octoroon [who] is made out to be a most despicable, cowardly villain" in *The Tragedy of Pudd'nhead Wilson*. It is ironic, Matthews pointed out to her audience, that this work was heralded by a literary critic as "'among the best of those productions which gives us hope for a distinctive American drama'" (175).[7]

Matthews's observations are particularly astute as they reflect upon white writers' condescending depictions of educated blacks; in literature no less than in life, she implies, the very idea of a literate, educated, upstanding black citizen must be obliterated in order to maintain black subservience and, most importantly, the white image of blacks as, to return to the words of David Walker, "talking apes, void of intellect, incapable of learning."[8] The educated Negro was a favorite with white writers; in evoking this character they could discredit it by transforming it into something negative or ridiculous. Citing the example of *Imperative Duty*, Matthews accused William Dean Howells of working "laboriously" to establish "the belief that the Negro possesses an Othello like charm in his ignorance which education and refinement destroys, or at best makes repulsive" (175). This, Matthews asserts, was the effect of Conan Doyle's writing as well; "like Howells, [he] also [paid] his thoughtful attention to the educated negro [*sic*]— making him in this case more bloodthirsty and treacherous and savage than the Seminole" (176). It was also the effect of Marie Therese Blanc's passing reference to black women in her 1895 *The Condition of Women in the United States: A Traveller's Notes*. In a book approaching three hundred pages, Matthews noted, a mere one hundred words were devoted to the condition of black women. Those one hundred words, which described a " 'Black Damsel' in New Orleans engaged in teaching Latin" and " 'a class of little Negro girls with faces like monkeys studying Greek,' " prompted Blanc to conclude that " 'the disgust expressed by their former masters seemed quite justified' " (176).

Matthews acknowledged that members of the "sensible public" recognized the absurdity of these degrading literary portrayals, receiving them with "jeers." But these literary mischaracterizations, "wholly inconsistent with anything short of a natural-born idiot!," made a tremendous impact on a wide readership nevertheless. "Stuff like this comes apace," she told her audience, "influencing the reading-world, not indeed thinkers and scholars; but the indiscriminate reading-world, upon whom rests, unfortunately, the bulk of senseless prejudice" (176). It was senseless prejudice that Matthews believed race literature would effectively work to dispel. Race literature would counter the mischaracterizations that in 1895 dominated the images of African Americans that circulated by print.

In challenging black women to become the producers, preservers, and distributors of race literature, Matthews reminded her audience that they would be building on a rich literary history with roots in the eighteenth century. Matthews points proudly to the writing of Phillis Wheatley and George W. Williams, which, she notes, was included in an anthology of American literature edited by H. L. Stoddard. She called Edward Blyden's essays and the published oratory of Alexander Crummell and Richard Greener "high specimens of sustained English, good enough for anyone to read, and able to bear critical examination, and reflect the highest credit on the race" (178). She praised William C. Nell's *Colored Patriots of the American Revolution* as "a scholarly, able, accurate book, second to none written by any other colored man" (178). In addition to the poetry of Paul Laurence Dunbar, Matthews singled out the autobiographies, novels, and essays of William Wells Brown, Frederick Douglass, Martin R. Delany, James McCune Smith, Archibald Grimké, and William Monroe Trotter. She also acknowledged the literary journalism of Samuel Cornish, John Russwurm, David Ruggles, I. Garland Penn, and T. Thomas Fortune, editor of the *New York Age*.

No less important to Matthews were the often-overlooked literary contributions of African American women. She commended the work of Ida B. Wells-Barnett, antilynching crusader and former editor of the Memphis, Tennessee, newspaper *Free Speech*, and pointed to Frances E. W. Harper's novel *Iola Leroy* as evidence of the "high literary qualities of which the race is capable" (178). Matthews also praised the literary and intellectual contributions of such other black women writers as Sarah Mapps Douglass and Grace A. Mapps, Charlotte Forten Grimké, H. Cordelia Ray, and Gertrude Mossell. She acknowledged that these literary contributions by male and female African American writers were "first beginnings," but argued that "they compare favorably with similar work of the most advanced people"; "all should be read," she counseled, "and placed in our libraries" (179). By making the literary productions of these writers publicly available, their past accomplishments would be preserved for the benefit of future generations. "Their lives and documents should be zealously guarded for the future use of our children," Matthews argued, not only to expose them to the pleasure associated with reading but also because "they familiarize the [black and white] public with the idea of the Negro owning and doing the brain work" (179–80) associated with the literary.

By cataloguing the past literary achievements of African Americans, Matthews offered her audience a sense of their literary heritage and implicitly communicated that, despite the widespread assumption that literary excellence could not spring from the pens of black authors, theirs was a tradition worthy of recognition and preservation. She also provided her listeners with an expansive definition of the boundaries of literature and the genres that might be considered literary. Matthews opened "The Value of Race Literature" with a definition of it: "By race literature," she told her audience, "we mean ordinarily all the writings emanating from a distinct class—not necessarily race matter; but a general collection of what has been written by men and women of that Race: History, Biographies, Scientific Treatise, Sermons, Addresses, Novels, Poems, Books of Travel, miscellaneous essays and the contributions to magazines and newspapers" (170). In refining and elaborating on this definition throughout her address, Matthews also offered a sense of race literature's purpose and the criteria by which it should be judged. "Race Literature does not mean things uttered in praise, thoughtless praise of ourselves, wherein each goose thinks her gosling a swan" (182), Matthews cautioned her audience. Rather than an outlet for false pride, Matthews insisted that race literature must fulfill more practical goals. It was, she argued, not a luxury but a "necessity as an outlet for the unnaturally suppressed inner lives which our people have been compelled to lead" (173).

That race literature emanated from the particular oppression faced by black Americans determined that it would differ and must be considered as distinct from American literature more broadly defined. "The conditions which govern people of African descent in the United States have been and still are, such as create a very marked difference in the limitations, characteristics, aspirations and ambitions of this class of people, in decidedly strong contrast with the more or less powerful races which dominate it" (170), Matthews said. She reminded her audience of the "statutes . . . carefully, painstakingly prepared by the most advanced and learned American jurists to perpetuate ignorance" among black people, laws whose sole design was to "[engender] servility and [beget] ox-like endurance" (170). Literature created by black Americans under these circumstances would "of necessity be different in all essential points of greatness . . . from what we may at the present time, for convenience, call American literature" (172). The experience of oppression out of which black literature arose would determine that it would not only expand the definition of American literature but also, in some respects, challenge it. She predicted that what she called "our Race Literature when developed would not only compare favorably with many, but will stand out pre-eminently, not only in the limited history of colored people but in the broader field of universal literature" (173).

Matthews identifies earlier black writers, including black women writers, as heroic, because they "dared to seek the sources of knowledge and wield a pen" (171) despite restrictions on their freedom and insults to their humanity. In calling for literary activities to form the foundation of the black women's club movement, she called on black clubwomen to assume this daring, heroic, and highly political stature as well. Matthews's turn from a general discussion of race literature to a specific consideration of the role of black women in its creation, consumption, and circulation comes toward the end of her address; but it is in the context of contemplating black women's dedication to literature and literary study that Matthews is able to assert: "Never was the outlook for Race Literature brighter" (184). Her optimism is largely due to the fact that what she considered to be a "literary movement" (183), a movement located in and driven by the political interests and concerns of black women, was already underway in the impulse among black women to form coalitions. Matthews used her address to inspire and challenge black clubwomen, who, she argued, must renew and extend their understanding of the importance of literary activism and their commitment to the production, preservation, consumption, and circulation of literature. What was at stake should black clubwomen not become literary activists, Matthews suggested, was nothing less than the future of the race. She closed her address with the following words of warning: "Unless earnest and systematic effort be made to procure and preserve for the transmission to our successors, the records, books and various publications already produced by us, not only will the sturdy pioneers who paved the way and laid the foundation for our Race Literature, be robbed of their just due, but an irretrievable wrong will be inflicted upon the generations that shall come after us" (185).

Matthews's appeal, situated as it was in the context of this public arena of political organization, was appropriately directed. By their mere presence at the First Congress of Colored Women, her audience, composed of black women actively seeking the means of defending and defining themselves and, by extension, all members of their race, presented themselves as ready to act and receptive to appropriate strategies that might prove politically effective. Indeed, as leaders in the black women's club movement and members of black women's clubs, many of those present at the First Congress of Colored Women had already begun to meet the literary challenges Matthews placed before them. In her address Matthews singled out the literary journalism of Boston's Woman's Era Club whose newspaper, the *Woman's Era*, she heralded as "a record of Race interests gathered from all parts of the United States" (183). Matthews praised the staff of the *Woman's Era* for "shrinking at no lofty theme, shirking no serious duty, aiming at every possible excellence, and determined to do their part in the future uplifting of the race" (183). Inspired by the literary accomplishments of women such as those behind the *Woman's Era*, Matthews believed that other black women, whose attendance at the Congress underscored their readiness to act and desire for direction, would inspire and sustain a literary movement that would alter the consciousness of the nation.

THE THRESHOLD OF WOMAN'S ERA

I have identified the immediate impetus for the assembly of the First Congress of Colored Women, and for Matthews's address on the value of race literature, as a moment of particular crisis. Combined with the other distinct injustices that they faced, what Jacks's letter signified to those black women responsible for organizing the meeting was a direct political attack in response to which a distinct form of political intervention was needed. As had antebellum black Americans facing the crisis of slavery and question of free black identity in the Antebellum North, black women turned to literature and to literary activism in this post-Reconstruction context as a means of addressing the particular political crises they faced. By positioning literature as a potentially powerful political tool for African Americans, Matthews echoed not only her early nineteenth-century ancestors but also those contemporaries who, in recent years, had similarly posited the political implications of literary work and textual production for black Americans. Indeed, the relationship between literature and political power was a standard feature of the public discourse of late nineteenth-century black women. Two years before Matthews's address to the First Congress of Representative Women, Frances E. W. Harper and Fannie Barrier Williams, both of whom would become major figures in the black women's club movement, had in different ways advanced their own perspectives on what Matthews would concisely articulate as the value of race literature. These articulations are telling, for they help us to see the different ways in which literacy and the importance of literary work rose again and again to the top of black women's political agenda in the last decade of the nineteenth century.

Although an advocate of women's suffrage, Harper was, as a black woman, especially sensitive to the necessity of cultivating forms of self-representation and political intervention that did not depend on suffrage. Her insistence that there were multiple arenas in which political power was already available to black women was something exemplified by her own life: throughout her long career as a writer and public speaker, Harper gained access to the means of representing herself and assuming political power even without the right to vote. Until they gained access to official channels of political participation, Harper believed that women must avail themselves of alternative means of claiming political power and representing themselves.[9] She herself had claimed such authority through her literature, which, in addition to reflecting the society in which she lived, took as its "mission" the task of changing it. Through her writing Harper worked to intervene in the political sphere and promote social change by creating literature that would "awaken in the hearts of [her] countrymen a stronger sense of justice" and "inspire" black Americans to "embrace every opportunity, develop every faculty, and use every power God has given them to rise in the scale of character and condition, and to add their quota of good citizenship to the best welfare of the country."[10] Literary representation allowed Harper to become "a power" who used her writing as a medium through which to "grapple with the evils which threaten[ed] to undermine the strength of the nation."[11]

This understanding of her own ability to command political presence through media such as literature lay at the foundation of Harper's address to the Congress of Representative Women, held in conjunction with the World's Columbian Exposition in Chicago in 1893. Harper was one of a handful of black women who were permitted to speak before the Congress of Representative Women, and her participation followed a bitter struggle on the part of African Americans to be represented at all at the World's Columbian Exposition. In a nation plagued with lynchings and widespread racial injustices, African American leaders considered their exclusion from the World's Columbian Exhibition a pointed and pernicious effort to neglect the plight and the accomplishments of black Americans. Despite the brouhaha that surrounded their inclusion on the program, the six black women selected to address the Congress did not hesitate to touch on the issues with which they were most concerned, including the sexual exploitation of black women and the complicity of white women in that exploitation. These concerns demanded direct confrontation and, as Harper argued before her audience, it was time for women—even and especially black women—to use their considerable power to confront them. Even without suffrage, women must find ways to "come into [their] political estate," Harper argued. Today, she stated, "women hold in their hands influence and opportunity, and with these they have already opened doors which have been closed to others." Harper cited literature as one of the ways in which women had become "rival claimant[s]" in the arena of political power traditionally believed to be

accessible only to those who could vote.[12] Armed with this understanding of women's political power and the multiple possibilities for
claiming it, Harper boldly and optimistically challenged her audience
to reimagine themselves as on "the threshold of woman's era."[13]

In her address to the same Congress of Representative Women,
Fannie Barrier Williams echoed and supported Harper's position by
pointing explicitly to the pivotal role black women's literary production would play in the transformation of their position in the United
States. In Williams's opinion, black women's negative reputation had
everything to do with their lack of public representation. "Less is
known of our women than of any other class of Americans," she
lamented. "No organization of far-reaching influence for their special
advancement, no conventions of women to take note of their progress,
and no special literature reciting the incidents, the events, and all
things interesting and instructive concerning them are to be found
among the agencies directing their career. There has been no special
interest in their particular condition as native-born American women.
Their power to affect the social life of America, either for good or for
ill, has excited not even a speculative interest."[14] Deploying an urgent
and forceful tone, Williams cast her predictions for the future of black
women in the United States in terms of the potential impact of literary
representation. "The exceptional career of our women will yet stamp
itself indelibly upon the thought of this country," she proclaimed. She
predicted that black women would distinguish themselves in part
through their future contributions to and impact on artistic production. "In less than another generation," she told her audience, "American literature, American art, and American music will be enriched by
productions having new and peculiar features of interest and excellence." She concluded: "American literature needs for its greater variety and its deeper soundings that which will be written into it out of
the hearts of these self-emancipating women."[15]

Williams's comments here speak not only to the incompleteness of
American literature without the sound of black women's voices but
also reflect the belief of black women of similar educational achievement in the last decade of the nineteenth century that the development of black women's literary voices would itself facilitate their empowerment and recognition as citizens. At the heart of an effort to
develop and nurture black writers and literary work by African Ameri-

can women during this time was the need to counteract prevailing and limiting assumptions that black women were immoral and ignorant, entirely unqualified for participation in the American body politic. Excluded from the nation's civic life according to conventions of both race and gender, these women believed that the status of their voices could provide the only true measure of collective race progress. If black men were, as protofeminist Anna Julia Cooper described them in 1892, a "muffled chord," then black women were the "mute and voiceless note" of the race: virtually silenced, they had "no language—but a cry."[16] In addition to this complex racial positioning, black women also found their voices neglected or obscured in terms of the gender-related concerns that faced all women. Literary study and the production of literary texts would help black women emerge from this voicelessness. Through their literary activities, they would develop ways to fashion and represent themselves, criticizing and challenging the injustices and inequalities that surrounded and oppressed them.

The "woman's era" that resulted at the turn of the century from the concerted efforts of black women like Fannie Barrier Williams, Frances E. W. Harper, and Victoria Earle Matthews, along with their lesser-known counterparts, to cultivate and publicly present their voices through literary means stands in stark contrast with historian Rayford Logan's characterization of the same period as the "nadir" of black experience in the United States. The emergence of a powerful and empowering woman's era in the midst of the disempowering barrage of discriminatory laws and racial violence of the 1890s points to a central irony: these years of debilitating racial conflict and exclusion were the very years that found black women banding together to demand that they, in the words of Fannie Barrier Williams, "be known and recognized for what we are worth."[17] The need for public forms of representation made this period particularly conducive to literary production and exchange, both as an individual pursuit and as a collective endeavor. As Elizabeth Ammons notes in her study of Frances E. W. Harper, the woman's era "simultaneously reflected and fostered the sense of powerfulness, mission, and possibility necessary to the emergence of art not just by scattered individuals . . . but by women as a group."[18] While black women would be excluded from the most overt and visible forms of political agency well into the twentieth century, the evolution of the woman's era in the last decade of the nineteenth century saw black women in greater and greater numbers becoming literary activists by engaging in print culture in the context of black women's clubs. These women recognized and acted on the idea that the woman's era Harper proclaimed at the Congress of Representative Women could not wait to come about until women were allowed to vote. Rather, it would emerge because those whom Williams rightly called "self-emancipating women" would free themselves by challenging and enriching the society and the culture through a combination of political activism and literary self-representation.

How did black women become literary activists? What did their literary activities, performed in the context of black women's clubs and the club movement, look like? What were they able to accomplish through literary endeavors? What limitations did they encounter in their literary work? For the remainder of this chapter I will explore a number of ways black women conceived of literary work in the context of the club movement. Of the various literary endeavors with which black women's clubs and black clubwomen were simultaneously engaged at the turn of the century, my discussion will focus primarily on three particular kinds of literary work, all of which were fundamentally interrelated: club papers, which, initially delivered in the intimate setting of the local club meeting, laid the groundwork for the more public presentations that were essential to the success of black clubwomen's political ambitions and public service projects; club newspapers, the most prominent of which was the *Woman's Era*, that provided black clubwomen a venue through which to communicate with one another and to bring before a national audience the products of their literary work; and clubwomen's reading practices, the choices for which allowed clubwomen to negotiate the boundaries of culture and assert definitions of literature expansive enough to include their own writers and literary habits. At the heart of all of these activities, as we shall see, was the sociability provided by the context of the club itself. In the face of tremendous challenges, clubwomen depended on one another to provide the constructive feedback that would help them to develop and strengthen their literary talents and sustain their confidence in themselves and enthusiasm for their work.

Throughout the discussion that follows, it will become evident that, at the turn of the century, black women put literature and print to work as a means of meeting the needs of their local and national communities, but it was an instrument of their own personal fulfillment as well. In this, their literary activities functioned simultaneously as private, intimate practice and public manifestations of power. Roger Chartier has observed that the power of literacy is a "power more effective than that of public office."[19] Excluded from public office and other official avenues of government agency, black clubwomen drew on the power of literacy and literature to effect change for themselves and for their communities. Through literature and printed texts, they advanced their own education in ways that augmented their capacity for carrying out the public service projects that would reshape their communities. By imagining themselves, through their reading and literary work, as a part of a larger national movement and culture, clubwomen forged bonds with one another that allowed them to participate in the political life of the nation in unprecedented ways.

In looking at the various kinds of literary activism with which black clubwomen were engaged at the turn of the century, what also becomes evident is the extent to which black clubwomen balanced what was socially acceptable about their activities with that which pushed the boundaries of middle-class womanhood. One aspect of the cultural and educational work of their coalitions emphasized modesty, selflessness, and benevolence, traditional elements of middle-class womanhood that were considered essential for middle-class black women to cultivate and communicate, through their dress, actions, and words, for the social and moral betterment of the race. But their collective literary activities also fostered the conditions and an environment in which black women were able to cultivate the autonomy, authority, and self-interest necessary to effectively develop ways of addressing their own political agenda. The tension between these directives is everywhere evident in the ways that black clubwomen talked about their literary work and their political agenda.

"TO DISCOVER AND UNCOVER HIDDEN CAPACITIES"

In a June 1895 meditation on black women's "special and growing interest" in commencement exercises, Fannie Barrier Williams wrote: "Women who have daughters capable of culture can do nothing better for womankind, as well as for the daughters, than to give them the advantage of a college training, or an education that will have an equivalent value in the quality of their intelligence." In encouraging black women to do everything in their power to ensure that their daughters were given the most complete education possible, Williams pointed not to the primacy of the university experience itself but to the importance of the "mental discipline and culture that are the most important furnishings of a university education." The great majority of black women at the turn of the century were denied access to venues of higher education, and those who did go to college were often offered limited and inferior academic curricula. But developing mental discipline and the skills associated with culture and its acquisition was recognized as essential to black women's public service efforts and their increased visibility at the end of the nineteenth century. Such talents, Williams noted, "will save us from many humiliating mistakes in our public efforts."[20] Williams's comments effectively isolate the correlation made by black clubwomen at the turn of the century between their own education and the success of the public work they wished to accomplish. With limited opportunities for black women to educate themselves in formal academic settings, black women's clubs provided an alternative and supplemental context in which to acquire and practice the skills they needed to confidently and effectively enter public and organizational life.

The association that Williams identified between personal betterment and social betterment was at the center of the black women's club movement at the turn of the century. Clubwomen's primary social interests—providing welfare services, building community institutions, defining the position and the capabilities of black women and of African Americans generally, and voicing protests against racial injustice—were integrally linked to their own education and intellectual abilities. In order to effectively perform as public activists, they needed to work individually and collectively to enhance their abilities as articulate speakers, persuasive writers, and critical thinkers. These skills, clubwomen believed, difficult to measure or document in and of themselves, would form the basis of their more readily measurable and immediately visible material accomplishments. Although material accomplishments were perceived as the outward signs of successful endeavors for the public good, clubwomen understood their self-education and self-improvement exercises to be an equal if not more important gauge of black women's potential for effecting change. "Some people's measure of good is an entirely material one," observed clubwoman Florida Ridley in a paper titled "Opportunity and Privileges of Club Life," delivered at a public meeting sponsored by the membership of Boston's Woman's Era Club in October 1896. "They recognize little that cannot be seen or handled, and consider nothing an advantage that does not add to material prosperity. We are all too much under the control of material things, and too slow to recognize the power of thought," Ridley observed. She admitted that a "woman's club may not build a home for the unfortunate, but if it opens the eyes and the hearts of its members to the condition of these unfortunates, if it considers the ways in which their misfortune might be averted, if it extends its intelligence and influence over the conduct of those who have the institution under management, it is fulfilling its mission." Ridley's comments underscore black clubwomen's belief that their ability to improve existing conditions depended on preparation and study. Only when armed with a critical understanding of the reasons behind poverty, Ridley insists, can effective strategies be developed to prevent it. And while black clubwomen might not be the ones who build the institution, their ability to effectively lobby those with the power to change policies and appeal to "those who have the institution under management" may prove a productive means of effecting significant and long-lasting change.[21]

Ridley's comments are a part of an address delivered at the first of a series of public Sunday afternoon meetings that, according to a description in the club's newspaper, "drew a large crowd of women interested in the work [of the Woman's Era Club] and men, curious to know just what the work [of the club] meant." Her comments were geared primarily toward this latter group, described as "skeptical and quite prepared to smile with superior indifference." It was onlookers like these who often dismissed the organized work of black women with the analysis that their "women's clubs mean nothing but 'talk, talk.'" That Ridley was prepared to respond to this critique acknowledges the assumptions about the nature and value of women's talk against which black clubwomen labored to assert the legitimacy of the many dimensions of their clubwork. Women's talk—most commonly associated then as it remains today with negative and derogatory terms, the most familiar and resonant of which is gossip—was seen as strictly trivial, largely vacuous, and essentially social. In outlining the work of women's clubs, Ridley embraced but critically revalued the association between women and talk: rather than a woman's weakness, she forced her audience to reconsider women's talk in positive terms, as an essential channel of communication and, finally, as a medium for positive communal change. "It is true the club is all talk," she told her audience, "it was created to furnish opportunities to talk." Calling a woman's "general felicity of language" her "strongest medium," Ridley persuaded her audience to imagine an atmosphere in which women's talk constituted substantive work: their talk, she argues, is "the result of thought."[22]

The verbal relationships and relationships to language forged in the context of women's clubs allowed clubwomen to enter a space, both physical and psychological, where they could seriously engage, first, with one another, and then, with the profound issues that surrounded them and threatened to destroy their communities. The twofold nature of this process should not be overlooked, although it was not always embraced with the openness displayed by Florida Ridley. In speaking about their clubwork, black women often devised strategies to emphasize that aspect of their work that was explicitly focused on community service, often downplaying self-education and the component of the club activities that centered on social interaction and their own intellectual advancement. This tendency to suggest that self-education was merely a fortunate by-product of their benevolent activities is well illustrated in the following report on the activities of the Woman's Era Club, the club in which Florida Ridley was a member: "the work for humanity in [the] way of interesting oneself in public affairs leads to self-culture and an active interest in the laws of education."[23] In truth, however, black women's significant accomplishments in the realm of public service could not have been possible without the "self-culture" and practical skills learned and the confidence derived from the educational programs that regularly took place in the intimate setting of the club meeting. Unlike the meetings of men's societies, which historically emphasized public debates and literary competitions, African American women's clubs focused their attention on reading, conversation, and mutual support; their meetings centered on exercises that would nurture the membership, pushing them to acquire and practice the skills that they would put to use in the effective public presentation of their words and their ideas.

The preparation and presentation of club papers is one example of these exercises. Clubwomen prepared papers to be read orally before the membership on a great variety of subjects. As Florida Ridley's paper on "Opportunity and Privileges of Club Life" indicates, a self-conscious reflection of the impact and importance of club life for black women was a popular area of exploration, especially as the women's club movement reached its maturity. Meditations on the benefits of club life were one way that black women reflected their primary concern with women and their changing roles. Clubwomen presented papers on the benefits of physical exercise that encouraged women to develop strong bodies to physically support their strength of mind and character.[24] They reflected on every aspect of what they called "Domestic Science." While these papers practically addressed black women's traditional responsibilities in the home, they also re-imagined the boundaries of domestic roles, often presenting concrete alternatives to the traditional patterns they saw reflected around them. In her paper on "Domestic Science," for instance, Ellen Bartelle Deitrick outlined her belief in a "division of labor." All household labor, she asserted, "will be better done when women evolve some plan by which cooking may be done by a highly skilled and scientific cook, laundering by an equally accomplished laundress and general cleaning by another expert specially trained for this branch of work." Although she believed that "young women should begin to learn domestic science by going through every operation from cleaning stoves and building fires to the artistic arrangement of a parlor," Deitrick was confident that, banded together, women could make more of their domestic skills, including combining them with business savvy. "I see no reason why the women of Boston should not, in some . . . fashion, start and build up a co-operative laundry," she proposed.[25]

Deitrick's paper on domestic science points to the ways in which, through club papers and the discussions they prompted, black women participated in debates through which different ideologies of womanhood were advanced and shaped. Her suggestion that the various domestic tasks be in some sense "professionalized," not only for greater efficacy but also as a way to form a union of women and turn a profit, is just one example of the way that black clubwomen recognized and embraced their own shifting status and the possibilities and implications of taking on new and different roles. Even as they continued to emphasize the importance of their domestic obligations, for instance, black women like Deitrick actively imagined a world outside of their homes and began to picture the various ways in which they might participate in it. Through their club papers and the discussions that they inspired, black women were able to actively explore just what, in practical terms, Frances E. W. Harper meant when she declared in 1893 that women stood on "the threshold of woman's era."

Titles of their club papers indicate the extent to which these explorations negotiated a critical balance between asserting new roles for women and affirming traditional responsibilities. Often the tension between women's traditional responsibilities and the goals of the "new woman" was vividly apparent because these perspectives were literally positioned side by side. For instance, in the fall of 1895, the Tuskegee Woman's Club heard two papers at one meeting, both of which addressed the topic "Woman and her Work." Miss M. M. Fleming's paper on "Women in the Home" maintained that "the ideal woman in a home" was "worth having." It was followed by Miss Leonora L. Chapman's paper on "Woman in Business," which, according to the club's report, "introduced facts and portrayed the business capacity of the new woman with a zest that created a fervor in the breasts of those who are advocating some of her principles."[26] From the record of this meeting, there is no indication that these aspects of women's work were considered in opposition with one another, nor was the membership required to favor one paper or its position over another. Rather, by examining the subject from two perspectives, members of the Tuskegee Woman's Club could gain exposure to multiple ideas which they could use to consider their own positioning.

It is worth noting that these papers on women's work were delivered at the Tuskegee Woman's Club's "first literary meeting of the current year," a fact that underscores the close connection between the clubs' literary endeavors and their political dialogues.[27] What was "literary" and educational about the club papers was not only their subject matter, although the dissemination of information on a variety of topics was clearly an important aspect of their work. Through the club paper, black women drew on myriad rhetorical skills, all of which they would need to be successful in their public service work. Not the least of these was the ability to work collectively. As clubs investigated a specific topic or concern, they organized their presentations in such a way as to involve as many members as possible. For example, when the Tuskegee Woman's Club discussed "The Education of Negro Girls," on 7 October 1895, seven members prepared short papers that allowed the women present to conduct an in-depth discussion of the history, present, and future of black women's education. The evening began with Miss Mattie Child's paper, "The Early Education," in which she

> recalled the days of toil and pain that attended those who struggled in secret for a little learning. "Present Methods," by Miss Milla Hadley gave a marked contrast over that of years ago and a corresponding feeling of thankfulness was aroused in her hearers. "Defects in Present System," were strongly pointed out by Mrs. Young, who gave the danger of extremes, one-sidedness, and the lack of simple thoughtness in small things. "Suggestion[s] for Future Improvement" by Miss Sarah Hunt were timely. Miss Hunt gave her hearers some of the benefits she received from her summer course taken at Cottage City. "Home Training," by Mrs. Irene Bond, struck a keynote that gave no uncertain sound, but vibrated throughout with the idea of its vital importance. "School Training," by Miss S. Belle Bransford prompted each member to the serious duties that are involved in the work of training our student girls. "Training for Society," by Miss Eliza Adams, brought out more duties for mothers and others in training the daughters in habits of economy, in modesty, in uprightness and honesty in dealing with others.[28]

All of the components of this presentation required the presenters to conduct research, whether formally or informally, and the division of the larger topic, "The Education of Negro Girls," into smaller subtopics introduced its own lesson in organization. Because club papers were traditionally read before the membership, they required that their authors demonstrate both written and oral presentation skills. Criteria for judging the quality of papers presented orally before the clubs were extensive. Club women wished to come away from their meetings "highly entertained and instructed"; they demanded that the content of the papers delivered before them be both "practical and profitable."[29] Those who both "spoke with ease and crowded much thought into [their] . . . paper[s]" received the highest praise.[30]

It is impossible to underestimate the centrality of the club paper to the mission and the objectives of black women's clubs. Josephine St. Pierre Ruffin, president of Boston's Woman's Era Club, reflected explicitly on this centrality in her address before the membership on the occasion of their second anniversary. Her comments are addressed to the Woman's Era Club specifically but pertain to the importance of the club paper for turn-of-the-century black women's clubs generally. "The especial aim of this club is to promote and foster a spirit of unity and helpfulness in every needed direction among its members, to discover and uncover hidden capacities," she began. "The club paper has done much in this way, bringing to the light talent among our women which had only to be discovered to reflect credit on any people." Opportunities to produce, present, critique, and discuss club papers provided a black clubwoman with a definitive way to "realize how much more potent for good she is when she combines with other like-minded women and they utilize the endowments of each for the benefit of all."[31] The experience of preparing and delivering club papers was directly responsible for giving clubwomen the confidence to pursue other, more ambitious goals. For instance, in 1892, their first year of organization, the women of the Sierra Leone Club of Lawrence, Kansas, interspersed papers on home training and domestic economy with "Current Topic Talks." "The knowledge we gained made a generous impression upon us, and it was concluded that if we could help ourselves in short talks and a few hours of study each day, that much good could be accomplished if we founded an industrial school." By January 1894 plans for establishing that school were "moving along nicely," and the women had "adopted a resolution to the effect that we would use every effort this year to get means to purchase a lot and erect a cottage for the salvation of our girls." Although the women of the Sierra Leone Club defined themselves as " 'queens of the fireside,' as all of us are wives and almost all mothers," their intellectual training and accomplishments moved them well outside of this limited realm.[32]

In addition to being shared among the immediate membership at club meetings, club papers reached an audience beyond that of the local club in three critical ways. At the end of the nineteenth century, as more and more black women's clubs were created, clubwomen who were members of one organization were invited to address the members of other black women's clubs, whether locally or when traveling to another city. Maria Baldwin, a member of Boston's Woman's Era Club, traveled across the river to Cambridge to deliver a paper on "The true hold of the poet on the people."[33] When visiting New York the president of the Woman's Era, Josephine St. Pierre Ruffin, attended a meeting of New York's Woman's Loyal Union in 1895, where she read "a very interesting paper."[34] Such visits offered clubwomen unfamiliar yet still sympathetic audiences before which to present their work. It also allowed clubwomen in various locations to hear the perspectives of others and hear about the work of other clubs.

Second, clubwomen throughout the country were called on to serve as delegates to national conventions. At the first annual meeting of the National Conference of Colored Women, held over a three-day period in July 1895, for instance, eleven clubwomen delivered papers before the audience. In addition to Victoria Earle Matthews's paper on "The Value of Race Literature," these included Ella L. Smith's paper on "Woman and the Higher Education," Anna Julia Cooper's paper on the "Need of Organization" among women, L. C. Carter's paper on "Industrial Training," and Margaret Murray Washington's paper on "Individual Work for Moral Education."[35] In fact, so "many fine papers prepared for the conference remained unread" that organizers predicted they "might have been in session a week and then not have exhausted [them]selves." So impressive was the quality of the papers at this first national conference that organizers suggested that, collected, they "would make a credible book."[36] The success of the first convention ensured that national conventions of black clubwomen would convene each summer, each one presenting another opportunity for them to present their work.

Growing interest in the regional organization of clubwomen also offered opportunities for black clubwomen to deliver papers outside the context of the club with which they were locally affiliated. At the first annual meeting of Colorado's Federation of Women's Clubs, for example, Mrs. Ida DePriest, a member of the Woman's League of Denver, contributed a paper to a conversation on the "Trend of Popular Literature." Of all the subjects addressed at the conference, this "was considered one of the hardest, if not the most difficult subject under discussion." More challenging still was DePriest's status as one of the few black representatives to attend the meeting; she was "one of the two colored delegates sent from the Woman's League of Denver."

DePriest's paper posed the question "to what extent may we accept . . . the conclusions of others without personal investigation" and argued in part that "only when the motive, intention, and apparent purpose of an act is known, and when a calm and comprehensive survey of the subject is taken, have we any right to express conclusions." The response to her paper suggests both the value of the intimate context of black women's local organizations and the importance of black women actively seeking venues beyond the space of those local organizations to present their work. Surely the content of DePriest's paper and the quality of its delivery benefited from her past experience preparing and presenting similar papers before the sympathetic membership of her home organization, the Woman's League. More importantly, DePriest's success before an audience composed for the most part of white women at the first annual meeting of the Colorado Federation of Women's Clubs illustrates the extent to which black clubwomen capably represented themselves through their literary work; in doing so, they redefined black womanhood for those who were skeptical about a black woman's intelligence or her capabilities. DePriest's presentation proved "an agreeable surprise to the women" at the meeting, who found her to be "equal to the occasion." The other "colored delegate" who attended the meeting, Mrs. Lizzie Olden, president of the Woman's League, was also able to alter the audience's perception of black womanhood through the paper she delivered. In "The Club as a Factor in Bettering Social and Civic Conditions," Olden argued that those "who are called our best women have little right to their title unless they make use of their talents and their leisure for the benefit of the community." Her paper was well received, and she was "frequently applauded." Both women, in this case, were able to use their literary presentations to help others begin to recognize and appreciate them in terms of their dignified self-presentation and significant intellectual abilities.[37]

Successfully exposing their texts to the scrutiny of others, both those who supported as well as those skeptical about the intellectual abilities of black women, gave African American clubwomen a sense of confidence in their critical writing. It also offered them a tangible sense of the potential impact of its public presentation. Coupled with the skills that clubwomen acquired in the context of conducting research for their club assignments and forming and presenting their opinions before the membership of their local clubs, club papers became the building blocks of other, more public documents that black women produced and disseminated. The creation and dissemination of these public documents, which had their roots in private literary exercises, became central to fulfilling the political objectives of black women's clubs.

The members of Boston's Woman's Era Club, for instance, came to fully appreciate the value of print as a means of widely publicizing injustices and communicating the political position of club members when in 1894 they used a printed text to respond to an especially heinous and, in the last decade of the nineteenth century, seemingly ubiquitous crime: lynching. In response to a particular incident, members of the Woman's Era decided that the time had come to give public voice to their disapproval. In the past they had written resolutions and composed other documents to express their opinions and communicate their outrage; for the most part, however, these documents had not been publicly issued or widely distributed and had therefore not attracted a great deal of attention. This time they composed a leaflet that communicated their protest and provided valuable information on the subject of lynching; these leaflets were printed and "sent in every direction." The effectiveness of the members' intervention was apparent from the acknowledgments they received from those who read their leaflet and learned from it. Through widespread dissemination, the leaflet made its way into the hands not only of the general populace but also of influential persons who "announced their intention of doing something toward awakening public sentiment." "Large demands for the leaflets have been made," the club reported, "two hundred being called for at one time and a postal note being received from St. Louis calling for as many as could be spared." The success of this effort indicated to members of the Woman's Era that print offered them the means to address a range of issues that affected African Americans in the United States. "This reception of the leaflets has revealed to the club a line of work which has been little used and which the club can incorporate with its other work with advantage," they wrote of their experience. "This is the publication and circulation of matter that refers especially to the race, not alone, but also such matter as shall be for the advancement and encouragement of the race and to quote from our constitution 'to collect all facts obtainable, showing the moral, intellectual, industrial and social growth, and attainment of our people.' " Their conclusion that "the receipt of leaflets . . . among the colored people generally South and West could be but a welcome and hope-inspiring feature" of their work suggests that it was a strategy they would turn to again and again in their capacity as public servants.[38]

For other black women's clubs, the dissemination of print was a central mission from their inception, and their accomplishments on this front were significant. The "object" of the Woman's Loyal Union of Brooklyn and New York, for instance, was "the diffusion of accurate and extensive information relative to the civil and social status of the Afro-American." Through print, they believed, African Americans might make "intelligent assertion[s] of their rights," and turn the "attention of conscientious, conservative, thinking people at large . . . to the injustice" of the treatment of African Americans.[39] Led by Victoria Earle Matthews, whose own literary ambitions included the "determination to write a series of text books, historical primers for the youth of the race, which will trace the history of the African and show that he and his descendants have been prominently identified with every phase of this country's history including the landing of Columbus," the tremendous literary achievements of this organization are not surprising. One of their first projects suggests their firm understanding of the power of the printed word and their determination to tap into it to relay accurate information about African Americans to a broader public. "Realizing the wrongs perpetuated upon our race in the South, the injury occasioned by opinions that have been freely expressed in several leading magazines and newspapers, as to the retrogression of the race morally," the club set out to "ascertain the truth of such statements" by conducting their own survey. Headed by Matthews herself, the membership of the Woman's Loyal Union "wrote a set of questions, submitted them to the executive board with the hope of their approval, and expressed the desire to have said questions sent to the ministers, school teachers and other representative men and women throughout the country for the purpose of eliciting from them the true statistics of our people morally."[40] Praised as "comprehensive and pointed," the questionnaire was considered an effective tool for fulfilling its design: "to gather from the most reliable sources facts as to the mental, moral and financial position of our people." "The circular is an intelligent step in the right direction," wrote one source in praise of the project; "the Loyal Union evidently intends gaining a clear understanding of the situation, and without doubt that is the way to undertake any broad work."[41]

Practice as researchers, writers, and presenters of papers in the intimate setting of club meetings prepared black women for the demands of issuing their writing in more public forums and formats. Statistics offered by the recording secretary at the second anniversary celebration of the Woman's Era, for instance, suggest the extent to which black clubwomen made use of these literacy skills and the authority with which they were associated. In the preceding year, clubwomen had shown their support for the antilynching crusade of Ida B. Wells-Barnett by responding in print to "all attempts to retard her influence"; their "letters of protest" had been sent to various individuals as well as to "the leading papers of New York and Boston." In addition, they submitted twenty-five petitions "for the forwarding of the Blair Joint resolution," which they hoped would reach "the highest officials in the state and prominent citizens."[42] "In accordance with that clause of the constitution . . . which provides for the dissemination of race literature," the Woman's Loyal Union spent much of its 1899–1900 season circulating "the important leaflet[,] 'An Address to the People of the United States,' prepared by Prof. Jesse Lawson and issued by the National Afro-American Council." Organized by the chairman of the literature committee, this effort resulted in the distribution of over two hundred leaflets. "The object to be gained by such circulation," they articulated in their end-of-year report, was "to fully furnish that dominant class [with] an accurate statement of the true condition and progress of the race." To accomplish this, their strategy was to send the pamphlet "primarily to those who need enlightenment on the present position of the Afro-American[,] such persons to be reached either directly or through the co-operation of others known to be favorably disposed."[43]

Clubwomen's commitment to the distribution of print and their belief that leaflets, pamphlets, and other printed texts could engage multiple communities in the service of African American progress remained at the center of their reform efforts. In 1896 the newly formed governing body of African American women's clubs listed "some of the things clubs in the association are pledged to consider

Reading rooms established by organizations such as the YMCA were one of the places African Americans found access to books, magazines, and other printed material at the beginning of the twentieth century. YMCA Reading Room and Office, La Boca. *Jesse Alexander Photograph Collection, Prints and Photographs Division, Schomberg Center for Research in Black Culture, The New York Public Library, Astor, Lenox and Tilden Foundations.*

this year": "To attack the chain gang system of the South, the separate car law, to do rescue work in the alleys and slums of our great cities, and for the plantation woman and child, the founding of homes for our indigent, and to show greater interest in the fallen and the wayward."[44] The clubs used every effort to uplift "the fallen and the wayward" and to criticize legal and extralegal racism in America. Toward that end, they distributed their own writing and that of others who shared their politics. Frances E. W. Harper expressed this commitment when, early in 1903, she wrote to the Reverend Francis Grimké, pastor of the influential 15th Avenue Presbyterian Church in Washington, D.C., regarding a series of sermons he had delivered on lynching. After thanking Grimké for sending her a printed copy of one of these sermons and praising its "manly refusal to accept the verdict of the mob in the cases of lynching," Harper suggested an alternative means of disseminating this powerful discourse throughout the white community. "Do these sermons have a circulation outside of our people?" she asked. "Could there not be some contrivance planned by which your sermons would reach larger audiences than they do now? Could not the council plan for their circulation, and the women's clubs be induced to scatter them among the white people in different localities?" Harper's promise to Grimké that "after New Year's day I will get a few from you to distribute" may seem like a hopelessly small gesture in light of the huge and fast-growing problems with which the black community grappled at the beginning of the twentieth century, but it serves as a reminder that these seemingly small individual and group actions laid the groundwork for the more widespread forms of public protest that were to come.[45]

"A POSITIVE NECESSITY"

Certainly one of the most important ways black women were able to bring their club papers and other critical and creative writing before a wider audience was through the publications that they themselves sponsored and produced. Although such publications took a variety of forms, the largest and most prominent of these was the *Woman's Era*, a newspaper begun in Boston in 1894 and initially produced by the membership of Boston's Woman's Era Club. Conceived by its founders as "the organ of the Woman's Era Club," the *Woman's Era* was from its inaugural issue "devoted to the interests of Women's Clubs, Leagues, and Societies throughout the country." It provided black women with a way to document "the work our women are doing everywhere," and "carefully record it for future reference."[46] In January 1895 the creation of the *Woman's Era* was heralded by the membership of the Woman's Era Club as "the most important event of the year."[47] Simply put, no other venue provided black women in the last decade of the nineteenth century with the space in which to publish their work and let their voices be heard. "None of our male contemporaries can find space in their papers for this information," the editors underscored. The exclusion of their work from all other publications made it necessary for women to realize that "only through the columns of a paper controlled by themselves will the hard and beneficent work they are doing all the time be made known to the world, and so bring to them the respect and the dignity they so richly deserve."[48]

From its inception, it was the *Woman's Era*'s practice to publish as many club papers as it could accommodate in each issue. True to this commitment, the first issues of the *Woman's Era* included a series of papers on domestic science and on women's health and beauty that had recently been delivered before the Woman's Era Club, where they had "led to an interesting discussion."[49] Also included in the first issues was a variety of other literary work produced by clubwomen, ranging from a celebration of the life of Lucy Stone, which described her as an "ardent, consistent and persistent abolitionist" who dedicated herself after emancipation to "the work of freeing her sex from the many legal disabilities under which they rested," to a serialized short story by Eva Lewis titled "A Domestic Scene."[50] The quantity and the variety of the writing included in these first issues of the newspaper points to the plethora of material received by the paper's editors in response to their request that the members of black women's clubs send in their literary contributions for publication. In fact, the editors were immediately forced to apologize for the impossibility of including all that they had received. "It would take a paper twice the size of the WOMEN'S ERA [*sic*] to accommodate the matter that has come in for this issue," the editors informed their readers in the first issue of the newspaper.[51] Undiscouraged, clubwomen continued to send their written work to the staff of the *Woman's Era* in great quantities. Periodically the editors felt it necessary to recognize and issue an apology for the considerable number of essays they received but were unable to print. "So many fine papers come to us from the women of Kansas City," reads one such note, prominently placed on the first page of the *Woman's Era*'s November 1895 issue. "It is indeed unfortunate that we are not able to print them all."[52]

The importance of the *Woman's Era* as both a site of publication and a source of literary reading for black clubwomen in the 1890s cannot be underestimated. It was one thing to read a paper before the membership of a local literary society; it was quite another for black women to see themselves in print, to know that their work was reaching a national audience, and to begin to think of themselves as readers, public speakers, and published authors. As Victoria Earle Matthews communicated to the newspaper's editors in a letter excerpted in the first issue of the *Woman's Era*, the newspaper was a "positive necessity—for as the trend is toward organization among our women as among others, it will truly serve not only as a centralization of ideas, but will stimulate and encourage and revive the hopes of those now earnestly engrossed in the work of organization of women generally."[53] At the heart of Matthews's understanding of the importance of the *Woman's Era* is the emphasis it places on sharing and the exchange of texts and ideas among black women. These were essential to validating black women's literary and public service efforts and to communicating to them a sense of broader coalition. In the words of one Kansas City clubwoman, "the possession of such a magazine as the ERA will give force to the movement and contribute largely toward welding the various organizations into one complete whole, thus rendering work for the race more effective."[54]

One of the most important things that the *Woman's Era* facilitated was the sharing of news and reports from the various black women's clubs throughout the country. Much of the paper's first issue was devoted to "News From the Clubs," a column that offered readers a brief introduction to the organization and activities of a range of clubs. In addition to information on the Woman's Loyal Union, the Washington Colored Woman's League, and the Woman's Era Club itself, the *Woman's Era* carried news of the Kansas City League, the Woman's Loyal Union of New Bedford, Massachusetts, Boston's Primrose Club, the Golden Rule Club of Cambridge, Massachusetts, Providence,

Rhode Island's Working Women's League, The United Daughters of Zion, the Lodge of Good Templars, and the Invincibles.[55] Subsequent issues of the newspaper introduced readers to a similar range of black women's organizations and the diversity of their activities, and the *Woman's Era* eventually appointed local editors to report on the club activities in their state. These accounts supported the "especial work" of the *Woman's Era*: "the binding together of our women's clubs, to give a knowledge of the aims and works of each to help in every way their growth and advancement and bring the colored women together in great and powerful organization for the growth and progress of the race."[56] Exchanges between women's organizations proved useful on the most basic levels. For instance, when members of the Woman's Era Club held a benefit carnival in Boston, they offered a description of it in the pages of the *Woman's Era*, as well as this explanation of why the description was included: "Other leagues may find in this rather detailed account [of the carnival] some useful suggestions which may be used to their advantage."[57] In fact, good use was made of this information. After reading of the Woman's Era's success, the Women's Working Club of Berkley, Virginia, "held a six days' carnival . . . which was successful in every way." "Using the Women's Era [*sic*] carnival as a model," the members "carried out the project with enthusiasm and energy." "Nothing of the kind has ever been given in Berkley before and its success was instantaneous and complete," the members reported to the *Woman's Era*. This account of their great success would certainly provide an example for and inspire confidence in other clubs that wished to organize a similar event.[58]

This example only begins to suggest the range of material black women found in the pages of the *Woman's Era* to encourage and assist them in their endeavors. On a practical level, descriptions of other clubs, their constitutions, governance, mode of organization, and activities provided readers of the newspaper with models from which to fashion their own organizations. Writers for the *Woman's Era* recognized that "everywhere our women are feeling fresh inspiration for organized work," and each month they received "many letters . . . inquiring into the methods of forming leagues." The "published reports upon the leagues," they claimed, "are the best answers that can be given."[59] Inherent in this response is the self-conscious understanding that while a "club model" could be provided, there was no such

thing as a "model club." "Every club must work out its own salvation[,] adapt itself to the peculiar needs of its members," the members
of the Woman's Era insisted. Assisting other African American women
in forming their own local clubs meant pointing them toward "the
methods of successful clubs now in good working order." Members of
the Woman's Era were willing to "cite the methods of [their] own
club," but they also suggested that women seeking to form clubs also
consider "reports from such clubs as the Loyal Union, the Washington
League, the Kansas City League, for other, different models." These
were readily available in the pages of the *Woman's Era.*[60]

The *Woman's Era* was instrumental in helping black women to
organize the first Congress of Colored Women in the summer of 1895;
soon after this meeting it became the official organ of the National
Federation of Afro-American Women. With the merger of the National Federation of Afro-American Women and the National League
of Colored Women in July 1896, the *Woman's Era* "was chosen by the
joint commission on union as the official organ of the united body,"
known as the National Association of Colored Women.[61] Long before
taking on this official status, however, the key importance of the
Woman's Era in bringing women together and helping them to make
their voices heard in public arenas was widely recognized. This importance was expressed by clubwoman Fannie Barrier Williams in a letter
to the newspaper's readers that appeared in its third issue. She wrote:

> At the very time when race interest seems at such a low ebb, when
> our leaders seem tongue-tied, dazed and stupidly inactive in the
> presence of unchecked lawlessness, and violent resistance to Negro
> advancement, it is especially fortunate and reassuring to see and feel
> the rallying spirit of our women voicing itself in words of hope,
> courage and high resolves in a journal that seems to spring out of the
> very heart and peculiar needs of our women.
>
> I know of no other publication having for its existence and possi-
> bilities such inspirations and rare opportuneness as your bright jour-
> nal. The WOMAN'S ERA is the face of our colored women turned
> upward to the star of hope. It is the timely message of love and
> sympathy from colored women to women everywhere. It happily
> suggests that we can do so much for each other in all the most
> important interests of our lives that we will have more time and
> reason for courage than for despair. To thousands of our women your

paper will come as the first intimation of the wideness of the world about them and the stretch of human interest and sympathy. Thousands of them will discover their own strength and a certain sense of importance in this gradual coming together of our women all over the land in clubs and leagues organized for high purposes.[62]

Early in 1897 the *Woman's Era* ceased publication; in its place a new paper, the *National Association Notes*, was begun, and it served as the official organ of the National Association of Colored Women.[63] Published under the direction of Margaret Murray Washington, wife of Booker T. Washington, in Tuskegee, Alabama, to some extent the *National Association Notes* echoed the conservative tone of its leadership.[64] In terms of encouraging the formation of black women's clubs and validating their activities it was, however, similar in form, content, and function to the *Woman's Era*. Perhaps most importantly, it continued to provide black women who were new to clubwork with both practical information toward setting up their own organizations and programs and the inspiration necessary to persevere. By the end of the nineteenth century the black women's club movement had infiltrated the deep South, and African American women there benefited from the example of the clubwork of their sisters in other locales. "The women of our city have been inspired by what has been accomplished through the Mothers' Council at Tuskegee [a part of the network of clubs and departments that made up the network of the Tuskegee Woman's Club]," wrote one such clubwoman from Opelika, Alabama, whose brief letter was printed in the *National Association Notes* in November 1899. "They are awakened to a new sense of their duty and have organized themselves," she wrote of her peers. "On October 28th we held our first meeting and discussed the subject, 'How shall we rear our children?'"[65] The *National Association Notes* nurtured such burgeoning efforts at coalition by publishing lists of topics for study and discussion and summaries of clubs' activities, projects, and events. These items would prevent those who were new to clubwork, like the women of Opelika, from feeling isolated in their efforts. In the pages of the newspaper, clubwomen found a wealth of information to arouse their understanding of the possibilities of their coalition and to serve as a basis from which to consider their own objectives and shape a program to meet them.

By claiming the right to represent themselves and exercise authority over the terms in which they described themselves and their activities, black women used the *Woman's Era* and *National Association Notes* to refute the negative and thoughtless representations of black womanhood that surrounded them. In the media, black women found themselves represented as the "Frankenstein product of civilization," to quote Eleanor Tayleur, whose article "The Negro Woman: Social and Moral Decadence" appeared in *Outlook* magazine in 1904. Tayleur's presentation of the educated African American woman as "a girl" who goes to school "session after session, for eight to ten years, without achieving anything more than the ability to read and write like a child in the second grade" was countered in the pages of the *Woman's Era* and *National Association Notes* with feature articles about notable black women and their outstanding achievements.[66] By highlighting Josephine St. Pierre Ruffin's leadership of the Woman's Era Club and her successful organization of the Conference of Colored Women, by focusing on the extraordinary ambitions and literary abilities of Victoria Earle Matthews and Ida B. Well-Barnett's brave antilynching crusade, by recording the artistic achievements of musician Blanche Washington, and the commercial savvy of ice merchant Georgianna Whitsel, the newspapers put into circulation among other black women the tremendous accomplishments of their peers.[67] In addition to highlighting the activities of the visible leaders among them, the newspapers also recognized the importance of paying tribute to the tremendous accomplishments of what the *Woman's Era*'s literary editor Medora Gould called "that great army of woman workers, the home-makers, whom it would be impossible to call by name, but to whom as a race we owe far more than we do to a few teachers and scribblers here and there."[68] Rather than distinguishing these individuals by name, a daunting task considering the sheer numbers involved in the black women's club movement, the *Woman's Era* and the *National Association Notes* offered them recognition by recording and quantifying their accomplishments. Most of the four hundred women who made up the membership of the Tuskegee Woman's Club, for instance, went unnamed in their end-of-year report, issued at the end of May 1899. Yet their accomplishments, which included the distribution of "sixteen hundred books, papers, pictures, cards and magazines," were recorded in the *National Association Notes* in June of that year. Statistics published on the work of individual clubs, such as Sarah N. Johnson's "Report of Work Among the Colored People," printed in the *National Association Notes* in February 1901, offered an invaluable glimpse of the anonymous work of individual clubwomen, whose accomplishments of the previous year had included: "42 public meetings, 20,280 pages of literature distributed . . . 500 garments made, 5 colored children placed in good homes . . . 420 orders given for food and coal to the needy[, and] $403.85 [raised] this year."[69] This sort of distinction was central not only to reshaping the white public's impression of black women and their capabilities; at a time when black women could not but be discouraged by the multiple ways that Jim Crow and racism circumscribed their lives and limited their opportunities, such recognition also insisted that they more clearly recognize and appreciate their own talents and achievements.

"AUTHORS OF WORTH AND LITERARY STANDING"

So far in this chapter I have outlined the various ways that black women's clubs at the turn of the century, although not exclusively "literary" in nature, conceived of literary work as central to fulfilling their material and political aims. I have explored the ways that black clubwomen considered the creation and the distribution of printed texts a primary strategy toward publicly redefining black womanhood and in turn, transforming the conditions under which African Americans lived. The racism and poverty that engulfed African American communities proved formidable adversaries; in the context of women's clubs, however, print offered black women a way to concentrate and make use of their own power. Particularly through the vehicle of the club paper, I've suggested, clubwomen moved from the examination and critique of existing social formations to the development and implementation of alternatives of their own. Inherent in the printed texts with which they engaged is their belief that the production, circulation, and consumption of these texts—by both sympathetic and hostile audiences—would open the doors of greater possibility and lead to concrete material change. This appropriation of writing and use of printed texts was a radical affront to the gendered expectations and associations that had long been associated with writing. Histori-

cally, as we have seen, while women have been encouraged to participate in the relatively passive activity of reading, their access to textual
production has been limited. Although throughout the nineteenth
century women knew how to write, they were typically discouraged
from using this skill in public and political ways. Throughout their
club movement, black women stretched the boundaries of gender by
seizing the power of written texts as their own.

I now wish to turn to another significant aspect of their clubwork:
reading. Because reading, as opposed to writing, was more readily associated with gendered notions of literacy and literary study, it is possible to overlook the ways in which it was integral to the challenge
launched by black clubwomen against the negative stereotypes assigned to them and the hostile environments in which they lived. But
cultivating the habit of reading was an integral component of black
clubwomen's conception of literary work as a strategy of resistance.
Simultaneously at work in this strategy were two impulses. First,
through their reading, black clubwomen wished to consume those
texts that had traditionally been defined as high culture, thus associating themselves with the prestige identified with genteel society. Second, black women used their reading and literary conversations to
challenge the traditional boundaries of culture and to question and
expand what was considered "literature." Their reading included the
"masters" of English Literature; but it included texts by African American and women authors as well, and their methods of study introduced them to a broad range of genres not traditionally considered
literary. These agendas may seem contradictory, representing an internal contest between factions that played itself out in the context of
black women's clubs. But throughout the club movement clubwomen
revealed them to exist side by side, the tension between them reflecting the complexity of African American women's dual commitment at
the turn of the century to working both within the black community,
to improve the knowledge and opportunities of their own people, and
outside of it, to change the hearts and minds of those who oppressed
black people.

Historians of the black women's club movement have more fully
explored the emphasis clubwomen placed on reading texts that represented the dominant high culture of the period and their subscription
to an ideology that supported their appraisal of it as superior.[70] If black

[handwritten margin note at top: What reading meant not just in their lives; but their lifes as citizens]

women's lack of culture and refinement anchored their reputation as immoral and fundamentally incapable of intellectual thought, some clubwomen believed that the acquisition of the skills and habits associated with high culture and refinement would contribute to their redefinition. Reading texts associated with this tradition was a way for black women to simultaneously identify with and consume the culture and prestige connected to literature. In the words of Josephine St. Pierre Ruffin, black women suffered from the "impossibility of mingling freely with people of culture and learning." Fundamentally "shut . . . out of physical touch with the great world of art, science and letters" that formed the basis of the genteel tradition, they were also shut out from the social status with which it was associated.[71] The context of the clubs helped black women gain access to this world in two ways: as the clubs recreated the atmosphere of culture from which black women were isolated, they also prepared black women to interact with other women of culture in mixed-race social groups.

In their literary choices and in the ways that clubwomen talked about their reading is evidence of the extent to which they believed in the importance of exposure to culture as defined by others whose esteem they coveted. This perspective and its accompanying association of culture with moral standing was directly advanced by clubwoman Charlotte Hawkins Brown, organizer and president of the North Carolina State Federation of Negro Women's Clubs. Many echoed her belief that black people would meet with more social recognition from "Nordics" if they adopted the social practices and customs of what she termed "peoples of refined tastes." She subscribed to a strictly traditional definition of culture. "Culture," she argued, "is the discipline of the mental and moral powers manifest in the ease, grace and poise one exhibits in the performance of one's life. It is the result of the development of the intellect and the appreciation of the aesthetic."[72] As Anne Ruggles Gere notes, Brown "points to the connection between culture and the moral betterment of persons by describing it as regulating both mind and morality."[73] Brown believed that, for black women, acquiring culture required special and sustained effort. "Culture may be achieved through intensive training and continued practice," she wrote.[74] Only through a rigorous program of training and practice, one that could take place in the context of black women's clubs, would black women acquired the culture that

[handwritten margin note: parallel w-clau]

would transform them into people worthy of recognition and respect. When paired with a concern for the "social graces," Brown believed that in the study of fine literature, art, and music lay what she termed "cultural security."[75] A classical education in these subjects, Brown trusted, would produce refined black women who garnered respect.

The focus of many black women's clubs at the turn of the century reveals the extent to which gaining access to the "great world of art, science and letters" meant engaging in a course of reading that included such "masters" of the genteel tradition as John Milton, Sir Walter Scott, William Cullen Bryant, and John Ruskin. A survey of two black women's clubs in Denver, Colorado, in the spring of 1895, for instance, indicates the classical nature of their reading. The focus of the Clio Club was on the "study of historical periods," which included topics such as the "invasion of Europe by the Barbarians and its results," "The Crusades and their effects upon European Civilization," "The Sieges of Paris," and "The mythical and romantic element in early English History." Members mastered these topics by "covering the literary, artistic, and social growth of each epoch." The Round Table Club had also pursued what they called "historical studies" in part through an examination of literary texts; their focus throughout their 1895 season was on Shakespeare's historical plays.[76] In addition to suggesting the content of their reading, both of these programs illustrate clubwomen's tendency to organize their reading around historical time periods or significant events. Their interest in history, especially in European history, underscores the extent to which they subscribed to the belief that to study "life . . . as is found in history" was to gain exposure to "life as it really is."[77] Something about this history and the texts that documented it, they believed, was authentic, real; to study it was to tap into the aura and prestige with which it was associated. The works of Shakespeare are representative of the texts considered the pinnacle of high culture and sanctioned as classics. Through contact with these texts, black clubwomen wished to label themselves as "lovers of higher literary criticism," which they associated predominantly with readers of those "great" writers such as Thomas Carlyle, Thomas Macaulay, Alfred Lord Tennyson, and William Makepeace Thackeray.[78]

Were this representative of the sum of black women's reading, or even the bulk of it, it would be easy to conclude that clubwomen were

exclusively interested in acquiring high culture as defined by mainstream society. While the authority that these authors and their literary texts held for black women readers is undeniable, what is more
striking and, I argue, more prevalent about their reading is the extent
to which it also questioned established literary standards and traditional literary values. Their attention to texts that definitively lay
outside conventional canons of literature, such as those by African
Americans and by women, highlights their desire to recalibrate the
value of those works. By reading texts by members of their own race
and those by women alongside texts determined by mainstream academic circles and the dominant cultural tradition to be "authors of
worth and literary standing," black women demonstrated the extent
to which they both embraced and chafed against standard notions of
culture.[79] This tension forced a reassessment and redefinition of what
constituted literature and literary study in crucial and lasting ways.

Given their understanding of the importance of textual representation, it is unsurprising that black clubwomen were especially interested
in books by and about African Americans. In the last decade of the
nineteenth century, they readily embraced the notion that literature by
African Americans was one of the many kinds of literatures worthy of
their attention. Surely the prominence in the club movement of Victoria Earle Matthews, whose interest in literature by African Americans and status as a writer was highlighted in a profile included in the
May 1894 issue of *The Woman's Era* and who was remembered in the
aftermath of the 1895 convention as its "star," contributed to black
clubwomen's growing appreciation for literature by members of their
own race. Another contributing factor was the impulse, as literary and
women's clubs increased in size and resources, to subdivide literary
study into various areas of focus. The Brooklyn Literary Union provides an example of this and underscores the novelty of this organizational plan. Enthusiastically announcing a "splendid program" for its
ninth season, the Union also announced that they had incorporated
into their program "an entirely new idea." Their ambition, which they
admitted was, "if not new in thought, new in practical application,"
was to create "eighteen reading circles, each with an independent
director, to conduct discussions on given nights." In addition to circles
on English Literature, French Literature, American Literature, and
Children's Literature, a circle on Afro-American Literature was estab-

lished. "Such an innovation has many advantages," wrote one representative of the Brooklyn Literary Union. "It will not only concentrate the efforts of progressive minds," she remarked, but also "[give] impetus to intellectual activity."[80]

Lest club members be deceived into thinking that little Afro-American literature existed, they would only have to turn to the column called "Literature Notes" in *The Woman's Era* to be informed about the variety of texts that were available. Written by literary editor Medora Gould, the "Literature" column was a regular feature of *The Woman's Era*. A selection of notices from it offers insight into what its readers would have found there. Gould's first "Literature Notes" included an announcement of the recent publication, "in one volume of the entire poetical works of Henry Wadsworth Longfellow." This was an "event worthy of special attention," as Gould informed her readers, because "a thorough knowledge of Longfellow is part of the education of every American." The same column also included the announcement that "Harper's Magazine for March contains an interesting contribution entitled 'The New England Negro,' by Miss Jane DeForest Sheldon. It treats of the time when slaves were owned extensively throughout Massachusetts and Connecticut, and the period immediately following their emancipation." Gould also noted that " 'Negro Stars in All Ages' is the title of a new book by W. H. Quick of North Carolina," and directed readers toward "a recent issue of 'The Texas Illuminator,' a race paper published in San Antonio, Texas," that "contains a well written article urging Neg[r]oes to become shareholders in a new railroad now in process of construction in that state."[81]

This inaugural column is representative of the range of literary interests that Gould cultivated among her readership. In her column Gould kept her readers abreast of the work of Thomas Hardy, Rudyard Kipling, Robert Louis Stevenson, Arthur Conan Doyle, W. D. Howells, Alfred Lord Tennyson, Henry James, Judge Tourgee, George Cable, James Lowell, Thomas Wentworth Higginson, Edgar Allan Poe, and Oliver Wendell Holmes. But she also directed them to texts by and about African Americans and other people of color in notices such as the following: "The Chautauquan for October last contains an article entitled 'The Southern Negro Woman,' by Olive Ruth Jefferson"; "The American Citizen Company also publishes a book by

J. Robert Love, M.D., of Port Au Prince, Hayti, called 'The Indictment, the Testimony, and Verdict, or Proofs, that Romanism is not Christianity' "; "An Attractive Little Volume is that entitled 'Aunt Lindy.' Its author is Victoria Earle, the *nom de plume* assumed by Mrs. Wm. E. Matthews, the President of the Woman's Loyal Union of New York. . . . The heroine is a typical woman of the negro [*sic*] race, whose heart is warm, whose hand is skillful and whose life is devoted to the service of her Maker"; and " 'The Work of Afro-American Woman' is a daintily bound volume whose author is Mrs. N. F. Mossell . . . Mrs. Mossell's commendable object in writing this book was to do for the women of her own race what had already been done for other women more favorably circumstanced."[82] The texts to which these entries refer would have been disparaged in mainstream literary conversation, first because of their authorship and subject matter, but also because in many cases they are not representative of genres traditionally recognized as literary. Gould's recommendation of them despite this is indicative of the ways in which clubwomen took into consideration their own needs and their own definitions of literary value when selecting their reading. It is implausible, for instance, that Mossell's *The Work of Afro-American Woman* would have been deemed important reading by established literary standards of the time; in the eyes of black women, however, this text was invaluable. Its relevance for clubwomen lay not only in the subject of Mossell's study, which, in outlining the important contributions made by black women, responded to the imperative identified by Victoria Earle Matthews, who insisted that the "lives and records" of black Americans must be "zealously guarded for the future use of our children" (Matthews, 179–80). The very fact of Mossell's authorship also served as its own assertion that black women could be major contributors to cultural production.

Gould's review of *The Work of Afro-American Woman* is especially notable because it advances a very different definition of culture and literary value than that articulated by Charlotte Hawkins Brown. In keeping with Brown's assessment, Gould's comments on Mossell's text imply that she recognized and appreciated that literature could have a transformative value for black women. Whereas for Brown the value of literature was that by associating with it black women would merit the approval of whites, Gould was more concerned with the ways that literature would help prepare African Americans to more fully address their racially and socially defined concerns. Her praise of the book and its author emphasizes this. "The plan of the book is quite comprehensive," Gould wrote, "containing reference [to the] work of our women in whatever lines in which they have achieved success, and is interspersed with interesting personal notes." Of Mossell's accomplishment Gould noted: "She has gathered together much valuable information and presents it to her readers in a clear, bright and entertaining manner, and no one can read the little volume without feeling a deeper interest in the progress of his race, and gaining much inspiration for nobler and better work in the future."[83] This last comment is perhaps the most revealing, as it clarifies Gould's understanding of literary value and her wish to expand the definition of culture to which black women adhered. While the writing of Tennyson, Kipling, or Shakespeare maintained a certain value for black women, from Mossell's text they gained information about their own people, which would in turn help them to become more active agents on behalf of the race.

This definition of literary value ensured that black women who tried their hand at authorship at the turn of the century would find an audience for their writing in the membership of African American women's clubs. Avid readers of the publications of their sisters, clubwomen also took the lead in promoting and distributing their work among one another and in their communities. A listing on the back cover of the program at the Conference of Colored Women in 1895 informed those delegates who attended of the most recent publications by black women, copies of which could be found "on the literature table in the reception room." In all, ten titles were included, ranging from Anna Julia Cooper's *A Voice From the South* and Mossell's *The Work of Afro-American Woman* to Mrs. A. A. Casneau's "Guide to Artistic Dress Cutting and Making" and Miss Rachel Washington's "A Guide to the Study of Harmony."[84] Among the novels that Victoria Earle Matthews recommended to her audience during her address at the convention was Frances E. W. Harper's *Iola Leroy*. In 1899 Pauline Hopkins presented her novel *Contending Forces* to the membership of the Woman's Era Club where it met with "instant success." Hopkins's indication that she would be "glad to give readings before women's clubs in any section of the country" suggests that she imagined African American clubwomen as a primary audience for her work. This impression is reinforced by the fact that, when published in 1900, the book was marketed both by and to black clubwomen. Solicited as agents by the publisher, Boston's Colored Co-Operative Publishing Company, they were promised a "liberal commission."[85] Clubwomen also served as local agents for Ida B. Wells-Barnett's *A Red Record*, which was reviewed in the *Woman's Era*.[86]

This rehearsal of African American authors and texts should not obscure the very real anxieties black clubwomen felt about the difficulty of knowing what to read. As they encountered recommendations for texts by Harper, Hopkins, and other African American writers that affirmed the value of their texts, they were also reminded of the importance of reading "real" literature, the definition of which did not include works by African Americans. Warnings about the dangers of "bad books" and, more to the point, about the imperative of choosing wisely lay at the base of public statements about reading. "The moment we enter the world of books that moment a great *personal* responsibility rests upon us," wrote Sarah E. Tanner, principal of New Jersey's Bordentown Industrial School, in an essay on reading written for inclusion in the *Woman's Era*. "Not only is it necessary to acquire the habit of reading, but also the habit of selecting carefully what we read . . . This in itself will greatly develop our intellectual tendency, and then we will learn to appreciate the good and the beautiful." Tanner's advice was succinct: "To gather information read histories, biographies and travels. Read the best novels and romances, authors like Sir Walter Scott, George Eliot, Thackeray, Dickens and Hawthorne. Do not read about authors and imagine you have read the authors themselves, but with great care *study* the masters of the art of literature, authors like Milton, Dante, Shakespeare, Bacon, Goëthe, Cervantes, Schiller, and others."[87] Even Gould, whose perspectives on what clubwomen should read were much more inclusive than Tanner's, acknowledged that the purpose of her column was to offer guidance to clubwomen in the selection of their reading. "It is not only necessary to know what to read, but it is also necessary to know what not to read," she wrote in her first column.[88] Leslie Wilmot, who regularly contributed a column to the *Woman's Era* called "Chats With Girls," also acknowledged the difficulty of knowing what to read and encouraged young people to steer clear of what she called "bad books" by applying Emerson's criteria of selection. "The importance of reading the best books is self-evident," she wrote. "Perhaps Emerson's three rules may aid us in selecting the best. First. 'Never read any but famed books. Second. Never read a book which is not a year old. Third. Never read anything you don't like.' "[89]

These assertions of cultural authority are important, for through them we are reminded that one component of the black women's club movement was about some black women regulating the lives and activities of others. Leaders of and spokeswomen for the black women's club movement were predominantly middle class, which, as historian Deborah Gray White argues, was associated more firmly at the turn of the century with " 'style of life' than with gross economic income."[90] As the motto of the black women's club movement, "Lifting As We Climb," implies, these middle-class women took it upon themselves to educate their poorer sisters in the values and the behavior associated with middle-class respectability. The context of club life provided an ideal network through which middle-class black women communicated and thus reinforced the standards they believed that black women of lower classes and social positions should adopt. In fact, by highlighting the difficulty of selecting books and the dangers of not knowing what to read, leaders of the club movement demonstrated their own apparent superiority in matters cultural, strictly regulating the kinds of reading and types of literary activities in which club members engaged while reinforcing simultaneously the insecurities of some clubwomen and their own authority. Ironically, one effect of this was the reproduction of the very hierarchy of culture that classified all African Americans and their literary contributions as outside the ranks of "real" culture. As White cogently argues, in this and other instances clubwomen proved themselves to be "allied, not united"; race and gender affinity insisted that they work together, but not without vivid reminders that some would lead, and some would follow.[91]

As we have seen, leaders of the club movement who simultaneously adhered to and resisted traditional versions of culture also struggled to know whose "authority" to follow: at times, their confidence in their own flagged, leaving visible insecurities. To negotiate these anxieties, black women found ways of connecting authors of their own race—whose works would hardly be considered "famed" by traditional literary standards—and those confirmed figures of "real" literature with whom they wished to be associated. Their promotion of African American poet Paul Laurence Dunbar provides a prime example of their use of the endorsement of an established white author, in this case William Dean Howells, to "authenticate" the writing of an African American. "Paul Laurence Dunbar is recognized as a true poet by the first critics of America and his little volume, 'Majors and Minors' will be welcomed as a contribution to real literature," reads a brief announcement in the *Woman's Era*. "There is hardly a recent circumstance that means more to the race than this. As Mr. Howells says it is probably through the arts that nations are to be brought together and hostilities and prejudices to disappear."[92] In part, it is what "Mr. Howells says" that gives this writer of this review, and the clubwomen who read it, the confidence to call Dunbar a "true" poet and associate him with "real" literature. Howells's own connection with "real literature" had been bolstered by Medora Gould in an 1895 column: his work "is of priceless value," she had written. "He has the ear of all that is best and most cultured in this republic."[93] But while Howells's endorsement of Dunbar's work is one reason for clubwomen's praise of Dunbar, his appreciation for Dunbar as "a poet of undisputed talent" also forced clubwomen to consider the absurdity of literary standards that would exclude a man's work from the ranks of "real" literature simply because of his "pure African blood." The pride and confidence with which this writer offered her own assessment of Dunbar's poems as "elegant in construction, and ringing and musical in every line" suggests that Howells's authenticating function began a crucial process of literary reevaluation.[94]

Given their attention to texts associated with the genteel tradition, the extent to which clubwomen embraced Dunbar's so-called dialect poems is also striking. Praising these poems in particular as "remarkable . . . masterpieces of their kind," the editors of the *Woman's Era* reprinted Dunbar's "When De Co'n Pone's Hot" in the fall of 1896.[95] Their validation and embrace of these poems must be seen in the context of the larger literary and political debate in the black community and in black women's clubs at the turn of the century over what Zora Neale Hurston would later term "Negro Characteristics." In 1894 these editorial comments were included in the pages of the *Woman's Era*:

There are those who firmly believe that the sooner the colored man loses and forgets his characteristics, the better it be for himself and other Americans. In a lecture delivered in Boston some time ago, George W. Cable advised the colored people to make all haste to drop those marks distinctly negroid, to strive to write like a white man, dress like a white man, and talk like one, and so hasten on the day when they will be distinguished only as "Americans." Others believe just as firmly that the best good of the race is served by preserving all characteristics that are worth preserving, that we have attributes of mind and characteristics of expression that might rather be copied by the other race rather than dropped by us.

This editorial's conclusion, that "it can but help to dignify the race to preserve its anecdotes and songs," is in keeping with clubwomen's celebration of Dunbar's poetry.[96] His dialect poems are particularly distant from the "high" literary style of Shakespeare or Milton (or for that matter, Howells), and yet clubwomen's appreciation for the literary value of his work remained strong. It inspired black clubwomen to believe with confidence that "more poets, more artists, more musicians [would] develop among [African Americans] in time, and the world [would] be forced to acknowledge them and the people from whom they spring."[97]

In part, the concern with guiding readers toward appropriate literary selection echoed in the comments of Tanner, Gould, and Wilmot had as much to do with gendered expectations about women readers that solidified as the nineteenth century drew to a close as it did with racial projections that designated black women incapable of the sophisticated thought required for serious intellectual inquiry. As Andreas Huyssen has noted, the "political, psychological, and aesthetic discourse around the turn of the century consistently and obsessively genders mass culture and the masses as feminine, while high culture, whether traditional or modern, remains the privileged realm of male activities."[98] Anything that was not high culture became associated with mass culture, and thus both feminine and inferior. Inherent in this formulation was a discourse that articulated widely held assumptions about women as readers, the most predominant of which was the expectation that their reading lacked integrity.

Gould's acknowledgment in her columns of a "lack of knowledge among women" that must be remedied were they to be taken seriously is only one example that suggests that she, to some extent, had internalized the gendered understanding of a woman's reading that was dominant at the turn of the century. "The average woman is content to read the sensational news, the fashion, and the society columns," she wrote, "and pass over the more solid material as uninteresting."[99] One way black clubwomen struggled against this presumption about women readers was by heeding advice such as that advanced by Sarah E. Tanner and planning courses of study that focused on those "solid" authors widely associated with the traditionally male realm of high culture and its institutions. But they also spent considerable time in the context of their reading and literary discussions questioning the absolute judgment of others and asserting the validity of those literary genres with which women were disparagingly associated. In response to widespread criticism about women's reading of "light novels," for instance, Gould spoke in their defense in one of her columns. "Although the reading of light novels may be a frivolous waste of time, and if carried to excess positively harmful," she began, "a wholesome light story is both refreshing and restful, especially to those whose reading is in the line of study." One aspect of a woman's reading, she insisted, must focus on the pleasure derived from reading a good book; a "light novel" could provide this sort of entertainment and diversion because it "paints a picture that quickly fades into indistinctness, but leaves behind a pleasant impression." Gould recommended that "a few light novels wisely interposed between serious study, break the current of habitual thought and invite a return to more normal and less strained conditions of the mind. They who can take the novel of the day for what it is worth and make the right use of it, have learned that the mind needs recreation as truly as the body needs exercise." Her conclusion—that the reading of so-called light novels is "a good habit that can very easily become a bad one"—clearly articulates the importance of intellectual rigor and the danger of excessive "light reading"; but it also suggests that women must make their own decisions about when and under what circumstances this sort of reading is constructive.[100]

Inherent in Gould's reassessment of "light reading" is a radical understanding that women—including black women—played a significant role in thinking about literary culture and determining literary merit. In part this was by virtue of their being the primary consumers of literary texts, especially novels. "It is we women who are responsible for the present trend in literature," she asserted in September 1894, "for it is the women who do the novel reading."[101] In keeping with the authority inherent in this perspective, Gould used her column to keep black women abreast of the work of literary women who would have been entirely excluded from the traditional ranks of high culture. These included a host of older female writers Gould regarded as worthy of greater attention such as E.D.E.N Southworth, as well as "new" writers such as Mary E. Wilkins, Agnes Repplier, and Sarah Grand. Black clubwomen's attention to Grand's work is especially noteworthy, for it illustrates that they read with discriminating and critical eyes. According to Anne Ruggles Gere, Grand's 1893 novel *Heavenly Twins* was widely read by clubwomen in every social location. Gere points to the radical content of the novel, which addresses issues like the "unequal education of men and women, the double sexual standard, and the burdens and depression marriage brings to women."[102] Gould's comments on the novel in her column imply that, although black women were drawn to the subject of *Heavenly Twins*, they were not impressed with the novel itself. Gould first wrote of Grand in July 1894, describing her to readers as "a very womanly woman" who "holds her opinions with a man-like firmness." Revisiting the subject of Grand and her novel two months later, Gould's comments appear to be in response to critical evaluations of *Heavenly Twins*. "Those who have read Sarah Grand's 'Heavenly Twins' and, aside from the high purpose of the story, found it uninteresting, will find the author at her best in 'Our Manifold Natures,' a collection of short stories which were written previous to the production of her long story."[103] One thing that Gould reveals here is an appreciation for the many levels on which the novel might be appreciated. Although black readers may have found the text interesting from the perspective of its insistence that women adopt new roles for themselves or because it suggested the importance of uncovering topics of conversation that deserved open discussion, their assessment of it as "uninteresting" may have been a reflection of their judgment of the book's aesthetic appeal.

Gould's comment suggests that she encouraged black women to read critically and to openly voice their perspectives on and interpretations of literature; she illustrated that this would, in turn, refine their ability to think critically about and succinctly voice their opinions of the world in which they lived. In June 1894 she published the remarks of one female reader who illustrated this connection. The reader noted that "throughout all fiction, aside from five ideal characters of Shakespeare, there is not a mother who is an admirable character." This reader blamed the omission of positive maternal figures on women themselves, who neither sought nor looked to themselves to create these models. "Content with too low a standard," women "did not claim the culture that men looked upon as their exclusive right." Her reading was instrumental in convincing this clubwoman that women must take responsibility for creating more accurate representations of themselves. "The women of the new school," she wrote, must "hold a different view of life." They must consider it the "duty of the wife and mother to keep in touch with the world about her, and to represent the highest culture attainable."[104] In this way, she advocated, women could replace inaccurate and inadequate literary representations of women and mothers with portraits they themselves created. These comments offer some sense of the way that women used their reading to think broadly about literary representation and give insight into the kinds of critical discussions that took place in the context of women's clubs.

By way of concluding this discussion of black women's reading in the context of the club movement, I wish to make two final points. First, as the content of their reading stretched the boundaries of traditional definitions of literary value, their approach to reading and to the study of authors and texts contradicted traditional literary methods. Although clubwomen often called their literary meetings "classes," their literary practices suggest the extent to which their approach to texts was radically different from those found in turn-of-the-century academic settings.[105] Some clubs followed a model established in academic classrooms; but women's clubs generally eschewed the practices and terms of literary study associated with the academy. For instance, the culture of reading cultivated by black women's clubs deemphasized one authoritative perspective on literary texts; instead, it encouraged women to determine for themselves the importance of various aspects of the texts they read. When reading Scott's *Ivanhoe*, for instance, members of the Woman's Era were given "a set of questions on the novel . . . to which answers were to be formed" in advance of the meeting at which the novel was discussed. Members understood that answers were to be determined "according to one's opinion after careful reading." Both the questions and the various responses were discussed at the meeting. These questions—for instance, "In an historical novel what should the novelist reject and what reproduce?"; "What is the artistic effect of the introduction and notes?"; and "Point out the chief elements of contrast between the characters of Richard and John, Ivanhoe and Athelstane, the Jolly Hermit and the Cistercian Monk, Rebecca and Rowena"—were sufficiently open-ended to insist that there were no "right" answers. Rather, the questions and the format of the meeting were designed to emphasize the importance of careful reading, of individual interpretation, and of "being able to form and hold one's own opinion."[106] Accounts of literary discussions at club meetings insist that differing opinions were embraced. In a study of Nathaniel Hawthorne's *The Scarlet Letter*, for example, club members discovered that they "had various opinions on its merits." A report on the meetings indicated contrasting critical appreciation of the novel. "One girl could see no reason why it should be classed among the great novels. She thought it, morbid and dull. . . . Another girl could find no words to equal her admiration for this really fine book and read extract after extract of the best passages." Neither perspective on the novel was disparaged by the membership and the meeting was not competitive or combative. On the contrary, although the members had different impressions of the novel, they were able in their discussion of it to find common ground. After hearing a variety of papers that considered various aspects of the novel and its author, a discussion of the novel's setting propelled club members into conversation on communities in general, at the conclusion of which they "decided to devote some time to searching for information on that subject."[107]

This club's study of community sprang from a conversation about the community of Brook Farm to which Hawthorne refers; that their interests and the conversation evolved out of material uncovered in their reading is a typical pattern manifest in records of black women's clubs at the turn of the century. Their interest in community probably had more to do with the community service projects they had planned than any abstract sense of scholarly discipline or rigor. The flexibility this suggests is characteristic of the literary work of black women's clubs. So too is the great variety of ways that black women interacted with their reading, and this is the final point that I wish to make.

Among the many fascinating ways that black clubwomen interacted with reading and made the literary texts they studied their own was to animate them with their own voices and bodies. In transforming texts into living performances of all kinds, they brought the texts to life. Many clubs turned each literary meeting into a performance of sorts. The Tuskegee Woman's Club, for instance, described an "evening with 'Mr. Rudyard Kipling'" in this way: "As the roll was called, each member responded with an appropriate quotation. The music, which was sung, was also the word of Kipling. A sketch of the life of Kipling was well rendered by Mrs. E. J. Scott. The other members recited different poems from the great author."[108] This description is of an intimate meeting at which only clubmembers were present; but black women designed similar and more elaborate performances to which members of the larger community were invited. At the completion of their study of Longfellow, members of Charleston, West Virginia's Charleston Women's Improvement League hosted a "Longfellow evening," to which the public was invited. That the evening was held at one of the members' houses suggests something of its informal atmosphere; yet the members planned and performed a formal program that included a variety of different kinds of interactions with Longfellow's writing. The "program . . . rendered" included "recitations and music [that] were taken from that author, an essay giving the conditions under which certain poems were written and an essay with a description of his life."[109] Such an evening, which addressed Longfellow's literary contributions through music, recitations, essays, and dramatic readings of quotations, would have demanded the involvement of the entire membership of the Charleston Women's Improvement League. This performance serves as a reminder that black women's clubwork offered a means of making literature and culture accessible, not only for themselves but for African American communities generally.

So successful were such public performances at bringing literature into the community that clubwomen adopted similar methods to make the work of black authors more widely known and appreciated. Although Atlanta's Chautauqua Circle included in their program of study works by Milton, John Ruskin, and Sir Walter Scott, they chose to present their work on African American authors when they hosted their first reception for their husbands. The record of this public performance indicates that "The Negro in Literature and Art was a master production by Mrs. Watson. She showed unlimited research. . . . Mrs. Ross read an excellent paper on Gems from Negro writers. She quoted some of their choice selections."[110] Such presentation before a limited and theoretically sympathetic audience laid the groundwork for clubwomen to appreciate the potential impact of public performances before wider and more varied audiences. Clubwoman Mary Church Terrell's explanation of why she wrote the Phillis Wheatley Pageant-Play suggests her understanding that, for some audiences, the performance of literary texts and the animation of literary lives would contribute to the prominence of notable African Americans more effectively than print alone. Terrell's pageant-play was written to be performed by African American schoolchildren who, she was aware, learned a great deal about the achievements of the nation's white heroes but "know comparatively little about the creditable things which their African forebears have done."[111] In telling the story of the eighteenth-century African poet Phillis Wheatley and the reception of her poetry, Terrell's production communicated that Wheatley was such a forbearer, embedded in the nation's literary tradition and worthy of the pride and respect of contemporary schoolchildren.

"WE MUST GO OUT INTO THE NATION AND CHANGE IT"

Terrell's concern for making literature, including literary figures and texts about members of her own race, accessible to African Americans of different ages and educational levels is representative of black clubwomen's commitment to what I will call public literacy. In transforming themselves into literary activists at the turn of the century, these women sought to communicate to wider and wider audiences the power of literature and its centrality to the future of the race. They believed that printed texts of all sorts had the capacity to serve the needs of the black community in a way that no other medium could. The work of the Woman's Loyal Union is exemplary of the kind of literary activism that captured the imagination of black clubwomen. As they gathered information about the needs of their communities through research projects and club papers, they put this information into print as a way to reach as wide an audience as possible. A club report issued in the summer of 1895 summarizes their activities. "We are now turning our time and attention to the circulation of printed matter in the form of leaflets, which have been suggested to us by the answers contained in the replies to the circular letters. We have already printed for distribution, at a small price within the reach of all, leaflets addressed to 'Parents and Guardians,' and will soon have another, 'The Sanctity of Home,' to be followed by others—all of which are written by members of our Association. In this way we hope to reach the masses, and do more effectual good than spoken words to the few."[112]

By relying on print to help amplify their voices, clubwomen trusted that textual means of representing themselves and sharing these representations with others would lead to the improvement of the quality of their lives and the lives of others of their race. Another manifestation of their literary activism and their commitment to public literacy can be seen in the clubs' dedication to establishing physical institutions such as libraries and reading rooms that would encourage and sustain their own literary interests and that of their communities. Again, the efforts of the Woman's Loyal Union in this area are representative. "The work claiming the interest of the association at present," reported H. Cordelia Ray on behalf of the Woman's Loyal Union in 1896, "is the establishment of a library and reading-room, where may be gathered, primarily, works written by colored authors, or those that discuss the race question." Although these texts were their principal interest, they planned that the "scope of the library . . . [would] be broad, as it is expected to include in time all works of standard value in literature."[113] Boston's Woman's Era Club also set their sights on the distribution of literature, establishing a "stationery table" at the New England Hospital for Women and Children. Offerings at the table included "a collection of the best books and photographs of colored authors," including works by Frederick Douglass, W. E. B. Du Bois, Paul Laurence Dunbar, Archibald Grimké, and William Wells Brown. Included with this list of distinguished male writers was the work of three black women: Alice Ruth Moore, Rachel Washington, and A. A. Casneau.[114] Members of the Tuskegee Woman's Club hosted "book receptions" and other literary events "for the purpose of getting good books for the library of the Tuskegee Normal and Industrial School."[115]

In the last years of the nineteenth century and well into the twentieth century, these efforts by black clubwomen to promote public literacy made a tremendous impact in black communities throughout the nation. Whereas the black women's club movement had gotten its start and was driven in the early years by the leadership of women in northern cities like New York and Boston, black women in other locales, particularly in the South, took up the challenge of establishing literary culture and forming libraries to serve their communities in great numbers. Judia C. Jackson's report on the activities of her women's club in Athens, Georgia, illustrates something of the ingenuity and personal sacrifice that was a component of their efforts. "A movement is on foot with the Literature Committee to establish a reading room by each member contributing his individual property, viz., magazines, papers, books, etc., also by soliciting aid of the same kind from friends who are circumstanced in this way." Her optimism about the project's success was evident in her vision of its future: "The members favor the project," she wrote, "and we mean to have this develop into a library."[116] Charleston, South Carolina's Phyllis [*sic*] Wheatley Literary and Social Club worked to establish a small library with limited resources in a similar way. According to their records, members compiled "a list of books on Negro Life or by Negro authors" and each member "drew a book which she was expected to purchase. By exchanging them, the club had at its disposal a wide range of interesting and informative material." Combined with a subscription to *Mentor* magazine, this reading material carried club members "far afield." One club member's description suggests the international focus of their reading: "South Africa, India, South America—all came within our mental vision. Chapters of Du Bois' Darkwater were reviewed at several meetings," and the "entire programme of one meeting was devoted to Africa's Contribution to World Civilization." The club also donated books to the local Y.W.C.A. and provided the Avery Institute, a school for African Americans with which many of the club's original members were affiliated, with a subscription to *Reader's Digest*.[117]

At the heart of their efforts was the importance of spreading knowledge about African American authors and their literary contributions. Clubwomen recognized that this knowledge was particularly valuable for black youth. The Ladies Auxilliary of Washington, D.C., chose as the focus of their literary study in the winter of 1897 "the lives of characters of our own race to whom only casual attention has been given; as for instance Sojourner Truth, Phyllis [*sic*] Wheatley, Crispus Attucks, Harriet Tubman, and others." "This is a matter which should commend itself to all," noted Josephine Bruce in her capacity as the club's president and spokeswoman, "but it is of especial importance to the rising generation that they should be familiar with the valorous lives and self-sacrificing deeds of those in their own ranks, so that in an interchange of views, a Douglass may be placed beside a Washington, a Harriet Tubman beside a Joan of Arc."[118] That they named their women's clubs again and again after past African American female literary figures like Phillis Wheatley and Sojourner Truth, as well as those literary luminaries of their own time like Frances E. W. Harper and Ida B. Wells-Barnett, serves to underscore the extent to which these figures captured their imagination and served to inspire them to excel in their own literary efforts. As they worked to uncover more information on these figures through their own literary work, they appreciated that among the most important beneficiaries of their efforts would be black girls. "This is the kind of work that makes our women ready for the opportunities that are opening for them," wrote clubwoman Dora Cole in reference to the literary work of what she called "an interesting and noteworthy institution," Philadelphia's Educational Club. "This is the 'Woman's Century,' it is said, and although colored women come in last in the American scheme of life, it behooves the girls of our race to equip themselves so as to act their parts worthily."[119]

Although black women's clubs made heroic strides toward equipping their membership and the youth of their community with the resources and critical skills they needed to fully participate in the world around them, Cole's observation that "colored women come in last in the American scheme of life" compels us to focus on some sobering facts about the women's club movement. For the most part, white women's organizations continued to resist forming alliances with black women, supporting instead a racist and patriarchal order that perpetuated discrimination against all black people. And in spite of the rise to relative visibility and prominence of a number of black female intellectuals like Frances E. W. Harper, Fannie Barrier Williams, Ida B. Wells-Barnett, Anna Julia Cooper, Victoria Earle Matthews, Josephine St. Pierre Ruffin, Pauline Hopkins, and Mary Church Terrell, African

American male intellectuals continued to undervalue the role of their female counterparts. That the literary and intellectual contributions of black women continued to be deemed inferior even by other African Americans is perhaps best exemplified by their categorical exclusion from the founding of the American Negro Academy in 1897. This intellectual community, fashioned as an "organization of Colored authors, scholars and artists" with the expressed intent of "raising the standard of intellectual endeavor among American Negroes," included in its membership such distinguished figures as Alexander Crummell, Francis Grimké, and W. E. B. Du Bois. From the beginning, these founders deliberately designed the American Negro Academy to be open only to "men of African descent."[120] Although the absolute exclusion of women was clearly communicated in the organization's constitution, one invited member felt so strongly about this policy that, on reviewing the document, he felt it necessary to reiterate his position as "decidedly opposed to the admission of women to membership." Inherent in his unsolicited rationale for their exclusion is evidence of his superficial knowledge and understanding of the intellectual work of African American women in the last decade of the nineteenth century. His stated belief that "literary matters and social matters do not mix" demonstrates how some men continued to devalue the literary work of black women because they continued to value a belief that literature was a man's realm and not the "proper" sphere of women's work.[121]

In addition to these external factors, it is also important to recognize the various other costs of club work at the turn of the century. In addition to the class and gender tensions addressed by Deborah Gray White in her study of the black women's club movement, it is crucial to note that at this time of such great literary activism, faced with the responsibility of creating literature and participating in forums that might encourage conversations around broad issues of gender and the reimagination of African Americans' role in society, black women were often frustrated by the nature of their literary interaction.[122] "It has been a bitter disappointment to me," wrote Mary Church Terrell in her 1940 autobiography, *A Colored Woman in a White World*, "that I did not succeed as a short story writer."[123] As president of the National Association of Colored Women from 1896 to 1901, and noted journalist and public speaker in the first decades of the twentieth century, Terrell achieved unsurpassed popularity. For all her apparent success,

however, Terrell's unfulfilled aspirations to be a writer of imaginative literature left her with the impression that there was no "literary atmosphere" during the very time when the greatest percentage
of educated African American women were involved with literature
through their clubwork. She found it impossible to focus on her own
literary aspirations because of her deep and utterly time-consuming
commitment "to assist in the thousand and one things which we try to
do to promote the welfare of the race."[124] Her sense of disappointment
in her literary achievements is especially poignant because she felt that
her artistic aspirations were very much a part of her political goals. For
many years, she wrote, she thought that "the Race Problem could be
solved more swiftly and more surely through the instrumentality of
the short story or novel than in any other way."[125] Her failure as a
short story or novel writer, she felt, was indicative of her limited
success as a political activist.

Terrell's personal correspondence and memoir leave an especially
detailed record of one writer's frustration with the public and political
demands placed upon the creativity of all African Americans, female
and male, by the social and political climate of the turn of the century.
The very diversity of their responsibilities made their literary lives all
the more difficult. She was only one of many would-be African American imaginative writers who gave voice to individual laments over the
lack of any strong role for imaginative literature by black writers in
the public arena in the late nineteenth- and early twentieth-century
United States. By speaking frankly about her literary disappointments, Terrell puts into perspective the limitations that resulted from
laying claim to a collective black public voice. "If I had lived in a
literary atmosphere, or if my time had not been so completely occupied with public work of many varieties, I might have gratified my
desire to 'tell the world' a few things I wanted it to know. I do not
regret the time and energy consumed serving others. I cannot help
wondering, however, whether I might not have succeeded as a short-
story writer, or a novelist, or an essayist, if the conditions under which
I lived had been more conducive to the kind of literary work I so
longed to do."[126] In spite of Terrell's repeated efforts to have her short
stories and other works of fiction published, she was met with constant rejection from publishers who advised her to address "The Race
Problem" through her public lectures and occasional essays rather

than through imaginative writing. Terrell recognized fiction as a vehicle capable of reporting, critiquing, and reflecting on the social and historical circumstances of black people in the United States. Overwhelmed by or uninterested in the potential political power of Terrell's fiction, however, publishers criticized and refused to print her creative works. Her archives are filled with rejection letters that echo the words of one publisher: "perhaps you are too intent on reforming this world than on creating an imaginary world of your own, after the artist's fashion."[127]

Inherent in this typical dismissive editorial response to Terrell's fiction are questions about the power of written expression and the relative effectiveness of different genres for the promotion of causes linked to the black race. Terrell's conviction that short stories and novels would act to promote conversations around and, eventually, introduce solutions to "The Race Problem" was due in part to her impression that these genres would reach those unlikely to attend lectures or read political treatises or pamphlets. She believed a "conspiracy of silence" existed on the part of the American press.[128] "Editors will accept anything which makes colored people appear ridiculous, criminal, or undesirable," Terrell reprimanded the editor of *Harper's Magazine*, "but they will reject anything which shows the obligations against which they are obliged to contend, the thousand and one humiliations to which they are subjected every minute in the day and the injustices of which they are the victims at the white man's hands."[129] Her own experience led her to believe that no editor would accept for publication literary materials that set forth the "conditions under which Colored people actually live today—their inability to secure employment, the assault and battery constantly committed upon their hearts, their sensibilities and their feelings."[130]

Terrell's desire was to create in fiction not only those major characters whose lives of impoverishment and exploitation challenged them to survive as individuals but also portraits of black Americans that would accurately represent the range of their backgrounds and social and occupational contexts. The sense of personal disappointment in her literary work that was communicated again and again to publishers in personal correspondence and exposed in her autobiography remained otherwise masked behind what was, by all appearances, a thriving literary career. In retrospect, however, Terrell's hidden frustration exposes the fact that although literary work introduced black women at the turn of the century to public voice and provided them with the means to greater political activism, it did not always give them the luxury of freely representing their own individual, artistic voices. Her autobiography reveals the bitterness that resulted from a lifetime of literary disappointments: "Nobody wants to know a colored woman's opinion about her own status or that of her group," she wrote. "When she dares to express it, no matter how mild or tactful it may be, it is called 'propaganda', or is labeled 'controversial'. Those two words have come to have a very ominous sound to me. I cannot escape them; they confront me everywhere I go."[131] The principal irony of Terrell's story is captured in the fact that, as a columnist for *The Woman's Era* in the last decade of the nineteenth century, she was able to freely and forcefully encourage black women to persevere in their literary pursuits through anecdotes that celebrated black women's efforts and their ability to become "masters" of language. At the same time, however, she herself was effectively silenced by political demands that kept her from fulfilling her true artistic desires.[132]

Terrell's suppression of her artistic aspirations in order to fulfill the more immediately pressing demands of political agitation that came with being, to quote the title of her autobiography, a "colored woman in a white world," is representative of the many challenges that faced the black women who ushered in the Woman's Era. By urging black women to form and participate in clubs and by advancing literary work as a political weapon, some leaders of the black women's club movement, like Mary Church Terrell, were themselves forced to forgo their own deeply felt need to be cultural workers in order to fulfill their appointed duty as political advocates. Others, like Anna Julia Cooper, struggled intensely through their work to negotiate the social expectations of popular images of "true womanhood" and the conventions of decorum that accompanied them, as well as assumptions about the separation of female and male domains and the limiting political discourse of manhood. Despite the significant achievements of the black women's club movement in the last decade of the nineteenth century, its leaders must also have been disheartened by the prospect of measuring "progress" that was slow in coming and often difficult to see at all. Well into the twentieth century, white men continued to abuse black women physically and sexually. For the most part, white women did not recognize that they shared with black women a common experience of oppression and remained hostile to the prospect of working with them or welcoming them into their clubs. And even as the women's club movement proved to be one of the most effective means of organizing and mobilizing black people, it continued to be underappreciated by black male leaders who continued to disparage black women's intellectual abilities.

These and other observations must, however, be contrasted with the measurable impact of the black women's club movement, not only in terms of its effect on the development of literary activism in the turn-of-the-century United States but also in the experiences of individual clubwomen who credit the transformation of their lives to their work as members of black women's clubs. These women worked effectively through their clubs to protest lynching, the convict lease system, and job discrimination, while demanding improvements in educational opportunities and the right to vote for all African Americans. Signs of the impact and the effectiveness of the black women's club movement are also embedded in the memoirs and personal recollections of clubwomen themselves, many of whom have documented in detail the extent to which their lives were transformed by their literary and political activity in black women's clubs. In her memoir *Lemon Swamp and Other Places*, for instance, Mamie Garvin Fields tells of Mary Church Terrell's visit to Charleston, South Carolina, where she spoke to the community's black women at the local A.M.E. Church. "I'll never forget the night she spoke," Fields wrote of Terrell's visit. "We have our own lives to lead, she told us. . . . We must care for ourselves and rear our families, like all women. But we have more to do than other women. . . . We must go out into the nation and change it. Above all, we must organize ourselves as Negro women and work together." At the end of her address Terrell challenged her audience to form clubs and work collectively to effect change in their community. According to Fields, the impact of this invitation to activism was monumental. "The women hardly knew what to do when Mrs. Terrell got through speaking. We felt so stirred up, nobody wanted to wait till morning to pick up our burden again. Everywhere you might look, there was something to do."[133]

Fields's memory of her reaction to Terrell's address is especially poignant in light of the ambivalence Terrell retrospectively expressed over the politically consuming life she led and its cost in terms of her unfulfilled aspirations to be a writer of imaginative literature. Taken together, Fields's recollections of her enthusiasm and Terrell's of her disappointment underscore that the Woman's Era had two, contradictory sides. While club work and literary activism must be celebrated for the ways in which it enabled black women to find the means to greater public voice and political power, we must also remember that this did not necessarily mean that they were able to fully and freely experiment with their own individual voices or pursue their personal aspirations. As political activists, they were able to make significant steps to improve the lives of black people and sustain black communities, but they were often forced to suppress their individual voices in order to present a unified and unifying narrative that would ameliorate and protect the collective experience of all African Americans. This contradiction epitomizes the conflicting claims that would continue to be made on the African American "literary woman" throughout the twentieth century: one, the fundamental human need to affirm the specificities of one's personal experience, however "typical" or "atypical," through reading and writing; the other, the no less compelling imperative to use literature to express solidarity with those whose lives and sufferings take similar forms from similar causes. The role of imaginative literature Terrell and others envisioned would be realized by the writers of the Harlem Renaissance, but these dual claims would only intensify as the social and political climate of the first decades of the twentieth century placed more and more demands on the literary endeavors of all African Americans, male and female.

5

Georgia Douglas Johnson and
the Saturday Nighters

In the previous chapters I have traced the development of African American literary societies from their beginnings in the nineteenth century, exploring how these societies worked to disseminate literacy and literary sensibility and functioned as forums for the creation of a democratic consciousness throughout the nineteenth and into the twentieth century. While the records of these earlier literary coalitions allowed me to consider the complex interplay between literary societies and the institutions that have historically supported them, such as the black press and political organizations like the National Association of Colored Women, these sources have not permitted me to focus on the specific ways that literary societies provided the catalyst for the personal, political, and artistic development of particular individuals. The story of the Saturday Nighters, a literary society formed in Washington, D.C., in the 1920s, allows me to do this.

The Saturday Nighters had not one but two beginnings. The literary society first began as an informal study group coordinated in 1921 by Jean Toomer, the author commonly credited with launching the Harlem Renaissance with the 1923 publication of *Cane*. Its more formal and lasting manifestation occurred under the leadership of Georgia Douglas Johnson who, throughout the 1920s, welcomed both well-known and unknown black writers into her Washington, D.C., home on Saturday evenings to read literature and discuss and critique their own work and that of their contemporaries. Examining how the Saturday Nighters met the quite different needs of its two founders will reveal how specific individuals were served by the literary societies in which they participated. In the years prior to the publication of *Cane*, Toomer was searching for a sense of literary and intellectual community and raising questions about racial identity. Like so many other black literary artists of the 1920s, Toomer struggled to find a community that would endorse and lend focus to his literary endeavors. His correspondence with Georgia Douglas Johnson in 1919 and 1920 illustrates his need for an intellectual context as well as an outlet for exchange that would allow him to confidently establish his place in the complex literary world of the 1920s. It was in light of these imperatives and conditions that the Saturday Nighters first began meeting.

The more formal beginning of the Saturday Nighters and the group's ultimate success can be attributed almost exclusively to the energy and magnetic personality of its leader, Georgia Douglas Johnson, who was herself a gifted and ambitious writer. From the living room of her S Street home in Northwest Washington, D.C., Johnson provided a spiritual and intellectual center for many of the most well-known Harlem Renaissance writers. Her house, which she referred to as "Half-way House," was just that; it served as a refuge from the interracial hostility that marked the post–World War I landscape, the heady chaos of New York City's Harlem, and the elaborate social and cultural traditions of "colored Washington." In part because of her age and family responsibilities, Georgia Douglas Johnson neither "aspire[d] to leave Washington for New York" nor felt "obliged to simply forget [her] artistic ambitions," as Constance MacLaughlin Green implies was true of all Washington, D.C., writers and intellectuals in the 1920s.[1] Rather, Johnson recognized that the artists, including herself, who through their work would give the Renaissance its color and shape needed the imaginative and intellectual environment she sustained in her home on Saturday evenings. The sanctuary she created there offered a rare, liberating combination of honest and open fellowship and rich intellectual exchange. For those interested in literature and committed to the craft of writing, Johnson provided the leadership necessary to foster an atmosphere that was both friendly and constructively critical; these were important elements frequently missing from a movement that alienated individuals and undermined talent as often as it nurtured it. In turn, Johnson's own literary ambitions and her creative energy were sustained by her interaction with those who gathered in her home on Saturday nights. In seeking out her company and in sharing with her their ideas and their unfinished manuscripts, these writers and intellectuals expanded her literary identity and enriched her work and career as a writer.

Traditionally, accounts of the acclaimed African American literary renaissance of the 1920s have linked the unprecedented outpouring of literary and artistic production by African Americans to New York City's Harlem, which, by the end of World War I, was well on its way to becoming what prominent writer and civil rights advocate James Weldon Johnson called "the greatest Negro city in the world."[2] Johnson's celebration of Harlem as the "intellectual [and] the cultural . . . center for Negroes in the United States" was included in *The New Negro*, Alain Locke's renowned anthology of the literary and artistic achievements of black Americans.[3] Published in 1925, *The New Negro* simultaneously documented and applauded black artists' newfound sense of confidence and purpose as expressed through their achievements in the arts. Scholarly assessments of the period have largely shared the celebratory tone of earlier representations, portraying the Harlem Renaissance as a time when, to quote Langston Hughes, "the Negro was in vogue."[4] An appreciation for the Saturday Nighters complements these representations and allows for a more nuanced understanding of this period in African American literary history. Rather than highlighting the public celebrations of Harlem in its heyday, or the acclaimed publications of the decade, an analysis of the Saturday Nighters provides insight into one of the most important of those informal institutions where the cultural productions of the Harlem Renaissance were first presented, supported, and made ready for public consumption.

"TO THROW A LITTLE FIRE IN THEIR HEARTS"

The story of Jean Toomer's early years as a struggling writer offers a necessary corrective to conventional notions of the accomplishments and popularity of black writers in the 1920s. Toomer was hardly overflowing with confidence in his own imminent success or latent talent;

on the contrary, by 1921 he was in dire need of the artistic support and intellectual energy a successful literary society might offer. After years of dislocation and distractions, he was trying to sustain a period of optimism and the creative energy brought on by a decision to return to Washington, D.C., where, in addition to helping his uncle, Walter Pinchback, run the Howard Theater, he was finally able to concentrate on his writing. Returning to Washington had its drawbacks, the most daunting of which was that by doing so Toomer would be returning to the world of his grandfather, the prominent Reconstruction lieutenant governor of Louisiana and former United States senator, P. B. S. Pinchback. Toomer's relationship with his family was strained, and his determination to maintain physical distance from Washington, D.C., can be seen in the series of random educational pursuits that required him to relocate from Madison, Wisconsin, to Chicago to New York City within a relatively short period of time. Although much of his grandfather's considerable wealth had been squandered through his weakness for gambling, evidence suggests that Toomer's family offered him some albeit limited financial assistance; he received from them little else in the way of support, however, and Toomer felt especially stifled by the authority embodied in his grandfather, who he felt had "never taken art seriously, and me, as a writer and musician still less seriously."[5]

Toomer's time in New York had proved financially difficult, and although returning to Washington was not ideal, he considered it an option that would allow him the most freedom to write. In a letter dated 4 June 1920, written to Georgia Douglas Johnson just before his departure from New York, Toomer made clear the impossibility of relying on his grandfather as a source of significant financial support: "for not only has he done much for me—it would greatly inconvenience him to do more."[6] Nevertheless, his experience in New York had been emotionally exhausting and intellectually deadening, and returning to Washington would reduce the expenses that were making a career as a writer seem virtually impossible. Earlier efforts to secure a sponsor had failed. Toomer told Johnson that he had appealed to "a man of means who was supposed to be kindly disposed toward men of talent," but this man was, in the end, unwilling to sponsor him. "I found," Toomer reported of this attempt to seek patronage, "that what little I have done and my personality were not sufficient to convince him that a loan of $5000 would be a good investment." Both Toomer's temperament and his timing were probably to blame for his failure to interest a sponsor. Whereas by the mid-1920s patronage agreements between black authors and wealthy white art lovers were commonplace, his relatively early appeals appeared too risky to be attractive. "What he seemingly desires," Toomer said of one potential patron, "is that a man already have achieved some recognition from critics and the public. He is unwilling to trust his own judgement in the matter."[7]

For his own part, Toomer was unwilling to sacrifice his aesthetic sensibility or his exclusive authority over his work in order to meet the demands of someone else. As an artist, his priority was satisfying himself. Toomer would not disguise this commitment even to secure the promise of financial backing. "I made it plain to him that a man of my taste and judgement could not possibly give the public anything until a certain proficiency in technic [*sic*] had been acquired, and that it was in order to secure this technic, for this and no other reason, that I desired and needed the money," he told Johnson. Toomer's summary of the affair suggests his disdain for the mixing of business and art: "His business sense," he wrote to Johnson, "seems to have dominated whatever art impulses he may have had."[8]

Without the support of a wealthy patron, returning to Washington and to the watchful and usually critical eye of his grandfather presented itself to Toomer as less distasteful than the alternative—holding down a job. This was a life he tried and did not like, primarily because it gave him no time to write. In a brief postcard sent to Johnson at Christmas 1919, Toomer gave his impression of life as a member of the working class: "Most of my energies have gone into work, work at the shipyards," he wrote. "Now, I know their life, so I've quit. I'll have more time to write."[9] Toomer found daily employment, particularly manual labor of the sort he was exposed to as a welder in a New Jersey shipyard, to be "dull and stupid"; under these tedious conditions, the "desire to express [oneself] and to live a great full life . . . fretted itself away in inconsequential action."[10] Returning to that world was unthinkable: "It is with somewhat of a shudder," he wrote to Johnson, "that I contemplate dulling the fine sensibilities and eagerness that now is mine by working in some ill-paid employment."[11]

Although self-conscious about his youth (Toomer described himself early in 1920 as an "immature youngster"), he was at the same time acutely aware of his artistic potential and driven to cultivate the talents he possessed.[12] His assessments of himself reflect his sharpening understanding of the process involved in becoming an artist. Although he believed himself capable of literary greatness, he recognized the distance he had to go before he would achieve his full potential. "It will be some years before Jean Toomer the thinker, the feeler, the man in love with life in toto, passions, vices, sorrows, despairs—all of life, will be able to put half of what is in him on the cool surface of a white sheet of paper," he wrote of himself in January 1920. "As yet I am far from the finished artist. But even now I have opinions, ideas, ideals, which I'll tell, straight from the shoulder, to anyone who asks for them."[13]

This passionate self-assessment of Jean Toomer the artist was prompted by a disappointing encounter with W. E. B. Du Bois in which Du Bois failed to remember Toomer and, in Toomer's opinion, to express adequate enthusiasm for his work. "Yesterday I called Dubois [*sic*]," Toomer wrote to Georgia Douglas Johnson in January 1920. "At first he didn't even remember me, even after mentioning the fact that you and he had talked of me. In fact, it wasn't until I chanced to mention my hike up here, that the light burst through—or rather filtered through—it wasn't a very strong light." Although Du Bois had "ended [their conversation] by saying that if [Toomer] would send some of [his] stuff to the office he would be glad to look it over," Toomer's initial reaction was lasting. "Now I really had expected more," Toomer lamented, acknowledging that Du Bois's response to him had been typical, rather than extraordinary. "Any editor would have said as much as that," Toomer admitted. "Anyone with an ounce of curiosity (literary or otherwise) in his make up would rather like to look over new material." Toomer had assumed that Du Bois would be more interested in his writing, and Du Bois's failure to take an interest in him personally was quite a blow. "I had thought he wanted to get in touch with me, even possibly know me," Toomer said. "Does he expect to do so by looking at my writings?"[14]

As Toomer's experience with Du Bois illustrates, breaking into the literary world and being accepted by its old guard was no easy feat for a young black writer, even one with such obvious talents as Jean Toomer. In Du Bois, Toomer saw not simply a literary insider; having given up on the idea of securing a patronage agreement, Toomer's hope that Du Bois would want to "know him" suggests his hope that Du Bois would serve as a role model, a literary mentor.[15] The disappointment of that encounter epitomized all of the other disappointments Toomer had experienced in his efforts to develop his literary talents, bruising his pride and increasing his feelings of isolation both as an individual and as an artist. So acute was his sense of detachment from the literary world that even the romantic notion of the "creative poverty" of the artist was lost on him. "I have tested for myself the salutary effects of comparative poverty and privation," he told Johnson in June 1920. "I now say, for myself at least, that such things only dwarf the soul, weaken the body, dull the mind and prohibit fruitful activity."[16]

Toomer's tremendous sense of isolation and displacement in the years preceding his return to Washington, D.C., culminated in a nervous breakdown. Physically, he recovered by retreating for a time to a cabin in the Catskills; mentally, the treatment he required could only be found in the company of others. Soon after returning to New York City, he attended a literary gathering that in retrospect he considered to be a pivotal event in his development as a writer. "Here was the first gathering of people I had ever seen in my life—people who were of my own kind," he wrote of this experience. "It was simply a matter of learning to speak their language."[17] Toomer's letters to Johnson during the first six months of 1920 suggest that he felt the beginnings of an important transformation taking place within himself. "What a growth may take place within a man in a few short months," he wrote to Johnson in June 1920. "As I look back on last year it seems as if my soul was then in poverty. My responses to the great and the beautiful are now so keen and poignant that the feeble sensitivity of my former self seems as but [a] faint current in a body half alive." Toomer had been, he wrote, "instinctively withdrawn into myself." Now, at the beginning of the summer of 1920, he felt himself a new man, once more in control of the world around him and more confident of his abilities and objectives. "It . . . is indicative of my approaching strength and maturity that whereas formerly the vital but divergent activities of [New York City] did but pull me in their wake and leave me dizzy and bewildered, I now can somewhat master them and turn them to my own purposes," he wrote optimistically to Johnson. He closed his letter to her with the following prediction: "I really feel as if my future and whatever possibilities may lie therein will be determined by what strides I make in the next few years. Now surely it is my impressionable period, and my formative one."[18]

A number of things seem to have crystallized for Toomer in 1920, in terms of both his understanding of his needs as a fledgling writer and his tentative recognition of how he might begin to fulfill those needs. While Toomer recognized his own literary abilities, he was also growing to appreciate the fact that becoming a writer took more than raw talent; it also required the passage of time and a nurturing process that could occur neither overnight nor in isolation. Toomer's restless wandering from city to city and his experimentation with different academic and professional environments had prevented him from settling into the literary apprenticeship that was a necessary part of every writer's development. Furthermore, Toomer's letters to Johnson suggest his realization that without the support of his family, the financial backing of a wealthy patron, a mentoring relationship with an experienced writer like Du Bois, and regular contact with others who shared his interests and his dedication to the literary life, he lacked the very support systems that were crucial to his literary preparation. What Toomer saw, however fleetingly, at the literary gathering he attended in New York was the value of literary community; kindred spirits or, in his words, "people who were of my kind" existed in the literary world, and they could support him and help him develop as a writer. This realization validated his own literary and intellectual pursuits and solidified his determination to surround himself with others who shared his interests and goals. Once settled in Washington, D.C., he took it upon himself to form a coalition of writers and intellectuals who would provide him with the networks of support and intellectual stimulation that were essential to his artistic development.

In January 1921 Toomer enthusiastically contacted Howard University professor and literary luminary Alain Locke to inform him of the development and progress of his new literary society. "I have managed to hold two meetings of a group . . . whose central purpose is an historical study of slavery and the Negro, emphasizing the great economic and cultural forces which have largely determined them. The aim is twofold," Toomer explained, "first, to arrive at a sound and just criticism of the actual place and condition of the mixed-blood group in this country, and, second, to formulate an ideal that will be both workable and inclusive." "The first group came together a week ago Wednesday," Toomer reported. "I outlined the purpose of the meetings, and tried my best to throw a little fire in their hearts. Also gave out a few books for study and report. Last night [at the group's second meeting] Miss Scott had prepared 'An Historical Sketch of Slavery' by T. R. R. Cobb, while Henry Kennedy covered, and really in a fine way, the same subject dug mostly out of Wells. This coming Wednesday I shall take up 'Twenty Years of an African Slaves [*sic*].' "[19]

Although Toomer recognized that their first two gatherings represented only modest beginnings, his ambitions for the group were high. "The meetings should at least provide material for conversation other than the commonplace and trivial," he told Locke. In addition to discussions around proposed historical and cultural topics, the group would also share and critique their own creative work: "As a natural outgrowth of [the discussion] should come the reading of original efforts." Toomer included in his letter to Locke a partial list of those who had participated in the inaugural meetings of Toomer's group; it included "Mary Burrill, Georgia Johnson, Miss Scott (of Howard), Mary Craft, E. C. Williams and Henry Kennedy." His invitation to Locke to attend a meeting of the literary society reveals a certain degree of self-consciousness but also Toomer's sense of the group's importance and potential. "The subjects may be a trifle elementary for you," Toomer began, "but now that we seem to be underway, I certainly would like to have you join us—whenever the time will permit."[20]

This scant description of this group's activities leaves little concrete evidence of their particular focus or of the substance of their discussions. Nevertheless, given Toomer's own family background, his questions about racial definition, and his struggle to find a meaningful identity in succeeding years, it is possible to speculate more fully on their agenda and the impact of their meetings on the development of Toomer's understanding of his own racial positioning and aesthetic commitment. The group's focus on the economic and cultural forces that shaped the Negro points to their interest in the intersection of history and the current position and social circumstances of African Americans in the United States. Their initial investigation into the historical context of slavery through readings on the subject, Toomer felt, would help them to understand more fully the social and political contours of the post–World War I landscape, especially as they concerned race. The particular aims Toomer identified in his correspondence with Locke further isolate the objectives underlying the group's inquiry into the history of the nation's African Americans and their present circumstances. By identifying this population as "them" rather than "us," Toomer signaled his own understanding of his position as at least partially removed from the history and present condition of black Americans; yet he also expressed the perception that only through an investigation of the experiences of this group could he begin to determine the place and positioning of the "mixed-blood group," the people with whom Toomer himself identified throughout his adolescence, young adulthood, and into the period during which *Cane* was written. What was the relationship between the mulatto aristocracy, the group that had assumed public leadership of African American life after emancipation, and those black people who, in the first two decades of the twentieth century, left the South and flooded northern cities as a part of the Great Migration? What was the place of people with mixed racial and ethnic strains in a nation increasingly obsessed with absolute racial and ethnic definition? What was behind the American obsession with blackness, and how might this nation find the courage, much less the vocabulary, to address the racial and social complexity embodied in light-skinned black people?

That these questions were central and pressing for Toomer and for those who formed the cohort of Washington, D.C.–based artists and intellectuals with whom Toomer met in 1921 is unsurprising. Toomer's own racial background was mixed, and his complexion was such that, according to one of his friends, "he would have had no trouble passing for white."[21] His family was deeply embedded in Washington, D.C.'s light-skinned black aristocracy, which achieved its clearest definition and greatest prominence in the first decades of the twentieth century. Toomer consciously entered this world in 1910 when, upon his mother's death, he moved to Washington, D.C., where he lived with his grandparents. There he attended the famous M Street High School (later Paul Laurence Dunbar High School), where many of the children of Washington's African American elite were enrolled. Toomer's description of that society, written early in the 1930s, is telling, for it captures an accurate interpretation of this group's historical construction as well as Toomer's nostalgic and essentialized imagination of it.

In the Washington of those days—and those days have gone by now—there was a flowering of a natural but transient aristocracy, thrown up by the, for the, creative conditions of the post-war period. These people, whose racial strains were mixed and for the most part unknown, happened to find themselves in the colored group. They had a personal refinement, a certain inward culture and beauty, a warmth of feeling such as I have seldom encountered elsewhere or again. A few held political posts of prominence. Some were in government positions. Others were in the professions. One was a municipal court judge. Several were in the real estate business. All were comfortably fixed financially, and they had a social life that satisfied them. They were not pushing to get anywhere or be anything other than what they were. Without bitterness, but with a sweetness and warmth that I will never forget, they were conscious that they were and had something in themselves. The children of these families became my friends.[22]

Toomer's recollections that "these new friends of mine were not conscious of being either colored or white" and that they "had never run up against the color line" may seem unlikely to modern readers, but they effectively isolate the setting in which Toomer found himself when as a teenager he arrived in Washington, D.C. His description of this world as one of financial and cultural comfort accurately captures the confidence of Washington, D.C.'s light-skinned colored upper class, which, historian Willard B. Gatewood Jr. argues, was the center of the nation's black aristocracy from the end of Reconstruction until at least World War I.[23] Composed mainly of racially mixed people who, as Toomer describes it, "happened to find themselves in the colored group," the world in which Toomer moved was more socially than racially conscious; seeing themselves as neither black nor white, their aspirations were to achieve first-class American citizenship through achievements in education, business, and culture.

By the beginning of the 1920s this world was rapidly vanishing, and its disappearance forced its members to think more critically about racial identity and their place and position in both the white and black worlds. The success of Jim Crow laws and practices and the influx of tens of thousands of African Americans from the rural South to the North in the first decades of the twentieth century, combined with racial and economic fears exacerbated by the nation's involvement in World War I, ensured a hardening of racial lines. Black Americans everywhere—no matter how negligible their African heritage or how genteel their social performance—realized that their ambitions for integration into American society were viciously resisted. As Jean Toomer's distinction between "them" and "us" suggests, members of this light-skinned aristocracy continued to think of themselves as different from the black masses; but in the wake of World War I, and particularly after the "Red Summer" of 1919, when race riots broke out in major U.S. cities, including Washington, D.C., all African Americans became subject to ever-stricter lines of racial demarcation, and it became increasingly obvious that the tendency of white America was simply to lump all blacks together regardless of their racial heritage, color, or social or economic standing. Striking legal evidence of this impulse can be seen in the removal of the category "mulatto" as a racial group from the U.S. Census after 1920, a definitive step toward eliminating any connection between blacks and whites and ostensibly maintaining white racial purity and integrity. This and other developments served as proof of the virulence of racism and forced members of the colored aristocracy to recognize an affinity with the black masses, or at least to question their relationship to them.

The place of the mulatto aristocracy to which Toomer's ancestors belonged was further destabilized by the rise of a new black elite, which, as Gatewood notes, "had emerged in urban black communities [by the 1920s] and posed a serious threat to the place traditionally occupied by the old upper class in the black social structures." This new elite, Gatewood argues, was unconcerned with distinguished ancestry, and "unlike the old upper class, whose occupations brought them into frequent contact with upper-class whites, was tied almost exclusively to the black ghetto and [was] less concerned about assimilation into the larger society."[24] The new black elite had very different social and, most importantly, cultural priorities and aesthetic values from those established by the black aristocracy to which Toomer's grandparents belonged. Rather than embracing the notion that they could demonstrate an intellectual and social parity with white Americans through the appreciation of the traditional artifacts of high culture associated with American genteel society, the new black elite increasingly came to value subjects that related to the Negro's slave and folk past and cultural forms with origins in the black community.

In the context of this period of transition, Toomer's participation in a literary collective whose object was to assess "the actual place and condition of the mixed-blood group in this country" and to formulate an "ideal that [was] both workable and inclusive" was an impulse with personal as well as artistic ramifications. Personally, the years surrounding his formation of that literary group were ones in which Toomer consciously and critically engaged in an assessment of racial categories and their social meanings. At the heart of this inquiry was an effort to articulate the fullness of his own identity in a world that was determined to reduce it to the limiting poles of black and white. Pressing the literary society to study African American history and to consider the status of mixed-race Americans was one way for Toomer to consider his own relationship to race, racial identity, and the historic circumstances behind these conceptions. But also at stake in Toomer's critical assessments of race were questions about artistic standards, content, and form. Whereas the black aristocracy had traditionally immersed themselves in literature and in art that was in keeping with what was most highly valued by their counterparts in white society, Toomer's encouragement of this literary group to delve into the history of black America suggests a desire to question the conventional boundaries of genteel cultural production dictated by his aristocratic ancestry. In wishing to push the group's conversation beyond the "trivial and commonplace," Toomer seems to have recognized both the difficulty and the importance of transcending the superficially cultured, cosmopolitan setting in which most of the group's members lived. Combined with their multiracial, advantaged backgrounds, social protocol dictated that, in their usual conversation, they were only secondarily inclined to confront issues of racial identity and class affiliation. But in the intimate setting provided by the literary society, Toomer seems to have been anxious to acknowledge the primary importance of these issues, addressing them both through historical reading and creative efforts.

Toomer's writing from this time offers evidence that his desire to work through questions of race and class was essential to both his personal identity and his sense of artistic direction; indeed, his comments in a biographical note written in 1922 to the editors of the *Liberator*, a magazine that had just accepted two pieces of his writing, indicate that he had come to find these issues intertwined.

Racially I seem to have (who knows for sure?) seven blood mixtures: French, Dutch, Welsh, Negro, German, Jewish and Indian. Because of these, my position in America has been a curious one. I have lived equally amid the two race groups. Now white, now colored. From my own point of view, I am naturally and inevitably an American. I have striven for a spiritual fusion analogous to the fact of racial intermingling. Without denying a single element in me, with no desire to subdue, one to the other, I have sought to let them function as complements. I have tried to let them live in harmony. Within the last two or three years, however, my growing need for artistic expression has pulled me deeper and deeper within the Negro group. And as my powers of receptivity increased, I found myself loving it in a way that I could never love the other. It has stimulated and fertilized whatever creative talent I may contain within me.[25]

These comments reinforce the observation that the years surrounding Toomer's involvement in the Washington, D.C., literary society were the ones in which his association with the African American race was the most profound; ironically, these were the same years in which Toomer began to disavow traditionally defined racial categorization entirely. He voices here both his embrace of African American culture and his impulse to distance himself personally and politically from the unalterable racial categories that dominated American life and the intolerable racial order that resulted from them. Toomer embodied his tentative identification with African American culture in *Cane*, a text whose view of the United States is filtered through the veil of Negro life, North and South. But even this text points to Toomer's understanding that the "racial situation in the United States" was "an incredibly entangled situation" in which the "familiar categories" of racial identification would not hold.[26] By 1930 Toomer was able to more fully articulate the "workable ideal" that he had sought to uncover in part through the study, in the context of the Washington, D.C., literary circle, of his own place in the history of black life and in the American racial conflicts of the 1920s. In response to James Weldon Johnson's request to include portions of *Cane* in an anthology of Negro writing he was compiling, Toomer forcefully explained that he could not be included in such a work. "My poems are not Negro poems," he wrote, "nor are they Anglo-Saxon or white or English poems. My prose likewise. They are, first, mine. And, second, in so far as general race or stock is concerned, they spring from the result of racial blendings here in America which have produced a new race or stock." "The old divisions into white, black, brown, red, are outworn in this country," he would write in 1931. He came to believe that there was "a new race in America. I am a member of this new race," he asserted. "It is neither white nor black nor in-between. It is the American race, differing as much from white and black as white and black differ from each other."[27] Toomer's perspective reflected not only his personal identification but a political position he would continue to refine throughout his life.

Certainly many circumstances and events shaped the development of Toomer's thinking on this subject in the years preceding the publication of *Cane*, and there are many reasons not to place undue emphasis on the importance of the literary coalition he formed in 1921. Records do not exist to document the group's progress or fate. If Toomer's effort to begin a literary society sprang from his keen sense of his own need for it, he was also aware of the weaknesses of Washington's literary community that made his group particularly susceptible to failure. As he had discovered from experience, black Washington's "society" was not always hospitable to passionate intellectual pursuits, nor was it conducive to generous, cooperative efforts. "We need something to cement us," Toomer wrote to Locke. "That something can only spring out of a knowledge, out of certain fundamental facts which we share in common. It is the lack of such a basis that I largely attribute our failure to get together in the past."[28] It is also important to note that Toomer's regular involvement in the group was relatively short-lived. In September 1921 Toomer left Washington, D.C., to spend three months in Sparta, Georgia, where he served as the substitute principal for the Sparta Agricultural and Industrial School. There, he lived among black people and gathered material for *Cane*. Rather than the intellectual discussions of African American history that took place in the context of the literary society, it was this trip that Toomer identified as pivotal to both his personal and artistic development. In 1922 he wrote: "A visit to Georgia last fall was the starting point of almost everything of worth that I have done. I heard folk-songs come from the lips of Negro peasants. I saw the rich dusk beauty that I had heard many false accents about, and of which, till then, I was somewhat skeptical. And a deeper part of my nature, a part that I had repressed, sprang suddenly to life and responded to them. Now, I can not conceive of myself as aloof and separated. My point of view has not changed; it has deepened, it has widened."[29]

Toomer's involvement in the literary society can only be seen as one of the things that sustained him and prepared him to see, historicize, and value Negro life in a new way. What *Cane*'s vignettes address so clearly and yet with such complexity are precisely the issues around which Toomer's literary society was initially focused: the fate of African American people and their culture, as represented both by rural black life in the South and that of mixed-blood America. Juxtaposing archetypal figures from southern black life with colored aristocrats in the North as well as the new, middle-class "black bourgeois" and the newly arrived black masses who, in the first decades of the twentieth century, had changed the face of northern cities like New York, Washington, D.C., and Chicago, *Cane* expresses the complexity of the racial situation in the United States as Toomer came to understand it. Rather than perpetuating the genteel fictions that members of the black middle and upper classes used to identify themselves as different and apart from the black masses, *Cane* reflects Toomer's understanding of the lasting impact of American slavery on all African Americans regardless of their class or color. It also outlines what he saw to be the Negro's fate: absorption into American culture.[30] Throughout *Cane*, but most particularly in the extended narrative, "Kabnis," with which the text concludes, Toomer was able to articulate the clash of contradictory identities that fueled his own anxieties about his racial and intellectual position in the United States. Included in this piece is a fictional representation of the anguish and injury involved, for mixed-race members of the middle and upper classes like Toomer himself, in the nation's obsession over race and racial categorization. Toomer would go on to deny his own black identity and, for the most part, the issues of race and class that must nevertheless have continued to dog him; but in the pages of *Cane* he was able to give voice to the unspeakable chaos that was attendant upon them.

"CONTACTUAL INSPIRATION"

Although the exact fate of the group that formed as a result of Toomer's original instigation is unknown, the promise of the collaborative evenings spent in the intellectually challenging and personally liberating company of other writers and intellectuals seems to have remained in the minds of those first involved in Toomer's effort. Members of Toomer's original society were soon regulars at Georgia Douglas Johnson's house on Saturday nights. Georgia Douglas Johnson was a woman of tremendous energy, much of which she channeled into her effort to create for the writers who gathered in her home on Saturday nights an atmosphere that was both intellectually stimulating and properly supportive. She was a gifted organizer who managed to raise children and hold down a busy household while at the same time establishing a career as an award-winning writer of poetry and drama. After her husband's death, Johnson was employed full time in order to meet the needs of her family; she was nevertheless able to maintain her focus on her own writing while also welcoming into her life and home the most talented and energetic writers of the Harlem Renaissance. In fact, these elements of her life—her creative and intellectual work and her organization of the Saturday Nighters—were inseparable. Johnson relied on the aesthetic and intellectual stimulation that she herself generated as the leader of the Saturday Nighters to sustain her energy as a creative writer. But there is no doubt that the Saturday Nighters was formed in part for the benefit of a younger generation of writers that Johnson realized was in need of a literary community; in Johnson's living room they found themselves in the company of an experienced writer, a literary mentor, and a dynamic personality.

Like Jean Toomer, Langston Hughes also noted that the Washington, D.C., of the 1920s was not conducive to literary community. His recollection of it is particularly forceful. In a scathing essay published in the August 1927 issue of *Opportunity* and titled "Our Wonderful Society: Washington," Hughes recorded his perception of and relationship to the nation's capital. After hearing throughout his youth that "Negro life in Washington . . . was the finest in the country, the richest, the most cultured, the most worthy," Hughes found Washington society to be hollow, presenting a facade of culture with no substance. It was, he discovered, especially devoid of literary sensibility. "I knew Jean Toomer's home was Washington and I had read his book 'Cane' and talked about it with other readers in New York and Paris and Venice," Hughes recounted. "I wanted to talk about it in Washington, too, because I had found it beautiful and real. But the cultured colored society of the capital, I mean those persons who always insisted that they were cultured, seemed to know little about the book and cared less." Hughes noted the irony of a city uniquely capable of nurturing its black artists that simply chose not to. "I thought it amazing, too, that a young playwright of ability and three or four poets of promise were living in Washington unknown to the best society. At least, I saw nothing being done to encourage these young writers, for the leading women's clubs appeared to be founded solely for the purpose of playing cards, and the cultured doctors and lawyers and caterers and butlers had little concern for poets and playwrights." Hughes concluded with this biting condemnation: "In supposedly intellectual gatherings I listened to conversations as arid as the sides of the Washington monument."[31]

One of the few aspects of Washington, D.C., that Hughes remembered "with pleasure" was Georgia Douglas Johnson's literary evenings, where the hostess "conversed with charm and poured tea on Saturday nights for young artists and writers and intellectuals."[32] Universally, Johnson's literary evenings were enjoyed and appreciated. And it was not only the writers who went on to become famous who found Johnson's living room to be an oasis of intellectual activity and warmth. Albert Rice, a native-born Washingtonian who would become a little-known writer of the period, considered Washington, D.C., to be "a center of Babbitts, both black and white"; from his perspective, its one redeeming quality was that "Georgia Douglas Johnson lives there and on Saturday nights has an assembly of likeable and civilized people." From the safe space she created in her living room, many of these writers moved toward their literary maturity, toward New York, and toward "fame and infamy."[33]

Of the origins of the Saturday Nighters, Johnson would later recount this particular narrative: "Years ago—Jean Toomer said to me 'Mrs. J—Why don't you have Weekly Conversations among the writers here in Washington?' It was difficult for me to arrange as home duties had about consumed me before Saturday night, however, I did make an attempt and we began the Saturday evening talks which continued through about ten years and came to life intermittently now and then to the present."[34] In contrast to most of black Washington's "society" events, Saturday evenings at Johnson's house were intellectually rich and stimulating. The group of writers and intellectuals they brought together would otherwise have remained isolated, both from the larger Washington society and from one another. In Johnson's living room they read their writing aloud, exchanged criticisms, talked about the latest books they had read and argued their views on literature, art, and politics. Like Jean Toomer's informal study group, their critique of one another's work and debates over art and aesthetic value introduced ways to sort through complicated issues of black representation and identity. In the context of the Saturday Nighters, they discovered what often seemed elusive elsewhere: encouragement, community, and the ever-accepting nature of Georgia Douglas Johnson herself. In a world of strict social rules and little acknowledgment of individual sensibility, Johnson possessed a special gift. Often all she offered to the young writers was an attentive ear and quiet enthusiasm. But these were precisely the elements missing in the world of young black artists of the 1920s. The writers with whom she met on Saturday evenings recognized and appreciated her magnanimity. Langston Hughes's characterization of the formation of the Saturday Nighters captures this. In *The Big Sea* he wrote that "Georgia Douglas Johnson . . . turned her house into a salon *for us* on Saturday nights."[35] Johnson was a tremendously supportive person with a talent for both listening and giving encouragement; what she was able to offer the young writers and intellectuals with whom she associated was a gift she appropriately termed "contactual inspiration."[36]

Johnson's generosity with this gift was apparent long before she began the Saturday Nighters. Toomer's letters to Johnson, for instance, provide an example of the relationship she had with younger writers. Evident in Toomer's correspondence is the extent to which he trusted her and depended on her friendship, kindness, and encouragement; he also seemed to depend on her critical feedback on his early writing. They shared "the writer's point of view," as Toomer once put it, and much more. "Your letter filled quite a gap by its close feeling and understanding," he wrote to her from New York City in March 1920. "While it may be true that one's head may be swelled by praise . . . it is equally certain that lack of real appreciation tends to drive one within oneself, too much so, and so is bad."[37] For the ever-introspective Toomer, Georgia Douglas Johnson was a sounding board against which he could voice his struggles to find a meaningful place in the world. Admitting to her that "these last few months have easily been the biggest of my life," Toomer shared with Johnson both the joys and the frustrations of this monumental period.[38] He could be honest with her about his feelings of isolation and his acute awareness of his difference. "The farther I go, the more I develop, every rung of the ladder I leave behind seems to have clinging to it some person I used to feel in close sympathy with," he wrote to Johnson in February 1920. "Not that they have gone back, but that my life values seem to be developing at a different rate than theirs." He admitted to her that "no one in this city can I truly call a true friend, that is, one who truly understands me, and I him." Although Toomer said he was "not lonesome" and knew "there are quite a few who in their good way are friends . . . everytime I meet and leave them, I feel something lacking. It is distressing." Although it is clear that Johnson was a prolific and inspired letter writer, and she and Toomer had a fulfilling epistolary relationship, he closed this and many other letters by expressing his desire to see Johnson. "I can't in a letter tell the evolutions," Toomer lamented. "I'm coming down to Washington before so very long, and perhaps I can hint at them then."[39]

Over the years, young and established writers would also long to see Johnson, making the trek from all over Washington, D.C., as well as from New York and other cities throughout the United States, to visit with Johnson in her home. Her S Street residence would be among the first places they stopped after being abroad. Her correspondence reveals the major and minor figures of the Harlem Renaissance who passed through her home. In the summer of 1922 she wrote to Alain Locke, telling him that Jessie Fauset had recently visited.[40] She had also met recently with Jean Toomer and Zora Neale Hurston. A few weeks later, in another letter to Locke, she asked about Claude McKay and mentioned that Waldo Frank had joined them for an evening.[41] From time to time she invited Locke to be present at a meeting of the Saturday Nighters, suggesting topics for presentation that might be of interest to the group. "We (Mamie + I + all the rest) want to hear all about your trip some fine Saturday evening at . . . my house," she wrote him in September 1922, just after his return from a summer in

Members of The Dark Tower, a literary organization
created in 1928 by A'lelia Walker, daughter of Madame
C. J. Walker. Painted on the walls of the room in which
they met in A'lelia Walker's Harlem mansion were
poems, including Countee Cullen's "The Dark Tower"
and Langston Hughes's "The Weary Blues." *"The Dark
Tower" (circa 1929); photographer, James Van Der Zee.* ©
Donna Musserden Van Der Zee.

Berlin.[42] When his travels took him away from Washington, Locke would receive cheerful notes from Georgia Douglas Johnson such as this one: "Shall we not have a . . . little literary festival when you come home? Will you bring Mr. McKay with you?"[43]

After leaving Washington, D.C., and their weekly involvement with the Saturday Nighters, the extended "family" formed by the group continued to rely on regular contact with and the soothing "presence" of Georgia Douglas Johnson, even if they did not always like (or could not read) what she had to say.[44] Johnson closely monitored their transitions to New York or Europe; she worried about and affectionately offered counsel to them. When Bruce Nugent arrived in New York City in 1926, for instance, he reported that he was "truly leading the life of a fiction artist. Going to all amusements, cabarets, parties, dinners, etc; and starving quite frequently." Cheerfully, he continued: "I don't mind starving, tho, because after all ones [*sic*] biography should be interesting and entertaining." Nugent anticipated Johnson's concern and the practical advice that would arrive with her next letter. "When you write please don't scold," he told her. "Don't tell me I should put aside my meagre pennies (when I have them) and alot [*sic*] myself only so much a day and *that* for food. Of course, I know I should."[45] Johnson did become a maternal figure for many of the Saturday Nighters, but her interest in their professional development and her role as a colleague and mentor always came first.[46] Nugent implies this when he closes his letter by telling her that he had "met most of the people [she] told [him] to meet" and asking her to try to secure a few subscriptions for the journal *FIRE!!*, the first (and last) issue of which would appear in November 1926.[47]

Although the meetings that took place on Saturday evenings in Georgia Douglas Johnson's living room were opportunities for writers to exchange opinions and think critically about the literature of the day—their own and that of others—this critical edge disguised itself in an attitude that was indeed quite festive. Current literature was reviewed with a certain lightheartedness. "We read your poems in the Dogest [*sic*] and the other magazine," Johnson reported to Countee Cullen in a 1927 letter. "We loved the one about the walls of the heart best of all. In fact," Johnson admitted, "we had fun showing how rediculously [*sic*] weak the other poems were beside yours."[48] Memories of the good times at Georgia Douglas Johnson's house on Saturday nights sustained writers through the tensions of their day-to-day personal and professional lives. In a letter to Johnson in which he expressed his nervousness over the announcement of the *Opportunity* awards, Bruce Nugent spoke nostalgically about returning to what he lovingly called "The Circle." "When I come down to a Saturday night—please let miss Carson [*sic*] make eggnog to go with the shrimp salad—or fish cakes + tea." He signed his letter "with regards to the circle."[49]

Composed of serious-minded individuals intent on improving their writing and their understanding of literature, the Saturday Nighters also enjoyed one another's company and used their reunions to share laughter as well as constructive criticism and literary advice. After leaving the group to settle in New York City, Bruce Nugent wrote to Johnson, speculating on why she had not had the time to answer his previous letter. "I wrote you a marvelous letter from New Bedford describing the place," he wrote, "a letter which you apparently placed in your file of poems and promptly lost, serving tea to the remnants of the old and plantlings of the new 'Circle.' Yes, I'm afraid that my greatest work of literature, genius, beauty, psychology, and ego, was laid away so that you (and the circle) could eat delightful fish with your fingers." Nugent captures something of Johnson's personality and energy, as well as his own nostalgia for the group, in the letter's close. "Or may hap it was laid on a sheaf of poems, still wet from the fingers of budding geniuses, while you searched for your glasses, which after perched on the end of your nose, failed even to disclose the cause of their being so perched. All of which means nothing. All of which discloses that I envie (I meant to spell it with a y) the remnants and the plantlings." In addition to suggesting that he had found nothing in New York to match or replace his experience with the Saturday Nighters, his conclusion simply yet concisely articulates his nostalgia for the warmth and fellowship he knew in Washington: "God only knows when I will get to D.C."[50]

While it is obvious that Johnson wanted and worked to make the Saturday Nighters a congenial group, it is important to note that it was also firmly under her control. She took it upon herself to invite talented but undiscovered individuals she came across to participate in the Saturday Nighters' weekly meetings and did not hesitate to mention the names of those whose work she believed should receive recog-

nition to the prominent literary figures whose influence she knew
could advance their careers. She promoted one such writer in a note to
Alain Locke: "There is a man in Richmond who has written a most
remarkable book—It's like Milton."[51] While the door was always open
to new members, and members were welcome to bring their friends
and literary colleagues to the meetings, Johnson acted decisively if she
felt that a new attendee might limit the Saturday Nighters' productivity. The gentle but firm control she exerted over the group is confirmed by J. C. Byars, a Washington journalist and poet. In his 1927
anthology of Washington writers he noted that Johnson monitored
those who attended her Saturday evening meetings: "If dull ones
come, she weeds them out, gently, effectively."[52]

Held together by Johnson's dynamic personality and her clear vision
of the importance of community to the creative artist, the Saturday
Nighters was a society through which the most prominent literary and
intellectual minds of the 1920s, as well as lesser luminaries of the
decade, passed. Johnson's own partial list of "salon attendees" suggests
her great capacity for embracing a variety of personalities and talents.
In addition to well-known Harlem Renaissance figures Jean Toomer,
Langston Hughes, Countee Cullen, Jessie Fauset, Wallace Thurman,
William Stanley Braithwaite, Charles S. Johnson, Zora Neale Hur-
ston, Arna Bontemps, Alain Locke, and Kelly Miller, two of the most
prominent members of the "old guard," James Weldon Johnson and
W. E. B. Du Bois, made appearances at Johnson's house. "Regulars"
included Alice Dunbar-Nelson, Mary "Mamie" Burrill, Gwendolyn
Bennett, Chandler Owen, Willis Richardson, Lewis Alexander, Marita
Bonner, Mollie Gibson Brewer, Grant Lucas, Angelina Weld Grimké,
Effie Lee Newsome, Richard Bruce Nugent, Montgomery Gregory,
Rebecca West, Ann Spencer, Wright Cuney, E. C. Williams, B. K.
Bruce, Glen Carrington, Mae Miller, Adella Parks, Frank Horne, and
Mae Howard Jackson.[53] White writers also came from time to time; for
instance, Waldo Frank was a guest of Jean Toomer.[54]

Throughout the 1920s Johnson's living room was a place where the
famous and the not-yet-famous could meet and talk about literary
subjects. It was in this and similar contexts that much of the daily
work of the writers of the Harlem Renaissance was done. Publicly, the
work of these artists appeared in collections like *The New Negro* and
the little magazines of the period like *FIRE!!*, as well as major publica-

tions such as *Opportunity, Messenger,* and *Crisis*; it was recognized through the contests these magazines sponsored and celebrated at awards dinners like the one held at the Civic Club in New York in March 1924. It was in places like the private Washington, D.C., home of Georgia Douglas Johnson, however, where Harlem Renaissance writers struggled with their literary work and where that work found its first audience. The literary community that Johnson created in her home through the Saturday Nighters was safe and supportive. Working together, black writers shared their work and critiqued the writing of their peers; the review they received from one another was welcome and constructive, and it helped them to shape the work they later published. It also led to debates on a set of diverse and challenging aesthetic, intellectual, and theoretical questions that faced black writers as they struggled to be true to themselves, their art, and their race.

"I AM TRYING TO WRITE"

While Johnson's instigation of the Saturday Nighters was in part altruistic, the society also served her by meeting a complex set of her own needs. In creating a meeting place for writers and intellectuals in her Washington, D.C., home, Johnson built and sustained the conditions under which emergent writers—including and especially herself—could thrive. In addition to her capacity as an organizer, Johnson was also an active reader and, by the time she began the Saturday Nighters, an accomplished writer. As an intellectual, Johnson craved the substantive and stimulating discussions that took place in her home on Saturday nights. As a writer, she needed to be exposed to the critical discourse that circulated on these evenings around her own literary creations and those of her peers. But Johnson was also firmly entrenched in that stifling Washington, D.C., society that Toomer, Hughes, and others passed through and remembered with disdain; in keeping with the expectations of this world, public etiquette dictated that she serve as a social hostess. By entertaining literary luminaries and promoting an intellectual atmosphere, Johnson was able to adequately perform this role without being consumed by its superficiality. In associating herself with the intellectual crowd that gathered in her house on Saturday evenings, Johnson simultaneously fulfilled the expectations of bourgeois respectability and expanded the boundaries of the world in which she lived.

This balancing of social protocol and intellectual desire is representative of the balancing acts that Johnson performed in a number of areas of her life. Johnson's age alone at the time of the Harlem Renaissance made her something of an anomaly, a fact of which she was acutely aware.[55] Born in 1877, she was both old enough to have lived through the formation of the National Association of Colored Women and young enough to assume a key role as an impresario and an author during the Harlem Renaissance. Whereas many of the female writers of the Harlem Renaissance defied traditional gender conventions by remaining unmarried and without children, Johnson was a wife and a mother and, after her husband's death in 1925, the primary wage earner in her family. After launching the Saturday Nighters, she was routinely surrounded by the most progressive gay, lesbian, and bisexual writers and intellectuals of the time, and she herself seems to have transgressed the boundaries of sexual convention by having at least one affair; yet she allowed little of the progressive sexual attitudes to which she was exposed or the complexity of the life she led to appear explicitly in her poetry. Similarly, at a time when black artists were expected to take on more expressly political voices and subjects in their work, Johnson remained reluctant to substantively address the racial situation or her experiences as a black woman in her writing, preferring instead to rely on and recycle older formulas of genteel feminine expression. While the authors who visited her home would go on to redefine African American letters, challenging Victorian notions of literary "correctness" while forcefully asserting a new black identity through their writing and contributing to the maturing modernist thrust of American literature generally, Johnson remained socially and professionally at the intersection of two eras, not entirely Victorian in her behavior and artistic expression, but not exactly modern, either. Ironically, although the group she organized was credited with helping the artists of the Harlem Renaissance find and strengthen their voices, Johnson would come to use the centrality of her role as the leader of the Saturday Nighters as a mask behind which she could disguise the awkwardness of her position. More than anything else, Johnson coveted recognition as a writer and involvement in literary community; this desire prompted her to pursue a literary career, but it also seems to have played a part in limiting the development and the promise of her writing. In seeking a place in the literary record of the twentieth century, Johnson chose to assure herself of some degree of recognition by aligning herself with the expressions of feminine emotion that had long been the subject of women's poetry. This made her writing easy to praise, as endorsements from William Stanley Braithwaite, W. E. B. Du Bois, and Alain Locke in the forewords of Johnson's three earliest collections of poetry illustrate. But, against a backdrop of male poets whose writing was more daring and more original, it was also easy to dismiss. Her role as a literary hostess, also a part of the feminine posture she adopted, was a way for her to ensure that she would remain at the center of the literary community and maintain contact with the vibrant intellectual world to which she would not otherwise fully belong. In establishing the Saturday Nighters, Johnson created a space where she herself could claim and regularly perform that artistic identity through which she wished to define herself and see her life's work.

For Johnson, establishing herself as a serious writer and achieving literary success was synonymous with making connections with others whose reputations were firmly established or whose talent was evident. These connections clearly served to quicken the pace of her life and offered the promise of her own success and recognition. She communicated something of the excitement she found in receiving this sort of endorsement of her literary talent and creative energy in a third-person statement she wrote for Countee Cullen's *Caroling Dusk* (1927). In it she described her initial foray into the literary world. "Dean Kelly Miller at Howard University saw some of her poetic efforts and was pleased. [William] Stanley Braithwaite was his friend and he directed her to send something to him at Boston. She did so, and then began a quickening and a realization she could do it!"[56] Miller and Braithwaite's early encouragement stands in contrast to Johnson's husband's lack of enthusiasm for her creative writing. Henry Lincoln Johnson "didn't think much of his wife's longing for a literary career" and "tried to discourage the idea," believing that "a woman should take care of her home and her children and be content with that."[57] Although his disapproval did not stop her from writing or prevent her from beginning the Saturday Nighters sometime around 1921, it must at times have been disheartening. In contrast, Johnson received from her mentors and from those who joined her in literary discussion on Saturday nights a wholly different sense of her own self-worth, one that was dependent on her femininity but not entirely limited to her position as a mother, a wife, and a housekeeper.

Johnson married her husband "Link," as he was called, in 1903; in 1910, when they relocated from Atlanta to Washington, D.C., she had two young sons. Link Johnson went on to establish a law firm in Washington and was appointed Recorder of Deeds in the Taft Administration in 1912. His role as an influential politician dictated that she would participate in the activities of elite black society and maintain a "proper" social relationship with other prominent ladies of their set. Despite these responsibilities, the Johnson's dining room table was more often crowded with books, literary journals, papers, and a typewriter than it was laid for tea, a fact that Link Johnson seems to have grown accustomed to. In her diary, Alice Dunbar-Nelson tells the story of a visit to the Johnsons' house in 1921 during which she tried to teach Georgia Douglas Johnson how to wear hats. "Georgia wanted to know how to put on hats, and I began to teach her," Dunbar-Nelson wrote. "She really did not know how, and I made her practise and practise [*sic*] again and again." Johnson's husband "seemed so glad" that Dunbar-Nelson was "teaching his wife an essential thing that he suggested luncheon," which his wife ordered him to prepare. When he had finished fixing the meal, Dunbar-Nelson recalled, "he had to push away papers, manuscript, junk from the dining room table to make room for his tray, for Georgia has her machine, and all her literary stuff in the dining room." As they dined, Georgia Douglas Johnson showed Dunbar-Nelson "the manuscript for her new book."[58] While Dunbar-Nelson's account of Link's enthusiasm over the prospect of his wife's mastering the "essential" art of hat-wearing indicates his underlying concern with her obligation as a member of Washington's black upper class to appear stylishly outfitted in society, her emphasis in retelling the story of her visit also points to Johnson's fierce determination to maintain her identity as a serious writer. Link Johnson's preparation of lunch for his wife and her guest as they leisurely looked over Johnson's manuscript suggests the extent to which Johnson simultaneously challenged traditional gender roles and worked to socialize herself by shaping her attire, for instance, in ways that supported them.[59]

As Dunbar-Nelson's description suggests, Johnson's identity as writer was very important to her, and she dedicated considerable time and energy to it. Link Johnson's prominent and profitable career meant that Georgia Douglas Johnson did not have to work outside of her home; in this situation, Johnson was a prolific writer. She published her first volume of poetry, *The Heart of a Woman and Other Poems*, in 1918; it was followed in 1922 with a second volume, *Bronze*. These collections established Johnson's reputation as the premier female Negro poet of the twentieth century, even as they dictated the qualified terms in which her art would be viewed by her contemporaries. In his foreword to *The Heart of a Woman*, her literary mentor William Stanley Braithwaite wrote that "the poems in this book are intensely feminine and for me this means more than anything else that they are deeply human. We are yet scarcely aware, despite our boasted twentieth-century progress, of what lies deeply hidden, of mystery and passion, of domestic love and joy and sorrow, of romantic visions and practical ambitions, in the heart of a woman."[60] As both Gloria T. Hull and Claudia Tate have noted in their analyses of Johnson's work, Braithwaite's assessment of Johnson's poems begins to progressively credit them with speaking for and to humankind rather than only for and to women; but he is unwilling to pursue this line of analysis, resorting instead to well-worn sentimental phrases about the "reality of woman's heart" and the "secrets of woman's nature."[61] James Weldon Johnson's comments about the collection in *The Book of Negro Poetry*, published in 1922, reveal even more about how Johnson's poetry was viewed and received. "It may be that her verse possesses effectiveness precisely because it is at the pole opposite to adroitness, sophistication," he wrote. "Through sheer simplicity and spontaneousness" he added, her poems communicate "a note of pathos or passion that will not fail to waken a response, except in those too sophisticated or cynical to respond to natural impulses."[62] James Weldon Johnson's attribution of spontaneity to Johnson's verse, his description of them as "sheer simplicity," and his positioning of Johnson's poetry as the opposite of adroitness and sophistication are representative of the reductive and simplistic ways that Johnson's poetry was viewed, especially by those male literary figures whose opinions and endorsements shaped the burgeoning literary renaissance. Their praise of Johnson's work was essential to her development as a writer; but the terms in which they encouraged her underscored their understanding that the quality of a woman's poetic expression was located in its emotion. Despite the suggestion inherent in their words that her work was somewhat trivial and certainly not comparable to the more sophisticated literary endeavors of their male counterparts, Johnson would cling to these gendered standards throughout her life.

Without detracting from her impressive literary career or denying her very real artistic talent, both Gloria T. Hull and Claudia Tate suggest that Johnson's desire to be a recognized poet was such that she embraced the idea of having "the heart of a woman," cultivating a feminine voice and the poetic imagination that went with it rather than pursue topics or forms of expression that fell outside its parameters. As Tate notes, as a black woman writing at the beginning of the twentieth century and against the unfolding literary landscape of the New Negro Renaissance, "the choices for Johnson may very well have been to be a 'lady poet' or to receive no recognition at all."[63] Although modern readers will recognize the ways in which Johnson's poetry is, as Hull has described it, "quietly seditious," it is cloaked in the mantle of "articulate helplessness" that was a prerequisite of feminine expression.[64] Writing in this predictable way, Johnson received wide recognition and support, and by 1922 she was widely acclaimed as an accomplished black female poet. This endorsement of her literary talent probably made her less and less willing to develop her writing in significant ways, or to venture beyond the formulaic feminine verse on which her reputation had been built to address in more challenging ways some of the increasingly complex aspects of her identity and experience. Even when she did explore these topics, she did so in a way that underscored the extent to which she was fulfilling the social obligations of a "lady poet." "My first book was the Heart of A Woman," Johnson recalled in a biographical note sent to Arna Bontemps in 1941. "It was not at all race conscious. Then someone said—she has no feeling for the race. So I wrote Bronze—it is entirely racial and one section deals entirely with motherhood—that motherhood that has as its basic note—black children born into the world's displeasure."[65]

The poems in *Bronze* depict typical racial situations, expressing tender sympathy for a downtrodden race; for them Johnson was acknowledged as an adequate writer of racial poetry. Missing from Johnson's writing here and elsewhere, however, is what Tate describes as the "complex critical sensibility that shaped her own life and vision."[66]

Johnson's own mixed-race background—her mother was part Chero-
kee, and her paternal grandfather was English—and her class affiliation determined that her racial identification was as complicated as
was that of her friend and fellow Washingtonian, Jean Toomer. And
yet this culturally complex world visibly penetrated little of her early
poetic expression. The poems in *Bronze*, for instance, are so tightly
cloaked in indirection that they do little to reveal in any substantive
way Johnson's own racial consciousness or concerns.

Similarly, Johnson's complicated sexual life remained veiled behind
a poetic technique that favored the ambiguous emotional expressions
associated with feminine sensibility. Even Johnson's very good friends
were only vaguely able to see through these veiled utterances to imagine the complicated secrets she was hiding behind her poetry. Speculating in her journal about the poems that made up Johnson's third
collection of poems, *An Autumn Love Cycle*, published in 1928, Alice
Dunbar-Nelson wrote: "You might call it poetic inspiration but it
looks suspiciously to me as if Georgia had an affair, and it had been a
source of inspiration to her." In fact, Johnson seems to have had at
least one affair, with none other than W. E. B. Du Bois. It is unclear
when this relationship began or ended, but it seems to have predated
Johnson's husband's death. By 1926 their relationship was such that it
warranted this seductive note from Du Bois, sent to Johnson from
Moscow. "I am thinking of you," he wrote. "I'd like to have you here.
I'm coming to see you at midnight. Please come down half dressed
with pretty stockings. I shall kiss you."[67] Johnson never explicitly
wrote about her relationship with Du Bois and, according to David
Levering Lewis, she "never seems to have deceived herself about the
prospect of becoming the second Mrs. Du Bois."[68] But this was certainly another situation in which Johnson must at times have perceived herself as a marginal figure.

She found refuge from the ambiguities that dominated so many
aspects of her life in the literary salon she hosted on Saturday nights.
There, her centrality—indeed, her dominance—was unsurpassed.
Regardless of what her colleagues thought about her writing, they
believed in her excellence as a literary hostess. Under these circumstances, it is no wonder that Johnson thought of her home as a "half-
way house": for her it was a refuge from the anonymity that always
threatened to envelop her literary career, a place where she was con-

fident in her role and sure of its importance. It was also a place where she took the time and created the space to imagine and maintain an intellectual identity, no small feat for herself or her literary colleagues amidst the hustle and bustle of busy lives, the complicated social and racial relations of the urban North, and the strain of familial and financial obligations. She promoted the image of her home as a half-way house, placing herself at the center of it. "I'm half way between everybody and everything," she would write, "and I bring them together."[69]

Link Johnson's death in the fall of 1925 following a third stroke brought with it significant change for Johnson. With both of her sons enrolled at Dartmouth College, she needed to work. For the next decade Johnson sought employment in various capacities to support herself and her children. For much of that time she was employed by the Department of Labor, and most of her extant correspondence carries its letterhead. Although the demands on her time and energy—both before but especially after her husband's death—were extraordinary, Johnson remained dedicated not only to her own writing but to her work as a literary mentor as well. Her ability to fulfill so many responsibilities and keep up with her own creative writing seemed, at times, impossible. On the occasion of her first-place award in the *Opportunity* literary contest for her play *Plumes*, Johnson reflected on her struggle to find the time to dedicate to her writing: "If I might ask of some fairy godmother special favors, one would sure be for a clearing space, elbow room in which to think and write and live beyond the reach of the Wolf's fingers."[70] Her closest friends and colleagues also wondered how she could escape "the Wolf's fingers." Literary mentor William Stanley Braithwaite was concerned enough about her writing, in light of the pragmatic responsibilities that filled her life, to contact her at the beginning of 1926 to ask: "How goes your own work?"[71] Her own work was, in fact, at its peak. In 1926 her play *Blue Blood* was awarded honorable mention in the *Opportunity* drama contest. In November of the same year, she wrote to Countee Cullen to report that the "corrected and ready . . . copy of 'The Cycle' [was] with Zona Gale," who was to help her find a publisher for it. She sent him an uncorrected copy of the manuscript, hoping he could "get something from it" despite the fact that it was "not in such fine order."[72] By May 1927 Johnson decided to send the manuscript of *An Autumn Love*

Cycle to Harper Brothers in New York. She appealed to Countee Cullen again for his assistance. "It occurs to me," she wrote to him in May 1927, "that perhaps you would be so kind as to talk to somebody there about it and me. Perhaps it would have a chance then."[73]

Johnson's relative success as a writer was due in no small measure to her perseverance in asking for criticism from other literary figures and her persistent determination to be published. She did not hesitate to ask her colleagues for prepublication editing or appeal to them to write inspiring introductions to her work. When she needed help, she sought it out, as she did of Alain Locke in March 1919. "Dear Mr. Locke," she wrote, wasting no time getting to the substance of her letter. "I wish someone to go over a manuscript with me in a critical way." Calling her request a "strictly business transaction," she promised to limit her appointment to "one hour of your time" to "lay my material before you and have the benefit of your great advantage."[74] By 1925 Locke still made a point of reserving time to review Johnson's work. In a note dated 11 August 1925 she wrote to him by way of a reminder: "I hope you can come around and look over the manuscript[s] as you so kindly consented to do, either Friday or Saturday evening of this week or one night next week as we can arrange." She closed this message by enthusiastically informing him of another just-completed manuscript in need of review. "I have finished a mighty good play called 'Blue Blood.' I would like you to read it. Zora Neale is interested in it."[75]

As Alice Dunbar-Nelson noted in 1921, it was no small thing that Johnson was courageous enough to do what Dunbar-Nelson called "the big thing"—allowing others to read and critique her work. "Georgia has done the big thing in letting [Alain] Locke, [W. E. B.] Du Bois, and [William] Braithwaite weed out her verses until only the perfect ones remain," Dunbar-Nelson noted in her diary, obviously impressed by Johnson's work after having read the manuscript of a collection of poems. "What she has left are little gems, characterized by a finish of workmanship that is seldom seen in our people."[76] While critical readers certainly exposed Johnson to what must at times have been painful reviews of her work, it is apparent that sometimes they also did her the disservice of disguising much of what they really thought about her writing under polite flattery, offering her much-needed support but not the tough critical eye that her writing demanded to develop and improve. Johnson regularly exchanged work-in-progress with Jean Toomer and was no doubt encouraged by his positive response. "I like 'The ashen-dusted trail,' " he wrote to her on one occasion. "Fine rhythm and word choice, just the words." His comments on her work generally echoed those of William Stanley Braithwaite and James Weldon Johnson: "I read your lines and I swear that as love lyrics aiming not at the rhythmic subtleties and virtuosities of the genius but at the true expression of emotion and feeling filtered thru the imagination they come nearer my heart than anything I've ever read." Toomer's comments to others regarding her writing, how-ever, suggest that he was not always completely honest with Johnson when he offered his opinion of her work. In 1922 he wrote to John McClure, editor of the *Double Dealer*, citing these criticisms of her writing: "Too much poetic jargon, too many inhibitions check the flow of what I think to be real (if slender) lyric gift."[77] Although privately Toomer's opinions about her writing were at times disparag-ing, he remained a supporter of her work and one of its first readers. He often closed letters to her in which he reviewed her work by appealing to her to "Send me some more."[78] It is as if he understood that his support for her work was imperative for her, both personally and professionally. He expressed as much in a note to Johnson that accompanied a review he had written of *Bronze*. His review of *Bronze*, he explained, was both a statement meant for publication as well as a personal endorsement of her talent. "I'm enclosing a review of BRONZE," Toomer wrote. "I think [it] will do you good. Its brevity should make it suitable for almost any publication. It's yours. Send it where you will. Or, if you'd rather, keep it for yourself."[79]

Although not everyone was as outwardly complimentary of John-son's writing as was Jean Toomer, she still managed to attract impor-tant literary figures to write satisfactory introductions and publication blurbs for her work. In calling on W. E. B. Du Bois, for instance, to write the foreword to the collection *Bronze*, the enormously ambi-tious Johnson was acutely aware that association with Du Bois's name "would add to the distinction and appeal of the book."[80] The intro-duction that Du Bois wrote suggests the extent to which Johnson was dependent on the support of others, even if that "support" was not always entirely flattering. "Those who know what it means to be a colored woman in 1922—and to know it not so much in fact as in feeling, apprehension, unrest, and delicate yet stern thought—must read Georgia Douglas Johnson's BRONZE," Du Bois wrote. "Much of it will not touch this reader and that, and some of it will mystify and puzzle them as a sort of reiteration and over-emphasis. But none can fail to be caught here and there by a word—a phrase—a period that tells a life history or even paints the history of a generation."[81] As Gloria T. Hull posits in her biographical study of Georgia Douglas Johnson, his last, patronizing paragraph implies what a coup it was to have any word from "the great Du Bois."[82] "I hope Mrs. Johnson will have a wide reading," he wrote. "Her word is simple, sometimes trite, but it is singularly sincere and true, and as a revelation of the soul struggle of the women of the race it is invaluable."[83] Du Bois's remarks here and elsewhere reveal his fundamental inability to consider lyrical verse as "serious" poetry. In his failure to sustain a genuine tribute to Johnson or to elaborate on even the more positive remarks he made about her work, Du Bois's comments reduce Johnson's achievement in *Bronze* to a series of clichés about femininity and stereotypes of feminine artistic sensibility.

That Johnson had to publish *An Autumn Love Cycle* at her own expense in 1928, despite her one act play *Plumes* having won first prize in an *Opportunity* writing contest a year earlier, suggests that many of Johnson's early literary mentors had come to share Du Bois's luke-warm assessment of her work. It also suggests that the literary mode in which she had achieved success no longer had a substantive audience. But these observations only begin to reveal the difficulties Johnson encountered when trying to see her work into print. Her poetic style was one obstacle; another was that many publishers did not consider her "popular enough as a writer to make [her work] pay."[84] This pronouncement did not deter Johnson from pursuing her own methods of both networking and promoting herself. The publishers "do not know how hard I work on my own sales," Johnson mused to Countee Cullen, discussing pragmatically the alternative channels through which she might boost interest in her own publications. "Through the newspapers for which I write I am able to do a tremendous amount of advertising. . . . I get [my books] into the schools and libraries."[85] Given her reputation as a center of the Washington, D.C., literary community and her contact with the most famous of the Harlem Renaissance writers, Johnson's perspective on literature and literary figures was considered valuable. She was a popular speaker at literary societies in Washington, D.C., as well as cities like Chicago and Atlanta. This was one venue through which she could promote her work as well as that of her peers. Cullen was the beneficiary of her praise, for instance, on an evening in November 1929. "I talked to a literary club here last night," she wrote to Cullen the next day, "and I told them that I thought you far surpassed Keats and pointed to your poetry as an example of what we should try for in literature both as for standard and content."[86]

Johnson's willingness to make public appearances, her determination to promote literary community, and her selfless nurturing of the work of others surely prevented her, on some level, from becoming a more accomplished writer. Despite her own best efforts and willingness to expose her writing to the critical eyes of her peers, she rarely had the time or mustered the courage to give her writing the polish it needed. By 1947 Johnson reported that she had thirty unfinished book manuscripts stored away. As her friend Cedric Dover pointed out in a letter to Johnson at the time, the sheer number of unpublished books suggested the extent of Johnson's divided attention over the years. "Now the blunt truth about your 30 books," Dover wrote. "Anyone who has written 30 unpublished books has been pouring out words for years, without much thought for selectiveness, audience, and the making of publishable books." His advice to her: get serious. "At this point there is only one productive course: write nothing more until you have thoroughly sifted and weeded out all this material and reduced it to manageable proportions." He suggested that "three or four novels could advantageously, if the scenes are similar, be cut down to one." Knowing Johnson's belief that all writers needed the critical eyes of others to produce their best work, he warned her that those she turned to for comment needed to be as strict with her as she needed to be with herself. He advised her to "try to discuss plans and progress with a severely critical, not flattering, friend, and with other writers." His last piece of advice suggested that she needed to be more realistic about the final stage in the process as well—getting published. "Finally," he wrote, "get each completed item brutally vetted by a harsh critic who knows something about publishing—and before long you'll see a series of Georgia books being published."[87]

Dover's observation, "You have too many irons in the fire: all warm, none red hot," was astute.[88] For this reason and others, Johnson became known not primarily for her writing but for her generous spirit and as an invaluable mentor to great writers. Few who knew her underrated the value of this role. William Braithwaite even believed it to be grounds for awarding Johnson a Rosenwald Fellowship. "This can be the best of your rewards," he wrote to Johnson in December 1944, when she was being considered for the award, "this opportunity which the fellowship grants you to complete your long delayed revisions and compositions, and thus not only enrich our Literary possessions, but create in them better understanding, a higher and purer spirit of fellowship between the races and in our democracy." "You fully deserve this opportunity," he continued, "not only on the score of your gifts as a writer but also for the valuable services you have rendered through your contributions to both American and racial Literature . . . and the encouragement and counsel given in the past to youthful aspirants in letters who have since honored by accomplishments our native art."[89]

The Saturday night gatherings in Johnson's home took place regularly from about 1921 until about 1928; they then took place sporadically into the 1930s. A number of factors contributed to their demise. Surely one of these was the fall of the stock market in 1929 and the resulting Great Depression, an event that effectively ended the vogue of the Negro by changing the economic status of white patrons whose financial commitment to African American art and artists had augmented the movement. But Johnson's own financial responsibilities, coupled with her diminished stamina and general disillusionment, were also factors in the disbanding of the Saturday Nighters. "I haven't been keeping the group together for I have not been feeling fit for a year or two," Johnson wrote to Langston Hughes in an undated note written on Department of Labor stationery. "In fact I have to work so hard that I cannot stay up on Saturday nights anymore." Johnson hoped that this lull in literary activity would be merely a hiatus and not the end of her career as a writer or mentor. "Link [her eldest son] has finished, passed the bar and begun to work so I can see a wee bit of light through the dense wood before me. Pepe [her youngest son] finishes next year. If they hurry and get onto their feet I shall be able to straighten up and try my wings before they are too wesk [*sic*, weak] to carry me far." Still, her outlook had already begun to shift from that of an active intellectual to one of a nostalgic sage. "I have been fortunate in having the friendship of all of you winged artists," she wrote to Hughes. "It has been one of my blessings. Somehow all that I have missed in the big ways of the world with its fanfare of trumpets, have more than been compensated for through the fragrant friendships I have known."[90]

Johnson did seem to regain her energy, but only to have it sapped again, this time not by financial concerns but by the same dilemmas and limitations that seemed always to plague black writers. Between 1935 and 1939 she submitted at least five plays to the Federal Theater Project, the U. S. Government's effort to begin a nationwide, federally funded theater as a part of President Roosevelt's New Deal and Works Progress Administration. Three of the plays that she submitted specifically address the subject of rape and lynching; two others are historical pieces on slavery and the slaves' desire to escape to freedom. Dedicated to the promotion of amateur playwrights and experimental productions unlikely to be produced through other venues, the Federal Theater Project should have been a perfect match for Johnson's dramas. As Winona Fletcher notes, however, Johnson's plays were too politically charged for the Federal Theater Project evaluators. Their readers' reports dismissed four of the five plays she submitted on various grounds; they were especially critical of the plays that addressed lynching, calling one melodramatic and expressing their disbelief that in another Johnson had suggested that a lynching might occur without provocation. Their most telling comment was reserved for the play that they approved, "A Sunday Morning in the South," a one-act drama that also addressed the subject of lynching. This drama was deemed acceptable not for its particular artistic merit but because, according to one reader, "it is not offensive to either group."[91] Johnson's playwriting and her work with the Krigwa Players in New York City in the late 1920s had prepared her to see the theater as a particularly powerful and effective means of relaying social protest. The rejection of her social protest dramas by the Federal Theater Project must have been discouraging, for in addition to confirming white America's persistent denial of wrongdoing in their treatment of African Americans, it revealed the extent to which the writing of black authors continued to be monitored for its "acceptability" with little regard for artistic merit.

Ultimately, it was not that Johnson's wings were too weak; rather, without time and, after the demise of the literary evenings in her home, without the support and intense intellectual stimulation of some of the best literary minds, Johnson's work and her well-being suffered. Johnson's correspondence is increasingly punctuated by the refrain "I am trying to write." "I am trying to write that biography of Mr. Johnson," she once wrote to Langston Hughes, "its [*sic*] a very difficult task because for one thing I haven't any leisure. The mornings are full of tasks and at night I am too weary to think."[92] In another letter to Hughes written during the same era Johnson wrote, "I feel so burdened and can't shake the feeling of a load off." "You are a carefree boy," she told Hughes, demanding playfully that he "tell [her] the secret" of his optimism. Johnson was acutely aware that her talent as an advisor did not make her especially good at hearing or taking her own advice. "Funny thing," she wrote to Hughes, "I am forever telling somebody how to [be carefree], and yet I am not able to do it for myself."[93]

In an effort to coax Johnson out of the state of frustration and disappointment into which she had fallen by the 1950s, Hughes advised that she write about something she knew well—the Saturday Nighters. "Why don't you do an article for *Phylon* about those wonderful literary evenings which the writers of Washington used to enjoy at your house?" he suggested to her in a letter dated 24 November 1957. In advancing this idea, Hughes was able not only to recommend a concrete publishing venue, but he also acknowledged the importance of Johnson's role in promoting literary community. "Certainly those evenings are a part of literary history and you are the one who should make a readable record of them," he told her.[94] Johnson apparently did make a record of the Saturday Nighters; one of the unpublished books listed in her "Catalogue of Writings" is titled "Literary Salon." Her brief description of the piece implies that it is the story of the Saturday Nighters: "Literary Salon is the story of literary gatherings that began under Taft's administration and continued into the years indefinitely with even now and then meetings of those who regather in the capital. It began with Jean Toomer, Langston Hughes, Countee Cullen, Alain Locke, etc., at 15th and 'S', N.W., and was the place where many of the splendid young writers of the present-day received their contactual inspiration."[95]

Although Johnson's manuscript recounting the literary evenings held in her home appears not to have survived, Johnson's "S Street Salon" was not forgotten. Others recorded the importance of the Saturday Nighters and documented Johnson's role as the spiritual center of that group. The importance of the group was, perhaps, most easily understood not by the artists who had themselves been present in Johnson's home but by a new generation of "fledgling" writers who had heard about the Saturday Nighters and wished for a similar literary community. In March 1958 Johnson received a letter from Paul Breman, who was in the process of putting together an anthology of selections that stressed "racial themes." "I have read about your Saturday Evening Salon," he wrote. "Could it have been in Langston Hughes' autobiography The Big Sea? . . . It is a pity that the younger generation does not have a meeting-place any more, it would mean so much just now." What these writers needed, Breman implied, was a supportive literary community in which to sort through their ideas and think critically about their writing. "Some of the poets now in their early twenties show some talent, yes," he wrote to Johnson, "but most of their work is made up of a sort of uncorrelated frustration which harms their poetry more than anything."[96]

The need to find a forum in which to work through the "uncorrelated frustration" of the writer's life had served as the catalyst behind the beginning of the Saturday Nighters. Johnson's involvement in the Saturday Nighters was at its peak in the 1920s; long after she stopped holding regular meetings of the group, she continued to seek forms of literary community that might replicate or replace it. Her participation in The Writers' Club, Inc., a Washington, D.C.-based group of black writers that Johnson was invited to join in 1941, as well as The Professional Writers' Club, an all-women's group, placed her once again in the context of active black artists, writers, and intellectuals. According to the constitution of The Writers' Club, the "organization exist[ed] for the purpose of stimulating more creative writing among those who have had their writings accepted by periodicals or publishers of note."[97] Both of these groups' emphasis on publication should have provided just the structure and encouragement that Johnson needed to complete the many projects she had underway: one of the mottoes of The Professional Writers' Club was "Let's remember that a manuscript in the desk drawer will never sell!"[98] But, according to fellow members of The Writers' Club, although diligent about her work, Johnson was not the enthusiastic and energetic personality she had been as the engine behind the Saturday Nighters. Although after 1948 Johnson attended The Writers' Club's meetings regularly until it disbanded in 1960, fellow member Dorothy Porter Wesley remembered her as "very stiff, still, and quiet" at the meetings.[99] She participated in the activities of the club by reading her poetry aloud, but she remained reserved. It is possible that a combination of her age, her continual struggle to maintain her focus and to publish after the promising but relatively brief flurry of literary recognition in the 1920s, and her lack of a leadership position in The Writers' Club led her to feel alienated and prevented her from fully participating in the intellectual work that surrounded her.

"LITTLE KNOTS OF PEOPLE WRITING, AND READING"

At the height of their activities, the Saturday Nighters was recognized as an important institution where writers and intellectuals gathered regularly to exchange ideas about literature and to talk about their writing. As literary interest and opportunities expanded for black Americans in the 1920s, similar circles were formed and acknowledged for their ability to support black writers and intellectuals throughout the country. Most of the individuals who took part in these literary societies remained anonymous. Unlike the Saturday Nighters, they won no *Opportunity* writing contests, they were not honored at dinners in New York City, and if their writing found its way into print at all it was by way of the miscellaneous pamphlets and broadsides that the literary societies themselves pulled together, paid for, and distributed in their communities. The stories of these small literary societies that met in domestic spaces throughout the nation in the 1920s and provided a context for the private reading and critiquing of literature complement the more formal and more familiar history of the Harlem Renaissance, its flamboyant personalities, and the public literary performances for which it is renowned.

Charles S. Johnson, editor of *Opportunity* from 1923 to 1928, recognized these small literary enclaves as essential but lamented their isolation; in his words, they were in need of "informal literary intelligence" to expand their number and their influence.[100] Officially, *Opportunity* was the organ of the National Urban League, but Charles Johnson's particular interests dictated that the content of the magazine would include "aspects of the cultural side of Negro life that have long been neglected" as well.[101] By mid-decade its expanding literary focus came to include the columns "Ebony Flute," written by Gwendolyn Bennett, and "The Dark Tower," by Countee Cullen; both were begun in direct response to increased interest in literature and, particularly, to the blossoming of literary societies. "The Ebony Flute" and, to a lesser extent, "The Dark Tower" provided news of literary societies, their membership, and their activities; both appeared regularly between 1926 and 1928. Dedicated to what she called "literary chit-chat and artistic whatnot," Bennett's column regularly carried news of the Saturday Nighters.[102] The July 1927 column was typical of her chatty, anecdotal tone: "The Saturday Nighters of Washington, D.C., met on June fourth at the home of Mrs. Georgia Douglas Johnson. Mr. Charles S. Johnson was the guest of honor. It was particularly pleasing to see and talk to Miss Angelina Grimké. She is a beautiful lady with ways as softly fine as her poems. The company as a whole was a charming medley. . . . E. C. Williams with his genial good humor; Lewis Alexander with jovial tales of this thing and that as well as a new poem or two which he read; Marieta [*sic*] Bonner with her quiet dignity; Willis Richardson with talk of 'plays and things' . . . and here and there a new poet or playwright . . . and the whole group held together by the dynamic personality of Mrs. Johnson . . . some poems by Langston Hughes were read."[103] Entries like this one brought "The Ebony Flute" and Gwendolyn Bennett high praise from the literary community. " 'I like the Ebony Flute,' " Georgia Douglas Johnson wrote to Bennett in the fall of 1926. William Stanley Braithwaite agreed, telling Bennett: " 'You have made *The Ebony Flute* attractive and interesting and I am looking forward to each month as a sort of personal chat with you about books and things.' "[104]

Month after month, in column after column, Gwendolyn Bennett illustrated through "The Ebony Flute" that the literary renaissance so intensely experienced in New York City's Harlem was indeed sweeping through black communities across the nation. "We who clink our cups over New York fire-places are wont to miss the fact that little knots of literary devotees are in like manner sipping their 'cup o' warmth' in this or that city in the 'provinces,'" Bennett reported in October 1926.[105] The effect of her words was not only to inform the New York writers and intellectuals that literary communities existed outside of the city; her reports had a tremendous impact on those "provincial" communities as well. Bennett received many notes like this one, the text of which she incorporated into her column for December 1926: "This is just a little line to say how much we enjoy the *Ebony Flute*," the letter began. "And when I say 'we' I mean a Saturday noon writers' organization, which Charles S. Johnson was good enough to help us form, when he was in Los Angeles a few weeks ago. We call ourselves the *Ink Slingers*."[106] Bennett's inclusion of the Ink Slingers' greeting in "The Ebony Flute" raised her readers' awareness of the indisputable fact that collective reading and writing groups were being formed everywhere. As Bennett reminded her readers, this intelligence disrupted New York's reputation as "the great book-publishing, book-consuming ogre." In the past, Bennett noted, "gossip of this and that thing concerning books and their makers would tend by centripetal force alone to precipitate into what groups in the great Metropolis are doing and thinking." But reading, writing, and other literary activities were alive and well in black communities outside of Harlem, a fact that organizations like the Saturday Nighters and the Ink Slingers proved and Bennett's column celebrated. "It is ever so refreshing," she wrote, "to be brought sharply up against the fact that here and there in other less motley cities are little knots of people writing, and reading . . . perhaps hoping and certainly thinking."[107]

As members of these small, literary "knots" moved from place to place, city to city, their influence was extended. Lewis Alexander, for instance, a poet and devoted member of the Saturday Nighters in the 1920s, became involved in a Philadelphia literary community called the Black Opals. In addition to regular meetings as a collective, the Black Opals also launched a literary magazine in 1927 to promote their work and their activities. The group's mission statement is written at the back of their first publication: "BLACK OPALS is the expression of an idea. It is the result of the desire of older New Negroes to encourage younger members of the group who demonstrate talent and ambition." The members of the Black Opals insisted that their association was a "movement" as well as a literary group; they believed that black literature should be a sanctuary for all black people and not just a select few and encouraged anyone interested in literary expression to contact and join them. "BLACK OPALS does not purport to be an aggregation of masters and masterpieces," reads a statement in the little magazine they published. "These expressions, with the exception of contributions by recognized New Negro artists, are the embryonic outpourings of aspiring young Negroes living for the most part in Philadelphia. Their message is one of determination, hope, and we trust power."[108]

Another group of note was the Saturday Evening Quill Club. Begun in Boston in 1925, it was "an organization of Boston writers" that included Dorothy West, Helene Johnson, Eugene Gordon, Florida Ruffin Ridley, Roscoe Wright, and Edythe Mae Gordon. In 1928 they put together the first issue of *The Saturday Evening Quill*, a collection of fiction, prose, poetry, essays, and illustrations that they were determined to issue annually. "Its purpose," they announced in "A Statement to the Reader" that appeared in the first issue, was "chiefly to present original work of Saturday Evening Quill Club members to themselves."[109] The publication was paid for "out of [the members'] own pockets and purses," and the first two issues were not offered for sale. Edited by Eugene Gordon, a member of the editorial staff at the *Boston Post* and himself a regular contributor to *Opportunity* and *Messenger*, the first issue of the *Quill* was very well received, a fact that was well documented in representative quotations printed on the first page of the next issue. "The magazine is artistic, meaty, and altogether credible," wrote a reviewer from *The Bostonian*. The *New York Amsterdam News* saw the *Quill* as the product of a worthy organization that would bring great good to the immediate community as well as the larger literary world. "It is good to see such movements as the Saturday Evening Quill Club," wrote their reviewer. "Of such things good literature will come. . . . Harlem writers should follow their example." W. E. B. Du Bois contributed his stamp of approval to the *Quill*, commenting that "of the booklets issued by young Negro Writers in New York, Philadelphia, and elsewhere, this collection from Boston is the most interesting and best. . . . It is well printed and readable and maintains a high mark of literary excellence." One critic imagined even more far-reaching goals for the organization and their successful publication. "The community is uplifted by the Saturday Evening

Quill Club's work," wrote Renzie Lemus. "It is the kind of stuff which makes the race problem solve itself."[110]

Those at the forefront of literary culture in the 1920s recognized that the work of the smaller literary societies outside of New York City and their independent publications were essential to ensuring the success, the overall effectiveness, and the impact of the black arts movement. In the "The Dark Tower," Countee Cullen went so far as to voice his optimism that the "Black Opals venture" might be able to "sweep the country as the little theater movement has done."[111] Noting that the Philadelphia-based group would soon be paying a visit to the Saturday Evening Quill Club in Boston, Gwendolyn Bennett envisioned the literary societies forming something of a national network. "Mayhap some year," she said, "both of these groups with one or two of New York's younger, newer Negroes will get together and go to visit the Ink Slingers in California."[112] These organizations ensured that the production of and interest in black literature would not die out as the market and appetite for black writing waned in the 1930s. They also enabled the impact of black literature to continue to expand beyond the bounds of formal educational institutions and traditional means of distributing literature, reaching out to black readers who might otherwise have been excluded from literary community.

Epilogue

BUILDING COMMUNITY IN CONTEMPORARY

READING GROUPS

The African American literary societies I have been looking at, from their origins in mutual aid societies at the turn of the eighteenth century to their efflorescence during and after the Harlem Renaissance, have historically been crucial to uniting black communities, illustrating the importance of collective endeavor, providing a network of support for African American intellectuals, playing a constitutive role in the formation of American literature, and influencing the development of a black public sphere. Transformed in the last decades of the twentieth century into reading groups and book clubs, contemporary literary societies continue to play important roles in black communities throughout the nation. These contemporary literary coalitions have not necessarily evolved directly from the earlier literary societies that have been the main focus of my research, and it is not my intention to argue that there is a continuity in organized reading groups from the early nineteenth to the beginning of the twenty-first century. Instead of suggesting such lines of descent, I would like to close my study by examining briefly the degree to which these contemporary literary societies are generally involved in the same particular set of issues, especially those issues involving the relationship between literary work and political activism, between collective study and a sense of community, between the practice of reading and the formation of literary history.

In August 1992 the *New York Times Magazine* ran an article announcing the repeal of one of the most strongly held beliefs in the publishing industry. "Publishers agreed that blacks don't buy books," the headline read. "Author Terry McMillan is proving them wrong." The article, titled "McMillan's Millions," told the story of the rise to widespread recognition and financial prosperity of author Terry McMillan, whose 1992 novel *Waiting to Exhale* had at the time been on the *New York Times* bestseller list for eleven weeks. The success of this, McMillan's third novel, had been anticipated: 385,000 copies were already in print, and McMillan had just sold the paperback rights for $2.64 million. Her public readings regularly drew audiences of over a thousand people. *Waiting to Exhale* would eventually be turned into a major motion picture, which, while not critically acclaimed, was wildly popular, especially among black viewers.[1]

For the publishing industry, McMillan's success—or what is still commonly referred to as the McMillan Phenomenon—was seen as nothing short of miraculous. As the *New York Times Magazine* so clearly articulated, commercial publishers have traditionally assumed that blacks don't read and that they don't buy books. "For years, the stereotypical response from publishers for not publishing black books was 'blacks don't read, there's no market because they don't buy hardcover books,'" said Calvin Reid, an editor at *Publishers Weekly*.[2] In 1987, however, the first printing of 5,000 copies of McMillan's first novel, *Mama*, sold out very quickly. While its publisher, Houghton Mifflin, had taken standard measures to see that the book was shipped to bookstores and received publicity and reviews, they were nevertheless shocked by its commercial success.

Rather than a miraculous and unexplainable phenomenon, McMillan's millions—in book sales and in her own financial profit—are directly attributable to her having taken control of her own marketing. Had McMillan been content to see her books marketed in the ways that the publishing industry has traditionally marketed books, statistics on the sales of her books may have fulfilled the industry's low expectations. But McMillan knew that a black book-buying public and a black readership existed, and that they were hungry to see their own creativity, aspirations, and experiences reflected in literature. To reach them, she launched an independent letter-writing campaign, writing to organizations that have traditionally been at the center of black communities and contacting local media to publicize her work. She sent letters to black bookstores, urging them to stock her books and encourage their clientele to read them. She also indicated her willingness to give readings from her work. Invitations poured in, and McMillan's reading tours took her into black communities throughout the nation where she read from her work and talked to the diverse groups of black readers who wanted to meet her. In the words of the owner of one black bookstore, Denver, Colorado's Hue-Man Experience, McMillan "worked black bookstores until she got that following"; but she also "worked" locations not traditionally associated with the marketing of books, including church meeting halls and other community centers in African American neighborhoods, sororities, and adult education programs such as the Union Settlement Association in East Harlem, New York.[3] Not only did black readers turn out to hear McMillan read, they bought her books in such numbers that, as the *New York Times Magazine* article attests, the publishing industry took notice. "What McMillan did with her letter-writing campaign, her endless reading tours, which included not just colleges but jazz clubs, community centers and smaller black bookstores, was to create a paradigm of how to sell to black American readers."[4] According to Cheryl Woodruff, one of only a handful of black editors in trade publishing in 1992, what was considered unique about the McMillan Phenomenon was that it was "made in the black community," dispelling widespread assumptions that black authors' books were read primarily by whites and a small group of black intellectuals.[5]

While McMillan's strategies of self-promotion and the subsequent success of her novels may have made black readers more visible to acquisitions editors who consider manuscripts by and about African Americans and to the marketing departments of the nation's mainstream publishing industry, the existence of a black readership and a black book-buying market is not new. Neither is the paradigm of how to sell books to black American readers that is suggested by McMillan's endless reading tours and her focus on those informal locations that have historically formed the center of black communities. McMillan's "whistle-stop campaign" is in fact reminiscent of earlier efforts to distribute literature to African Americans. Consider the success of itinerant bookseller Kathryn Johnson, for instance, who traveled throughout the north- and southeastern United States selling books by and about African Americans in the 1920s. Johnson well understood the importance of as well as the obstacles to getting books into the hands of black readers. Knowing that the broad-based approaches to bookselling favored by white America would neither cater to nor have an impact on the black community, Johnson loaded the back seat of her Ford coupe with books and went into black communities; there, she relied on the foothold she was given by a church or a local women's organization to attract the interest and gain the trust of the community. Like McMillan, Johnson paid attention to the cultural traditions of African Americans and tapped into the formal as well as the informal institutions that have always been central to the social and political lives of black people. In this way, Johnson located and served a black readership overlooked by traditional booksellers but eager to own books and to read them. "My books are like seeds," Johnson said of the impact of her work; "I believe they will grow and multiply into fine thoughts and deeds."[6]

Johnson's work in 1925 proved as newsworthy as the McMillan phenomenon of the late 1980s. Mary White Ovington, cofounder of the NAACP (National Association for the Advancement of Colored People) and herself no stranger to black communities, expressed nothing short of disbelief when she documented Johnson's activities for the trade journal *Publishers Weekly*. But Johnson was not alone in her understanding of the urgency of getting literature into black communities for the welfare of their citizens. "People need poetry," Mary McLeod Bethune told Langston Hughes in the summer of 1931. Her suggestion to him: "You must go all over the South with your poems."[7] The reading tour and the publications that resulted from Bethune's idea were motivated by Hughes's belief that white publishers made "little or no effort . . . to reach the great masses of the colored people"; nevertheless, he realized that literature was important to black Americans, in part because it was possible to "create an interest in racial expression through books."[8] His sensitivity to the particular needs of the black communities to which he traveled is reflected in the texts that he developed for his reading tours. "The Negro Mother and Other Recitations" consists largely of poems written to be appreciated by an audience with widely divergent literacy skills. Simple in diction and rhyme, inspirational in subject matter, these poems were not meant to be passively received; rather, they were meant to engender further literary activity such as memorization and performance. With texts such as this, Hughes intended to "mobilize the audiences of [his] public readings into a reading public" that imagined itself through literary texts and through reading and listening to poetry.[9]

To reach an even wider audience, Hughes designed and printed two inexpensive texts: a pamphlet version of "The Negro Mother and Other Recitations," which he sold for twenty-five cents, and illustrated broadside versions of single poems, which were available for ten cents each. In addition to selling them at readings, Hughes placed advertisements for these texts in black periodicals like *The Crisis*. The black reading public that responded to these advertisements was as determined as it was diverse. "Dear editor I me a reder of the Chris," begins one writer's 1932 request for several of the broadsides. Mrs. B. J. Anderson, president of the Periclean Club of Birmingham, Alabama, wrote to request a copy of Hughes's booklet for her club to display as a part of a week-long program on Negro writers and their literature. The purpose of their venture was "to acquaint the citizens of Birmingham with the achievement of Negroes in literature, and to increase their interest in the same." She closed her letter by adding that they would be "presenting Langston Hughes during the week and would especially like to have the little pamphlet of his poems."[10] The great numbers who placed orders for the inexpensive pamphlets or requested complimentary copies demonstrate the willingness of members of the black community to exercise their literacy and take on the role of literary activists. As Elizabeth Davey notes, "it was readers within [the communities Hughes visited]—primarily women—who circulated the poems further, lending the booklet, lecturing on the poems and the poets, and reading the poems aloud."[11]

Hughes's poetry recitals in the 1930s, the itinerant bookselling of Kathryn Johnson in the 1920s, and the extensive reading tours conducted in black communities nationwide by Terry McMillan in the late 1980s are all representative of the community-wide efforts undertaken to both recognize and develop those environments in which black readers would flourish. While the efforts to this end of Kathryn Johnson and Langston Hughes in the first decades of the twentieth century remained largely unrecognized, strategies used by Terry

McMillan and other black writers to disseminate their work to black readers and in black communities have, in the first decade of the twenty-first century, become highly visible. Mainstream publishing houses have begun to realize and appreciate the diverse ways that printed texts have traditionally found their way into black communities and into the hands of black readers. "The African-American community, through bookstores, black wholesalers and organization, have [*sic*] an extremely successful way of popularizing new and up-and-coming black writers that doesn't exist in the white community," said Leigh Haber, vice president and associate publisher of Scribners, a division of Simon and Schuster, in 1994. "Mainstream publishers didn't know it existed. They do now and have tapped into it."[12] A recognition of the importance of black bookstores and their role in the dissemination of books to black readers has been one sign of the rising awareness of publishers of the best ways to market books to black readers. Another is the diverse promotional tours planned for some black writers by their publishers, which are now as likely to include readings at sites central to black community life like black bookstores, community centers, or local book clubs as the prerequisite appearances at big chain superstores like Borders or Barnes and Noble.

In many ways, African Americans' interest in forming book clubs and reading groups is at the heart of the success of black authors and the newfound popularity of their literature. Since the late 1980s, paralleling the so-called McMillan Phenomenon has been tremendous interest among black Americans in forming book clubs and reading groups. As this book illustrates, book clubs and reading groups are not new to the black community. In the last decade, however, they have experienced a tremendous growth in number and variety. Although black women have been the most active in forming single-sex book groups, there are also men's book clubs, coed book clubs, and book clubs for singles and for couples. Mothers and daughters of all ages are uniting to participate in book clubs together and, to a lesser degree, parents are beginning to form book clubs to encourage reading among boys. Some book clubs are formed around their members' particular interests, while others bring together old friends for whom the reading group is a convenient excuse to make time to visit with one another. Some are supported by local bookstores or churches; like the book clubs of the past, however, many African American book clubs and reading groups meet informally, in a member's home. For this reason it is impossible to accurately estimate the number of black book clubs and reading groups currently in existence.

While their numbers are difficult to ascertain, members of black book clubs have been especially vocal about communicating the importance of their book clubs. This has been especially true of black women. Members agree that book clubs are about far more than the communal analysis of a good book. Although reading literature provides the catalyst for their coming together, the impact of black women's association with a reading group is usually felt on both an intellectual and an emotional or spiritual level. "The book club allowed me to place a priority on literature and make sure that I'd read a good book at least once a month," said Monique Greenwood of her involvement in the Go On Girl! Book Club. But "we never just come and talk about a book," said fellow book club member Tracy Mitchell-Brown. "We do talk about other things. The books jump start conversations."[13] This relaxed combination of the social and the intellectual facilitates conversations that would not take place in any other forum. When the Go On Girl! Book Club read *Double Stitch: Black Women Write About Mothers and Daughters*, for instance, members were asked to bring to the meeting pictures of their mothers; as the group discussed the text, they also reflected on their own familial ties. Members invited their partners to a discussion of Nathan McCall's *Makes Me Wanna Holler*. The result was a candid and riveting discussion of the book that led them to discuss their own relationships.

Greenwood, Mitchell-Brown, and Lynda Johnson-Garrett are co-founders of one of the most widely publicized and far-reaching black women's book clubs currently in existence. The Go On Girl! Book Club was begun in 1991 when the three women, colleagues at a New York-based fashion industry trade publication, began getting together over lunch to talk about the books they had read and their favorite authors. Seeking an open forum for the exchange of ideas and opinions, other black women soon joined them; the result was the Go On Girl! Book Club. Dedicated to maintaining the intimacy and productivity that made the experience valuable in the beginning, they limited their membership to twelve people but assisted other interested black women in creating spin-off groups. In 1995 the Go On Girl! Book Club formally incorporated itself as a national, nonprofit organization, with multiple chapters not only in New York but in dozens of cities across the country. In 1999 there were over two hundred members. Each year the entire membership reads the same twelve books, with each chapter discussing them at local, monthly Go On Girl! meetings. In selecting "quality works" by authors of African descent, they pay great attention to including fiction and nonfiction that deals with culture, politics, and other aspects of contemporary black life. The readings draw from a range of genres, including inspirational texts, short stories, biography, science fiction, mystery, and fantasy. In 1992 members read Toni Morrison's challenging novel *Jazz* as well as Terry McMillan's popular *Waiting to Exhale*; in 1994–95 they read *Volunteer Slavery*, the memoir of journalist Jill Nelson, as well as two of the classics of African American literature, Harriet Jacobs's *Incidents in the Life of a Slave Girl* and W. E. B. Du Bois's *Souls of Black Folk.*

Originally, the membership stayed abreast of the developments and activities of each local chapter through *Jambalaya: The Go On Girl! Gazette*; more recently, they have begun their own Web site, which includes information about joining the club and forming local chapters. Once a year the entire membership gathers at a meeting sponsored by one of the local chapters. In addition to taking care of the business of the organization and selecting the reading list for the coming year, the Go On Girl! Book Club Awards are conferred at this meeting. First given out in 1993 at a ceremony held in a Brooklyn jazz club, the awards honor authors selected from the year's reading list as well as publishers who have contributed in notable ways to the promotion of African American literature. The Go On Girl! Awards are meant to encourage responsible writing by authors of African descent. Recent honorees have included Gloria Naylor, Bebe Moore Campbell, Jill Nelson, Nathan McCall, Sonia Sanchez, and Octavia Butler; in addition, Beacon Press and other publishers have been awarded Go On Girl! Book Club Awards for their support of and dedication to publishing the writing of African Americans. The awards have contributed to the increasing visibility of this organization and a growing recognition of their widespread influence. Recent years have found authors and publishers communicating with the book club for guidance, feedback, or endorsement. Because each chapter is committed to exposing its local community to literature by writers of African descent, the group's impact has been felt locally as well. To ensure that positive environments exist in which reading can flourish for high school girls, they organize Junior Go On Girl! Book Clubs; in addition, they collaborate with bookstores and other organizations to host and sponsor literary events that will foster an appreciation for black literature throughout their communities.[14]

In addition to suggesting the ways black women might take on activist roles around spreading literacy and promoting literature by black authors in their communities, literary societies also provide a sense of community and a network of support that is often missing from their lives. Even the names of contemporary black women's book clubs, like Go On, Girl!, Literary Sisters, In the Company of My Sisters, Sister Sister, Herstory, and Black Women United in Literary Development (BUILD), suggest the extent to which they are educational but also inspirational and empowering. Book clubs provide the opportunity for black women, many of them avid readers, to remain intellectually engaged. Members remark that, unlike their formal educational experiences, the atmosphere in their book clubs is challenging and stimulating without being threatening. Much of the support black women derive from their experience in book clubs, however, extends beyond the intellectual. Book clubs give them a chance to come together and openly discuss issues that are central to their everyday lives but usually neglected or avoided there. "Most of us lead very integrated lives," said Karen Grisby Gates of her involvement with Babes on Books, a black women's literary group in Los Angeles. "We were feeling that we hadn't been able to keep in touch in a meaningful way with black girlfriends because we were ethnically isolated in the workplace. So this was a way to . . . have some sistership." Whereas the need for black institutions was once the result of segregation, ironically it is now integration that is creating the need for special black institutions. "Sistership" is increasingly important as black women become more and more successful at careers that locate them in situations where they are surrounded by few other people of color. "Some of us have been the first and only black people to do this or that," says Grisby Gates. "We're used to it, but in some ways a little tired of it because you always end up being a representative of the Negroes. What we missed [in our daily lives] was the chance to touch base with women on a defined and regular basis."[15]

In some respects, the interest shown by black Americans in forming book groups illustrates their exasperation with American society on a number of levels. While black people and other people of color are exposed on a regular basis to the dynamics of contemporary race relations and gender inequality, a deafening silence surrounds these issues in the course of public life. For African Americans, this silence can be debilitating. Discussions of literature in small groups suggest the possibility of humanizing the questions and debates that seem so distant from and irreconcilable with daily life. Angry that lessons in black history, literature, and culture were conspicuously absent from their formal education, many African Americans consider their membership in a book club as a way to educate themselves. That histories and historical fiction are particularly popular book club selections suggests the extent to which black Americans are hungry for stories of their own past. While stories of black leaders like Frederick Douglass and Martin Luther King Jr. are relatively well-known, black Americans are fulfilling their curiosity about other black leaders and previously neglected aspects of black history and culture through their reading groups. In a world where mainstream television and films have done very little to portray African Americans and other minorities in any but the most stereotypical ways, widespread contemporary interest in black book clubs suggests the extent to which black Americans have turned away from these media in favor of the diverse literature currently being produced by black writers.

Although scholars have documented that some readers turn to books as a means of escape from the tedium of their daily lives, reading for black Americans at the beginning of the twenty-first century has more to do with finding than losing themselves. "Even those of us who are the most privileged are deprived of positive images of ourselves and of opportunities to learn," mused Janus Adams, founder of Harambee: The Book Club for African-American Families and Friends, an African American mail order bookstore that operated much like the Book-of-the-Month Club. "For black people, it's suicidal not to have these images, and for nonblacks it presents distortion. It makes them expect a world that doesn't exist." Adams began Harambee in 1990 because "black literature [was] simply not available." Initially, Adams was inundated with orders; the book club has since gone out of business, evidence of the increased attention to black literature in local book superstores as well as an increase in the number and visibility of black bookstores. The growing audience for literature written by black Americans and the attention being paid to black writers by the publishing industry have paved the way for a variety of books that offer different voices and perspectives on the experience of being black in the United States. Through the combined efforts of black authors, booksellers, and those black readers who gather monthly to talk about books, black children at the beginning of the twenty-first century are more likely to be exposed to the rich literary legacy of black Americans. They are also more likely to think of themselves as readers and, potentially, as writers, than ever before. "These are exciting times," mused the manager of one black bookstore in Brooklyn, New York. "I'm watching black kids meet black writers for the first time. That's wonderful, because many thought all writers were dead white men."[16]

Another force that has had a tremendous impact on black readers, authors, and communities is Oprah's Book Club, a segment of *The Oprah Winfrey Show* launched in the fall of 1996. While interracial in membership, this book club, headed by a black woman and championing the writing of African American women, especially Toni Morrison and Maya Angelou, has influenced and been instrumental in the formation of local black book clubs. One of Oprah's intentions in presenting herself as a reader and conducting a television book club is to augment the public's understanding of African Americans, their culture, and the possibilities open to them. "Part of my calling," she asserts, "is to help people to think differently about me, me, black girl, born in Mississippi, 1954, the most racist state on earth."[17] Like earlier reading societies, she is intent on creating and spreading positive images of black people. Winfrey has spoken extensively about how important books and reading have been to her throughout her life. In a childhood marked by alienation, abuse, and loneliness, books were a means of transcending those negative experiences. As a reader, she was someone who belonged. "Getting my library card [as a child for the first time] was like citizenship," Winfrey recalls, "it was like American citizenship."[18] At the same time, Winfrey also found that reading gave her an affirmative vision of black womanhood.

Oprah's Book Club has been Oprah Winfrey's most successful venture to date as a talk-show host. Winfrey was aware that many of her viewers were already participating in their own local reading groups when she announced her intention to begin a television book club and "get the whole country reading again." In some respects, her on-air book club works in much the same way as an intimate local one would. After announcing the month's selection, Winfrey asks viewers to read the book and invites them to write to *The Oprah Winfrey Show*, relaying how the text affected them, what the characters meant to them, and how the story made them reflect on their own lives. From the letters and E-mail Winfrey receives, a handful of viewers are selected to have dinner with Winfrey and the author and participate in a discussion of the featured novel. Portions of the dinner are taped and aired during the show. A profile of the author and a short interview with him or her is also part of the broadcast. What distinguishes Oprah's Book Club is the number of technologies it employs to facilitate discussion of the text, which is potentially not limited to the time allotted to it on *The Oprah Winfrey Show*. In addition to communicating with *The Oprah Winfrey Show* via letters and E-mail, participants in Oprah's Book Club can also communicate with and post messages for one another in chat rooms established by Winfrey on America Online. They have also formed their own local book groups that meet independently but use Oprah's Book Club selections as their reading material.

Although some of her viewers were initially confused by the idea of a television book club (some believed that Winfrey would be giving books away, while others thought she wanted them to send books to her), many immediately communicated their enthusiasm for the idea. "I am 46 years old. And until this past year I have not read more than five books," wrote one viewer, in a letter shared by Oprah on the show. Another relayed that her "entire family has decided that this would be a fantastic thing to do together."[19] Even more impressive than the reaction of Oprah's loyal viewers was the impact of the book club on the publishing industry. The book Oprah chose as the book club's first selection, Jacquelyn Mitchard's *The Deep End of the Ocean*, had received lukewarm reviews when published in June 1996. Days after Oprah's announcement on 17 September 1996 that the novel would be the book club's first selection, it catapulted to number one on the *New York Times* bestseller list, and bookstores and publishers found themselves scrambling to acquire enough volumes of the novel to meet the demand. When the host chose Toni Morrison's third novel, *Song of Solomon* (1977), as her selection on 18 October 1996, Barnes and Noble

Members of The Literary Society, established in 1982 to enhance the independent reading, study, and understanding of African American literature, pose before a meeting in the home of a member, November 2001, New York City.

Booksellers reported that its chain had sold a remarkable 16,070 copies of the novel on that day alone; within two months, twice as many copies of the novel were sold as had been in the previous nine years of its publication. *Song of Solomon* too immediately appeared on the *New York Times* bestseller list. "I am surprised," said Oprah Winfrey in reaction to the success of the book club generally and to the phenomenal sales of *Song of Solomon* in particular. "I am surprised that we can put a 19-year-old book on a best seller list."[20] Morrison's reaction to the feat reflected that she, too, was impressed: "To give a book life larger than its original life is a revolution," she said.[21]

One reason for the great success of Oprah's Book Club is that it provides its "members" with a collective experience similar to that found in earlier literary societies as well as contemporary book clubs and reading groups. Never mind that Winfrey's is a "virtual" community; Oprah's Book Club allows her fifteen to twenty million daily viewers to imagine themselves as a part of and participants in a communal endeavor. Winfrey's own love for reading, her sense that books should be an integral part of people's lives, and her belief that they can bring people together clearly appeal to the daytime television public's desire to be a part of a larger community.[22] "I began buying Oprah's book selection so that I could be part of something bigger, to be connected to people," wrote a female viewer from Maine, who posted her comments on Oprah's Book Club in an online chat room. "I read her selections so I can be part of a group experience and then get to hear what the author has to say. Where [else] can you do that?"[23] Other postings confirm that Winfrey's viewers, many of whom are women who do not work and may therefore lack the sense of community associated with the workplace, seek a shared experience, something that is largely absent from their lives. The book club's success is also indicative of the extent to which texts, even if read in solitude, elicit in their readers responses that demand a forum for sharing. The thousands of letters addressed to Oprah's Book Club each month and the thousands of messages posted in online chat rooms attest to readers' deep desire to have a place in which to talk about what they have read. This effort by disparate readers to communicate with one another in a variety of ways illustrates what Toni Morrison asserted in her appearance as an Oprah's Book Club author: "Novels are for talking about and quarrelling about and engaging in some powerful way. However that happens, at a reading group, a study group, a classroom or just some friends getting together, it is a delightful, desirable thing to do. . . . Reading is solitary, but that's not its only life. It should have a talking life, a discourse that follows."[24]

In the past, literary societies served as informal schools for their members' political education; especially throughout the nineteenth century, they responded to African Americans' democratic aspirations and political desires. Winfrey's interest in texts and the focus of her book club is typically oriented more directly toward her viewers' personal, rather than political, responses to the texts they have read. Oprah admits that she chooses only those books "I have been emotionally moved by."[25] Her desire to hear from her audience how the books she has assigned affected them and her promise that they will change her viewers' lives underscores the extent to which the book club is in keeping with the emphasis on personal revelation and sentimental response that is at the heart of the talk-show format. Like the club's earliest selection, Mitchard's *Deep End of the Ocean,* a novel about a mother whose three-year-old son disappears when she turns her back for a second, many of the texts that Winfrey assigns explore the themes and topics that have traditionally provided material for the talk-show format. With Winfrey's guidance these texts become the catalyst for her studio audience's emotional confessions and personal transformations; their intimate responses, made public and aired worldwide for others to consume, elucidate the sympathy and empathy of Winfrey's television viewers. Winfrey wants readers to have a personal response to the texts she assigns: "That's what I love about books," she says. "You read about somebody else's life, but it makes you think about your own."[26] While some would argue that the personal literary encounters favored by Winfrey and encouraged by Oprah's Book Club are indeed political, they differ in degree and kind from the more overt political confrontations of earlier literary societies.

I have been stressing the emphasis in Oprah's Book Club on readers' personal fulfillment and personal responses to the text; in doing so, I do not want to overlook or underestimate the book club's social and political aspects. Oprah's Book Club has made tremendous contributions toward fostering literacy initiatives as well as creating a widespread appreciation for literature. There is no doubt that Oprah's Book Club has provided people with the incentive to buy books and to read them, no matter how superficial their reading has been. In addition, campaigns launched by Winfrey in connection with Oprah's Book Club have been instrumental in both increasing literacy and distributing literary texts. Winfrey asks publishers to donate 10,000 copies of her selections to libraries around the country. Her regular promotion of book drives has been instrumental to getting books into the hands of people who otherwise would not have easy access to them. As a result of a book drive in the fall of 1997, for instance, 15,000 books were collected and donated to the library at the Louisiana State Penitentiary in Angola, Louisiana. In June 1997 Winfrey formed a partnership with the Starbucks Coffee Company whereby all Starbucks stores would carry the Oprah's Book Club featured selection for the month; all proceeds from the sale of the books sold in the stores are funneled through the Starbucks Foundation to fund literacy initiatives in communities throughout the country. Oprah's Book Club has also brought a higher visibility to local book clubs that has permitted them to demonstrate for a national audience how book clubs might lead literacy campaigns in their communities. Representatives from Atlanta's Circle of Friends, for instance, a book club begun in 1994, appeared on *The Oprah Winfrey Show* on the occasion of the first anniversary of Oprah's Book Club. The club had just formed a community involvement group, identifying an Atlanta apartment complex as a community whose members would benefit from a literacy drive that included giving books to the complex's residents. Their efforts were so successful that they planned to organize another book drive, this time to benefit local residents of Habitat for Humanity properties.[27]

On the few occasions that Winfrey has assigned as Oprah's Book Club selections texts that do not lend themselves to immediate visceral and emotive responses and that instead require readers to engage in more complex discussions of textual analysis and interpretation, viewers have objected. Toni Morrison's *Paradise*, for instance, the most challenging book club selection to date, sparked viewers' complaints that the text was too difficult to read and understand. "Oprah, I was lost," admitted one member of the studio audience.[28] "I really wanted to read the book and love it and learn some valuable life lessons," another viewer told Winfrey, but "when I got into it, it was so confusing I questioned the value of a book that is that hard to understand

and I just quit reading it."[29] Given these responses, academics and other critics of Winfrey's methods and her endeavor might argue that Winfrey has created and caters to a facile readership that is unable to negotiate a difficult text. This criticism supports the conventional understanding that personal or emotional responses to texts come always at the expense of more intellectual reactions to them, and it points to the hierarchical relationship predominant in academic circles that privileges intellect over emotion. That the literary discussions that take place in the classrooms of the nation's top colleges and universities are different from discussions of literature conducted by Winfrey under the auspices of Oprah's Book Club is undeniable. While the qualities and scope of the discussions are dissimilar, however, one is not necessarily better or even more sophisticated than the other, as some academics have insisted. Rather than designations of superiority and inferiority, scholars of early twenty-first-century literacy and reading practices must bring to their research a recognition of and respect for what has always been true: there are many ways to know a book. Different readers come to texts for different reasons, and they bring different reading strategies to texts at different times. For members of the Bethel Historical and Literary Association, for example, reading and literary work was a means to articulating a political agenda. Members of the Saturday Nighters used their literary coalition as a place to draw inspiration for their own creative efforts and as a prepublication venue. Oprah's readers, who read in part for personal discovery, represent another way of interacting with literature. Their discussions typically begin with the text, and they enjoy the act of literary inquiry. Yet they also wish to reach beyond the text, and typical selections lead them into discussions about their own positioning as mothers or daughters, their experiences with death, loss, and grief, or the impact of race and racism in their lives.

One reason critics of Oprah's Book Club have maligned Winfrey's efforts is that she has combined two genres that are usually presented in opposition to one another: television and books. As a popular medium, television has been considered a form of distraction and a deterrent to "more substantive" activities like reading. Many, in fact, trace the decline of literacy to the advent of television. What the success of Oprah's Book Club underscores is that, just as readers approach texts with different interpretive methods and different ideas about the desired results of their reading, reading is associated with different locales. That Oprah's Reading Club is in fact initially a television event does not necessarily make it less valuable for its participants. Indeed, academic classrooms are not the only, or even the most significant, places where reading and literary study have historically taken place. For those traditionalists who devalue popular culture and value canonical literature, Winfrey's television reading program is emblematic of the breakdown of Western cultural standards, or what some have lamented as the closing of the American mind. What they are unwilling to realize is that Winfrey's use of the popular medium of television and her choice of reading selections, drawn from both popular literature and texts that are eligible for future canonization, complicates and challenges distinctions between elite and popular cultural forms and canonical and noncanonical literature in important ways. We saw that the black press in the nineteenth century was a vehicle through which early African Americans implicitly took part in debates about the formation of American literature and the voices it would include. Arguably, Oprah's Book Club and the local book clubs it has inspired can be seen as implicitly participating in contemporary debates about broadening the canon of American literature and expanding ideas about who reads, what is read, and how and where it is discussed.

The dispute between champions of the reading strategies traditionally associated with the academy and defenders of those engaged in Oprah's Book Club and other informal reading groups essentially comes down to the different value placed on different sites of reading. Rather than judging or dismissing these different situations of literary study, we might do well to appreciate the significant steps that alternative sites of literary interaction and exchange have taken toward democratizing both literacy and literary study. It is especially true that African American literary societies and reading groups have historically created these alternate sites of literacy, often as a challenge to those formal institutions that denied them access. These alternative sites were not only a challenge to the formal institutions; they also provided African American readers with a place to gain the kind of sustenance that many black intellectuals, especially black feminists, have defined as necessary for their intellectual growth. Barbara Christian, for instance, recalls that long before the writing of African American women was considered literature worthy of studying in academic settings, she discussed it with " 'ordinary' black women, women in the churches, private reading groups, women like my hairdresser and her clients, secondary school teachers, typists, my women friends." These conversations were conducted "with an intensity unheard of in the academic world." To these women, Christian reminds us, "this literature was not so much an object of study but was . . . life saving."[30]

It is worth pointing out that the three phenomena I have addressed here—Terry McMillan's marketing strategies, contemporary African American reading groups, and Oprah's Book Club—all identify sites of literacy and literary activity that for years went unrecognized by the publishing industry and other mainstream institutions in charge of disseminating literature. By focusing on the consumption rather than the production of literature we are made more aware of how different groups of readers respond to different marketing strategies. In addition to exposing the variety of places where readers in the United States gain access to literary texts and where reading takes place, Terry McMillan, groups like the Go On Girl! Book Club, and Oprah Winfrey have also inspired segments of the United States population not traditionally associated with literature or with reading to become readers. In doing this, they have made a significant contribution toward fulfilling the mission of the earliest African American literary societies.

Notes

1 Frederick Douglass, *Narrative of the Life of Frederick Douglass, an American Slave* (1845; reprint, New York: Penguin, 1983), 78–79.
2 Ibid., 82, 86–87.
3 Ibid., 84, 78.
4 Ibid., 119–20.
5 W. E. B. Du Bois quotes Booker T. Washington in *Black Reconstruction in America* (New York: Atheneum, 1992), 641.
6 W. E. B. Du Bois, *The Souls of Black Folk* (1903; reprint, New York: Penguin, 1989), 22–23.
7 Studies of slave literacy, including and especially Janet Duitsman Cornelius's *When I Can Read My Title Clear* (Columbia: University of South Carolina Press, 1991), have documented the extent to which, despite legislation designed to ensure their illiteracy, slave communities practiced literacy in a variety of ways. These studies confirm, as the story of Frederick Douglass illustrates, that while many slaves could not read, those who could often became the painstaking teachers of basic literacy for those who could not. Like Douglass, some slaves used their reading and writing skills to facilitate their escape from slavery; but others looked to the ability to read and write to transform their lives in more immediate ways and used their literacy to gain advantages for themselves and their fellow slaves within the institution of slavery. Taken together, recent studies of literacy and slave communities have complicated our understanding of the transmission and

uses of literacy among enslaved African Americans. For example, they document that the drive for literacy and schooling that exploded among ex-slaves in the wake of the Civil War was not the result of the work of only sympathetic white northern missionaries and educators. The extension of reading and writing skills throughout the black population was significantly accelerated by an informal network of literate and semiliterate black educators who disseminated literacy in their own communities both before and after Emancipation.

8   Frances Smith Foster, introduction to *Minnie's Sacrifice; Sowing and Reaping; Trial and Triumph: Three Rediscovered Novels*, by Frances E. W. Harper, ed. Frances Smith Foster (Boston: Beacon, 1994), xxi.

9   See Dorothy Porter, "The Organized Educational Activities of Negro Literary Societies, 1828–1846," *Journal of Negro History* 5 (1936): 555–76.

10   Toni Morrison, "Unspeakable Things Unspoken: The Afro-American Presence in American Literature," *Michigan Quarterly Review* 23 (winter 1989): 11.

11   Du Bois, *Souls of Black Folk*, 205.

12   See especially Houston A. Baker Jr., *Blues, Ideology, and Afro-American Literature: A Vernacular Theory* (Chicago: University of Chicago Press, 1984); and Henry Louis Gates Jr., *The Signifying Monkey: A Theory of Afro-American Literary Criticism* (New York: Oxford University Press, 1988).

13   Carl Kaestle, et al., *Literacy in the United States: Readers and Reading since 1880* (New Haven: Yale University Press, 1991), xiv.

14   Roger Chartier, "Texts, Printing, Readings," in *The New Cultural History*, ed. Lynn Hunt (Berkeley: University of California Press, 1989), 157.

15   Robert Darnton, "What is the History of Books?," in *Reading in America: Literature and Social History*, ed. Cathy N. Davidson (Baltimore: Johns Hopkins University Press, 1989), 27.

16   Ibid.

17   Michael Winship, "Afterword," in *Literary Publishing in America, 1790–1850*, by William Charvat (Amherst: University of Massachusetts Press, 1993), 95–96.

18   Wayne A. Wiegand includes a list of the objectives of the Center for the History of Print Culture in Modern America in his introduction to the Center's first publication. See "Introduction: Theoretical Foundations for Analyzing Print Culture as Agency and Practice in a Diverse Modern America," in *Print Culture in a Diverse America*, ed. Wayne A.

Wiegand and James P. Danky (Urbana: University of Illinois Press, 1998), 8.

19 Edward A. Goedeken, "Review: Print Culture in a Diverse America," H-Net Book Review, February 1999.

20 Wiegand, "Introduction," 7.

21 The story of Kathryn Johnson appears in an article written by Mary White Ovington, "Selling Race Pride," *Publishers Weekly* (10 January 1925): 111–14. Historians of the book will immediately recognize similarities between Johnson's "two-foot book shelf" and the "five-foot book shelf" marketed by P. F. Collier & Son beginning in 1909. Also known as the Harvard Classics, the collection was selected and promoted by Charles W. Eliot, president of Harvard University from 1870 to 1909, who had long supported the idea that every American should be engaged in a course of self-guided reading for self-improvement. His insistence—as marketed by Collier—that fifteen minutes of reading a day would result in a liberal education and his suggestion that a five-foot shelf could contain all of the books needed were ridiculed by critics who believed the collection was being advertised in such a way as to imply that knowledge could be acquired virtually effortlessly, through the ownership of books. While these books might confer the apparent status of the educated elite, critics charged, their ownership alone did not constitute an education. Although Johnson's project and Collier's five-foot shelf of books bear a striking resemblance, Johnson does not link the ownership of her selections to the trappings of an educated self or to material success. Rather than selling books that will be kept "for show," Johnson insisted on selling books "to persons who will read them." The value of the books was in their ability to communicate race pride and consciousness; in the development of race pride, she believed, lay the hope of progress and group advancement.

22 Ibid.

23 Carla Peterson, *Doers of the Word: African-American Women Speakers and Writers in the North (1830–1880)* (New York: Oxford University Press, 1995), 5.

24 See, for example, Katherine Bassard, "Gender and Genre: Black Women's Autobiography and the Ideology of Literacy," *African American Review* 26 (1992): 119–29.

25 For pushing me to question Anna Douglass's involvement in a literary society in the context of her illiteracy, I thank my colleague Maria Diedrich.

26 See especially Gary Nash, *Forging Freedom: The Formation of Phila-*

delphia's Black Community, 1720–1840 (Cambridge: Harvard University Press, 1988); James Oliver Horton, *Free People of Color: Inside the African American Community* (Washington, D.C.: Smithsonian Institution Press, 1993); James Oliver Horton and Lois E. Horton, *In Hope of Liberty: Culture, Community, and Protest Among Northeast Free Blacks, 1700–1860* (New York: Oxford University Press, 1997); Emma Lapsansky, " 'Since They Got Those Separate Churches': Afro-Americans and Racism in Jacksonian Philadelphia," *American Quarterly* 32 (1980): 54–78; and Julie Winch, *Philadelphia's Black Elite: Activism, Accommodation, and the Struggle for Autonomy, 1787–1848* (Philadelphia: Temple University Press, 1988).

27 Willard B. Gatewood, *Aristocrats of Color: The Black Elite, 1880–1920* (Bloomington: Indiana University Press, 1990), ix.

28 Robin D. G. Kelley, " 'We Are Not What We Seem': Rethinking Black Working-Class Opposition in the Jim Crow South," *Journal of American History* (June 1993): 77–78.

29 Shirley Brice Heath, "Toward an Ethnohistory of Writing in American Education," in *Writing: The Nature, Development, and Teaching of Written Communication*, ed. Marcia Farr Whiteman (Hillsdale, N.J.: L. Erlbaum Associates, 1981), esp. 27–32.

1 "DREADED ELOQUENCE"

1 The "Testimony and Confession" of Edward Smith is reprinted as Appendix Two in David Walker, *Appeal, in Four Articles; Together with a Preamble, to the Colored Citizens of the World, but in Particular, and Very Expressly to Those of the United States of America*, ed. Sean Wilentz (New York: Hill and Wang, 1965), 85–88. This quote is from page 85.

2 Ibid., 86; emphasis in original.

3 Ibid.

4 Peter P. Hinks, *To Awaken My Afflicted Brethren: David Walker and the Problem of Antebellum Slave Resistance* (University Park: The Pennsylvania State University Press, 1997), 145.

5 "Testimony and Confession" of Edward Smith, 86; emphasis mine.

6 Quoted in Hinks, *To Awaken My Afflicted Brethren*, 119.

7 The chief proponent of this perspective has been Sterling Stuckey, who argues that the *Appeal* was "the most all-embracing black nationalist formulation to appear in America during the nineteenth century." See Stuckey, *The Ideological Origins of Black Nationalism* (Boston: Beacon,

1972), 9. See also Sterling Stuckey, *Slave Culture: Nationalist Theory and the Foundations of Black America* (New York: Oxford University Press, 1987), 98–137.

8 Walker, *Appeal, in Four Articles*, 72.

9 In his 1841 defense of the claim to freedom of the Africans who had revolted on the *Amistad*, Adams observed that "circumlocutions are the fig leaves under which these parts of the body politic [the words "slave" and "slavery"] are decently covered"; John Quincy Adams, *Argument of John Quincy Adams before the Supreme Court of the United States, Appellants v. Cinque, and Other Africans, Captured on the Schooner Amistad* (1841; reprint, New York: New American Library, 1969), 39. For modern accounts of the ambiguities and contradictions of the Constitution, see Robert A. Ferguson, " 'We Hold These Truths': Strategies of Control in the Literature of the Founders," in *Reconstructing American Literary History*, ed. Sacvan Bercovitch (Cambridge: Harvard University Press, 1986); and Priscilla Wald, *Constituting Americans: Cultural Anxiety and Narrative Form* (Durham: Duke University Press, 1995).

10 For interpretive accounts of the appeals made by black petitioners to white Americans to live up to the promises of their revolutionary rhetoric, see Vincent Harding, "Wrestling Toward the Dawn: The Afro-American Freedom Movement and the Changing Constitution," *Journal of American History* 74 (1987): 718–39; and Gary Nash, "Black Americans in a White Republic," in *Race and Revolution* (Madison, Wis.: Madison House, 1990), 57–87.

11 James Forten Sr., *Letters from a Man of Colour* (Philadelphia, 1813), 1.

12 Leonard P. Curry, *The Free Black in Urban America, 1800–1850* (Chicago: University of Chicago Press, 1981), 216, emphasis in original.

13 My notion of the "public sphere" has been shaped by recent scholarship that has responded to Jürgen Habermas's formulation of the term. Habermas identified the bourgeois public sphere as a "space" in which citizens interact with one another in reasoned discourse. Recent criticism of this formulation has focused on Habermas's failure to recognize the possibility of alternative, nonbourgeois public spheres. Within a society stratified along lines of race, class, and gender numerous publics, or "counter-publics," might exist, signaling the variety of public arenas in which people participate. For an especially convincing reformulation of Habermas's concept of a "single, comprehensive, overarching public," see Nancy Fraser, "Rethinking the Public Sphere: A Contribution to the Critique of Actually Existing Democracy," *Social Text* 25/26 (1990): 56–80.

14 Quoted in the *Richmond Enquirer*, 28 January 1830.

15 "Walker's Appeal No. 1," *Liberator*, 8 January 1831, 6. In the wake of Walker's "mysterious" death, Garrison began a dialogue on the subject of David Walker and his pamphlet in the inaugural issues of the *Liberator*. Although Garrison's first response was to condemn the "general spirit" of the text, later comments imply his support for the "many valuable truths and seasonable warnings" found in its pages (*Liberator*, 29 January 1831, 17). Garrison published many perspectives on Walker's *Appeal*, including those from southern newspapers. Additional insight into Walker's text and its reception in the South can be derived from Clement Eaton, "A Dangerous Pamphlet in the Old South," *Journal of Southern History* 2 (1936): 323–34; Jane H. Pease and William H. Pease, "Walker's *Appeal* Comes to Charleston: A Note and Documents," *Journal of Negro History* 59 (1974): 287–92. In addition, Hinks's full-length study of David Walker, *To Awaken My Afflicted Brethren*, offers a detailed analysis of Walker's life and the context in which the *Appeal* was written and distributed.

16 *Boston Daily Courier*, 22 March 1830.

17 Letter to the editor from "Leo," *Liberator*, 29 January 1831, 17.

18 Response to "Leo," *Liberator*, 29 January 1831, 17, emphasis mine.

19 Hinks, *To Awaken My Afflicted Brethren*, 181.

20 *Freedom's Journal*, 16 March 1827, 3. In April 1828 the Boston group met again "for the purpose of enquiring whether the Freedom's Journal had been conducted in a manner satisfactory to the subscribers and to the Coloured community at large." Their endorsement of the newspaper as "well worthy of our unremitted exertions" underscores their unwavering support. See "Original Communication," *Freedom's Journal*, 25 April 1828, 38.

21 For a complete discussion of the intellectual background of the *Appeal*, including the extent to which Walker was influenced by the work of writers for *Freedom's Journal*, see chapter 4 in Hinks, *To Awake My Afflicted Brethren*. Walker was also supported the newspaper *Rights of All*, successor to *Freedom's Journal*; see the *Appeal*, 67.

22 Jupiter Hammon, *An Address to the Negroes In the State of New York* (1787), reprinted in *Early Negro Writing*, ed. Dorothy Porter (Boston: Beacon, 1971), 319.

23 *Boston Daily Evening Transcript*, 28 September 1830; emphasis in original.

24 Theodore S. Wright, "The Progress of the Antislavery Cause" (1837),

reprinted in Carter G. Woodson, ed., *Negro Orators and Their Orations* (New York: Associated Publishers, 1925), 87–88.

25   Quoted in Hinks, *To Awake My Afflicted Brethren*, 71. My brief discussion of the development and influence of antebellum black Freemasonry is indebted to Hinks's detailed discussion; see especially pp. 70–76.

26   Walker's Speech to the Massachusetts General Colored Association was printed in *Freedom's Journal*, 19 December 1828. It is also reprinted as Appendix I in the Hill and Wang edition of the *Appeal*; the quotes are from 80–81.

27   "Minutes of the Fifth Annual Convention" (1835), in Howard H. Bell, ed., *Minutes of the Proceedings of the National Negro Conventions, 1830–1864* (New York: Arno Press, 1969), 26–27.

28   For encouraging me to consider more fully Walker's connection to the black Freemasons and other antebellum fraternal coalitions, I thank Robert S. Levine. Levine's own forthcoming work on Walker, which I read in manuscript as *Forgotten Readers* was going to press, shares my interest in Walker's newspaper work and his Masonic commitments. See "Circulating the Nation: The Missouri Compromise, David Walker's *Appeal*, and the Rise of the Black Press," in Todd Vogel, ed., *The Black Press: Literary and Historical Essays on the "Other" Front Page* (New Brunswick: Rutgers University Press, 2001).

29   Harding, "Wrestling Toward the Dawn," 719.

30   Michael Warner, *Letters of the Republic: Publication and the Public Sphere in Eighteenth-Century America* (Cambridge: Harvard University Press, 1990), 67.

31   Ferguson, " 'We Hold These Truths,' " 2.

32   Studies of these communities and their emergence after the Revolutionary War include Ira Berlin, "Time, Space, and the Evolution of Afro-American Society on Mainland British North America," *American Historical Review* 85 (February 1980): 44–78; James Oliver Horton, *Free People of Color*; James Oliver Horton and Lois E. Horton, *In Hope of Liberty*; Leon Litwack, *North of Slavery: The Negro in the Free States, 1790–1860* (Chicago: University of Chicago Press, 1961); Jane H. Pease and William H. Pease, *They Who Would Be Free: Blacks' Search for Freedom, 1830–1861* (New York: Atheneum, 1974). For community-specific studies, see Gary Nash, *Forging Freedom*; Julie Winch, *Philadelphia's Black Elite*; George A. Levesque, *Black Boston: Negro Life and Culture in the Antebellum City* (New York: Garland, 1994); Roi Ottley

and William Weatherby, eds., *The Negro in New York: An Informal Social History* (New York: Oceana Publications, 1967); Graham Russell Hodges, *Root and Branch: African Americans in New York and East Jersey, 1613–1863* (Chapel Hill: University of North Carolina Press, 1999); and Letitia Woods Brown, *Free Negroes in the District of Columbia, 1790–1846* (New York: Oxford University Press, 1972).

33 An 1849 inquiry into the condition of Philadelphia's blacks indicated the great popularity but transitory nature of mutual aid societies in the first half of the nineteenth century. It compared an 1849 list of African American mutual aid societies with one of 1847 and found that the number had increased from 80 to 106. However, of the 80, more than half had disappeared or taken new names. See *Statistical Inquiry into the Condition of the People of Color of Philadelphia* (Philadelphia: Society of Friends, 1849), 22–23. Horton, in his study of free blacks in eighteenth- and early nineteenth-century America, *Free People of Color*, states that "throughout the first generation of the nineteenth century, 'African' remained the name of choice for most black groups" (153).

34 William Douglass, *Annals of the First African Church in the United States of America, Now Styled The African Episcopal Church of St. Thomas* (Philadelphia: King and Baird, 1862), 16. Reference to this will be cited as Douglass, *Annals*.

35 "Laws of the African Society" (1796), reprinted in *Early Negro Writing*, 9.

36 Homi K. Bhabha, "Of Mimicry and Man: The Ambivalence of Colonial Discourse," *The Location of Culture* (London: Routledge, 1994), 86. All other quotations in the paragraph are also from p. 86.

37 William H. Robinson, ed., *The Proceedings of the Free African Union Society and The African Benevolent Society, Newport, Rhode Island, 1780–1824* (Providence: The Urban League, 1976), 22. References to this text will be cited as "Newport."

38 Winch, *Philadelphia's Black Elite*, 6.

39 For a more detailed treatment of black death and burial rituals in the eighteenth and nineteenth centuries, see Angelika Krüger-Kahloula, "Tributes in Stone and Lapidary Lapses: Commemorating Black People in Eighteenth- and Nineteenth-Century America," *Markers: The Annual Journal of the Association for Gravestone Studies* 4 (1989): 33–102.

40 Alexis de Tocqueville remarked the inhumane treatment given to blacks even in death. "When the Negro dies, his bones are cast aside,

and the distinction of conditions prevail even in the equality of death. Thus, a Negro is free, but he can share neither the rights, not the pleasures, not the labor nor the afflictions, nor the tomb of him whose equal he has been declared to be; and he cannot meet him upon fair terms in life or in death." *Democracy in America* (New York: Vintage, 1955), vol. 2, 27.

41 My general understanding of the Jacksonian era has been particularly enhanced by Harry Watson's work on the subject. See especially *Liberty and Power: The Politics of Jacksonian America* (New York: Hill and Wang, 1990).

42 William Hamilton, *An Address to the New York Free African Society for Mutual Relief, delivered In the Universalist Church, January 2, 1809*, reprinted in *Early Negro Writing*, 37. References to this text will be cited as Hamilton.

43 William Whipper, *An Address Delivered in Wesley Church on the Evening of June 12, Before the Colored Reading Society of Philadelphia, For Mental Improvement* (1828), reprinted in *Early Negro Writing*, 107. References to this text will be cited as Whipper, *Address*.

44 *Statistical Inquiry*, 22–23.

45 Whipper, "Original Communications," *Freedom's Journal*, 20 June 1828, 98.

46 The Constitution of the Colored Reading Society of Philadelphia does not specify the exact amount of its initiation and membership fees, and I have been unable to locate this information elsewhere. Where available, these figures would be difficult to place into context without some indication of the average income of free blacks during this time. Studies of the economic condition of African Americans in antebellum America reveal relatively little about the actual wages earned by free blacks in their various occupations; my research in this area is ongoing. Property-holding statistics, such as those compiled by Leonard Curry in the Appendix of *The Free Black in Urban America, 1800–1850*, suggest that very few blacks were financially secure; as a rule, blacks were restricted to the fields of domestic service and common labor.

47 Whipper, "Original Communications," 98. This announcement makes clear that the Reading Room Society forbade the inclusion of "every book which is chimerical or visionary" from its library.

48 Joseph Willson, *Sketches of the Higher Classes of Colored Society in Philadelphia* (Philadelphia: Merrihew and Thompson, 1841), 27.

49 George Maurice Abbot, *A Short History of the Library Company of Philadelphia* (Philadelphia: n.p., 1913), 3.

50　"Philadelphia Library Company of Colored Persons," *Hazard's Register of Pennsylvania*, 16 March 1833, 186 (page is numbered incorrectly in original; it should be 176).

51　*Minutes and Proceedings of the First Annual Meeting of the American Moral Reform Society, Held at Philadelphia* (1837); reprinted in *Early Negro Writing*, 238.

52　Pennsylvania Abolitionist Society, *The Present State and Condition of the Free People of Color in the City of Philadelphia* (Philadelphia, 1838), 30.

53　*Address and Constitution of the Phoenix Society of New York, and of the Auxiliary Ward Associations* (1833); reprinted in *Early Negro Writing*, 141. References will be cited as "Phoenix."

54　Samuel Cornish, "A Library for the People of Color," *Colonizationist and Journal of Freedom*, February 1834, 306–07. This letter was first printed in the *New York Observer*.

55　The following report of a "Boston Minor's [*sic*] Exhibition" appears in the 21 May 1831 issue of the *Liberator*. "We are highly gratified, (with other gentlemen and ladies,) on witnessing [the Boston Minors'] third Exhibition at the meeting-house in Belknap-street on Monday evening last. The pieces were selected with remarkable discrimination, and spoken with accuracy and effect: some of the dialogues went off in a very clever style. Considering that these youthful performers are entirely self-instructed, they give promise of future advancement" (83).

56　Samuel Cornish, "Phoenix Library—Donations," *The Emancipator*, 4 February 1834.

57　"A Phoenixonian," "To the Editors of the Colored American," *Colored American*, 16 February 1839, unpaginated.

58　The *Weekly Advocate* (later renamed the *Colored American*) printed an "extra" edition 22 February 1837 to report a meeting held by the black community at the "Phenix [*sic*] rooms." The purpose of the meeting was to discuss recent events affecting free people of color in the state of New York. Their discussion led to a draft of a petition calling for (1) the repeal of laws authorizing the holding of persons to service as slaves in the state of New York; (2) the right to trial by jury being granted to persons of color within the state arrested and claimed as fugitive slaves; and (3) an alteration of the constitution, so as to give the right of voting to all male citizens of the state on the same terms, without distinction of color. Members of the black community were "requested to go to the Phenix [*sic*] rooms which will be open for that purpose every day for a few days, from 3 o'clock till 9 in the evening, and put their names to the petition." The *Colored American* 1 July 1837 edition reports the closing of the "Phoenix school"; its trustees were no longer "able to pay the rent." The school, which consisted of "thirty five or more young misses—all of respectable families, and in the most interesting, and important stage of female education," may have been the last of the Phoenix Society's educational network as it was originally conceived.

59 "A Phoenixonian," "To the Editors of the Colored American," *Colored American*, 16 February 1839, unpaginated. The fate of the Phoenix Society's library is undocumented. Reports of the Phoenixonian Society's need for a library had appeared previously in the *Colored American*. A critique of the Phoenixonian Society's anniversary exercises in 1837 included this comment: "Were they blest [*sic*] with a good Library, and some philosophical apparatus, they might acquire a fun[d] of general, and practical knowledge, which would qualify them for any, and every station in life." See "Phoenixonian Literary Society," the *Colored American*, 8 July 1837, unpaginated.

60 "To Our Friends and Subscribers," *Colored American*, 7 January 1837, 1.

61 "To the Editor of the '*Colored American*,'" *Colored American*, 3 February 1838, unpaginated.

62 "Proposal and Plan of a Newspaper for the People of Color," *Colored American*, 4 March 1837, unpaginated.

63 An announcement of the eighth anniversary celebration of the Phoenixonian Literary Society and an invitation to the public to attend is included in the *Colored American*, 3 July 1841. Sometime after this celebration, the Phoenixonian Literary Society became known as the Hamilton Lyceum; see the announcement, titled "Mental Entertainment," in the *Colored American*, 25 December 1841. After 1841, the activities of all early African American literary societies become much more difficult to follow. One reason for this is that the *Colored American*, a great supporter of African American literary societies, stopped publication.

64 "Address to the Female Literary Association of Philadelphia, on their First Anniversary, By a Member," *Liberator*, 13 October 1832, 163.

65 These metaphors were cultivated by whites as well as by African Americans. Expressing his pleasure over the formation of Philadelphia's Female Literary Society, Garrison wrote: "It puts a new weapon into my hands to use against southern oppressors." See William Lloyd Garrison to Sarah Mapps Douglass, 5 March 1832. Anti-Slavery Col-

lections. Boston Public Library/Rare Books Department. Courtesy of the Trustees.

66 "To the Public," *Hazard's Register,* 12 March 1831, 163–64.

67 Reporting on a meeting at the African Meeting House in New Haven, Connecticut, one attendee made the following observation, which was recorded in a letter to the editor of *Freedom's Journal* and printed in the 17 August 1827 issue: "Sorry am I to say, that the number assembled was very few. Females, be it written to their credit, composed a large majority; in fact, the spirit of enquiry among them, whether derived from their mother Eve or not, is always greater than among an equal number of males. Hence we find so many more of them engaged in the active duties of Societies, which have not only the moral improvement of man in mind, but whose aim is also, to disseminate the charities and necessities of life among the poor and sick."

68 "Summary," *Freedom's Journal,* 24 August 1827, 95.

69 The constitution was sent to Garrison by Frederick A. Hinton, one of the Philadelphia agents for the *Liberator*. Although the constitution was printed under the title "Female Literary Association" in the *Liberator* on 3 December 1831 (196), members apparently did not see it in print. Early in 1832, their secretary, Sarah Mapps Douglass, wrote to Garrison to ask "Did any person forbid the publication of the F.L.A. forwarded to you by our friend Mr. Hinton[?]" In a long letter filled with praise for their efforts, Garrison replied that "a copy of the Constitution of the Female Literary Association, which was forwarded to me some time since, was duly received; but I accidently mislaid it, and was thus prevented giving it *immediate* insertion." He closed the letter with this note: "Remember that we have now a Ladies' Department for the Liberator. Pray occupy it as often as possible with your productions, and get others of your Society to do the same." See Sarah Mapps Douglass to William Lloyd Garrison, 29 February 1832, and William Lloyd Garrison to Sarah Mapps Douglass, 5 March 1832, Anti-Slavery Collections. Boston Public Library/Rare Books Department. Courtesy of the Trustees.

70 Garrison's comments appeared in the 30 June 1832 issue of the *Liberator,* 103. At the time of his visit the society was "composed of about twenty members"; Garrison noted that their membership was "increasing, and full of intellectual promise." Garrison's claim that he began publishing the writing of members of the Female Literary Association not only for their merit but "in order to induce the colored ladies of other places to go and do likewise" echoes the Female Literary

Association's own reasons for wanting their constitution published in the pages of the *Liberator*. In the words of secretary Sarah Mapps Douglass, "Our design in wishing it published was, that our sisters of other cities might be induced from our example to form similar associations." See Sarah Mapps Douglass to William Lloyd Garrison, 29 February 1832. Anti-Slavery Collections. Boston Public Library/Rare Books Department. Courtesy of the Trustees.

71 The constitution of the Female Literary Association was printed in the *Genius of Universal Emancipation*, December 1832, 29–30. Subsequent quotations in this paragraph are from this text.

72 Surely the Pennsylvania legislature's stringent proposals restricting the movement of free African Americans in the state and their determination to see that fugitive slave laws were enforced was in part a response to Nat Turner's Rebellion. In August 1831, Turner and a host of followers began a violent uprising around Southampton, Virginia. Although the rebellion was quickly stopped, the idea of blacks having successfully taken up arms against whites was lasting, and repercussions were felt in the North as well as the South. Legislation designed to restrict the activities of free blacks was almost immediately proposed. One month after Nat Turner's execution, for instance, on 17 December 1831, a motion was submitted to the Pennsylvania legislature requesting that authorities consider the expediency of a law barring free blacks from entering the state. See *Journal of the House of Representatives of the Commonwealth of Pennsylvania* 56 (1831–32), 48. For a more complete analysis of this legislative activity, see Julie Winch, *Philadelphia's Black Elite*, 132.

73 "Address," *Liberator*, 21 July 1832, 114–15.

74 "Mental Feasts," *Liberator*, 21 July 1832, 114.

75 Constitution of the Female Literary Association, *Genius of Universal Emancipation*, December 1832, 29–30. For fuller consideration of this society and its membership and an exploration of other female literary societies in antebellum Philadelphia, see Julie Winch, "'You Have Talents—Only Cultivate Them': Philadelphia's Black Female Literary Societies and the Abolitionist Crusade," in *The Abolitionist Sisterhood: Women's Political Culture in Antebellum America*, ed. Jean Fagan Yellin and John C. Van Horne (Ithaca: Cornell University Press, 1994), 101–18. Winch remarks parenthetically that the societies she discusses "assumed literacy" among their members (102). My research generally calls into question the assumption that basic literacy was a definitive prerequisite for membership in an antebellum literary society. But the

highly educated membership of the Female Literary Association and the extent of their literary activities support Winch's claim that everyone in this group was able to read and write.

76   L. H., "Duty of Females," 124. Although Dorothy Porter asserts (by including the piece "Duty of Females" in *Early Negro Writing*) that the author of these words, L. H., is a woman of color, I disagree. Although L. H. appears sympathetic to the plight of black Americans, she never aligns herself with them in the way that other black writers of the period do. In comparison to the writing of Maria Stewart, for example, whose writing is filled with references to "we" and "our people," L. H. actually distances herself from the black population. Consider her reference in "Duty of Females" to the part women can play in the education of free people of color: "It is the intelligence of [free people of color] which will advance *their* cause; and it is *their* ignorance which will retard it" (125; emphasis mine). See L. H., "Duty of Females," reprinted in *Early Negro Writing*, 123–26. The piece was originally published in the *Liberator*, 5 May 1832, 70.

77   Quoted in "Annual Meeting of the American Equal Rights Association: Second Day's Proceedings," *The Revolution*, 27 May 1869, 321–22. For a cogent discussion of the role of African American women in the context of the project of racial uplift, see Linda Perkins, "Black Women and Racial 'Uplift' Prior to Emancipation," in *The Black Woman Cross-Culturally*, ed. Filomina Steady (Cambridge, Mass.: Schenkman, 1981), 317–34.

78   Sander Gilman, "Black Bodies, White Bodies: Toward an Iconography of Female Sexuality in Late Nineteenth Century Art, Medicine, and Literature," in *Race, Writing, and Difference*, ed. Henry Louis Gates Jr. (Chicago: University of Chicago Press, 1986), 223–61, traces the linkage between the icon of the Hottentot female and the image of the black female as the source of unrestrained sexuality, corruption, and disease. Gilman uses various disciplines to examine the merging and manifestation of this theme with perceptions of the black female as Other in the nineteenth century.

79   Carla Peterson, *Doers of the Word*, 18.

80   On the identity of "Ada" see James Forten Sr. to William Lloyd Garrison, 23 February 1831. He writes: "As you are not acquainted with the author of 'Ada' and of 'A,' I have discovered by accident that these pieces were written by one of my Daughters." Anti-Slavery Manuscripts, Boston Public Library/Rare Books Department. Courtesy of the Trustees.

81 "Adah" is the name of one of Lamech's two wives; in Hebrew, "Adah" means "ornament" but, according to *The New Westminster Dictionary of the Bible*, "since Lamech's other wife was named 'Zillah' (meaning in shadow), 'Adah' may signify brightness." See Henry Snyder Gehman, ed., *The New Westminster Dictionary of the Bible* (Philadelphia: Westminster Press, 1970), 15. Todd Gernes's research on Sarah Forten and the poetry she published under the pen name "Ada" radically refigures what critics have long understood to be the corpus of Sarah Forten's writing published under that name. Gernes cogently argues that many of the poems commonly attributed to Sarah Forten are in fact the work of Eliza Earle Hacker, a little-known white Quaker poet who lived from 1807 to 1846. Both women adopted the pen name "Ada," both were avid abolitionists, and the literary output of both authors, especially in the 1830s, was copious. In effect, over time the writing of Eliza Earle Hacker has been erroneously attributed to Sarah Forten to the extent that the two women "have been merged . . . into a single African-American persona" (231). Gernes's recovery and historical reassessment of the two, individual authors goes far to recover the identity of Eliza Earle Hacker and the integrity of Sarah Forten, and exemplifies the difficulty of identifying—much less critically assessing—nineteenth-century women writers. See Gernes, "Poetic Justice: Sarah Forten, Eliza Earle, and the Paradox of Intellectual Property," *The New England Quarterly* 71 (June 1998): 229–65.

82 Catherine M. Sedgwick, *Hope Leslie; or Early Times in Massachusetts* (New York: White, Gallaher, and White, 1827), 40, 39–40.

83 For my own analysis of the Female Literary Association's exchanges I am indebted to Marie Lindhorst's "Politics in a Box: Sarah Mapps Douglass and the Female Literary Association, 1831–1833," *Pennsylvania History* 65, no. 3 (1998): 263–78.

84 Zillah, "To A Friend," *Liberator*, 30 June 1832, 103.

85 "A Colored Female of Philadelphia," "Emigration to Mexico," *Liberator*, 28 January 1832, 14.

86 Preamble to the constitution of the Garrison Society, *Liberator*, 16 February 1833, 26. The Garrison Society should not be confused with the Garrison Literary and Benevolent Association. Organized in New York City in 1834, the Garrison Association's membership consisted of boys and men, aged four to twenty. For an announcement of this society's formation and its constitution, see the *Liberator*, 19 April 1834, 63.

87 Willson, *Sketches*, 108.

88 Anna Julia Cooper's comments on the controversial admission of "lad-

ies" to the "gentleman's course" of education in her essay "The Higher Education of Women" (1892) suggest something of the anxiety that surrounded the introduction of women to higher education during this time. "It was thought to be an experiment—a rather dangerous experiment—and was adopted with fear and trembling by the good fathers, who looked as if they had been caught secretly mixing explosive compounds and were guiltily expecting every moment to see the foundations under them shaken and rent and their fair superstructure shattered into fragments" (49). Surely the preparation offered by literary societies reassured black women in their intellectual ability and contributed to the confidence and courage needed to pursue higher education in this hostile environment. See *A Voice from the South* (1892; reprint, New York: Oxford University Press, 1988).

89 Address delivered at an exhibition of the Young Ladies Literary Society, 27 December 1837. Printed in the *Colored American*, 3 February 1838, 14–15, as "Extract" (the quote appears on page 15).

90 William Lloyd Garrison to Sarah Mapps Douglass, 5 March 1832. Anti-Slavery Manuscripts. Boston Public Library/Rare Books Department. Courtesy of the Trustees.

91 Maria W. Stewart, "An Address Delivered Before the Afric-American Female Intelligence Society of America," reprinted in *Maria W. Stewart: America's First Black Woman Political Writer: Essays and Speeches*, ed. Marilyn Richardson (Bloomington: Indiana University Press, 1987), 53. References to this speech will be cited as "Afric-American."

92 The constitution of Boston's Afric-American Female Intelligence Society was printed in the *Liberator*, 7 January 1832, 2. Although their central focus was reportedly literary, the group seems to have also operated to some extent as a mutual aid society. It maintained a fund for the benefit of "any member of [the] society, of one year's standing . . . who may be taken sick."

The largest women's literary societies in the 1830s and 1840s seem to have consisted of about thirty members. In *Sketches of the Higher Classes of Colored Society in Philadelphia*, Joseph Willson outlines the organization and activities of the Minerva Literary Association, a literary society formed by thirty African-American "ladies" in October 1834. Boston's Afric-American Female Intelligence Society, founded in 1832, maintained a comparable membership during this period. New York societies mentioned by Willson include the Ladies Literary Society (1834) and the Female Literary Society (1836).

93 Maria W. Stewart, "Religion and The Pure Principles of Morality, The Sure Foundation On Which We Must Build," reprinted in *Maria W. Stewart*, 30.

94 Ibid., 29.

95 Maria W. Stewart, "An Address Delivered At the African Masonic Hall, Boston, 27 February 1833," reprinted in *Maria W. Stewart*, 60.

96 Ibid., 59, 58.

97 Ibid., 60.

98 Ibid., 59.

99 This quote is drawn from the preamble to the constitution of the Afric-American Female Intelligence Society, printed in the *Liberator*, 7 January 1832, 2.

100 Stewart, *Religion and The Pure Principles of Morality*, 30.

101 Stewart, "Lecture Delivered at the Franklin Hall, Boston, September 21, 1832," reprinted in *Maria W. Stewart*, 47, 48.

102 Stewart, "Religion and The Pure Principles Of Morality," reprinted in *Maria W. Stewart: America's First Black Woman Political Writer*, 38.

103 Ibid., 37.

104 Ibid., 33.

105 Stewart, "Lecture Delivered at the Franklin Hall, Boston, September 21, 1832," 48; Stewart, *Religion and The Pure Principles of Morality*, 37.

106 Lora Romero, *Home Fronts: Domesticity and Its Critics in the Antebellum United States* (Durham: Duke University Press, 1997), 63.

107 Stewart, "Mrs. Stewart's Farewell Address To Her Friends In The City of Boston," reprinted in *Maria W. Stewart*, 68.

108 Stewart, "An Address Delivered At The African Masonic Hall," 63.

109 Stewart, "Mrs. Steward's [*sic*] Essays," *Liberator*, 7 January 1832, 2.

110 William Lloyd Garrison to Maria W. Stewart, 4 April 1879, reprinted in *Maria W. Stewart*, 89.

111 "For Sale at this Office," *Liberator*, 8 October 1831, 163. Stewart's name and that of her husband were misspelled as "Steward" in the both the pamphlet and the advertisement for it that Garrison printed in the *Liberator*. In other places it is misspelled as "Stuart"; see, for instance, the *Liberator*'s announcement of Stewart's "Farewell Address," 28 September 1833 (reprinted in *Maria W. Stewart*, 65).

112 Stewart, "Mrs. Stewart's Farewell Address To Her Friends in the City of Boston," 70.

113 Stewart, "An Address, Delivered at the African Masonic Hall," 57.

114 According to one race leader of the time, William C. Nell, "even [Stewart's] Boston circle of friends" opposed her public activities; see letter from William C. Nell, *Liberator*, 5 March 1852, 39.

115 Stewart, "Mrs. Maria Stewart's Farewell Address to Her Friends in the City of Boston," 70.

116 Reverend Alexander Crummell, quoted in Dorothy Sterling, ed., *We Are Your Sisters: Black Women in the Nineteenth Century* (New York: Norton, 1984), 158. Crummell, who knew Stewart in New York, reported that "she became a member of a 'Female Literary Society,' and I remember listening, on more than a few occasions, to some of her compositions and declamations" (Sterling, 159). According to Dorothy Porter, there were at least two such groups in New York City at the time: the New York Female Literary Society and the Ladies Literary Society of the City of New York. See Porter, "The Organized Educational Activities of Negro Literary Societies, 1828–1846," 557.

117 Marilyn Richardson, Introduction to "Part II: Later Life," in *Maria W. Stewart*, 82–83. The full title of Stewart's final publication is as follows: *Meditations From The Pen Of Mrs. Maria W. Stewart, (Widow of the late James W. Stewart), Now Matron Of The Freedman's [sic] Hospital, and Presented in 1832 to the First African Baptist Church and Society of Boston, Mass., First Published by W. Lloyd Garrison and Knap [sic], Now most respectfully Dedicated to the Church Militant of Washington, D.C.*

118 Roland, "Moral," *Liberator*, 1 March 1834, 36; "To the Societies of Colored Females for Mutual Improvement," *Liberator*, 8 March 1834, 38.

119 J. C. B., "Literary Societies," *Liberator*, 30 August 1834, 139.

120 James Forten Jr., *An Address Delivered before the American Moral Reform Society, August 17th, 1837*, reprinted in *Early Negro Writing*, 238.

121 Ibid.

122 Letter from "Long Island Scribe," *Colored American*, 2 June 1838, 59.

123 "Literary Societies," *The Colored American*, 5 October 1839, unpaginated.

124 Henry Louis Gates Jr., *The Signifying Monkey*, 51.

125 "Female Literary Association," *Liberator*, 3 December 1831, 196.

126 Letter from Theodore Weld, *Liberator*, 12 April 1834, 57.

127 Editorial, *Genius of Universal Emancipation* 3 (1833): 90.

128 In fact, the literary activities of free blacks probably played a large part in the escalation of racial tensions in northern cities in the 1830s and 1840s. As Emma Lapsansky notes in her study of race relations in

antebellum Philadelphia, "blacks' rising ambitions and designs for upward mobility . . . threatened to jostle the established social order" (62). Lapsansky's discussion outlines the ways in which the accomplishments and successes of the black community increased white hostility toward blacks and aggravated race relations. See Lapsansky, " 'Since They Got Those Separate Churches'."

2 SPREADING THE WORD

1 See Frederick Douglass, *Narrative of the Life of Frederick Douglass, an American Slave*, 81–87. Few stories of the impact of the acquisition of public voice are more powerful than that of Frederick Douglass. While still a slave, Douglass acquired a copy of Caleb Bingham's *Columbian Orator*; among other examples of powerful rhetoric he found in it was the story of a slave who, in the course of a series of conversations, persuaded his master that slavery was wrong. "The reading of these speeches," he wrote in *My Bondage and My Freedom*, "added much to my limited stock of language, and enabled me to give tongue to many interesting thoughts, which had recently flashed through my soul, and died away for want of utterance." What Douglass describes is how his reading literally transformed him, giving him the voice that would eventually allow him to enter the public sphere. See Douglass, *My Bondage and My Freedom* (1855; reprint, Urbana: University of Illinois Press, 1987), 99–101. The quotation is from page 100. Douglass speaks of the impact of what he read in the *Columbian Orator* in similar terms in *Narrative of the Life*, 83–84.

2 "Examiner," "Characteristics of the People of Color—No. 3: Literary Character," *Colored American*, 16 May 1840, unpaginated. Readers should note that the pagination of antebellum black newspapers is inconsistent (and often inaccurate); for instance, the *Colored American* was paginated consistently only in 1838 and from March to December 1841. Whenever possible I have included page numbers in my citations; in all cases the citations given are indicative of the most complete information available.

3 Henry Louis Gates Jr., "From Wheatley to Douglass: The Politics of Displacement," in *Frederick Douglass: New Literary and Historical Essays*, ed. Eric Sundquist (New York: Cambridge University Press, 1990), 52.

4 *Christian Recorder*, 27 December 1862, 206.

5 Benedict Anderson, *Imagined Communities: Reflections on the Origins and Spread of Nationalism*, rev. ed. (London: Verso, 1991), 6.

6 Ibid., 7.

7 For discussion of the role of print in the formation of nationalism and "imagined community," see ibid., 62–63, 74–75. The quotation is from page 62.

8 African American historian Garland Penn's groundbreaking history of black journalism, *The Afro-American Press and Its Editors* (1891; reprint, New York: Arno Press, 1969), laid the groundwork for future historians to consider the early black press primarily in the context of abolitionist efforts when he observed that *Freedom's Journal* "contended for our freedom from bondage, or our deliverance from a human curse which then seemed riveted about us with a most tenacious grip" (27). Later studies that consider *Freedom's Journal* and other antebellum black newspapers as abolitionist publications include Frederick G. Detweiler, *The Negro Press in the United States* (College Park, Md.: McGrath, 1968), 35–37; Carter R. Bryan, "Negro Journalism in America Before Emancipation," *Journalism Monographs* 12 (September 1969): 8–10; Roland E. Wolseley, *The Black Press, U.S.A.* (Ames: Iowa State University Press, 1971), 17–18. Edwin Emery, *The Press and America* (Englewood Cliffs, N.J.: Prentice-Hall, 1972), 219, stresses the abolitionist focus of *Freedom's Journal* but mentions that the paper had other content as well.

9 Frederick Cooper, "Elevating the Race: The Social Thought of Black Leaders, 1829–1850," *American Quarterly* 24 (December 1972): 606. Cooper adds, "articles on slavery were often reprints from other journals, while the editors themselves wrote about other subjects" (606). The editors shared this perspective: "We would not be unmindful of our brethren who are still in the iron fetters of bondage. They are our kindred by all the ties of nature; and though but little can be effected by us, still let our sympathies be poured forth, and our prayers in their behalf, ascend to Him who is able to sucour them." See "To Our Patrons," *Freedom's Journal*, 16 March 1827, 1.

10 "Why we should have a Paper," *Colored American*, 4 March 1837, unpaginated.

11 "To Our Patrons," *Freedom's Journal*, 16 March, 1827, 1. As Frankie Hutton notes in her study of the antebellum black press, *The Early Black Press in America, 1827–1860* (Westport, Conn.: Greenwood Press, 1993), "many of the newspaper's editors were active abolitionists outside of their editorships whereas their newspapers were pragmatically

focused on upbeat news and activities from free black communities"
(4). Hutton's analysis of the early black press provides the most complete recent assessment of it; especially useful is the first part of her
study in which she concentrates on the editors of the earliest black
newspapers and their beliefs. Further details on the lives of the editors
of the early black press are available elsewhere. I have not focused on
them here as I am interested in *Freedom's Journal* and the other publications I address in this chapter as institutions rather than as reflections of their editors' own desires and beliefs.

12 Reverend Samuel Cox, "Recommendations," *Freedom's Journal*, 23
March 1827, 4. Along with the editors' own perspective on their primary audience, this comment calls into question earlier assumptions
that, because of the illiteracy rate in the black population, the majority
of the readers of *Freedom's Journal* were white. In the northern states,
my research suggests a higher literacy rate than has traditionally been
assumed. By 1850, the census reports that 86 percent of black Bostonians were literate; by 1860, that number had risen to 92 percent. The
reliability of census figures, especially concerning people of color, and
the very definition of literacy they assume are problematic. Furthermore, literacy rates in New England and along the Atlantic seaboard in
the nineteenth century were not typical of the entire United States.
But these figures do suggest the extent to which literacy was both
known and manifest by African Americans long before the Civil War.

13 "To Our Patrons," *Freedom's Journal*, 16 March 1827, 1.

14 "Proposals for Publishing the Freedom's Journal: Prospectus," *Freedom's Journal*, 25 April 1828, 37. The same column was reprinted in the
16 May and 30 May 1828 issues of the newspaper.

15 Evidence of the mixture of hostility and resentment that brewed in
northern, urban spaces filled the pages of the white press at the end of
the 1820s. It is perhaps best captured in the series of cartoons produced
by caricaturist Edward Clay titled "Life in Philadelphia." Clay's cartoons, popular in both the United States and England, ridicule the
strivings and aspirations of urban, upwardly mobile African Americans.
As broadsides, they were published by William Simpson and C. S. Hart
in Philadelphia and by Tregear and several other publishing houses in
London. Nancy Reynolds Davison offers a cogent analysis of Clay's
caricatures in her study "E. W. Clay: American Political Caricaturist of
the Jacksonian Era" (Ph.D. diss., University of Michigan, 1980).

16 For a fuller analysis of the development and growth of urban spaces in
the antebellum free North and the lives of free blacks within these

spaces, see Gary B. Nash, *Forging Freedom*, esp. chap. 7; Emma Lapsansky, " 'Since They Got Those Separate Churches' "; James Oliver Horton, *Free People of Color*; James Oliver Horton and Lois E. Horton, *In Hope of Liberty*.

17 *African Repository* 1 (1825): 68.

18 *African Repository* 4 (1828): 118. As Peter P. Hinks asserts, *Freedom's Journal* was "probably begun in part as a response to the publication two years earlier of the ACS [American Colonization Society] organ *African Repository*." The creation of the *African Repository* in 1825 had fueled the rapid growth of the American Colonization Society in part because it contributed dramatically to the Society's ability to communicate its message to a wide audience and facilitated the organization of its supporters. See Hinks, *To Awaken My Afflicted Brethren*, 101.

19 As James Oliver Horton and Lois E. Horton note in their study of free blacks in the antebellum United States, "the expansion of the franchise for white men [in the first decades of the nineteenth century] was often accompanied by the restriction or elimination of the franchise for black men." The Hortons discuss black voting rights in *In Hope of Liberty*, 167–70; the quotation is from page 168. The extent to which free blacks were excluded from traditional means of political expression and participation can be seen in the fact that in New York City, out of a black population of 12,575, only 16 voted in 1825. See Philip S. Foner, *History of Black Americans* (Westport, Conn.: Greenwood Press, 1975), 517–20; statistics on page 520.

20 "Education, No. 1," *Freedom's Journal*, 30 March 1827, 10.

21 "To Our Patrons," *Freedom's Journal*, 16 March 1827, 1.

22 "To Our Patrons," *Freedom's Journal*, 16 March 1827, 1. All quotations in this paragraph are from this source.

23 As was customary of all antebellum newspapers, much of the material that appeared in *Freedom's Journal* was reprinted from other publications in the United States and England.

24 "Effects of Slavery," *Freedom's Journal*, 16 March 1827, 4. The letter appeared originally in New York's *Christian Advocate* and was reprinted in *Freedom's Journal*.

25 "Foreign News," *Freedom's Journal*, 27 May 1827, 43.

26 As Kenneth D. Nordin notes, "since *Freedom's Journal*'s target audience was essentially semi-literate, the strategy of making the paper entertaining was a sound one." See Nordin, "In Search of Black Unity: An Interpretation of the Content and Function of *Freedom's Journal*," in *Journalism History* 4 (winter 1977–78): 126.

27 Charles C. Andrews, "New York African Free School," *Freedom's Journal*, 9 November 1827, 138. In his letter, Andrews called it "a pleasing fact" that *Freedom's Journal* joined "three hundred well selected volumes" in the school's library. His pride in the collection is evident in the anecdote he relayed to readers of the newspaper: "One of our little scholars, aged about ten years, was questioned on some astronomical and other scientific subjects a few months ago, by a celebrated and learned doctor of this city; the boy answered so readily and so accurately to the queries, [and] was at last asked, how it was that he was so well acquainted with such subjects. His reply was, that he remembered to have read of them in the books in the School Library."

28 "African Free Schools in the United States," *Freedom's Journal*, 18 May 1827, 38.

29 Advertisement: "B. F. Hughes School, for Coloured Children of both Sexes," *Freedom's Journal*, 16 March 1827, 4. Similar advertisements and announcements appear throughout the paper.

30 "School Notice," *Freedom's Journal*, 2 November 1827, 136.

31 "To Our Patrons," *Freedom's Journal*, 16 March 1827, 1.

32 See *Freedom's Journal*, 14, 21, 28 February 1828 and 21 March 1828.

33 "Dick the Gentleman," *Freedom's Journal*, 27 April 1827, 26.

34 "To the Senior Editor," *Freedom's Journal*, 31 August 1827, 99.

35 "Libraries," *Freedom's Journal*, 5 October 1827, 119. For a valuable history of the nineteenth-century middle-class culture of self-control, see Mary Ryan, *The Cradle of the Middle Class: The Family in Oneida County, New York, 1790–1865* (Cambridge: Cambridge University Press, 1981), esp. chaps. 2 and 4.

36 "R," "For the Freedom's Journal," *Freedom's Journal*, 1 June 1827, 46.

37 "Letter, No. V. To Rev. Samuel E. Cornish," *Freedom's Journal*, 2 November 1827, 135.

38 "George M. Horton," *Freedom's Journal*, 8 August 1828, 153; "GEORGE M. HORTON," *Freedom's Journal*, 29 August 1828, 179; "GEORGE M. HORTON," *Freedom's Journal*, 12 September 1828, 194–95, emphasis in original. Horton's case is discussed and these passages are quoted in Gates, "From Wheatley to Douglass," 54–56.

39 "Muta," "Original Communications," *Freedom's Journal*, 27 July 1827, 78.

40 Ibid.

41 Samuel E. Cornish, "Original Communications," *Freedom's Journal*, 13 July 1827, 70. As Kenneth Cmiel argues in his study of linguistic usage in the United States, the "nineteenth-century debate over lan-

guage was a fight over what kind of personality was needed to sustain a healthy democracy" (14). In this context, the possession of literary character "implied far more than the ability to handle words deftly; it invoked larger concerns about audience, personality, and social order" (24). Literary character was always a reflection of the individual, but its focus was always civic as well. Early Americans looked to literary performances to distinguish individuals with the "cultivated sensibilities . . . needed to check their own self-interest and encourage a humane but unsentimental concern for the common good" (30). See Cmiel, *Democratic Eloquence: The Fight over Popular Speech in Nineteenth-Century America* (New York: William Morrow, 1990); he discusses the development of this understanding of rhetoric in the revolutionary era in the first chapter.

42 "Libraries," *Freedom's Journal,* 5 October 1827, 119.

43 "A Young Man," *Freedom's Journal,* 7 September 1827, 102.

44 "To Our Patrons," *Freedom's Journal,* 16 March 1827, 1.

45 "To Correspondents," *Freedom's Journal,* 2 November 1827, 136.

46 Untitled, *Freedom's Journal,* 16 March 1827, 2.

47 "FREEDOM'S JOURNAL," *Freedom's Journal,* 25 April 1828, 38.

48 "Miscellaneous: Reading," *Weekly Advocate,* 11 February 1837, unpaginated.

49 "Selection of Books," *Colored American,* 16 February 1839, unpaginated; "Solid Reading," *Colored American,* 20 July 1839, unpaginated. In the 1830s it was still common for all newspapers to reprint articles from other newspapers. This was one of the ways that the literary values embraced by the European American population were communicated to the black community. As Thomas Augst documents in his research on New York's Mercantile Library Company, the distinction between the business of reading and reading for amusement was hotly contested in the 1830s and 1840s. This process of literary valuation is reflected and paralleled in the discussions of literature that appear in the columns of the *Colored American.* See Augst, "The Business of Reading in Nineteenth-Century America: The New York Mercantile Library," *American Quarterly* 50 (June 1998): 267–305, esp. 292–99.

50 "Literary Societies," *Colored American,* 5 October 1839, unpaginated.

51 "Circular," *Colored American,* 16 June 1838, 69. Charges for the use of the facilities underscore Ruggles's commitment to making it accessible to all. "Strangers" were welcomed free of charge. All others were to pay according to how long they wished to use the library: yearly rates were

$2.75; monthly the charge was $0.25, and the library could be used for a week for 6 ½ cents.

52   Ibid.

53   *Weekly Advocate,* 7 January 1837, unpaginated.

54   "Title of this Journal," *Colored American,* 4 March 1837, unpaginated. The *Colored American* began publication on 7 January 1837 as the *Weekly Advocate,* with Samuel Cornish, former editor of *Freedom's Journal,* as its editor, Phillip Bell as proprietor, and Charles Ray as general agent. After two months, the publication was renamed the *Colored American* to signify the centrality of the black population's demand for full citizenship rights. It appeared under that name from the 4 March 1837 issue until it suspended publication with the 25 December 1841 issue. In 1838 Charles Ray became one of the paper's proprietors; the following year, after the withdrawal of Phillip Bell from the enterprise, Ray became the paper's sole publisher.

It is significant to note that the National Negro Conventions met annually from 1830 until 1835, when the convention was held in Philadelphia. The next National Negro Convention did not take place until 1843, when it met in Buffalo, New York. The publication run of the *Colored American* (1837–41) coincides roughly with the interval during which no national conventions were held.

55   "Our Undertaking," *Weekly Advocate,* 7 January 1837, unpaginated.

56   Original contributions published in *Freedom's Journal* often began with disclaimers that asserted the inexperience of the writer or made reference to the "better pens" who might be more suited to address the topic at hand. To some extent, the anxiety expressed in these introductory clauses must be taken at face value: because *Freedom's Journal* was one of the first publication venues available to black writers in the United States, its contributors were often giving voice to their very real inexperience. The writers' increasing experience, especially in the newspaper's second year of publication, suggests that these disclaimers of authority were also at times unauthentic. Surely the acknowledgments of "better pens" was to some extent a humbling strategy used by many experienced American writers throughout the nineteenth century. But rather than signs of their humility or lack of experience, these introductory remarks and apologies emphasize that the conditions under which black people lived in the United States often required strategies of representation and framing devices that would disguise the control and authority implied by the very act of writing. As Frances

Smith Foster argues, "such declarations are not accurate, nor were they meant to be"; she describes them rather as "masks" that "riff the readers away to new, different, and compelling interpretations" (165). Foster reviews the ways a handful of early African American authors, including Phillis Wheatley and Frederick Douglass, used this strategy in her groundbreaking book *Written by Herself: Literary Production by African-American Women, 1746–1892* (Bloomington: Indiana University Press, 1993). It should be noted that framing devices such as disclaimers were not entirely absent from contributions to the *Colored American*. Female writers were most apt to express apparent self-consciousness in their texts. In an article for the *Colored American* titled "Female Influence" (30 September 1837), a writer who signed her name "Ellen" included this paragraph: "There is a delicacy in a young and unknown female writing for the public press, which naught but my anxiety for the elevation of my people, and the improvement of my sex, together with the importance of the subject, could induce me to overcome. But with these objects in view, and with the consciousness of right, I feel impelled by an irresistible impulse, to incite the mind of community to the deep responsibility which rests upon them, in consequence of their neglect of a subject of such vital interest."

57　"Free Man of Colour," *Weekly Advocate,* 14 January 1837, unpaginated.

58　"Why we should have a Paper," *Colored American,* 4 March 1837, unpaginated.

59　Periodically, the *Colored American* ran a column titled "The Importance of Our Paper." In the beginning of the paper's second year, this column asked the question: "Without a paper—an organ of communication through which we may keep up an interchange of views, and maintain a unity of feeling and effort, how could we possibly sustain ourselves?" *Colored American,* 3 February 1838, 15.

60　"To Our Friends and Subscribers," *Colored American,* 7 January 1837, unpaginated; the editors introduced the *Colored American* as its readers' "ADVOCATE and FRIEND."

61　William Whipper, "To the Editor of the 'Colored American,'" *Colored American,* 3 February 1838, 15. Whipper, who in 1828 was one of the organizers of Philadelphia's Colored Reading Society, wrote to criticize the editor of the *Colored American* for not printing a letter expressing his opinion on the "principles and measures of the American Moral Reform Society," the organization with which he had been associated since its founding in August 1837.

62　*Colored American,* 1 April 1837, unpaginated.

63 "To Our Friends and Subscribers," *Weekly Advocate*, 7 January 1837, unpaginated.

64 "Original Communication," *Weekly Advocate*, 7 January 1837, unpaginated.

65 Table: "Vessels of War, in the U.S. Navy, 1836," *Weekly Advocate*, 7 January 1837, unpaginated. For subsequent installments of the same series, "A Brief Description of the United States," see the 14 and 21 January 1837 issues.

66 "Principal Features of the Various Nations of the Earth" and "Useful Knowledge: Life of Ben Franklin," *Weekly Advocate*, 28 January 1837, unpaginated.

67 "AMICUS," *Colored American*, 11 March 1837, unpaginated.

68 "Highly Important," *Colored American*, 14 January 1837. This announcement is repeated periodically, sometimes under the heading "Societies among the People of Color." See, for instance, the 21 January, 18 February, and 22 July 1837 issues of the paper. The overall objective of the newspaper in gathering this information was to create "a concise account of our various Benevolent and Literary Institutions to be carefully prepared from the most official sources" (7 July 1837). Societies were asked to send "a copy of their constitutions, or extracts therefrom: [and] also, answers to the following questions": "1. Male or Female; 2. How long since they were formed; 3. Who were the founders; 4. How many members; 5. Whether incorporated; 6. Names of present officers; 7. Whether Benevolent, Literary or Moral; 8. If Benevolent, how much is expended annually [for beneficial purposes]; 9. If Literary, what advancement made; 10. Whether they have a Library; 11. How many Volumes." Perhaps as an incentive to the societies to participate in the survey, the *Colored American* promised "To any society, or Secretary of a Society, who may send us answers to the above questions, or any other information relative to their respective institutions, (post paid) we will send several copies of the number containing the account of their Society" (29 July 1837). Despite these efforts, no such directory seems to have ever been created. Had the project been completed or, if completed, had the resulting directory of African American literary, moral, and benevolent associations survived, it would have offered a remarkable record of these institutions.

69 "Constitution and By-Laws of the Philadelphia Association for the Moral and Mental improvement of the People of Color," *Colored American*, 24 June 1837, unpaginated; John N. Templeton, "We, the young men of color of the city of Pittsburgh . . . ," *The Colored Ameri-*

can, 2 September 1837, unpaginated. The most prominent member of the Young Men's Literary and Moral Reform Society was Martin R. Delany. According to Delany's biographer Victor Ullman, the Young Men's Literary and Moral Reform Society was a new name for the Theban Literary Society, a coalition formed by Delany and a classmate, Molliston Clark, in 1832. Delany and Clark's use of this name reflects their knowledge of the rich history of the Egyptian city of Thebes and their appreciation for the vibrant intellectual traditions associated with this African civilization. According to Ullman, members of the Theban Literary Society "were occupied [during their meetings] with reading and criticism of each other's literary efforts and intellectual wanderings" (25). Ullman implies that the Theban Literary Society provided its members with a somewhat shallow experience when he comments that the atmosphere of the club was "quite divorced from the immediate problems of the day." The lifelong literary and political pursuits of both Delany and Clark, however, suggest that, while this early literary association may have been pretentious, it was neither devoid of substance nor did it remove its members from sincere engagement with the issues facing African Americans in the mid-nineteenth century. Significantly, both Clark and Delany went on to prominent and fulfilling literary careers, aligning themselves with publications whose commitment to the welfare of the black community was unwavering. Clark became a significant figure in the A.M.E. Church and served as the editor of its organ, the *Christian Recorder.* Delany began his own newspaper, the *Mystery,* in 1843; he became a coeditor with Frederick Douglass of the *North Star* (which would later become *Frederick Douglass's Paper*) in 1847. Delany's *Blake: or the Huts of America, A Tale of the Mississippi Valley, the Southern United States, and Cuba,* published serially in the *Anglo-African Magazine* between January and July 1859, and in the *Weekly Anglo-African* in 1861 and 1862, is one of the first novels to be written by an African American. Ullman's biography of Delany, *Martin R. Delany: The Beginnings of Black Nationalism* (Boston: Beacon, 1971), is a marvelous source of information on his life. Its usefulness to researchers, however, is limited, as his sources are largely undocumented. Similarly another source of information on Martin Delany, Dorothy Sterling's *The Making of an Afro-American* (New York: Doubleday, 1971), also suffers from its lack of specific documentation. Sterling discusses Delany's involvement in the Theban Literary Society and the Young Men's Literary and Moral Reform Society on pages 45–46.

70 "A Good Example," *Colored American,* 1 April 1837, unpaginated. These comments are made about the Female Benevolence Society of Troy, New York. A report on the fourth anniversary of this society appears on the first page of this issue.

71 "Constitution of the New-York 'Phoenix Society,'" *Liberator,* 29 June 1833, 104.

72 Sarah Melvin and Eliza Richards, "A Fair," *Colored American,* 23 December 1837, unpaginated; Charles B. Ray, "New Agencies," *Colored American,* 11 November 1837, unpaginated. In the 20 January 1838 issue, *Colored American* printed the note from the Ladies Literary Society that had accompanied the proceeds from the fair. "The expenses of the fair having been much greater than they anticipated," the society sent less than they had originally hoped; nevertheless, they wrote, "while they regret the smallness of the sum, [they] are buoyed up with the hope that it may be of some benefit to the Paper."

73 "Examiner," "Characteristics of the People of Color—No. 3: Literary Character," *Colored American,"* 16 May 1840, unpaginated.

74 "W.," "We take this opportunity . . . ," *Weekly Advocate,* 18 February 1837, unpaginated.

75 Ibid.

76 "File Your Papers," *Weekly Advocate,* 7 January 1837, unpaginated.

77 "Our Undertaking," *Weekly Advocate,* 7 January 1837, unpaginated.

78 "The Cheapest Publications in the World!: Whole Library for Twelve Dollars," *Colored American,* 9 June 1838, 64. "The Christian Library" is advertised as "handsomely bound in sheep, fine paper, and in separate volumes, consisting of 64 of the most valuable Standard religious and Scientific Works, elegantly printed, without any alteration."

79 See "Household Libraries," *Colored American,* 7 July 1838, 80. This list of seven guidelines emphasizes the importance of a physical space for study, respect for books, and general economy as much as it does the acquisition of the texts themselves: "1. Select a room, or at least a corner of some room, where the Bible and other books, together with inkstand and paper, shall be kept. [. . .] 2. Obtain a good, convenient book case, and writing table, or desk, or both. Let the dust be brushed off, daily used, and kept constantly neat and clean. 3. Whenever a book has been taken into another room for use, let it always be returned to the library for safekeeping. 4. Avoid subscribing for books, unless you feel that the book cannot be published without a subscription. . . . 5. Lay out your money carefully. Buy no books but good ones. Select the best. Seek to make, from month to month, some increase to

the library. Learn your children, servants, and friends to use the books with care. 6. Admit no novels. 7. Select, in addition to religious works, books of reference, school books, scientific works, and philosophical, &c.—a few of the best productions of the best poets. In all departments get works of established and solid reputation." A library was cast as something that even those of the most modest economic stature could possess: "By pursuing this course a few years, every farmer and mechanic can have a library which will be of great value to his children, when he is gone, as well as to himself while living."

80 "The Blessing of Books," *Colored American,* 17 February 1838, 24.

81 "The Object of the NORTH STAR," *North Star,* 3 December 1847, 1.

82 "COLORED NEWSPAPERS," *North Star,* 7 January 1848, 2.

83 Review of *Poems on Miscellaneous Subjects, Frederick Douglass' Paper,* 15 September 1854, 2. In an effort to continue the promotion of her work, *Frederick Douglass' Paper* included in the next issue, published on 22 September 1854, one of Frances Ellen Watkins's poems, "The Slave Auction."

84 *North Star,* 3 August 1849, 3.

85 Frederick Douglass, review of *Narrative of the Life of Henry Bibb, North Star,* 17 August 1849, 2.

86 Quoted in Gates, "From Wheatley to Douglass," 58, 59. The New York branch of the American Anti-Slavery Society, led by James G. Birney and Lewis Tappan, took the lead in declaring Williams's narrative "wholly false"; they retracted their support for it and requested that publishers discontinue its sale in a statement printed in the *Liberator* on 2 November 1838. In fact, as Marion Wilson Starling has noted, attacks on the narrative's credibility had "not attacked the *substance* of the narrative to any considerable extent, but rather the *names* Williams had given his characters." Although the conditions of slavery Williams depicted were uncontested, his strategy of disguising the name of the place in which he was enslaved and the people with whom he had contact (a strategy Frederick Douglass would also adopt in the 1845 telling of his escape from slavery) destroyed the credibility of his narrative. For more detailed analyses of this case, see Starling, *The Slave Narrative: Its Place in American History* (Washington, D.C.: Howard University Press, 1988), 228–31 (the above quote is from page 230), and William L. Andrews, *To Tell a Free Story: The First Century of Afro-American Autobiography, 1790–1865* (Urbana: University of Illinois Press, 1986), 87–90.

87 "Narrative of Henry Box Brown," *North Star,* 28 September 1849, 2.

The *Narrative of Henry Box Brown, Who Escaped from Slavery Enclosed in a Box 3 Feet Long and 2 Wide* (Boston: Brown and Stearns, 1849) was ghostwritten by Charles Stearns, who claimed to have received the facts of the story from Henry Brown. Stearns also wrote an introduction to the *Narrative*. As Douglass emphasized in his review, however, Brown's experience as a slave may first appear to readers as atypical. His narrative included "stories of partial kindness on the part of his master" and "he never, during thirty years of bondage, received a whipping." These facts about the circumstances of Brown's enslavement are important, Douglass implies: although they fail to expose the institution of slavery as physically violent, they point in distinctive ways to the untold emotional and psychological brutality that drove Brown to risk his life to escape from bondage.

88 Ibid.

89 The 3 August 1849 issue of the *North Star* includes a note to readers informing them that "EXTRACTS from Mr. Peabody's review of Narratives of Fugitive Slaves, are crowded out this week. They will appear in [the] next number." It was included on the front page of the 10 August 1848 issue of the *North Star*. Ephraim Peabody's review mentions but does not extensively review two other slave narratives: the *Narrative of Henry Watson, a Fugitive Slave* (1848) and *Narrative of the Sufferings of Lewis and Milton Clarke* (1846). I have quoted here from the version of "Narratives of Fugitive Slaves" printed in the *Christian Examiner,* July 1849, 61, 62; the text runs from 61–93.

90 Theodore Parker, "The American Scholar," in George Willis Cooke, ed., *The American Scholar,* vol. 8 of *Centenary Edition of Theodore Parker's Writings* (Boston: American Unitarian Association, 1907), 37. "The American Scholar" was first delivered as a commencement speech at Colby College, 8 August 1849.

91 Andrews, *To Tell a Free Story,* 101–02.

92 Nathaniel Hawthorne, "The Pine Tree Shilling," *North Star,* 14 December 1849, 4; Herman Melville, "Tatooing," *North Star,* 2 June 1848, 4.

93 "Barton and Whittier," *North Star,* 26 January 1849, 4.

94 It should be noted that the entries in the "Literary Notices" column of the paper during this time may have been written by Douglass but are more likely the work of Julia Griffiths, Douglass's English comrade, financial supporter, and literary editor. While many of the earliest reviews in the *North Star* are signed with the initials "F. D.," indicating Frederick Douglass's authorship of them, assessment of the literary

choices made in the *North Star* and *Frederick Douglass' Paper* is complicated by the fact that the newspapers reveal few clues about the editorial processes by which literary selections or assessments were made.
During the height of *Frederick Douglass' Paper*'s popularity, Douglass
announced that Griffiths would take over as editor of the newspaper's
literary column, describing her as "a lady well qualified, by her talents,
tastes, industry, and acquirements, to discharge the duties of this department." It is likely that hers was the principal voice in making
many of the decisions about the selection of authors to be included in
the newspaper between 1850 and 1855. But, as Benjamin Quarles has
noted and as the name of the newspaper during this time unam-
biguously asserts, *Frederick Douglass' Paper* was "to an unusual degree
the product of one man's thinking." For Douglass's announcement of
Griffiths's role as literary editor, see "Prospectus of the Eighth Volume
of 'Frederick Douglass' Paper,'" *Frederick Douglass' Paper*, 8 December
1854, 2. Quarles's comments about *Frederick Douglass' Paper* are included in his *Frederick Douglass* (Washington, D.C.: Associated Publishers, 1948), 83. For a detailed discussion of the relationship between
Douglass and Griffiths, see William S. McFeely's *Frederick Douglass*
(New York: Simon and Schuster, 1991), 163–82.

95 J. G. [Julia Griffiths], "Literary Notices," *Frederick Douglass' Paper*,
29 April 1852, 2.

96 In *Martin Delany, Frederick Douglass, and the Politics of Representative Identity* (Chapel Hill: University of North Carolina Press, 1997),
Robert S. Levine skillfully traces the public debate between Douglass
and his former coeditor, Martin R. Delany, waged in the pages of
Frederick Douglass' Paper, on the subject of *Uncle Tom's Cabin*. As
Levine points out, the disagreement between these two well-respected
men was not motivated by the publication of Stowe's novel alone, and
although the text itself became the tangible focus of their debate, they
were also, to some extent, struggling over the right to be the "main
voice" in the black community (60). The novel's publication coincided with the April 1852 publication of Delany's *The Condition, Elevation, Emigration, and Destiny of the Colored People of the United States*
(reprint: New York: Arno Press, 1968), in which he expressed his
mounting doubts about the effectiveness of white abolitionists and his
disillusionment with the possibility that blacks could elevate themselves in the United States. Delany sent a copy of *Condition* to Douglass in May 1852. But whereas *Frederick Douglass' Paper* quickly heralded Stowe's novel as a literary sensation bound to have a tremendous

impact on the status of African Americans in the United States, the newspaper entirely neglected the publication of Delany's *Condition,* failing to review it or even announce its appearance. That Douglass ignored this work, choosing instead to focus the attention of his readers on the thinking and perspective of a white woman whose text promoted both religious otherworldliness and colonization, was to Delany astonishing and infuriating. Surely it contributed to the overwhelming sense of disillusionment he expressed in a letter to William Lloyd Garrison, who had directly criticized his emigrationist treatise while openly praising Stowe's colonizationist novel. "I have no hopes in this country," he wrote. "[I have] no confidence in the American people" (quoted in Levine, 70).

Specifically, Delany found *Uncle Tom's Cabin* to be racist and paternalist. Despite his own suggestion expressed in *Condition* that emigration might be best for African Americans, he was also troubled by Stowe's apparent advocacy of Liberian colonization. But as Levine points out, behind Delany's various criticisms of *Uncle Tom's Cabin* lurked a broader but equally pressing question: "Can a white writer such as Stowe faithfully represent the black experience in slavery?" (75). Delany had reflected on this question in *Condition,* arguing that "Our elevation must be the result of *self-efforts,* and the work of our *own hands*" (45). In this light, Delany felt that Douglass was misguided in championing *Uncle Tom's Cabin* as a text with the potential to improve the condition of blacks in the United States. He believed that Douglass relied too heavily on the words and ideas of whites at the expense of talented black leaders and their perception of the black community's particular needs and interests. "We have always fallen into great errors in efforts of this kind, giving to others [more] than the *intelligent* and *experienced* among *ourselves,*" Delany wrote in April 1853 on the subject of Douglass's promotion of Stowe as a representative voice for black Americans. "In all respect and difference [*sic*] to Mrs. Stowe, I beg leave to say that she knows nothing about us, 'the Free Colored people of the United States,' neither does any other white person—and consequently, can contrive no successful scheme for our elevation; it must be done for ourselves." See Martin L. Delany to Frederick Douglass, letter of 20 March 1853, *Frederick Douglass' Paper,* 1 April 1853, 2. Levine's chapter on the Douglass-Delany debate (58–98) was instrumental in my understanding of Douglass's literary objectives in his newspaper.

97 Frederick Douglass, "The Heroic Slave," reprinted in *The Life and*

Writings of Frederick Douglass, Volume 5, ed. Philip S. Foner (New York: International Publishers, 1975), 476. My reading here follows that of Levine; see *Martin Delany, Frederick Douglass, and the Politics of Representative Identity,* 83–85.

98   *Dred Scott v. John F. A. Sandford,* 19 Howard 393 (1857), 404–05.

99   Thomas Hamilton, "Apology (Introductory)," *Anglo-African Magazine* 1 (January 1859): 3.

100 Jer. V. R. Thomas, "The Success of Our Paper," *Christian Recorder,* 16 September 1854, 79.

101 "Editor," "Our Expectation," *Christian Recorder,* 13 July 1854, 62.

102 Hamilton, "Apology (Introductory)," *Anglo-African Magazine* 1 (January 1859): 1. About Thomas Hamilton we know very little. In his "Apology" he described himself as " 'brought up' among Newspapers, Magazines." Boasting of his experience in the publishing industry, he summarized his lifelong aspirations and accomplishments in this way: "To become a Publisher, was the dream of his youth . . . and the aim of his manhood." In 1843, "while yet a boy," Hamilton established the *People's Press,* "a not unnoticed weekly paper," that denounced slavery and urged free blacks to refrain from participating in the nation's wars until their services were recognized and their freedom and equality guaranteed. The *People's Press* survived until 1847; it is unclear what Hamilton did in the twenty years between his publishing ventures.

103 Ibid., 4.

104 Ibid., 1.

105 Frances E. Watkins [Harper], "The Two Offers," *Anglo-African Magazine* 1 (September and October 1859): 288–91, 311–13; the quotations are both from p. 313.

106 Evidence suggests that most writers for these publications were unpaid, either by design or because the financial situation of the publication would not allow it. For instance, Thomas Hamilton insisted in his introductory comments to the first issue of the *Anglo-African Magazine* that literary contributions to the magazine, "when used, will be paid for, according to the means of the Publisher"; he had to admit at the end of the first year of his venture, however, that the "contributors to this Magazine have performed a labor of love—the publisher has not yet been able to pay them." See Hamilton, "Apology (Introduction)," *Anglo-African Magazine* 1 (January 1859): 4; and Hamilton, "The Anglo-African Magazine for 1860," *Anglo-African Magazine* (December 1859): 400.

107 M. M. Clark, "Prospectus of the Christian Recorder of the African Methodist Episcopal Church," in Daniel Payne, *History of the African Methodist Episcopal Church* (Nashville, Tenn.: Publishing House of the A.M.E. Sunday-School Union, 1891), 278–79.

108 "Books For Our Times," *Christian Recorder,* 23 January 1864, 15. This column appears regularly in the newspaper, sometimes under the heading "Books For The Times."

109 "Book Notices," *Christian Recorder,* 9 July 1864, 110.

110 Advertisements for "Our Own Book-Store" or "Our Very Own Book-Store" appear regularly in the newspaper. See, for instance, the *Christian Recorder,* 21 November 1863, 187.

111 "Editor's Repository: Our Duty to Aid Ourselves and Support Our Literature," *Repository of Religion and Literature, and of Science and Art* 5 (January 1863): 21.

112 Amos Gerry Beman, letter from Rev. Amos Gerry Beman, *Weekly Anglo-African,* 29 October 1859, 1.

113 "Poems, Anecdotes and Sketches," *Weekly Anglo-African,* 30 July 1859, 1.

114 "A New and Exciting Book [review of *Life of Rev. J. W. Longuen*]," *Weekly Anglo-African,* 1 October 1859, 1; a review of William C. Nell's *Colored Patriots of the American Revolution* was published in the 30 July 1859 issue of the *Weekly Anglo-African* (3); Child's work was reviewed in "New Books," *Weekly Anglo-African,* 2 June 1860, 2.

115 "Should the 'Anglo-African' Be Sustained?" *Weekly Anglo-African,* 9 June 1860, 2. This correspondent, whose name is not attached to the letter, refers here to the importance of "both the weekly and the magazine."

116 "Popularity of the 'Anglo-African,'" *Weekly Anglo-African,* 4 February 1860, 3.

117 "Anglo-African Lectures," *Weekly Anglo-African,* 15 October 1859, 2.

118 Ibid.

119 "Amusements," *Weekly Anglo-African,* 31 March 1860, 3.

120 Sigma, "Letter from Hartford," *Weekly Anglo-African,* 3 December 1859, 1.

121 Frances Smith Foster, introduction to *Minnie's Sacrifice; Sowing and Reaping; Trial and Triumph: Three Rediscovered Novels,* by Frances E. W. Harper, xxvi. Foster's essay provides an invaluable overview of the literary legacy of African Americans.

122 Ibid., xxxv.

123 M. M. Clark, "Prospectus of the Christian Recorder of the African

Methodist Episcopal Church," in Daniel Payne, *History of the African Methodist Episcopal Church*, 278–79. In 1855 the Book Concern entertained a proposal to change the newspaper into a monthly magazine: "Having duly considered all the circumstances in the case, and finding themselves without funds, and furthermore, without a reasonable prospect of obtaining sufficient means to sustain the semi-monthly publication of our paper, in its present form, the Book Committee have [*sic*] concluded that it be greatly to the advantage of the Book Concern, and the whole connexion, to change the present form of our little sheet from a semi-monthly newspaper to a monthly magazine." Apparently, there was little support for this proposition and the newspaper retained its status but continued to be published inconsistently. See "Proposed Change in The Christian Recorder," *Christian Recorder,* 18 August 1855, 130.

124 "Reasons why the Repository should be Continued and Patronized," *Repository of Religion and of Literature, and of Science and Art.* This announcement is reprinted on the inside back cover of virtually every issue of the *Repository;* see, for instance, January 1862.

125 Ibid.

126 J[ohn] M. B[rown], "Salutatory," *Repository of Religion and Literature, and of Science and Art 1* (April 1859): 1. See also: "Prospectus" (February 1862), unpaginated; John M. Brown, "A Word to Our Subscribers and Friends" (April 1861), 51.

127 E[lisha] W[eaver], "To Our Subscribers," *Repository of Religion and Literature, and of Science and Art* 4 (October 1859): 192.

3 LITERARY COALITIONS IN THE AGE OF WASHINGTON

1 Imprecise records make it very difficult to determine when these organizations disbanded.

2 It should be noted that while the Emancipation Proclamation, delivered by President Lincoln on 1 January 1863, freed all slaves living in the states "in rebellion against the United States," it did not free slaves in the states that had not withdrawn from the Union. Not until the ratification of the Thirteenth Amendment on 6 December 1865 was slavery officially and completely abolished in the United States.

3 The comments of John W. Cromwell, a member of the Bethel Historical and Literary Association and the Association's historian, supports this perspective. On the decline of participation in literary societies

after the Civil War, Cromwell notes: "with the close of the war and the advent of the elective franchise [literary societies] went to pieces; mainly because of the 'fresh fields and pastures new' for the main participants and their ruling spirits." Cromwell, *History of the Bethel Literary and Historical Association* (Washington, D.C.: R. L. Pendleton, 1896), 26 (hereafter cited as *History*). It should be noted that the Bethel Literary is interchangeably called the Bethel Historical and Literary Association and the Bethel Literary and Historical Association. I have followed the lead of the Moorland-Spingarn Research Center, Howard University, where the Association's records are housed.

4 Henry Louis Gates Jr., "The Trope of the New Negro and the Reconstruction of the Image of the Black," *Representations* 24 (fall 1988):131.

5 In his recent study of racial uplift ideology, *Uplifting the Race: Black Leadership, Politics, and Culture in the Twentieth Century* (Chapel Hill: University of North Carolina Press, 1996), Kevin Gaines offers detailed analysis of racial ideology, exposing the extent to which its emphasis on class distinctions and patriarchal authority ensured that it would remain a limited force against white oppression and discrimination. Gaines illustrates the extent to which the very meaning of racial uplift was contested at the beginning of the twentieth century; at its worst, he argues, racial uplift ideology neither supported nor lived up to democratic ideals of citizenship or social advancement.

6 "Literary Societies of Our People," *People's Advocate*, 5 July 1879, 2. Further evidence of the perceived sluggishness of literary culture in Washington, D.C., in 1879 can be found in the dismal turnout expected at the National Literary Convention of the United States, held in Baltimore in December 1879. While the announcement expressed its writers' "hope [that] all friends of literature will avail themselves of the opportunity to listen to the rising generation express their appreciation of knowledge," it also chastised the black community for its apathetic response to the call for participants in the conference. "We feel heartily sorry that there will not be but one representative of literature from our National Capitol, (Mr. Alexander H. Brooks) [whose address was titled 'Patronage, Emulation and Personal Necessity, as Promotive of Literary Exertion']. Nothing can be more plainly apparent than the colored race do not estimate properly the value of their educational interests and institutions in their intimate relations to their form of government and the necessity of their sustaining them in order to secure their own individual prosperity. Even teachers themselves exhibit apathy and indifference upon this subject, which are

indicative of their lack of personal concern in the pursuit of their profession." "The National Literary Convention," *People's Advocate*, 20 December 1879, unpaginated.

7 "A Good Sign," *People's Advocate*, 10 December 1881, 2. Evidence of renewed interest in serious literary study was not limited to Washington, D.C. The front page of the 25 September 1880 issue of the *People's Advocate* carried the announcement of the "GRAND LITERARY R-EOPENING [*sic*]" of Philadelphia's Bethel Historical and Literary Association. New York was also the home of a Bethel Literary and Historical Association. Smaller literary societies existed; see, for instance, the announcement in the *People's Advocate* for the Monday Night Literary Club, which, in November 1883, discussed " 'The Junius Letters', their authorship and their influence on English politics of the last century" (17 November 1883, 3). They also discussed "Charles Dickens, Works and Characters," and William Makepeace Thackeray; see the *People's Advocate* 24 November 1883, 3.

8 Lewis H. Douglass, "The Bethel Literary," *People's Advocate*, 10 December 1881, 3.

9 Le Duke, "Bethel Literary at Lincoln Mission," *People's Advocate*, 15 December 1883, 1.

10 Cromwell, *History*, 4.

11 Cromwell emphasizes the importance of the Bethel Literary's status as a popular organization: "When [the Bethel Literary was] first organized, there was no popular literary society here among the colored people, nor had there been, as far as is known, in any section of the city, any such organization that had lived at the furthest more than a few months, since the ANTE-BELLUM lyceums" (*History*, 26).

12 Several examples of such postcards are included in the Bethel Historical and Literary Association records at the Moorland-Spingarn Research Center at Howard University. One announces a meeting at which Paul Laurence Dunbar is scheduled to read a new poem. Like most of the postcards included in this collection, it is undated. See box 5-1, series B, folder 10. The second quotation is from Cromwell, *History*, 10.

13 Cromwell, *History*, 26.

14 Ibid., 4.

15 Ibid.

16 Ibid., 6.

17 Ibid., 5.

18 Ibid., 9.

19 Ibid., 8. According to Cromwell, "the noble Bereans opened their doors, and there for several weeks the sessions were held." Apparently this particular conflict was resolved fairly quickly, despite Stevenson's persistent efforts to destroy the Literary. Cromwell writes: "After the return of the meetings to their regular place on meeting in the [Bethel] Hall, which occurred after the removal of Dr. Stevenson, an ineffectual effort was made by him through third parties either to break up our meeting or force us to pass a series of resolutions stultifying the course of the Literary in its attitudes toward the Doctor." Although in the end the Literary survived this challenge, Cromwell acknowledges that "for quite a time there was confusion and disorder" (*History*, 9). The Association would continue to refuse alignment with specific religious or partisan interests, declaring in the fall of 1896 that it was "wholly non-partisan, non-political, non-sectarian, etc." See Papers of the Bethel Historical and Literary Association, box 5-1, series B, folder 6 (Minutes, 1895–1901), 14 November 1896 (hereafter cited as Bethel Minutes).

20 Cromwell, *History*, 9.

21 Ibid., 6. The relationship between the Bethel Literary and the A.M.E. Church seems to have remained strained if not competitive at least through 1896, when Cromwell wrote in the *History of the Bethel Literary and Historical Association* that the "reputation [of the Bethel Literary] has outstripped that of the Church of which it is an adjunct" (4).

22 The Moorland-Spingarn Collection at Howard University has records for the Bethel Historical and Literary Association from 1895–1913; minutes for the years 1895–99 are by far the most detailed and complete. Other sources suggest that the Bethel Literary existed beyond 1913. For instance, according to Alfred A. Moss Jr., Archibald H. Grimké apparently delivered a paper before the Bethel Literary in January 1915 titled "The Ultimate Criminal," which was also issued in pamphlet form as the American Negro Academy's Occasional Paper No. 17. See Moss, *The American Negro Academy: Voice of the Talented Tenth* (Baton Rouge: Louisiana State University Press, 1981), 175.

23 Cromwell, *History*, 3.

24 Ibid., 26–27.

25 "Bethel Literary," *People's Advocate*, 3 March 1883, unpaginated. The speaker of the evening was Dr. O. M. Atwood, who presented a paper on "Individual Development," and the meeting was described as "the most memorable session that has yet to be held in the history of the Bethel Literary."

26 Cromwell, *History*, 10–11.

27 Willard B. Gatewood, *Aristocrats of Color*, 214 (Gatewood summarizes the characteristics of what he calls the "black aristocracy" on pages 343–48); Cromwell, *History*, 7.

28 Le Duke, "Bethel Literary at Lincoln Mission," *People's Advocate*, 15 December 1883, 1.

29 Ibid.

30 Cromwell, *History*, 5.

31 Ibid. A full report of the meeting on eminent Negro women is included in the *People's Advocate*, 12 December 1881, 3.

32 Cromwell, *History*, 8.

33 Ibid. The titles, with their authors, are as follows: "The Negro in the 10th Census," by T. J. Minton; "Cooperation," by Professor James Storum; "The Future of the Negro," by Professor Cardozo; "African Experiences," by the Honorable J. H. Smyth; "Mohammedanism vs. Christianity," by Professor Greener; "The Negro in Journalism," by J. W. Cromwell; "The Negro in Business," by R. C. Douglass; "Heroes of the Anti-Slavery Struggles," by Mary Ann Shadd Cary; and "Skepticism among Negroes," by Rev. William Waring. Certainly not all topics discussed dealt directly with issues of race. Consider also the lecture entitled "Man," by Dr. Augusta, and Miss Belle Nickens's presentation on "Dress as a Fine Art."

34 "Bethel Literary," *People's Advocate*, 3 March 1883; reprinted in Cromwell, *History*, 13–14.

35 Cromwell, *History*, 7.

36 Ibid., 11.

37 Booker T. Washington, "The Atlanta Exposition Address," in *Up From Slavery* (1901; reprint, New York: Avon, 1965), 148.

38 See Bethel Minutes, 14 and 21 January, 4 February 1896.

39 Bethel Minutes, 17 March 1896.

40 Ibid., emphasis in original.

41 This contribution was recorded in the Bethel Literary's record book as a "Scholarship for Tuskegee Industrial and Normal School."

42 Bethel Minutes, 24 March 1896.

43 Ibid.; see also Cromwell, *History*, 26.

44 Quoted in Gaines, *Uplifting the Race*, 40.

45 At some point in the history of the Bethel Historical and Literary Association, enough members advocated industrial education that a resolution was passed: "Resolved; That it is the sense of this Association that the conditions that confront the Colored youth of the land,

demand the extension and further development of Industrial Education; and that we heartily indorse [*sic*] the efforts of W. C. Dodge, esq. in this direction, and ask that provisions be made in one of the educational bills now before Congress to extend aid to the District of Columbia by a grant of land the proceeds of which may be used in increasing the facilities for Colored youth to obtain Industrial Education." This document is undated, and I have been unable to pinpoint when this resolution was passed. See the Bethel Historical and Literary Association Records, box 5-1, series B, folder 11 (Resolutions), n.d.

46 Quoted in Gates, "Trope of the New Negro," 136. I have been unable to locate this article.

47 Quoted in "The New Negro: An Interesting Debate by the Bethel Literary Association," *Evening Star*, 22 January 1896. This article is pasted into the record book for the Bethel Historical and Literary Association as a summary of the meeting held on 21 January 1895.

48 Cromwell, *History*, 27.

49 Kelly Miller's presentation to the Boston Literary on 17 November 1902 provides a revealing example of the extent of the membership's intolerance of Washington's politics. The topic of Miller's lecture was higher education for the Negro; in it he mentioned Washington and included mild praise for Washington's abilities and his persuasiveness. Although Miller emphasized the benefits of higher education, members of the audience stood up one after another to attack Miller for his comments regarding Washington. According to the account of the meeting printed in the *Boston Guardian* on 22 November 1902, Miller was "nettled by the attack" and felt he had been misunderstood by his audience. See also the Minutes for the Boston Literary and Historical Association (hereafter cited as BLHA Minutes), 17 November 1902, from the Guardian Collection in the Special Collections at Boston University, box 11, folders 2 and 3.

50 Trotter, George Forbes, and a third black man, William Stott, met to discuss the prospect of beginning a newspaper in the fall of 1901. Trotter apparently provided the money that was needed to begin the venture, while Forbes contributed knowledge of the business gained through previous work for one of Boston's black newspapers, the *Courant*, in the 1890s. When the first issue of the newspaper was published on 9 November 1901, Trotter was listed on the masthead as the "Managing Editor." It was appropriate that the offices of the *Boston Guardian* were located in the same building that housed William Lloyd Garrison's *Liberator*; Trotter had been raised on stories of the aboli-

tionist era, and he considered his own work in the same radical tradition. According to Trotter's biographer, Stephen Fox, Trotter originally considered the *Guardian* a complement to his real estate business. By 1904, however, with the departure of his business partner George Forbes, Trotter abandoned the real estate business and dedicated himself full time to his work on the paper. His choice was accompanied by considerable financial difficulty and growing resentment of what he called the "high-tones and salaried crowd." Stephen R. Fox, *The Guardian of Boston* (New York: Atheneum, 1970), 78–79.

51 For an analysis of this deterioration, see especially Ray Stannard Baker, *Following the Color Line: American Negro Citizenship in the Progressive Era* (New York: Harper Torchbook, 1964), 120.

52 William Monroe Trotter, "Harvard College Class of 1895: Thirtieth Anniversary Report" (Cambridge, Mass., 1925), 303.

53 Trotter, *Boston Guardian*, 13 September 1902, 4.

54 Trotter, *Boston Guardian*, 23 May 1903, 4.

55 Trotter to Charles Chesnutt, 3 April 1901, Charles Chesnutt Papers. Records indicate that Chesnutt did not accept a speaking engagement before the Association until 1905. Originally scheduled to address the Association on 22 May 1905, he appears to have postponed this engagement until 25 June 1905, so that he might attend his son Edwin's graduation from Harvard University. The lecture that he gave was subsequently revised and published as "Race Prejudice: Its Causes and Its Cure," *Alexander's Magazine* 1 (July 1905): 21–26. See Chesnutt to W. Walter Sampson, 10 April 1905, *"To Be An Author": Letters of Charles W. Chesnutt, 1889–1905*, ed. Joseph R. McElrath Jr. and Robert C. Leitz (Princeton: Princeton University Press, 1997), 224. As the editors of this volume note, he may also have given a lecture or a reading in Providence, Rhode Island, around the same time. An undated letter, written in late January or early February 1905, to W. P. N. Freeman of Providence, proposes possible dates for an appearance there in conjunction with his anticipated visit to Boston.

56 "Historical Sketch" (hereafter cited as "Historical Sketch"), published 1 November 1904, source unknown; from the Guardian Collection in the Special Collections at Boston University, box 11, folder 3.

57 Evidently, the process of reading the names of each person presented for membership during the meeting was too time-consuming. At the 15 April 1901 meeting, a motion was passed "that in the future all names of persons desirous of becoming members of this Association shall be presented in writing and must be referred to, and approved by

the executive committee before being acted upon by the Association at the next meeting." BLHA Minutes, 15 April 1901.

58 Constitution and bylaws, Boston Literary and Historical Society (hereafter cited as BLHA Constitution), from the Guardian Collection in the Special Collections at Boston University, box 11, folder 3.

59 "Historical Sketch."

60 Individuals were eligible to be elected to office after having been members for at least three months, and the elections were conducted by ballot. Elections were held yearly at the first meeting in March, and officers assumed their new appointments immediately. Members served in their elected positions for one year, and were "never [to] be elected more than twice in regular succession" (BLHA Constitution).

61 BLHA Minutes, 7 October 1902.

62 BLHA Constitution; "Historical Sketch."

63 BLHA Constitution.

64 Following an extended discussion of the issue of nonmembers' speaking rights at the Association's 10 March 1902 meeting, the Reverend McMullen was called on to draft an amendment to the constitution to revise the policy on nonmember participation. This amendment was passed following an extended discussion on 7 April 1902.

65 BLHA Minutes, 1 April 1901. This sentiment was echoed from time to time by various members of the Association. For example, at a meeting on 2 December 1903, Mr. Butler Wilson thought it necessary to remind members of the intellectual nature of their assemblies. "We must be able to discuss all questions with our intellects," he commented toward the end of a particularly heated discussion of John Brown's execution, "and not with our passions."

66 BLHA Minutes, 3 November 1902.

67 BLHA Minutes, 13 January 1902.

68 Rev. J. H. McMullen, "The Needs of the Hour," BLHA Minutes, 7 October 1901.

69 See BLHA Minutes, 24 February and 24 March 1902.

70 BLHA Minutes, 7 April 1902.

71 Ibid.

72 BLHA Minutes, 22 April 1901. For another example of Negro military history from this period, see Booker T. Washington's collection *A New Negro for a New Century* (Chicago: American Publishing House, 1900). Steward was the son of United States Army Chaplain Theophilus G. Steward, a member of the American Negro Academy. In 1901 Charles Gould Steward served on the Boston Literary's executive

committee. It is interesting to note that Dr. Charles G. Steward, a dentist, was only one half of an extremely active literary couple. When he married in 1907, Steward was president of the Boston Literary and Historical Association. His wife, Maude Trotter, William Monroe Trotter's sister, was president of the St. Mark Musical and Literary Union, the other prominent, large, lecture-oriented literary society active in Boston at the turn of the century. A copy of their wedding announcement is reprinted in Adelaide Cromwell's *The Other Brahmins: Boston's Black Upper Class* (Fayetteville: University of Arkansas Press, 1994), 56.

73 BLHA Minutes, 13 May 1901. In 1903, Grimké was elected to serve as the president of the American Negro Academy.

74 Ibid.

75 Ibid.

76 Ibid.

77 BLHA Minutes, 19 October 1903. Only members of the Association "of two years' good standing" were eligible for election to the historical committee.

78 Wilson's comment is widely quoted; see, for instance, Everett Carter, "Cultural History Written with Lightning: The Significance of *The Birth of a Nation*," *American Quarterly* 12 (fall 1960): 347–57.

79 For a concise account of the protest against the film organized by black communities, see Thomas Cripps, *Slow Fade to Black: The Negro in American Film* (New York: Oxford University Press, 1977), chapter 2 ("The Year of The Birth of a Nation"), esp. 59–63. For an excellent general discussion of the film, see Michael Rogin's "'The Sword Became a Flashing Vision': D. W. Griffith's *The Birth of a Nation*," *Representations* 9 (winter 1985): 150–95.

80 BLHA Minutes, 1 April 1901.

81 Ibid.

82 BLHA Minutes, 15 April 1901.

83 Ibid., 9 February 1903. Rabbi Fleischer's address the Association was originally scheduled for 22 April 1902 but had to be rescheduled because of various "obligations." See the BLHA Minutes, 22 April 1902.

84 Ibid.

85 "Prof. Du Bois to Speak Here," *Boston Guardian*, 3 January 1903, 1.

86 "Ovation to Prof. Du Bois," *Boston Guardian*, 10 January 1903, 1.

87 W. E. B. Du Bois, "The Conservation of Races" (1897), reprinted in *W. E. B. Du Bois: Writings* (New York: Library of America, 1986), 822.

88 "Ovation to Prof. Du Bois," *Boston Guardian*, 10 January 1903, 1.

89 A partial list of members for the Boston Literary and Historical Association is included with the constitution and bylaws. Harper's visit to the association on 20 October 1902 is recorded in the minutes for that date. Her visit was also recorded in the *Boston Guardian,* 25 October 1902, 1. The title of Harper's address was "The Power of Example." According to the minutes, "Mrs. Harper then read some of her original verses which were highly appreciated."

90 "The Literary," *People's Advocate,* 31 December 1881, 3.

91 Jane Rhodes, *Mary Ann Shadd Cary: The Black Press and Protest in the Nineteenth Century* (Bloomington: Indiana University Press, 1998), 203.

92 Cromwell, *History,* 6.

93 Ibid., 22.

94 Terrell writes: "For years I attended regularly the weekly meetings of the Bethel Literary and Historical Society [*sic*], which is the oldest organization established by colored people in this country. In fact, I was the first woman to be elected president. Some of the most distinguished men, without regard to race or color, have appeared in this forum. After the speaker has finished his address, the audience is allowed to discuss the subject from the floor." Mary Church Terrell, *A Colored Woman in a White World* (1940; reprint, New York: G. K. Hall, 1996), 400.

4 READING, WRITING, AND REFORM IN THE WOMAN'S ERA

1 Frances E. W. Harper, *Iola Leroy, or Shadows Uplifted* (1892; reprint, New York: Oxford University Press, 1988), 246, 260, 262. Melba Joyce Boyd, *Discarded Legacy: Politics and Poetics in the Life of Frances E. W. Harper, 1825–1911* (Detroit: Wayne State University Press, 1994), 190–92, notes that the fictional literary society meeting recasts the social and political issues that faced newly freed black communities, as well as the variance of political attitudes and proposed strategies with which they confronted the challenges of citizenship. In doing so, Harper creates what Hazel Carby describes as "not [a] passive representation of history but [an] active influence within history." See Hazel V. Carby, *Reconstructing Womanhood: The Emergence of the Afro-American Woman Novelist* (New York: Oxford University Press, 1987), 95. Iola Leroy's paper "The Education of Negro Mothers" is probably a

reference to Harper's own essay "Enlightened Motherhood," which she delivered orally before the Brooklyn Literary Union on 15 November 1892. The essay is reprinted in *A Brighter Coming Day: A Frances Ellen Watkins Harper Reader*, ed. Frances Smith Foster (New York: Feminist Press, 1990), 285–92.

2   Harper, *Iola Leroy*, 262.

3   Victoria Earle Matthews, "The Value of Race Literature: An Address Delivered at the First Congress of Colored Women of the United States, at Boston, Mass., July 30th, 1895," *Massachusetts Review* 27 (summer 1986): 177. References to Matthews's "The Value of Race Literature" will subsequently be cited parenthetically by page number in the text.

4   Harper, *Iola Leroy*, 262.

5   Lewis H. Douglass, "The Bethel Literary," *People's Advocate*, 10 December 1881, 3.

6   J. W. Jacks [President of the Missouri Press Club] to Miss Florence Balgarnie, 19 March 1895. Jacks considered his letter a communication of courtesy, intending to inform Balgarnie "what sort of people you are taking so much interest in." Of African Americans in general Jacks wrote: "The negroes [*sic*] in this country are wholly devoid of morality." The bulk of Jacks's letter comments on African American women. His comments are accurately summarized in the following sentence: "The women are prostitutes and all are natural liars and thieves." Boston Public Library/Rare Books Department. Courtesy of the Trustees.

7   Due to what appears to be a typographical error, the line of Matthews's address in which she refers to "the Negro-hating Mark Twain" is missing from the text of "The Value of Race Literature" reprinted in the *Massachusetts Review*. It should appear on page 174. Another reprint of Matthews's address can be found in *With Pen and Voice: A Critical Anthology of Nineteenth-Century African-American Women*, ed. Shirley Wilson Logan (Carbondale: Southern Illinois University Press, 1995), 126–48; the quote is on page 132.

8   David Walker, *Appeal, to the Coloured Citizens of the World*, 61.

9   "What we need to-day is not simply more voters, but better voters," Harper argued before the Congress of Representative Women. "I do not believe in unrestricted or universal suffrage for either men or women. I believe in moral and educational tests." See Frances E. W. Harper, "Woman's Political Future," in *The World's Congress of Representative Women*, ed. May Wright Sewall (Chicago: Rand, McNally, 1894), 434–35.

10 Harper, *Iola Leroy*, 282.

11 Harper, "Woman's Political Future," 437.

12 Ibid., 435.

13 Ibid., 433–34. Harper's use of this phrase was a part of her efforts to establish the need for women to enter the political sphere: "Through weary, wasting years men have destroyed, dashed in pieces, and overthrown, but to-day we stand on the threshold of woman's era, and woman's work is grandly constructive. In her hand are possibilities whose use or abuse must tell upon the political life of the nation, and send their influence for good or evil across the track of unborn ages."

14 Fannie Barrier Williams, "The Intellectual Progress of Colored Women of the United States Since the Emancipation Proclamation," in *The World's Congress of Representative Women*, 696.

15 Ibid., 700.

16 Anna Julia Cooper, "Our Raison D'Être," in *A Voice From the South*.

17 Williams, "The Intellectual Progress of Colored Women of the United States Since the Emancipation Proclamation," 710.

18 Elizabeth Ammons, *Conflicting Stories: American Women Writers at the Turn into the Twentieth Century* (New York: Oxford University Press, 1991), 28.

19 Roger Chartier, "The Practical Impact of Writing," in *Passions of the Renaissance*, vol. 3 of *A History of Private Life*, ed. Roger Chartier (Cambridge: Harvard University Press, 1989), 137.

20 Fannie Barrier Williams, "Illinois," *Woman's Era*, June 1895, 4.

21 Florida Ridley, "Opportunity and Privileges of Club Life," *Woman's Era*, October and November 1896, 10.

22 Ibid.

23 "Report of the Woman's Era Club, Boston, Mass." (1896); reprinted in *A History of the Club Movement among the Colored Women of the United States of America* (Washington, D.C.: National Association of Colored Women's Clubs, 1902), 116. The Woman's Era Club met the first and third Monday of each month. Members were expected to pay $1.00 annually in dues. By 1896 the membership of the Woman's Era was listed as 133.

24 See, for example, the series of papers by Mary P. Evans printed in the *Woman's Era* in 1894, including: "Health and Beauty from Exercise: Paper No. 1," *Woman's Era*, 1 May 1894, 7; "Health and Beauty from Exercise: Paper No. 2," *Woman's Era*, 1 June 1894, 7; "Health and Beauty from Exercise: Paper No. 3," *Woman's Era*, July 1894, 7.

25 Ellen Bartelle Deitrick, "Domestic Science: Paper No. 2," *Woman's Era*, 1 May 1894, 6.

26 Elizabeth E. Lane, "Tuskegee Woman's Club," *Woman's Era*, November 1895, 4.

27 Ibid.

28 Ibid.

29 Elizabeth Piper Ensley, "Colorado Club Women," *Woman's Era*, November 1895, 12; "An Afternoon with the Boston Woman's Era Club," *National Association Notes*, 15 June 1897, 1.

30 Ensley, "Colorado Club Women," 12.

31 Details of the anniversary celebration, including a summary of Ruffin's comments, are recorded in the *Woman's Era*. See "England's Attitude," *Woman's Era*, February 1895, 12.

32 Annie King and S. H. Johnson, "Sierra Leone Club," *Woman's Era*, 1 May 1894, 2.

33 "Club Gossip," *Woman's Era*, 1 May 1894, 4.

34 Katie V. Carmand, "Report of the Women's [*sic*] Loyal Union of New York and Brooklyn," *Woman's Era*, August 1895, 5.

35 Cooper was a member of Washington, D.C.'s Colored Woman's League, and Washington belonged to the Tuskegee Women's Club. I have been unable to identify the club affiliations of Smith or Carter.

36 In the conference souvenir issue of the *Woman's Era*, the editors of the newspaper lamented that it was only possible to print these papers "singly, or at most doubly." They suggested, however, that the "papers especially prepared for the conference would make a credible book" and expressed their hope that "in some way or another, at some time or another, they may all be collected in one volume." See untitled announcement, *Woman's Era*, August 1895, 20.

37 Ensley, "Colorado Club Women," 12. The inclusion and seeming acceptance of these African American delegates at the meeting of the Colorado Federation of Women's Clubs contradicts the more common depictions of the experience of black women who wished to participate in the activities of and form affiliations with white women's clubs. In 1893 Fannie Barrier Williams was denied admission to the Chicago Woman's Club despite her high social standing and numerous contributions to the women's clubs in Illinois. The *Woman's Era*'s assessment of the situation was cogent: although she was "well equipped to help on the work the Woman's clubs are formed to do, the modicum of negro [*sic*] blood in her veins outweighed her eminent

fitness" ("The Chicago Woman's Club Reject Mrs. Williams," *Woman's Era*, December 1894, 20). As Anne Ruggles Gere notes in her discussion of the women's club movement, social segregation dictated that white women "saw very little of their African American peers," which allowed them to "develop and nurture highly distorted images" of them. Excluding black women from their midst was also a way white clubwomen asserted their own privilege and power. See Gere, *Intimate Practices: Literacy and Cultural Work in U.S. Women's Clubs, 1880–1920* (Urbana: University of Illinois Press, 1997), 164. Gere's study of women's clubs and clubwomen in a variety of social locations has been invaluable to my own work on the black women's club movement.

38 "The Woman's Era," *Woman's Era*, 24 March 1894, 4. The event that inspired members of the Woman's Era to create and distribute the leaflets is described as the "Denmark lynching." I have been unable to further identify this lynching, or even to determine whether "Denmark" is a location or proper name.

39 "News from the Clubs," "New York Letter," *Woman's Era*, 24 March 1894, 2.

40 S. Elizabeth Frazier, "Profile of Victoria Earle Matthews," *Woman's Era*, 1 May 1894, 1.

41 "Club Gossip," *Woman's Era*, July 1894, 4.

42 "England's Attitude," *Woman's Era*, February 1895, 13. Several times in the 1880s and 1890s Senator Henry W. Blair, a Republican from New Hampshire, introduced before Congress a bill that would provide for the distribution of surplus Federal funds to state schools in proportion to the prevalence of illiteracy. The bill was never passed. For examples of the kind of resolution the Woman's Era might have drafted, see Herbert Aptheker, ed., *A Documentary History of the Negro People in the United States*, vol. 2. (1951; reprint, New York: Carol Publishing Group, 1992), 648, 693–94, 710, 715.

43 "The Work of the Woman's Loyal Union of New York City," *National Association Notes*, April 1900, unpaginated.

44 "Work Suggested by the National Association," *Woman's Era*, October/November 1896, 3.

45 Harper, "Count on Me as a Subscriber," in *A Brighter Coming Day*, 322–23.

46 "To Our Correspondents and Subscribers," *Woman's Era*, January 1896, 16.

47 "England's Attitude," *Woman's Era*, February 1895, 13.

48 "To Our Correspondents and Subscribers," *Woman's Era*, January 1896, 16.

49 Ellen Barttell Deitrick, "Editorial Notes," *Woman's Era*, 24 March 1894, 7.

50 "Lucy Stone," *Woman's Era*, 24 March 1894, 1; Eva Lewis, "A Domestic Scene," *Woman's Era*, 24 March 1894, 14. The story continues in subsequent issues: see *Woman's Era*, 1 May 1894, 14; *Woman's Era*, 1 June 1894, 6–7.

51 Deitrick, "Editorial Notes," 7.

52 "Notes and Comments," *Woman's Era*, November 1894, 1. By way of paying tribute to these unincluded but appreciated contributors, the editors added: "It is said that the literary centre is going west."

53 Victoria Earle Matthews, letter to the editors of the *Woman's Era*, quoted Deitrick, "Editorial Notes," 7.

54 J. Silone Yates, "Kansas City Letter," *Woman's Era*, August 1894, 9.

55 "News From the Clubs," *Woman's Era*, 24 March 1894, 2–5. The location of the last three clubs is not included.

56 "Our Women's Clubs," *Woman's Era*, 1 May 1894, 8.

57 "Boston: The Woman's Era Club," *Woman's Era*, 1 May 1894, 3.

58 "News From the Clubs," *Woman's Era*, July 1894, 2–3.

59 "Club Gossip," *Woman's Era*, July 1894, 4.

60 "A Club Model," *Woman's Era*, November 1895, 10.

61 "National Association of Colored Women," *Woman's Era*, September 1896, 2.

62 Letter from Mrs. Fannie Barrier Williams, *Woman's Era*, 1 June 1894, 5.

63 Reportedly, Josephine St. Pierre Ruffin was not unhappy to see the *Woman's Era* cease publication; it had become a financial burden for her. See Josephine St. Pierre Ruffin to Mrs. Chiney, 24 March 1896, Ms.A.10.1.87, Josephine St. Pierre Ruffin Papers, Boston Public Library, Boston, Massachusetts.

64 Margaret Murray Washington's conservatism is notorious. The third wife of Booker T. Washington, she fully endorsed her husband's philosophy of industrial education and race accommodation. Washington's theory of women's roles in the racial advancement allowed her to pursue clubwork while remaining true to her husband's perspectives. Washington's editorship of the *National Association Notes* was controversial; some approved of its conservative tone, and others believed the paper needed to be more outspoken in its opposition to issues like segregation and lynching and more supportive of women's suffrage.

These conflicting perspectives came to a head in 1912, when at the National Association of Colored Women's biennial meeting Ida B. Wells-Barnett proposed that the editorship of the newspaper be an elected rather than an appointed position. Washington's leadership of the *National Association Notes*, she believed, had been unhealthy. From Wells-Barnett's perspective, it silenced black clubwomen: "Mrs. Washington had started the *Notes* on her own motion," she would later write, and "as long as she paid the expense out of her own pocket and had it printed at Tuskegee, the women felt a delicacy in finding fault with anything about it." The only way out of this dilemma, Wells-Barnett believed, was for the membership of the National Association of Colored Women to elect an editor "responsible to the body" for the contents of the *National Association Notes*. The motion did not pass, but it served to articulate many clubwomen's opposition to Washington's editorship. Ironically, at this same meeting, Washington was elected president of the National Association of Colored Women, a position she held until 1916. Although Washington seems to have been firmly in control of the paper throughout the beginning of the twentieth century, her name appears on its masthead as editor only between 1917 and 1922. Deborah Gray White offers a cogent assessment of Washington's position in the black women's club movement in *Too Heavy a Load: Black Women in Defense of Themselves, 1894–1994* (New York: Norton, 1999), 82–85. Wells-Barnett's recollections of the incident are included in her autobiography *Crusade for Justice: The Autobiography of Ida B. Wells*, ed. Alfreda M. Duster (Chicago: University of Chicago Press, 1970), 328–29.

65 "Club Notes," *National Association Notes*, November 1899, unpaginated.

66 Eleanor Tayleur, "The Negro Woman: Social and Moral Decadence," *Outlook* 76 (30 January 1904): 267, 269.

67 The accomplishments of Ruffin, Matthews, and Wells-Barnett are highlighted often in the pages of the *Woman's Era*. Profiles on Washington and Whitsel provide good examples of the kind of profiles of black women that appeared regularly in the newspaper. Washington was selected as the first to be featured in a column titled "Women Worth Knowing," *Woman's Era*, September 1894, 1; Whitsel is profiled in "An Ice Merchant," *Woman's Era*, June 1895, 1. The *Woman's Era* also began an "Eminent Women Series" that featured portraits of black women "now before the people as authors, lecturers and public workers"; these portraits were eventually collected and offered together as a

subscription incentive. See "Woman's Era Eminent Women Series," *Woman's Era*, October/November 1896, 15.

68 Medora W. Gould, "Literature Notes," *Woman's Era*, December 1894, 19. In making this comment, Gould was commending Gertrude Mossell's *The Work of Afro-American Woman*, published in 1894.

69 Sara N. Johnson, "Report of Work among Colored People," *National Association Notes*, February 1901, unpaginated.

70 See, for instance, Deborah Gray White, "The Cost of Club Work, the Price of Black Feminism," in *Visible Women: New Essays on American Activism*, ed. Nancy A. Hewitt and Suzanne Lebsock (Urbana: University of Illinois Press, 1993), 261. White argues: "The purpose of [black women's] literary, art, and music clubs . . . was to provide intensive training and continued practice, not in black culture, which was implicitly judged inadequate, but in the dominant high culture of the period."

71 Josephine St. Pierre Ruffin, "Editorial: Greeting," *Woman's Era*, 24 March 1894, 8.

72 Charlotte Hawkins Brown, "The Quest of Culture," Speeches, 1929, Series 1, Charlotte Hawkins Brown Papers, Library of Congress, Washington, D.C.

73 Gere, *Intimate Practices*, 193.

74 Brown, "The Quest of Culture."

75 Charlotte Hawkins Brown was the founder of the Palmer Memorial Institute, a school begun in 1902 for black youth located in Sedalia, North Carolina. The school's motto, "educational efficiency, spiritual sincerity, and cultural security," is representative of the formula Brown believed African American youth needed for success. Although Brown believed that students at the Palmer Institute should pursue a classical education, the preference of most of her northern white donors for "educational efficiency" manifests itself in its emphasis on agricultural and industrial classes. Brown's concern for African Americans' attention to character and manners is manifest in *The Correct Thing To Do—To Say—To Wear*, an etiquette guide published in 1940 that won Brown informal recognition as "The First Lady of Social Graces." For more information on Brown, see Constance Hall Marteena, *The Lengthening Shadow of a Woman: A Biography of Charlotte Hawkins Brown* (Hicksville, N.Y.: Exposition Press, 1977); and Tera Hunter, " 'The Correct Thing': Charlotte Hawkins Brown and the Palmer Institute," *Southern Exposure* 11, no. 5 (September/October 1983): 37–43.

76 Elizabeth Piper Ensley, "Colorado," *Woman's Era*, May 1895, 9.

77 Medora Gould, "Literature Department," *Woman's Era*, September 1894, 10.

78 Untitled Notice, *Woman's Era*, December 1894, 13.

79 Rosa Bowser, "Virginia," *Woman's Era*, June 1895, 9. Bowser, the *Woman's Era* correspondent from Virginia, voiced her own perspective on literary value: "One important point should be borne in mind, viz., the acquirement of an education, in the limited sense of the term, does not depend upon the number of books read nor the variety of literature, but upon the thorough study and digestion of the most important subjects by authors of worth and literary standing."

80 H. Cordelia Ray, "New York," *Woman's Era*, February 1895, 2. Of the plan to subdivide the Brooklyn Literary Union's literary studies into "eighteen reading circles" Ray wrote: "Such an innovation has many advantages. It will not only concentrate the efforts of progressive minds, but bring them into more immediate touch with the people, and thereby develop much that is latent among us, besides giving impetus to intellectual activity." Only seventeen circles were listed in a report given early in 1895; they were: English Literature, the French Revolution, Afro-American Literature, Biography, Ancient History, Domestic Science, Physiology and Hygiene, Political Science, Electricity, Sociology, Public Questions, French Literature, Music, American Literature, Children's Literature, Physical Culture, and Business Co-operation. The institution of literary circles and similar methods of dividing literary study into specific fields or "departments" placed greater emphasis on the director or leader of that department. Concern for that individual's expertise in the subject matter to be studied prompted Mrs. N. F. Mossell to make the following suggestion in 1896: "Some of our magazines might also inaugurate a correspondence course in English literature and history. It would give practice and experience to the teacher of the department, and it would help to solve the problem among many of our girls as to what they shall read, and what course of study or reading would be the most helpful toward supplying them with subjects for thought and hence for conversation." See N. F. Mossell, "The Open Court," *Woman's Era*, May 1895, 20.

81 Medora Gould, "Literature," *Woman's Era*, 24 March 1894, 10.

82 Medora Gould, "Literature," *Woman's Era*, 1 May 1894, 10; Gould, "Literature," *Woman's Era*, June 1894, 11; Gould, "Literature Department," *Woman's Era*, August 1894, 11; and Gould, "Literature Notes," *Woman's Era*, December 1894, 19.

83 Medora Gould, "Literature Notes," *Woman's Era*, December 1894, 19.

84 Program of the First National Convention of the Colored Women of America, Boston, Mass., 29, 30, 31 July 1895. Boston Public Library/ Rare Books Department. Courtesy of the Trustees.

85 "Prospectus of the New Romance of Colored Life, 'Contending Forces,'" *Colored American Magazine*, September 1900. Another account of this reading is offered in the *Woman's Era's* report for 1899, which was published in the *National Association Notes*. It reported that "an entertaining and interesting afternoon was spent at a Japanese Tea, given to Miss Pauline Hopkins, to aid her in the publication of her novel, 'Contending Forces,' portions of which she read." In this report Pauline Hopkins is listed as the secretary of the Woman's Era Club. "Report of the Woman's Era Club for 1899," *National Association Notes*, April 1900, unpaginated.

86 Sylvia Mann Maples, "Tennessee," *Woman's Era*, May 1895, 13. A portion of Maples's report on club activity in her state reads: "Miss Hattie Macafee is the agent at this point for Miss Wells' 'Red Record.' It tells of many men—negroes, of course—who have been hanged from the highest limb of the nearest tree for (in most cases) uncommitted crimes. It is, indeed, a red record; yea, even more, a blood-dyed death roll of the south."

87 Sarah E. Tanner, "Reading," *Woman's Era*, June 1895, 13.

88 Medora Gould, "Literature," *Woman's Era*, 24 March 1894, 10.

89 Leslie Wilmot, "Chats With Girls," *Woman's Era*, 24 March 1894, 11. Wilmot acknowledged that these were "three good rules but rather hard to reconcile unless the last presupposes each and every one to have perfect tastes."

90 Deborah Gray White, "The Cost of Club Work, the Price of Black Feminism," 259.

91 Deborah Gray White, *Too Heavy a Load*, 78.

92 Untitled Notice, *Woman's Era*, September 1896, 9.

93 Medora Gould, "Literature Department," *Woman's Era*, August 1895, 23.

94 Untitled Notice, *Woman's Era*, September 1896, 9. Interestingly, by the second decade of the twentieth century the popularity of Paul Laurence Dunbar was unsurpassed among clubwomen and his literary value went unquestioned. The Phyllis [*sic*] Wheatley Literary and Social Club's meeting in February 1918, at which they focused on Dunbar's work, is representative of the variety of ways that he was considered by clubwomen. The evening included "Quotations from

Dunbar," a paper titled "Dunbar's Poetry," a recitation of the poem "When Lucy Backslid," a paper titled "Dunbar's Prose Works," and a reading of "The Ode to Ethiopia." The meeting concluded with one clubwoman's "Personal Recollections of Dunbar." See Minutes of the Phyllis Wheatley Literary and Social Club, 26 February 1918, folder 3, Avery Institute Library, Special Collections, Charleston, South Carolina.

95 "Paul Dunbar's New Book," *Woman's Era*, January 1897, 7. Much of the "Literature Department" in the October/November 1896 issue of the *Woman's Era* was dedicated to announcing the pending publication of a collection of poems by Dunbar by the publisher Dodd, Mead & Co. The column included extensive quotations from Howells's introduction. See "Literature Department," *Woman's Era*, October/November 1896, 7.

96 "Negro Folk-Lore," *Woman's Era*, September 1894, 9.

97 Untitled Notice, *Woman's Era*, September 1896, 9.

98 Andreas Huyssen, "Mass Culture as Woman: Modernism's Other," in *Studies in Entertainment: Critical Approaches to Mass Culture*, ed. Tania Modleski (Bloomington: Indiana University Press, 1986), 191.

99 Medora Gould, "Literature," *Woman's Era*, 24 March 1894, 9.

100 Medora Gould, "Literature," *Woman's Era*, 1 May 1894, 10.

101 Medora Gould, "Literature Department," *Woman's Era*, September 1894, 10.

102 Gere, *Intimate Practices*, 219.

103 Medora Gould, "Literature Department," *Woman's Era*, September 1894, 11.

104 Medora Gould, "Literature," *Woman's Era*, June 1894, 11.

105 In the chapter "(Un)Professional Reading and Writing," Anne Ruggles Gere charts the efforts of the leading academic literary critics at the turn of the century, such as Thomas Wentworth Higginson, to devalue the literary practices of clubwomen. In part, she observes, this effort must be seen as a part of the effort to establish the legitimacy of English departments and the authority of literary studies in the American university. Accusing clubwomen of taking over literature—and ruining it by not adhering to the practices and terms that guided literary study in formal academic communities—was for English professors one way of deflecting attention away from the struggle that surrounded the professionalization of literary studies at the turn of the century. See Gere, *Intimate Practices*, 208–47.

106   "The Woman's Era Literature Department," *Woman's Era*, June 1896, 2; "The Study of the Novel: Ivanhoe," *Woman's Era*, June 1896, 3.

107   Leslie Wilmot, "Chats With Girls," *Woman's Era*, May 1894, 10–11.

108   R. J. Porter, "Club Notes," *National Association Notes*, April 1899, unpaginated.

109   Fannie C. Cobb, "Charleston, W. VA. Club Notes," *National Association Notes*, April 1900, unpaginated.

110   Minutes of the Chautauqua Circle (Atlanta, Ga.), 31 December 1913. The Chautauqua Circle Collection, Atlanta University Center, Robert W. Woodruff Library.

111   Mary Church Terrell, "Why I Wrote the Phyllis Wheatley Pageant-Play," Mary Church Terrell Papers, Moorland-Spingarn Research Center, Howard University, Washington, D.C.

112   Katie V. Carmand, "Report of the Women's [*sic*] Loyal Union of New York and Brooklyn," *Woman's Era*, August 1895, 5.

113   H. Cordelia Ray, "Report of the Woman's Loyal Union of New York and Brooklyn," reprinted in *A History of the Club Movement among the Colored Women of the United States of America* (Washington, D.C.: National Association of Colored Women's Clubs, Inc., 1902), 66.

114   Untitled Notice, *Woman's Era*, October/November 1896, 8.

115   "Club Notes," *National Association Notes*, November 1900, unpaginated.

116   Judia C. Jackson, "Club Notes," *National Association Notes*, March 1899, unpaginated.

117   Summary of Club Activities, 1920–21, Phyllis Wheatley Literary and Social Club Collection, Folder 1, Special Collections, Avery Institute, Charleston, South Carolina; Minutes of the Phyllis Wheatley Literary and Social Club, 14 December 1916, 19 October 1932, 21 October 1936, Avery Institute, Charleston, South Carolina.

118   Josephine B. Bruce, "The Ladies Auxilliary," *Woman's Era*, October/November 1896, 9.

119   Dora Cole, "Pennsylvania," *Woman's Era*, December 1894, 14.

120   As Alfred A. Moss Jr. notes in his study of the American Negro Academy, no copy of the constitution of the American Negro Academy has survived. I depend here on Moss's reconstruction of it from various sources. See Moss, *The American Negro Academy*, 25 n. 29. Moss presents a detailed study of the origins of the Academy, its activities, and its membership.

121   Theophilus G. Steward to Alexander Cromwell, n.d., quoted in Moss, *The American Negro Academy*, 38.

122 White, "The Cost of Club Work, the Price of Black Feminism," 247–69.

123 Mary Church Terrell, *A Colored Woman in a White World*, 234.

124 Terrell to a Mr. Reid, 19 December 1921, Mary Church Terrell Papers, Library of Congress.

125 Terrell, *A Colored Woman in a White World*, 234. In addition to her other literary activities, Terrell was also the first female president of the Bethel Literary and Historical Society and a member of the all-women's literary society, the Booklovers' Club, which she describes in her autobiography as "organized for the purpose of reading, reviewing and discussing books" (399).

126 Ibid., 237.

127 J. E. Spingarn to Terrell, 24 May 1922, Mary Church Terrell Papers, Library of Congress. Spingarn wrote to Terrell in his official capacity as the editor of Harcourt, Brace.

128 Terrell to "the Editor of *Harper's Magazine*," 29 March 1922, Mary Church Terrell Papers, Library of Congress.

129 Ibid. Terrell's letter also contained the following plea: "open up your columns, so that the colored man's point of view may shine forth every now and then. Your magazine is strong and can afford to take any stand it wants to take. I am not pleading for myself. Of course, I wish you would accept my story. That goes without saying, but I have very little hope. If it were a masterpiece of literature and told the story of a colored girl's plight on a Jim Crow Car, I fear it would not be accepted by Harper's Magazine. It would be against your policy, would it not?"

130 Mary Church Terrell to F. Arthur Metcalf, President, Home Correspondence School, 25 May 1916, Mary Church Terrell Papers, Library of Congress.

131 Terrell, *A Colored Woman in a White World*, 234.

132 Terrell was emphatic about the fact that it was her political work and not, for instance, her family or role as head of household that prevented her from doing the sort of literary work to which she aspired. Although she cites the "innumerable interruptions in the home" as an obstacle to writing for a woman, they were not insurmountable. "It is quite possible for a woman to succeed as a writer," Terrell wrote in her autobiography, "if she has nothing to do but look after her children and her home. But when exacting public work is added to her other cares, it is very difficult, if not impossible, to do so." *A Colored Woman in a White World*, 236.

133 Mamie Garvin Fields, *Lemon Swamp and Other Places: A Carolina Memoir* (New York: Free Press, 1983), 189–90. Fields does not give a date for Terrell's visit.

5 GEORGIA DOUGLAS JOHNSON AND
THE SATURDAY NIGHTERS

1 Constance MacLaughlin Green, *The Secret City* (Princeton: Princeton University Press, 1967), 209.

2 James Weldon Johnson, "Harlem: The Culture Capital," in *The New Negro*, ed. Alain Locke (1925; reprint, New York: Atheneum, 1992), 301.

3 Ibid., 311.

4 Langston Hughes, *The Big Sea* (1940; reprint, New York: Thunder Mouth's Press, 1986), 228.

5 Jean Toomer to Georgia Douglas Johnson, 4 June 1920. This letter is a part of the Georgia Douglas Johnson Papers at Howard University's Moorland-Spingarn Research Center (hereafter cited as GDJ Papers), box 2, folder 9. Toomer's accounts of his relationship with his grandfather vary. For instance, in an untitled autobiographical notebook written in 1936, Toomer suggested that, before his death, his grandfather had begun to appreciate his writing: "during the months immediately following [Toomer's return to Pinchback's Washington, D.C., apartment in 1919] he not only did not oppose me but he became my companion as never before, entering into talks and discussions with me, reading my papers, praising as well as criticizing them." Jean Toomer Papers, Yale Collection of American Literature, Beinecke Rare Book and Manuscript Library (hereafter cited as Jean Toomer Papers), box 22, folder 560.

6 Toomer to Johnson, 4 June 1920, GDJ Papers, box 2, folder 9.

7 Ibid.

8 Ibid.

9 Toomer to Johnson, Christmas 1919, GDJ Papers, box 2, folder 9.

10 Toomer to Johnson, 4 June 1920, GDJ Papers, box 2, folder 9.

11 Ibid.

12 Toomer to Johnson, 7 January 1920, GDJ Papers, box 2, folder 9.

13 Ibid.

14 Ibid.

15 As George B. Hutchinson argues in his study of Toomer's relationship with Washington's literary community, Toomer seems to have found a mentor in his relationship with Alain Locke. Locke was interested in Toomer's work, and Toomer found Locke's comments to be of great value. In August 1922 Toomer wrote to Locke to express his appreciation for Locke's help on an unspecified piece: "I liked your criticism," he wrote. "The cocoon *is* both tight and intense." Citing an undated note from Locke to Countee Cullen in which Locke refers to Toomer as one of his "spiritual children," Hutchinson points out that Locke considered himself a mentor to Toomer. See Hutchinson, "Jean Toomer and the 'New Negroes' of Washington," *American Literature* 63 (December 1991): 690–91. Early in 1922 Locke asked Toomer to send a carbon copy of *Cane* so that he could write a review that was ready to be published as soon as the book was released. See his letter to Jean Toomer, 4 January 1922, Jean Toomer Papers, MS 1, folder 151. Toomer also asked his publisher, Boni and Liveright, to send Locke a copy of *Cane* as soon as it was available. See Toomer to Locke, 17 August 1923, Alain Locke Papers, Moorland-Spingarn Research Center, Howard University (hereafter Alain Locke Papers), box 164–90, folder 12.

16 Toomer to Johnson, 4 June 1920, GDJ Papers, box 2, folder 9. The combined effect of relative poverty, isolation, and perhaps his less than enthusiastic reception by Du Bois and other literary legends placed a strain on Toomer's commitment to writing, and in 1920 he temporarily seems to have been prepared to pursue his interest in music. "Here of late the impulse of music has become unusually strong in me," he wrote in a personal letter to Georgia Douglas Johnson dated 4 March 1920. "I mean the desire to create music, not merely to interpret it." Toomer's description of his desire to become a musician and his description of the "musical ideas, stampeding for expression" suggest the extent to which he was committed to art as well as the lasting confusion over what form that art would take. In 1920 his desire to be a musician led him to contact "a man who is very proficient in music theory, with the idea in mind that [he] study under him." See Toomer to Johnson, 4 March 1920, GDJ Papers, box 2, folder 9. A mutual preoccupation with music may have been one of the things that cemented Toomer's friendship with Georgia Douglas Johnson. Johnson's interest in music was such that in 1902, after working as a school teacher for a decade, she resigned to attend the Oberlin Conservatory of Music for a year.

17 Toomer, quoted in David Levering Lewis, *When Harlem Was in Vogue* (New York: Oxford University Press, 1979), 63.

18 Toomer to Johnson, 4 June 1920, GDJ Papers, box 2, folder 9.

19 Toomer to Alain Locke, 26 January 1921, Alain Locke Papers, box 164–90, folder 12.

20 Ibid.

21 Mae Wright Peck to Therman O'Daniel, interview, 2 July 1980, printed in O'Daniel, ed., *Jean Toomer: A Critical Evaluation* (Washington, D.C.: Howard University Press, 1988), 28. Peck was romantically involved with Toomer in the 1920s.

22 "Outline of An Autobiography," reprinted in *The Wayward and the Seeking: A Collection of Writings by Jean Toomer*, ed. Darwin T. Turner (Washington, D.C.: Howard University Press, 1980), 85.

23 Willard B. Gatewood Jr., *Aristocrats of Color*, 39.

24 Ibid., 334.

25 Jean Toomer to the editors of the *Liberator*, 19 August 1922, reprinted in *A Jean Toomer Reader: Selected Unpublished Writings*, ed. Frederik L. Rusch (New York: Oxford University Press, 1993), 15–16.

26 Jean Toomer, "Incredible Journey," Jean Toomer Papers, box 18, folder 491.

27 Jean Toomer to James Weldon Johnson, 11 July 1939, in *A Jean Toomer Reader*, 106; Jean Toomer, "A New Race in America," in *A Jean Toomer Reader*, 105.

28 Toomer to Alain Locke, 26 January 1921, Alain Locke Papers, box 164–90, folder 12.

29 Jean Toomer to the editors of the *Liberator*, 19 August 1922, *A Jean Toomer Reader*, 16.

30 Toomer detailed his vision of the Negro in "solution" in a letter to Waldo Frank: "There is one thing about the Negro in America which most thoughtful persons seem to ignore: the Negro is in solution, in the process of solution. As an entity, the race is loosing [sic] its body, and its soul is approaching a common soul. If one holds his eyes to individuals and sections, race is starkly evident, and racial continuity seems assured. One is even led to believe that the thing we call Negro beauty will always be attributable to a clearly defined physical source. But the fact is, that if anything comes up now, pure Negro, it will be a swan-song. The negro [*sic*] of the folk-song has all but passed away: the Negro of the emotional church is fading. A hundred years from now these Negroes, if they exist at all will live in art. . . . The supreme fact of mechanical civilization is that you become part of it, or you get

sloughed off (under). Negroes have no culture to resist it with (and if they had, their position would be identical to that of the Indians), hence industrialism the more readily transforms them. A few generations from now, the Negro will still be dark, and a portion of his psychology will spring from this fact, but in all else he will be a conformist to the general outlines of American civilization, or of American chaos. In my own stuff, in those pieces that come the nearest to the old Negro, to the spirit saturated with folk-song: Karintha and Fern, the dominant emotion is a sadness derived from a sense of fading, from my knowledge of the futility to check solution. There is nothing about these pieces of the bouyant [*sic*] expression of a new race. The folk-songs themselves are of the same order. The deepest of them: 'I ain't got long to stay here.' "

"America needs these elements [elements contributing to the beauty of the South, of the African-American folk spirit]. They are passing. Let us grab and hold them while there is still time. Segregation and laws may retard this solution. But in the end, segregation will either give way, or it will kill. Natural preservations do not come from unnatural laws." See Jean Toomer to Waldo Frank, undated but probably written in the winter of 1922 or the spring of 1923, Jean Toomer Papers, box 3, folder 84.

31 Langston Hughes, "Our Wonderful Society: Washington," *Opportunity* 5 (August 1927): 226–27. Locke's comments on the intellectual life of black Americans in the nation's capital are also notable. "Negro Washington," he claimed in 1929, "contains more of the elements of an intellectual race capital proportionally than the Washington of political fame and power. . . . Had this possibility been fully realized by the Washington intelligentsia a decade or so ago, Washington would have outdistanced Harlem and won the palm of pioneering instead of having merely yielded a small exodus of genius that went out of the smug city with passports of persecution and returned with visas of metropolitan acclaim." Locke, "Beauty and the Provinces," *The Stylus* 2 (1929): 4. Locke had put this perspective more succinctly in a letter to Toomer in 1922: "Washington is stagnation," he said. Locke to Toomer, 17 October 1922, Jean Toomer Papers, box 4, folder 151.

32 Hughes, "Our Wonderful Society," 227.

33 Quoted in Ronald M. Johnson, "Those Who Stayed: Washington Black Writers of the 1920's," *Records of the Columbia Historical Society* 50 (1980): 494.

34 Quoted in John Sekora, "Georgia Douglas Johnson and Generational

Modernism: A Response to Jeffrey C. Stewart," *G. W. Studies* 12 (July 1986): 45. Sekora does not make it clear when or where Johnson recalled this.

35 Hughes, *Big Sea*, 216; emphasis added.

36 Johnson used the phrase "contactual inspiration" in a draft of an undated list of manuscripts that, according to Johnson, were "Ready for Publication"; see item 9, which she describes as a piece called "Literary Salon." The list is a part of Johnson's file at the Moorland-Spingarn Research Center, Howard University. If completed, the manuscript to which she refers seems not to have survived.

37 Toomer to Johnson, 4 March 1920, GDJ Papers, box 2, folder 9.

38 Toomer to Johnson, 20 February 1920, GDJ Papers, box 2, folder 9.

39 Ibid.

40 Johnson to Locke, 17 August 1922, Alain Locke Papers, box 164–40, folder 35.

41 Johnson to Locke, 31 September [*sic*] 1922, Alain Locke Papers, box 164–40, folder 35.

42 Ibid.

43 Johnson to Locke, 28 October 1923, Alain Locke Papers, box 164–40, folder 35.

44 Johnson's handwriting was notoriously illegible, and those who wrote to her begged her to type her responses to spare them from struggling to make out her penmanship. When leaving for Paris in September 1924, Jessie Fauset sent a note to Johnson encouraging her to write her there. "Georgie dear," she begged, "when you write do type it. I love your letters but when I open them my heart sinks because I never know what you are going to say; you have no idea how rarely I am able to read an entire letter through." (See Fauset to Johnson, 22 September 1924, GDJ Papers, box 1, folder 32.) Toomer shared Fauset's frustration and similarly pleaded with her regularly to "write me soon,—but Georgie *don't make me work too hard to read what you write!*" (Toomer to Johnson, 23 July 1923; emphasis in original). He congratulated Johnson when he received a letter from her that he could read, as he did on 27 August 1923: "This time your note was legible. Good!" (Toomer to Johnson, 27 August 1923).

45 Bruce Nugent to Johnson, n.d., GDJ Papers, box 1, folder 26. Although this letter is undated, it is apparent from its content that Nugent is just arriving in New York City. According to David Levering Lewis, it was at Johnson's house one Saturday night during the winter of 1925 that Bruce Nugent met and spent hours talking to Langston Hughes; this

was a turning point in his life. Nugent followed Hughes to New York and continued his literary work there. See Lewis, *When Harlem Was in Vogue*, 196.

46 Johnson had apparently expressed some motherly disapproval, for instance, in a letter to Jessie Fauset. She had apparently written to find out it if it were true that Fauset had bobbed her hair, and she made some comment about Fauset's bathing attire. Fauset's response was to the point: "I don't know what you mean by a one piece bathing suit. I had a little silk or rather satin dress, sleeveless with a belt around it. And under it I wore an 'Annette Kellerman'. I had on much more than the other girls. I have never gone bare-legged in public in my life, certainly not since I was seven. So that's that." Fauset to Johnson, 22 September 1924, GDJ Papers, box 1, folder 32.

47 Nugent to Johnson, n.d., GDJ Papers, box 1, folder 46.

48 Johnson to Countee Cullen, 1927, Countee Cullen Papers, Manuscript Division, Library of Congress (hereafter cited as CCP), reel 1, box 3, file 5.

49 Bruce Nugent to Johnson, n.d., GDJ Papers, box 1, folder 46.

50 Bruce Nugent to Johnson, also undated, GDJ Papers, box 1, folder 46.

51 Johnson to Locke, 31 September [*sic*] 1922, Alain Locke Papers, box 164–40, folder 35.

52 Introduction to Georgia Douglas Johnson's poems, in *Black and White: An Anthology of Washington Verse*, ed. J. C. Byars Jr. (Washington, D.C.: Crane Press, 1927), 42.

53 This list is compiled from a number of sources, including lists Johnson herself made of those who attended meetings of the Saturday Nighters and the recollections of others. One of Johnson's extant lists is located in the GDJ Papers, box 162–1, folder 4.

54 Although the Saturday Nighters' reaction to Waldo Frank is not documented, Johnson made a point of mentioning his visit to her home in a letter to Alain Locke: "Did you know Jean had things in the Double Dealer and the Liberator? Waldo Frank has been here, came around and spent an evening. Must tell you my impression of him." Johnson to Alain Locke, 31 September [*sic*] 1922, Alain Locke Papers, box 64–40, folder 35.

55 Johnson employed at least two contradictory strategies to deal with the "problem" of her age. On some occasions, such as her application for the Harmon Foundation in 1928, Johnson falsified her birth date to appear younger than she actually was. At other times she tried to make her age work to her advantage, pointing to the benefits of maturity. In

correspondence regarding her 1950 application to the Whitney Foundation, for instance, Johnson suggested she might be referred to as "the mother of the Negro Poets" and argued in support of her application that "one would need age in order to qualify for the thing I would do." Quoted in Claudia Tate, "Reading a (Woman) Poet of the New Negro Renaissance," introduction to *The Selected Works of Georgia Douglas Johnson* (New York: G. K. Hall, 1997), xxxv.

56 Biographical headnote, in *Caroling Dusk: An Anthology of Verse by Negro Poets*, ed. Countee Cullen (New York: Harper & Row, 1927), 74.

57 Floyd Calvin, "Georgia Douglas Johnson Fears She Won't Have Time To Complete All Of The Work She Has Planned," Pittsburgh *Courier*, 7 July 1928, 6.

58 Dunbar-Nelson, *Give Us Each Day: The Diary of Alice Dunbar-Nelson*, ed. Gloria T. Hull (New York: Norton, 1984), 87–88. A. Philip Randolph, president of the Brotherhood of Sleeping Car Porters, recalled Johnson's rare combination of graciousness and spunk in a letter to her in 1940. "I will never forget," he wrote to her, "the time when you got a few friends together at your home to meet Chandler Owen and myself, who were outlawed and recognized as ungodly radicals. You were among the very few who were willing even to listen to us and did it despite our criticism of your splendid husband and Judge Terrell." A. Philip Randolph to Johnson, 18 December 1944, GDJ Papers, box 2, folder 5.

59 In his autobiography of W. E. B. Du Bois, David Levering Lewis describes Link Johnson as "a conniving patronage seeker indifferent to [his wife's] literary aspirations." See *W. E. B. Du Bois: The Fight for Equality and the American Century, 1919–1963* (New York: Henry Holt, 2000), 184.

60 William Stanley Braithwaite, Introduction to *The Heart of a Woman and Other Poems*, by Georgia Douglas Johnson (Boston: The Cornhill Company, 1918), vii.

61 Ibid., ix. Gloria T. Hull, *Color, Sex, and Poetry: Three Women Writers of the Harlem Renaissance* (Bloomington: Indiana University Press, 1987), 157; Tate, "Rereading a (Woman) Poet of the New Negro Renaissance," xlviii.

62 James Weldon Johnson, *The Book of Negro Poetry* (New York: Harcourt, Brace, 1931), xliv.

63 Tate, "Rereading a (Woman) Poet of the New Negro Renaissance," xlvii.

64 Hull, *Color, Sex, and Poetry*, 158.

65 Quoted in Hull, *Color, Sex, and Poetry*, 160.

66 Tate, "Rereading a (Woman) Poet of the New Negro Renaissance," xli.

67 Alice Dunbar-Nelson, *Give Us Each Day*, 88; Du Bois to Johnson, 17 [illegible] 1926, GDJ Papers, box 162–1, folder 29.

68 Lewis, *W. E. B. Du Bois: The Fight for Equality and the American Century*, 183.

69 "Georgia Douglas Johnson, Noted Poet, Author, Dies," *Baltimore Afro-American*, 28 May 1966.

70 "The Contest Spotlight," *Opportunity* (July 1927): 204.

71 William Stanley Braithwaite to Johnson, 5 January 1926, GDJ Papers, box 1, folder 25. Braithwaite had enough faith in Johnson's stamina to add: "Somehow I feel 1926 ought to be a banner year for you."

72 Johnson to Cullen, 9 November 1926, CCP, reel 1, box 3, file 5.

73 Johnson to Cullen, 18 May 1927, CCP, reel 1, box 3, file 5. Despite her efforts to find a publisher for *An Autumn Love Cycle*, Johnson ended up self-publishing it, as she had her earlier collections.

74 Johnson to Locke, 19 March 1919, Alain Locke Papers, box 164–40, folder 35.

75 Johnson to Locke, 11 August 1925, Alain Locke Papers, box 164–40, folder 35. Johnson also found Langston Hughes to be a valuable critic of her work. "I remember the *S Street Evening* when you helped me with *Autumn Cycle*," Johnson wrote to Hughes in 1949. "Time and again you have answered my call." See Johnson to Hughes, 7 June 1949, Langston Hughes Papers, James Weldon Johnson Collection, Yale Collection of American Literature, Beinecke Rare Book and Manuscript Library (hereafter cited as Langston Hughes Papers), box 83.

76 Dunbar-Nelson, *Give Us Each Day*, 88.

77 Toomer to John McClure, 6 October 1922, Jean Toomer Papers, box 7, folder 22.

78 Toomer to Johnson, 4 March 1920, GDJ Papers, box 2, folder 9.

79 Toomer to Johnson, n.d., GDJ Papers, box 2, folder 9.

80 On 12 December 1921 William Stanley Braithwaite wrote to Georgia Douglas Johnson about *Bronze*: "About the introduction: that is really a thing you would have to decide but if Mr. Du Bois wrote an introduction there is no doubt it would add to the distinction and appeal of the book." This letter is included in the William Stanley Braithwaite Papers, Yale Collection of American Literature, Beinecke Rare Book and Manuscript Library.

81 W. E. B. Du Bois, foreword to *Bronze,* by Georgia Douglas Johnson (Boston: Brimmer, 1922), 7.

82 Gloria Hull, *Color, Sex, and Poetry,* 163. In her introduction to John-son's collected work, Claudia Tate acknowledges Hull's reading of Johnson's decision to use Du Bois's foreword to *Bronze* but also suggests that perhaps Johnson was trapped into using it—regardless of how Du Bois characterized her work—because she had asked him to write it on the advice of her friend William Stanley Braithwaite. See Tate, "Read-ing a (Woman) Poet of the New Negro Renaissance," xlviii.

83 Du Bois, foreword to *Bronze,* 7.

84 Johnson to Cullen, 18 May 1927, CCP, reel 1, box 3, folder 5. Of the many undated rejection slips collected in Johnson's file at Howard University, one from an Oklahoma City journal called *Seven* is rep-resentative. Completely impersonal, it is a mimeographed sheet on which is listed a number of categories. The following categories are checked off: "Title lacks originality," "trite," "trite phrases." See John-son's collection of rejection notices, GDJ Papers, box 1, folder 7.

85 Johnson to Cullen, 18 May 1927, CCP, reel 1, box 3, folder 5.

86 Johnson to Cullen, 11 November 1929, CCP, reel 1, box 3, folder 5.

87 Cedric Dover to Johnson, 16 July 1947, GDJ Papers, box 1, folder 27.

88 Ibid.

89 Braithwaite to Johnson, 27 December 1944, GDJ Papers, box 1, folder 25.

90 Johnson to Langston Hughes, n.d., Langston Hughes Papers, box 83. According to my calculations, Henry Lincoln Johnson Jr. would have finished law school in 1929, and Peter Douglas Johnson would have finished medical school in 1931. This note, then, was written in 1930.

91 Winona Fletcher includes this quotation from the Federal Theater Project's readers' reports in her biographical entry, "Georgia Douglas Johnson," in *Afro-American Writers from the Harlem Renaissance to 1940,* vol. 51; *Dictionary of Literary Biography* (Detroit: Gale Research Co., 1987), 161. Her cogent discussion of the five plays Johnson sub-mitted to the Federal Theater Project between 1935 and 1939 is on pp. 159–63.

92 Johnson to Hughes, n.d., Langston Hughes Papers, box 83.

93 Johnson to Hughes, n.d., Langston Hughes Papers, box 83.

94 Hughes to Johnson, 24 November 1957, Langston Hughes Papers, box 83.

95 Johnson's "Catalogue of Writing" and the list of writing she had "Ready for Publication" is included in the GDJ Papers, box 2, folder 17.

96 Paul Breman to Johnson, 13 March 1958, Georgia Douglas Johnson Papers, Manuscript Division, Library of Congress. See also the Georgia Douglas Johnson Papers at Howard University, box 1, folder 24.

97 The records of this club are located at the Moorland-Spingarn Research Center, Howard University.

98 I have quoted from the club's early "New Year's Resolution"—recorded in the agenda for their 10 October 1960 meeting: "We don't have to wait until January 1st, to make our New Club Year Resolutions—to get our visions out of wishful thinking and put them down on paper—to become better writers by doing more systematic work—to get our manuscripts in the mail and keep them moving until they are SOLD. Let's remember that a manuscript in the desk drawer will never sell!" This document is located in the GDJ Papers, Howard University, box 1, folder 8.

99 Dorothy Porter Wesley, quoted Tate, "Reading a (Woman) Poet of the New Negro Renaissance," xxxii.

100 Charles S. Johnson, "Editorials," *Opportunity* 4 (August 1926): 241. Charles Johnson's recognition of the importance of literary societies is in keeping with his astute understanding of the importance of literary community. Referring to "Johnson's *Opportunity* network," David Levering Lewis argues in his study of the 1920s that "sooner or later, the Harlem of Charles Johnson enveloped almost every young artist or writer" (*When Harlem Was in Vogue*, 126). In *The Big Sea*, Langston Hughes reinforces this perspective. "Mr. Johnson," he wrote, "did more to encourage and develop Negro writers during the 1920's than anyone else in America" (218). It was Johnson who organized the Civic Club dinner in New York City on 21 March 1924, widely hailed as a "coming out party" for the young black artists, writers, and intellectuals whose work would come to define the Harlem Renaissance. The idea for the dinner was apparently conceived, however, by Jessie Fauset, Gwendolyn Bennett, and Regina Anderson, who were all "members of a little literary club" at the time. See Fauset's letter to Alain Locke, 9 January 1933, Alain Locke Papers, box 164–28, folder 41.

101 "Editorials," *Opportunity* 1 (February 1923): 3.

102 Gwendolyn Bennett, "The Ebony Flute," *Opportunity* 4 (August 1926): 260.

103 Gwendolyn Bennett, "The Ebony Flute," *Opportunity* 5 (July 1927): 212.

104 Bennett, "The Ebony Flute," *Opportunity* 4 (October 1926): 322.

105 Ibid.
106 Bennett, "The Ebony Flute," *Opportunity* 4 (December 1926): 391.
107 Ibid.
108 *Black Opals: Hail Negro Youth*, vol. 1, no. 1, was published by the Press of Reading Advertising Service in the spring of 1927.
109 "A Statement to the Reader," *The Saturday Evening Quill* 1 (June 1928): 2.
110 All of these quotations can be found under the heading "Excerpts from Comments on the First Number of *The Saturday Evening Quill*," *The Saturday Evening Quill* 2 (April 1929): 2.
111 Countee Cullen, "The Dark Tower," *Opportunity* 5 (June 1927): 180.
112 Bennett, "The Ebony Flute," *Opportunity* 6 (February 1928): 56.

EPILOGUE

1 Daniel Max, "McMillan's Millions," *New York Times Magazine*, 9 August 1992, 20–26.
2 Calvin Reid, quoted in "A Renaissance for Black Authors," by Monte R. Young, *Newsday*, 6 July 1994, sec. B.
3 Clara Villarosa, quoted in Young, "A Renaissance for Black Authors."
4 Max, "McMillan's Millions," 24.
5 Cheryl Woodruff, quoted in "McMillan's Millions," 24.
6 Mary White Ovington, "Selling Race Pride," *Publishers Weekly* (10 January 1925): 111–14.
7 Mary McLeod Bethune to Langston Hughes, quoted in Elizabeth Davey, "Building a Black Audience in the 1930s: Langston Hughes, Poetry Readings, and the Golden Stair Press," in *Print Culture in a Diverse America*, ed. James P. Danky and Wayne A. Weigand (Urbana: University of Illinois Press, 1998), 223.
8 Langston Hughes to Walter White, executive secretary of the NAACP, 3 August 1931; quoted in Davey, "Building a Black Audience in the 1930s," 223.
9 Davey, "Building a Black Audience in the 1930s," 238.
10 Florence Duke to the Golden Stair Press, 1932, quoted in Davey, "Building a Black Audience in the 1930s," 228; B. J. Anderson to the Golden Stair Press, 12 January 1932, quoted in Davey, "Building a Black Audience in the 1930s," 228–29.
11 Davey, "Building a Black Audience in the 1930s," 229.
12 Leigh Haber, quoted in Young, "A Renaissance for Black Authors."

13 Monique Greenwood, quoted in "Getting Down with the Pleasure of Reading," by Valerie Burgher, *QBR: The Black Book Review* 3 (May/June 1993): 14; Tracy Mitchell-Brown, quoted in "Open a Book, and There's a Sister Inside," by Michel Marriott, *New York Times*, 16 July 1997, sec. C, p. 1.

14 Information on the Go On Girl! Book Club is available on their Web site: www.goongirl.org. Additionally, Monique Greenwood, Lynda Johnson-Garrett, and Tracy Mitchell Brown are the authors of *The Go On Girl! Book Club Guide for Reading Groups* (New York: Little Brown, 1999).

15 Karen Grisby Gates, quoted in David Holmstrom, "Book Clubs Become Touchstone for Black Women," *Christian Science Monitor*, 2 January 1998, 10.

16 C. J. Pose, quoted in Young, "A Renaissance for Black Authors," sec. B.

17 Oprah Winfrey to Willow Bay, "Oprah's Reading Campaign," Good Morning America Sunday (ABC), 19 January 1997, transcript #97011909-J02.

18 Oprah Winfrey to Willow Bay, "Oprah Talks Books," Good Morning America Sunday (ABC), 23 February 1997, transcript #97022309-J02.

19 Letters to Oprah Winfrey from Unidentified Women #13 and #12, "Newborn Quintuplets Come Home," *The Oprah Winfrey Show* (transcript), 18 October 1996, 15.

20 Oprah Winfrey, quoted in Doreen Carvajal, "Uneasy Marriage of Interests for Television and Publishers," *New York Times*, 10 November 1996, sec. 1.

21 Toni Morrison, "How'd They Do That?" *The Oprah Winfrey Show* (transcript), 18 November 1996, 13.

22 Without doubt, a part of what appeals to Oprah's viewers is the aura of Oprah herself. Some critics of Oprah's Book Club have used this fact to argue that Oprah has "excited less a reading revolution than a cult of personality." What Oprah's viewers hunger for, argues D. T. Max, for instance, is insight into Oprah herself, and the book club is "just another stop on the voyage of self-discovery Winfrey leads each and every day." To support his observation, Max cites the comments of Jacquelyn Mitchard, author of Oprah's Book Club selection *The Deep End of the Ocean*. "If you send my name to the 900,000 who bought 'Deep End of the Ocean' because of Oprah, it will mean nothing to them. There's no carryover. You learn quickly that Oprah's the brand name, not you." Max's research into Detroit-area book clubs, many of which were structured around Oprah's selections, revealed that this

perspective did not accurately reflect the entire impact of Oprah's Book Club. The city, he discovered in 1999, was "awash with book clubs." "Communally," he observed, their members were "engaged in an enormous conversation, with books at the center." Although Oprah supplied book clubs with the titles of the selections they would read, the clubs' engagement with the texts was determined by the interests of their members. See D. T. Max, "The Oprah Effect," *New York Times Magazine*, 26 December 1999: 41.

23 Quoted in "Fans Throw the Book at Oprah When She Blows Off a Novel," by Laura Lippman, *Buffalo News*, 3 October 1997: 9C.

24 Toni Morrison, "Book Club—Toni Morrison," *The Oprah Winfrey Show* (transcript), 6 March 1998, 9.

25 Oprah Winfrey, quoted in "Has Oprah Saved Books?" *USA Today*, 12 December 1996, 1D.

26 Oprah Winfrey, "Newborn Quintuplets Come Home," *The Oprah Winfrey Show* (transcript), 18 October 1996, 16.

27 For information about the Circle of Friends Book Club and their visit to *The Oprah Winfrey Show*, see Shandra Hill, "Club Sends Members to Meet Oprah Winfrey," *Atlanta Constitution*, 2 October 1997, 14D.

28 Unidentified Woman #6, "Book Club—Toni Morrison," *The Oprah Winfrey Show* (transcript), 6 March 1998, 3.

29 Unidentified Woman #7, "Book Club—Toni Morrison," *The Oprah Winfrey Show* (transcript), 6 March 1998, 3.

30 Barbara Christian, "But What Do We Think We're Doing Anyway: The State of Black Feminist Criticism(s) or My Version of a Little Bit of History," *Changing Our Own Words: Essays on Criticism, Theory, and Writing by Black Women*, ed. Cheryl Wall (New Brunswick: Rutgers University Press, 1989), 64.

Bibliography

ARCHIVAL SOURCES AND PERIODICALS

Readers interested in learning more about the publications listed here should consult *African-American Newspapers and Periodicals: A National Bibliography*, ed. James P. Danky (Cambridge: Harvard University Press, 1998). This two-volume bibliography, arranged alphabetically by title, accounts for over six thousand newspapers and periodicals by or about African Americans in the United States, Canada, and the Caribbean. Entries list the frequency of publication, subscription rates, publisher, and variations in title and place or frequency of publication. The bibliography also informs researchers where issues of the publications can be found, either on microfilm or hard copy. Readers should also note that increasingly, access to nineteenth-century African American newspapers and periodicals is available through web-accessible archives.

African Repository
Anglo-African Magazine
Avery Institute Library, Charleston, S.C., Special Collections
    Phyllis Wheatley Literary and Social Club Collection
Baltimore Afro-American
Beinecke Rare Book and Manuscript Library, Yale Collection of American Literature, New Haven, Conn.
    James Weldon Johnson Collection
        William Stanley Braithwaite Papers

Langston Hughes Papers

Jean Toomer Papers

Black Opals (Philadelphia, Pa.)

Boston Daily Courier

Boston Daily Evening Transcript

Boston Guardian

Boston Public Library, Rare Books Department, Boston, Mass.

  Anti-Slavery Collection

  Woman's Era Collection

Buffalo News

Christian Advocate (New York)

Christian Recorder (Philadelphia, Pa.)

Colonizationist and Journal of Freedom (Boston, Mass.)

Colored American Magazine (Boston, Mass.)

Courier (Pittsburgh, Pa.)

The Emancipator (New York)

Freedom's Journal (New York)

Genius of Universal Emancipation (Baltimore, Md.)

Hazard's Register of Pennsylvania

Liberator (Boston, Mass.)

Library of Congress, Washington, D.C., Manuscript Division

  Charlotte Hawkins Brown Papers

  Countee Cullen Papers

  Georgia Douglas Johnson Papers

  Mary Church Terrell Papers

Moorland-Spingarn Research Center, Howard University, Washington, D.C.

  Bethel Historical and Literary Association Papers

  Georgia Douglas Johnson Papers

  Alain Locke Papers

  Mary Church Terrell Papers

Mugar Library, Special Collections, Boston University, Boston, Mass.

  Guardian Collection

Mystery (Pittsburgh, Pa.)

National Association Notes (Boston, Mass.; Tuskegee, Ala.)

North Star (Rochester, N.Y.)

Opportunity (New York)

People's Advocate (Alexandria, Va.)

Repository of Religion and Literature, and of Science and Art (Baltimore, Md.)

Richmond Enquirer
Robert W. Woodruff Library, Atlanta University, Atlanta, Ga.
 The Chautauqua Circle Collection
The Saturday Evening Quill (Boston, Mass.)
Woman's Era (Boston, Mass.)
Weekly Advocate (New York)
Weekly Anglo-African (New York)
Western Reserve Historical Society, Cleveland, Ohio
 Charles Waddell Chesnutt Papers

ARTICLES AND BOOKS

Abbott, George Maurice. *A Short History of the Library Company of Philadelphia.* Philadelphia: n.p., 1913.
Adams, John Quincy. *Argument of John Quincy Adams before the Supreme
 Court of the United States, Appellants v. Cinque, and Other Africans,
 Captured on the Schooner Amistad.* 1841. Reprint, New York: New
 American Library, 1969.
Ammons, Elizabeth. *Conflicting Stories: American Women Writers at the
 Turn into the Twentieth Century.* New York: Oxford University Press,
 1991.
Anderson, Benedict. *Imagined Communities: Reflections on the Origins and
 Spread of Nationalism.* London: Verso, 1991.
Andrews, William L. *To Tell a Free Story: The First Century of Afro-
 American Autobiography, 1790–1865.* Urbana: University of Illinois
 Press, 1986.
"Annual Meeting of the American Equal Rights Association: Second Day's
 Proceedings." *The Revolution* (27 May 1869): 321–22.
Aptheker, Herbert, ed. *A Documentary History of the Negro People in the
 United States.* Vol. 2. 1951. Reprint, New York: Carol Publishing Group,
 1992.
Augst, Thomas. "The Business of Reading in Nineteenth-Century America: The New York Mercantile Library." *American Quarterly* 50 (June
 1998): 267–305.
Baker, Houston A. *Blues, Ideology, and Afro-American Literature: A Vernacular Theory.* Chicago: University of Chicago Press, 1984.
Baker, Ray Stannard. *Following the Color Line: American Negro Citizenship
 in the Progressive Era.* New York: Harper Torchbook, 1964.

Bassard, Katherine. "Gender and Genre: Black Women's Autobiography and the Ideology of Literacy." *African American Review* 26 (1992): 119–29.

Berlin, Ira. "Time, Space, and the Evolution of Afro-American Society on Mainland British North America." *American Historical Review* 85 (February 1980): 44–78.

Bhabha, Homi K. "Of Mimicry and Man: The Ambivalence of Colonial Discourse." *The Location of Culture.* London: Routledge, 1994.

"Book Club—Toni Morrison." *The Oprah Winfrey Show.* ABC. 6 March 1998.

Boyd, Melba Joyce. *Discarded Legacy: Politics and Poetics in the Life of Frances E. W. Harper, 1825–1911.* Detroit: Wayne State University Press, 1994.

Braithwaite, William Stanley. Introduction to *The Heart of a Woman and Other Poems,* by Georgia Douglas Johnson. Boston: The Cornhill Company, 1918.

Brown, Charlotte Hawkins. *The Correct Thing To Do—To Say—To Wear.* 1940. Reprint, New York: G. K. Hall, 1995.

Brown, Letitia Woods. *Free Negroes in the District of Columbia, 1790–1846.* New York: Oxford University Press, 1972.

Bryan, Carter R. "Negro Journalism in America Before Emancipation." *Journalism Monographs* 12 (September 1969): 8–10.

Burgher, Valerie. "Getting Down with the Pleasure of Reading." *QBR: The Black Book Review* 3 (May/June 1996): 14–15.

Byars, J. C., ed. *Black and White: An Anthology of Washington Verse.* Washington, D.C.: Crane Press, 1927.

Carby, Hazel V. *Reconstructing Womanhood: The Emergence of the Afro-American Woman Novelist.* New York: Oxford University Press, 1987.

Carter, Everett. "Cultural History Written with Lightning: The Significance of *The Birth of a Nation.*" *American Quarterly* 12 (fall 1960): 347–57.

Chartier, Roger. "The Practical Impact of Writing." In *Passions of the Renaissance.* Vol. 3 of *A History of Private Life,* edited by Roger Chartier, 111–59. Cambridge: Harvard University Press, 1989.

——. "Texts, Printings, Readings." In *The New Cultural History,* edited by Lynn Hunt, 154–75. Berkeley: University of California Press, 1989.

Chesnutt, Charles W. "Race Prejudice: Its Causes and Its Cure." *Alexander's Magazine* 1 (July 1905): 21–26.

——. *"To Be An Author": Letters of Charles W. Chesnutt, 1889–1905.* Edited by Joseph R. McElrath Jr. and Robert C. Leitz. Princeton: Princeton University Press, 1997.

Christian, Barbara. "But What Do We Think We're Doing Anyway: The State of Black Feminist Criticism(s) or My Version of a Little Bit of History." In *Changing Our Own Words: Essays on Criticism, Theory, and Writing by Black Women,* edited by Cheryl Wall. New Brunswick: Rutgers University Press, 1989.

Clark, M. M. "Prospectus of the Christian Recorder of the African Methodist Episcopal Church." In *History of the African Methodist Episcopal Church,* by Daniel Payne, 278–79. Nashville, Tenn.: Publishing House of the A.M.E. Sunday School Union, 1891.

Cmiel, Kenneth. *Democratic Eloquence: The Fight over Popular Speech in Nineteenth-Century America.* New York: William Morrow, 1990.

Cooper, Anna Julia. *A Voice from the South.* 1892. Reprint, New York: Oxford University Press, 1988.

Cooper, Frederick. "Elevating the Race: The Social Thought of Black Leaders, 1829–1850." *American Quarterly* 24 (December 1972): 604–25.

Cornelius, Janet Duitsman. *"When I Can Read My Title Clear": Literacy, Slavery, and Religion in the Antebellum South.* Columbia: University of South Carolina Press, 1991.

Cripps, Thomas. *Slow Fade to Black: The Negro in American Film.* New York: Oxford University Press, 1977.

Cromwell, Adelaide. *The Other Brahmins: Boston's Black Upper Class.* Fayetteville: University of Arkansas Press, 1994.

Cromwell, John W. *History of the Bethel Literary and Historical Association.* Washington, D.C.: R. L. Pendleton, 1896.

Cullen, Countee, ed. *Caroling Dusk: An Anthology of Verse by Negro Poets.* New York: Harper & Row, 1927.

——. "The Dark Tower." *Opportunity* 5 (June 1927): 180.

Curry, Leonard P. *The Free Black in Urban America, 1800–1850.* Chicago: University of Chicago Press, 1981.

Darnton, Robert. "What Is the History of Books?" In *Reading in America: Literature and Social History,* edited by Cathy N. Davidson, 27–52. Baltimore: Johns Hopkins University Press, 1989.

Davey, Elizabeth. "Building a Black Audience in the 1930s: Langston Hughes, Poetry Readings, and the Golden Stair Press." In *Print Culture in a Diverse America,* edited by James P. Danky and Wayne A. Wiegand, 223–43. Urbana: University of Illinois Press, 1998.

Davison, Nancy Reynolds. "E. W. Clay: American Political Caricaturist of the Jacksonian Era." Ph.D. diss., University of Michigan, 1980.

Delany, Martin R. *The Condition, Elevation, Emigration, and Destiny of the Colored People of the United States.* 1852. Reprint, New York: Arno Press, 1968.

de Tocqueville, Alexis. *Democracy in America.* 2 vols. 1835/1840. Reprint, New York: Vintage Books, 1955.

Detweiler, Frederick G. *The Negro Press in the United States.* College Park, Md.: McGrath, 1968.

Douglass, Frederick. "The Heroic Slave." In *The Life and Writings of Frederick Douglass.* Vol. 5, edited by Philip S. Foner, 473–505. New York: International Publishers, 1975.

——. *My Bondage and My Freedom.* 1855. Reprint, Urbana: University of Illinois Press, 1987.

——. *Narrative of the Life of Frederick Douglass, an American Slave.* 1845. Reprint, New York: Penguin, 1983.

Douglass, William. *Annals of the First African Church in the United States of America, Now Styled The African Episcopal Church of St. Thomas.* Philadelphia: King and Baird, 1862.

Du Bois, W. E. B. *Black Reconstruction in America.* 1935. Reprint, New York: Atheneum, 1992.

——. "The Conservation of Races." 1897. Reprinted in *W. E. B. Du Bois: Writings.* New York: Library of America, 1986.

——. Foreword to *Bronze*, by Georgia Douglas Johnson. Boston: Brimmer, 1922.

——. *The Souls of Black Folk.* 1903. Reprint, New York: Penguin, 1989.

Dunbar-Nelson, Alice. *Give Us Each Day: The Diary of Alice Dunbar-Nelson.* Edited by Gloria T. Hull. New York: Norton, 1984.

Eaton, Clement. "A Dangerous Pamphlet in the Old South." *Journal of Southern History* 2 (1936): 323–34.

Emery, Edwin. *The Press and America.* Englewood Cliffs, N.J.: Prentice-Hall, 1972.

Ferguson, Robert A. " 'We Hold These Truths': Strategies of Control in the Literature of the Founders." In *Reconstructing American Literary History*, edited by Sacvan Bercovitch, 1–28. Cambridge, Harvard Univerity Press, 1986.

Fields, Mamie Garvin. *Lemon Swamp and Other Places: A Carolina Memoir.* New York: Free Press, 1983.

Fletcher, Winona. "Georgia Douglas Johnson." In *Afro-American Writers from the Harlem Renaissance to 1940*, vol. 51 of *Dictionary of Literary Biography*. Detroit: Gale Research Co., 1987.

Foner, Philip S. *History of Black Americans.* Westport, Conn.: Greenwood Press, 1975.

Forten, James Sr. *Letters from a Man of Colour.* Philadelphia, 1813.

Foster, Frances Smith. Introduction to *Minnie's Sacrifice; Sowing and Reaping; Trial and Triumph: Three Rediscovered Novels,* by Frances E. W. Harper. Boston: Beacon, 1994.

———. *Written by Herself: Literary Production of African-American Women, 1746–1892.* Bloomington: Indiana University Press, 1993.

Fox, Stephen R. *The Guardian of Boston.* New York: Atheneum, 1970.

Fraser, Nancy. "Rethinking the Public Sphere: A Contribution to the Critique of Actually Existing in Democracy." *Social Text* 25/26 (1990): 56–80.

Gaines, Kevin. *Uplifting the Race: Black Leadership, Politics, and Culture in the Twentieth Century.* Chapel Hill: University of North Carolina Press, 1996.

Gates, Henry Louis Jr. "From Wheatley to Douglass: The Politics of Displacement." In *Frederick Douglass: New Literary and Historical Essays,* edited by Eric Sundquist, 47–65. New York: Cambridge University Press, 1990.

———. *The Signifying Monkey: A Theory of Afro-American Literary Criticism.* New York: Oxford University Press, 1988.

———. "The Trope of the New Negro and the Reconstruction of the Image of the Black." *Representations* 24 (fall 1988): 129–55.

Gatewood, Willard B. *Aristocrats of Color: The Black Elite, 1880–1920.* Bloomington: Indiana University Press, 1990.

Gehman, Henry Snyder, ed. *The New Westminster Dictionary of the Bible.* Philadelphia: Westminster Press, 1970.

Gere, Anne Ruggles. *Intimate Practices: Literacy and Cultural Work in U.S. Women's Clubs, 1880–1920.* Urbana: University of Illinois Press, 1997.

Gernes, Todd. "Poetic Justice: Sarah Forten, Eliza Earle, and the Paradox of Intellectual Property." *New England Quarterly* 71 (June 1998): 229–65.

Gilman, Sander. "Black Bodies, White Bodies: Toward an Iconography of Female Sexuality in Late Nineteenth Century Art, Medicine, and Literature." In *Race, Writing, and Difference,* edited by Henry Louis Gates Jr., 223–61. Chicago: University of Chicago Press, 1986.

Goedeken, Edward A. "Review of James P. Danky and Wayne A. Wiegand, eds., *Print Culture in a Diverse America.*" *H-LIS, H-Net Re-*

views, February 1999. 4 September 2001. ⟨http://www.h-net.
msu.edu/reviews/showrev.cgi?path=5581920986462⟩.

Go On Girl! Book Club. Home Page. 22 January 2001. The National
Chapter for the Go On Girl! Book Club, Inc. 4 September 2001.
⟨http://www.goongirl.org⟩.

Green, Constance MacLaughlin. *The Secret City*. Princeton: Princeton
University Press, 1967.

Greenwood, Monique, Lynda Johnson-Garrett, and Tracy Mitchell
Brown. *The Go On Girl! Book Club Guide for Reading Groups*. New
York: Little Brown, 1999.

Harding, Vincent. "Wrestling Toward the Dawn: The Afro-American
Freedom Movement and the Changing Constitution." *Journal of American History* 74 (1987): 718–39.

Harper, Frances E. W. *A Brighter Coming Day: A Frances Ellen Watkins
Harper Reader*. Edited by Frances Smith Foster. New York: Feminist
Press, 1990.

———. *Iola Leroy, or Shadows Uplifted*. 1892. Reprint, New York: Oxford
University Press, 1988.

———. "Woman's Political Future." In *The World's Congress of Representative Women*, edited by May Wright Sewall. Chicago: Rand, McNally,
1894.

Heath, Shirley Brice. "Toward an Ethnohistory of Writing in American
Education." In *Writing: The Nature, Development, and Teaching of
Written Communication*, edited by Marcia Farr Whiteman. Hillsdale,
N.J.: L. Erlbaum Associates, 1981.

Hinks, Peter P. *To Awaken My Afflicted Brethren: David Walker and the
Problem of Antebellum Slave Resistance*. University Park: The Pennsylvania State University Press, 1997.

Hodges, Graham Russell. *Root and Branch: African Americans in New York
and East Jersey, 1613–1863*. Chapel Hill: University of North Carolina
Press, 1999.

Horton, James Oliver. *Free People of Color: Inside the African American
Community*. Washington, D.C.: Smithsonian Institution Press, 1993.

———, and Lois E. Horton. *In Hope of Liberty: Culture, Community, and
Protest Among Northeast Free Blacks, 1700–1860*. New York: Oxford University Press, 1997.

"How'd They Do That?" *The Oprah Winfrey Show*. ABC. 18 November
1996.

Hughes, Langston. *The Big Sea*. 1940. Reprint, New York: Thunder
Mouth's Press, 1986.

——. "Our Wonderful Society: Washington." *Opportunity* 5 (August 1927): 226–27.

Hull, Gloria T. *Color, Sex, and Poetry: Three Women Writers of the Harlem Renaissance.* Bloomington: Indiana University Press, 1987.

Hunter, Tera. "'The Correct Thing': Charlotte Hawkins Brown and the Palmer Institute." *Southern Exposure* 11, no. 5 (September/October 1983): 37–43.

Hutchinson, George B. "Jean Toomer and the 'New Negroes' of Washington." *American Literature* 63 (December 1991): 683–92.

Hutton, Frankie. *The Early Black Press in America, 1827–1860.* Westport, Conn.: Greenwood Press, 1993.

Huyssen, Andreas. "Mass Culture as Woman: Modernism's Other." In *Studies in Entertainment: Critical Approaches to Mass Culture,* edited by Tania Modleski, 188–207. Bloomington: Indiana University Press, 1986.

Johnson, Charles S. "Editorials." *Opportunity* 4 (August 1926): 241.

Johnson, James Weldon. *The Book of Negro Poetry.* New York: Harcourt Brace, 1931.

——. "Harlem: The Culture Capital." In *The New Negro,* edited by Alain Locke. 1925. Reprint, New York: Atheneum, 1992.

Johnson, Ronald M. "Those Who Stayed: Washington Black Writers of the 1920's." *Records of the Columbia Historical Society* 50 (1980): 484–99.

Kaestle, Carl, et al. *Literacy in the United States: Readers and Reading Since 1880.* New Haven: Yale University Press, 1991.

Kelley, Robin D. G. "'We Are Not What We Seem': Rethinking Black Working-Class Opposition in the Jim Crow South." *Journal of American History* (June 1993): 75–112.

Krüger-Kahloula, Angelika. "Tributes in Stone and Lapidary Lapses: Commemorating Black People in Eighteenth- and Nineteenth-Century America." *Markers: The Annual Journal of the Association for Gravestone Studies* 4 (1989): 33–102.

Lapsansky, Emma. "'Since They Got Those Separate Churches': Afro-Americans and Racism in Jacksonian Philadelphia." *American Quarterly* 32 (1980): 54–78.

Levesque, George A. *Black Boston: African American Life and Culture in Urban America, 1750–1860.* New York: Garland, 1994.

Levine, Robert S. "Circulating the Nation: The Missouri Compromise, David Walker's *Appeal,* and the Rise of the Black Press." In *The Black Press: Literary and Historical Essays on the "Other" Front Page,* edited by Todd Vogel. New Brunswick: Rutgers University Press, 2001.

——. *Martin Delany, Frederick Douglass, and the Politics of Representative Identity.* Chapel Hill: University of North Carolina Press, 1997.

Lewis, David Levering. *W. E. B. Du Bois: The Fight for Equality and the American Century, 1919–1963.* New York: Henry Holt, 2000.

——. *When Harlem Was in Vogue.* New York: Oxford University Press, 1979.

Lindhorst, Marie. "Politics in a Box: Sarah Mapps Douglass and the Female Literary Association, 1831–1833." *Pennsylvania History* 65, no. 3 (1998): 263–78.

Lippman, Laura. "Fans Throw the Book at Oprah When She Blows Off a Novel." *Buffalo News,* 3 October 1997: 9C.

Litwack, Leon. *North of Slavery: The Negro in the Free States, 1790–1860.* Chicago: University of Chicago Press, 1961.

Locke, Alain. "Beauty and the Provinces." *The Stylus* 2 (1929): 4.

——, ed. *The New Negro.* 1925. Reprint, New York: Atheneum, 1992.

Marteena, Constance Hall. *The Lengthening Shadow of a Woman: A Biography of Charlotte Hawkins Brown.* Hicksville, N.Y.: Exposition Press, 1977.

Matthews, Victoria Earle. "The Value of Race Literature: An Address Delivered at the First Congress of Colored Women of the United States, at Boston, Mass., July 30th, 1895." *Massachusetts Review* 27 (summer 1986): 169–91.

——. "The Value of Race Literature: An Address Delivered at the First Congress of Colored Women of the United States, at Boston, Mass., July 30th, 1895." In *With Pen and Voice: A Critical Anthology of Nineteenth-Century African-American Women,* edited by Shirley Wilson Logan. Carbondale: Southern Illinois University Press, 1995.

Max, Daniel. "McMillan's Millions." *New York Times Magazine,* 9 August 1992: 20–26.

——. "The Oprah Effect." *New York Times Magazine,* 26 December 1999: 41.

McFeely, William S. *Frederick Douglass.* New York: Simon and Schuster, 1991.

"Minutes of the Fifth Annual Convention" 1835. Reprinted in *Minutes of the Proceedings of the National Negro Conventions, 1830–1864,* edited by Howard H. Bell, 26–27. New York: Arno Press, 1969.

Morrison, Toni. "Unspeakable Things Unspoken: The Afro-American Presence in American Literature." *Michigan Quarterly Review* 23 (winter 1989): 1–34.

Moss, Alfred A. Jr., *The American Negro Academy: Voice of the Talented Tenth*. Baton Rouge: Louisiana State University Press, 1981.

Mossell, N. F. *The Work of Afro-American Woman*. 1894. Reprint, New York: Oxford University Press, 1988.

Nash, Gary. "Black Americans in a White Republic." *Race and Revolution*. Madison: University of Wisconsin Press, 1990.

——. *Forging Freedom: The Formation of Philadelphia's Black Community, 1720–1840*. Cambridge: Harvard University Press, 1988.

"Newborn Quintuplets Come Home." *The Oprah Winfrey Show*. ABC. 18 October 1996.

Nordin, Kenneth D. "In Search of Black Unity: An Interpretation of the Content and Function of *Freedom's Journal*." *Journalism History* 4 (winter 1977–78): 123–28.

O'Daniel, Therman B., ed. *Jean Toomer: A Critical Evaluation*. Washington, D.C.: Howard University Press, 1988.

"Oprah's Reading Campaign." *Good Morning America Sunday*. ABC, WABC, New York. 19 January 1997. Transcript # 97011909-J02.

"Oprah Talks Books." *Good Morning America Sunday*. ABC, WABC, New York. 23 February 1997. Transcript # 97022309-J02.

Ottley, Roi, and William Weatherby, eds. *The Negro in New York: An Informal Social History*. New York: Oceana Publications, 1967

Ovington, Mary White. "Selling Race Pride." *Publishers Weekly* (10 January 1925): 111–14.

Parker, Theodore. "The American Scholar." In *The American Scholar*, edited by George Willis Cooke, 1–53. Vol. 8 of *Centenary Edition of Theodore Parker's Writings*. Boston: American Unitarian Association, 1907.

Pease, Jane H., and William H. Pease. "Walker's *Appeal* Comes to Charleston: A Note and Documents." *Journal of Negro History* 59 (1974): 287–92.

——. *They Who Would Be Free: Blacks' Search for Freedom, 1830–1861*. New York: Atheneum, 1974.

Penn, Garland. *The Afro-American Press and Its Editors*. 1891. Reprint, New York: Arno Press, 1969.

Pennsylvania Abolitionist Society. *The Present State and Condition of the Free People of Color in the City of Philadelphia*. Philadelphia, 1838.

Perkins, Linda. "Black Women and Racial 'Uplift' Prior to Emancipation." In *The Black Woman Cross-Culturally*, edited by Filomina Steady, 317–34. Cambridge, Mass.: Schenkman, 1981.

Peterson, Carla. *Doers of the Word: African-American Women Speakers and*

Writers in the North (1830–1880). New York: Oxford University Press, 1995.

Porter, Dorothy. "The Organized Educational Activities of Negro Literary Societies, 1828–1846." *Journal of Negro History* 5 (1936): 555–76.

——, ed. *Early Negro Writing*. Boston: Beacon, 1971.

Proceedings of the Free African Union Society and The African Benevolent Society, Newport, Rhode Island, 1780–1824. Providence: The Urban League, 1976.

Proceedings of the National Negro Conventions, 1830–1864. New York: Arno Press, 1969.

Quarles, Benjamin. *Frederick Douglass*. Washington, D.C.: Associated Publishers, 1948.

Ray, H. Cordelia. "Report of the Woman's Loyal Union of New York and Brooklyn." Reprinted in *A History of the Club Movement among the Colored Women of the United States of America*. Washington, D.C.: National Association of Colored Women's Clubs, 1902.

"Report of the Woman's Era Club, Boston, Mass." 1896. Reprinted in *A History of the Club Movement among the Colored Women of the United States of America*. Washington, D.C.: National Association of Colored Women's Clubs, 1902.

Rhodes, Jane. *Mary Ann Shadd Cary: The Black Press and Protest in the Nineteenth Century*. Bloomington: Indiana University Press, 1998.

Richardson, Marilyn, ed. *Maria W. Stewart: America's First Black Woman Political Writer, Essays and Speeches*. Bloomington: Indiana University Press, 1987.

Rogin, Michael. " 'The Sword Became a Flashing Vision': D. W. Griffith's *The Birth of a Nation*." *Representations* 9 (winter 1985): 150–95.

Romero, Laura. *Home Fronts: Domesticity and Its Critics in the Antebellum United States*. Durham, N.C.: Duke University Press, 1997.

Ryan, Mary. *The Cradle of the Middle Class: The Family in Oneida County, New York, 1790–1865*. Cambridge: Cambridge University Press, 1981.

Sedgwick, Catherine M. *Hope Leslie; or Early Times in Massachusetts*. New York: White, Gallaher, and White, 1827.

Sekora, John. "Georgia Douglas Johnson and Generational Modernism: A Response to Jeffrey C. Stewart." *G. W. Studies* 12 (July 1986): 45–46.

Smith, Edward. "Testimony and Confession." Appendix Two. In *Appeal, in Four Articles; Together with a Preamble, to the Colored Citizens of the World, but in Particular, and Very Expressly to Those of the United States of America,* by David Walker. Edited by Sean Wilentz. New York: Hill and Wang, 1965.

Starling, Marion Wilson. *The Slave Narrative: Its Place in American History*. Washington, D.C.: Howard University Press, 1988.

Statistical Inquiry into the Condition of People of Color of Philadelphia. Philadelphia: Society of Friends, 1849.

Sterling, Dorothy. *The Making of an Afro-American*. New York: Doubleday, 1971.

———, ed. *We Are Your Sisters: Black Women in the Nineteenth Century*. New York: Norton, 1984.

Stuckey, Sterling. *The Ideological Origins of Black Nationalism*. Boston: Beacon, 1972.

———. *Slave Culture: Nationalist Theory and the Foundations of Black America*. New York: Oxford University Press, 1987.

Tate, Claudia. "Reading a (Woman) Poet of the New Negro Renaissance." Introduction to *The Selected Works of Georgia Douglas Johnson*. New York: G. K. Hall, 1997.

Tayleur, Eleanor. "The Negro Woman: Social and Moral Decadence." *Outlook* 76 (30 January 1904): 266–71.

Terrell, Mary Church. *A Colored Woman in a White World*. 1940. Reprint, New York: G. K. Hall, 1996.

Toomer, Jean. *A Jean Toomer Reader: Selected Unpublished Writings*. Edited by Frederick L. Rusch. New York: Oxford University Press, 1993.

———. *The Wayward and the Seeking: A Collection of Writings by Jean Toomer*. Edited by Darwin T. Turner. Washington, D.C.: Howard University Press, 1980.

Ullman, Victor. *Martin R. Delany: The Beginnings of Black Nationalism*. Boston: Beacon, 1971.

Wald, Priscilla. *Constituting Americans: Cultural Anxiety and Narrative Form*. Durham: Duke University Press, 1995.

Walker, David. *Appeal, in Four Articles; Together with a Preamble, to the Colored Citizens of the World, but in Particular, and Very Expressly to Those of the United States of America*. 1829. Edited by Sean Wilentz. Reprint, New York: Hill and Wang, 1965.

Warner, Michael. *Letters of the Republic: Publication and the Public Sphere in Eighteenth-Century America*. Cambridge: Harvard University Press, 1990.

Washington, Booker T. *A New Negro for a New Century*. Chicago: American Publishing House, 1900.

———. *Up From Slavery*. 1901. Reprint, New York: Avon, 1965.

Watson, Harry. *Liberty and Power: The Politics of Jacksonian America*. New York: Hill and Wang, 1990.

Wells, Ida B. *Crusade for Justice: The Autobiography of Ida B. Wells.* Edited by Alfreda M. Duster. Chicago: University of Chicago Press, 1970.

White, Deborah Gray. "The Cost of Club Work, the Price of Black Feminism." In *Visible Women: New Essays on American Activism,* edited by Nancy A. Hewitt and Suzanne Lebsock, 247–69. Urbana: University of Illinois Press, 1993.

———. *Too Heavy a Load: Black Women in Defense of Themselves, 1894–1994.* New York: Norton, 1999.

Wiegand, Wayne A. "Theoretical Foundations for Analyzing Print Culture as Agency and Practice in a Diverse Modern America." Introduction to *Print Culture in a Diverse America,* edited by James P. Danky and Wayne A. Wiegand. Urbana: University of Illinois Press, 1988.

Williams, Fannie Barrier. "The Intellectual Progress of Colored Women of the United States since the Emancipation Proclamation." In *The World's Congress of Representative Women,* edited by May Wright Sewall. Chicago: Rand, McNally, 1894.

Willson, Joseph. *Sketches of the Higher Classes of Colored Society in Philadelphia.* Philadelphia: Merrihew and Thompson, 1841.

Winch, Julie. *Philadelphia's Black Elite: Activism, Accommodation, and the Struggle for Autonomy, 1787–1848.* Philadelphia: Temple University Press, 1988.

———. " 'You Have Talents—Only Cultivate Them': Philadelphia's Black Female Literary Societies and the Abolitionist Crusade." In *The Abolitionist Sisterhood: Women's Political Culture in Antebellum America,* edited by Jean Fagan Yellin and John C. Van Horne, 101–18. Ithaca: Cornell University Press, 1994.

Winship, Michael. Afterword to *Literary Publishing in America, 1790–1850,* by William Charvat. Amherst: University of Massachusetts Press, 1993.

Wolseley, Roland E. *The Black Press, U.S.A.* Ames: Iowa State University Press, 1971.

Wright, Theodore S. "The Progress of the Antislavery Cause." 1837. Reprinted in *Negro Orators and Their Orations,* edited by Carter G. Woodson, 86–92. New York: Associated Publishers, 1925.

Index

Elizabeth McHenry is Assistant Professor of
English at New York University.

Library of Congress Cataloging-in-Publication Data

McHenry, Elizabeth.
Forgotten readers: recovering the lost history
of African American literary societies /
Elizabeth McHenry.
p. cm. — (New Americanists; A John Hope Franklin
Center book)
Includes bibliographical references and index.
ISBN 0-8223-2980-8 (alk. paper)
ISBN 0-8223-2995-6 (pbk. : alk. paper)
1. American literature—African American authors—
Appreciation—United States. 2. American literature—
African American authors—History and criticism.
3. American literature—19th century—History and
criticism. 4. African Americans—Intellectual life—
19th century. 5. African Americans—Books and
reading. 6. African Americans in literature.
7. Literature—Societies, etc. I. Title. II. Series.
PS153.N5 M36 2002
028'.9'08996073—dc21   2002004448

mass culture   Huyssen   p. 235

Black woman   Reader :   224 —

Oprah : 306